END OF
THE BEGINNING

Tim Clayton & Phil Craig

CORONET BOOKS
Hodder & Stoughton

First published in Great Britain in 2002 by Hodder & Stoughton
A division of Hodder Headline
The right of Tim Clayton and Phil Craig to be identified as the Authors of
the Work has been asserted by them in accordance with the
Copyright, Designs and Patents Act 1988.

A Coronet paperback

1 3 5 7 9 10 8 6 4 2

A CIP catalogue record for this title is available from the British Library

ISBN 0 340 76681 6

Typeset in Bembo by Palimpsest Book Production Limited,
Polmont, Stirlingshire
Printed and bound in Great Britain by
Clays Ltd, St Ives plc

Hodder and Stoughton
A division of Hodder Headline
338 Euston Road
London NW1 3BH

Additional research by Frances Craig

Contents

Contents

Illustrations

Section 1

(IWM refers to the Imperial War Museum)

Looking from the 'Knightsbridge box' towards the 'Cauldron', 1 June 1942 (*IWM*)

Peter Vaux in 1942 (*Peter Vaux*)

Members of Vaux's team. Left to right: driver, Corporal Williams with 88mm shell, Peter Ashworth, Jim Marshall, Kenneth Paxton, Corporal Finch (*Peter Vaux*)

The interior of ACV2 drawn by Corporal Barrett (*Peter Vaux*)

Peter Vaux's Armoured Command Vehicle (ACV2) disguised as a lorry (*Peter Vaux*)

Harold Harper enjoys a brew at dawn (*Harold Harper*)

A 25-pounder gun in action (*IWM*)

Arthur Onslow, Viscount Cranley

Neville Gillman (*Neville Gilman*)

Three Crusader tanks of 4 County of London Yeomanry (the Sharpshooters), summer 1942 (*IWM*)

Don Bruce (*Don Bruce*)

115 squadron's armourers prepare for a mission. A Wellington bomber waits for its bomb load in the background, spring 1942 (*IWM*)

Edith Heap in RAF Pocklington's ops room (*Edith Kup*)

Flak over Brest in 1942, similar to that encountered by Don Bruce's Wellington (*IWM*)

Ariete Division postcard: 'Every day of battle brings us closer to our destination' (*Dougie Waller*)

Section 2

A Kittyhawk of Billy Drake's 112 'Shark' squadron takes off in a cloud of sand, loaded with a 250 pound bomb (*IWM*)

Ken Lee relaxes at the Gazira Sporting Club, Cairo (*Ken Lee*)

Section 3

German Commander's HQ in Guernsey (*Bundesarchiv, Koblenz*)
'Freedom from Fear' – Norman Rockwell's original painting for one of Roosevelt's 'Four Freedoms' posters (*Collection of the Norman Rockwell Museum at Stockbridge, Norman Rockwell Art Collection Trust. Printed by permission of the Norman Rockwell Family Agency Copyright © 1943 the Norman Rockwell Family Entities*)

Section 4

'There will be no retreat, none whatsoever, none!' Bernard Montgomery in front of a Grant tank (*Hulton Archive*)
Dougie Waller's photograph of Laurie Richmond
Dougie Waller and friends in Cairo, August 1942 (*Dougie Waller*)
A 6-pounder gun comes off its 'portee' (*IWM*)
The pennant Dougie Waller took from the first Panzer IV he knocked out at the battle of Alam Halfa (*Dougie Waller*)
Pilots of 260 squadron (*Lionel Sheppard*)
Ken Lee's snap of 260 squadron pilots being briefed before a bombing raid near Alamein
260 squadron's Warhawks take to the air in line abreast (*Ken Lee*)
German vehicles under air attack (*IWM*)
Neville Gillman's Crusader tank moves to Alamein on a transporter (*Neville Gillman*)
The Italian Folgore parachute division propaganda postcard (*Dougie Waller*)
Sherman tanks in action during the Battle of el Alamein (*IWM*)
Infantrymen near a burning German vehicle during the battle (*Hulton Archive*)
The much-feared German 88mm gun (*IWM*)
German prisoners after the Battle of El Alamein (*Hulton Archive*)

Maps

The Western Desert
May 1942

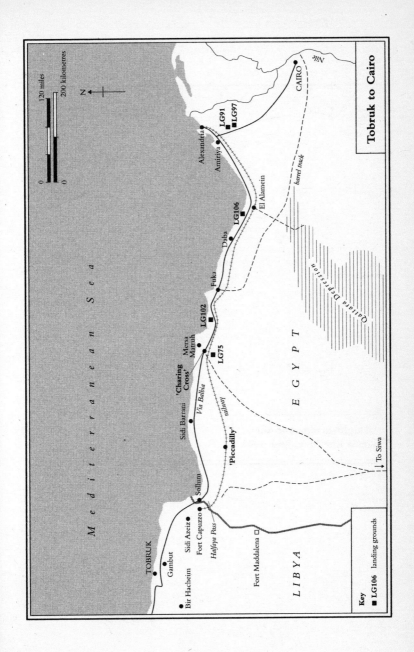

Tobruk to Cairo

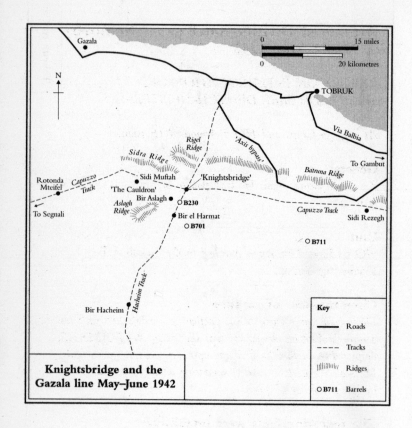

Knightsbridge and the Gazala line May–June 1942

7 Armoured Division Intelligence Summary No. 32, 24 May 1942

REPORT ON INTERROGATION OF
STABFELDWEBEL DEUTCH-MEISTER

At HQ 30 Corps and HQ 7 Armoured Division.

General
An unsatisfactory man. He was glad to be captured, and to be out of the war . . .

Unit
HQ 90 Light Division – attached to the Signals of the Engineering Section.

Circumstances of capture
He was marking a gap in a minefield . . . when his truck ran on a mine, killing his driver. He was shot at by the ITALIANS, despite the fact that he fired the appropriate Very light signals. Dislikes ITALIANS. After wandering all night he was picked up by our patrols at U 4322.

The following facts were established
(i) Part, at least, of HQ 90 Light Division is in the area SW of SEGNALI.
(ii) 155 Lorried Infantry Regiment is definitely there, and probably 900 Engineering Battalion.
(iii) HQ 90 Light Division is in direct wireless communication with HQ Panzerarmee Afrika.
(iv) Some GERMAN tanks are in that area also (on one occasion he mentioned 50, and on another 300). These are part of 5 Tank

Regiment (21 Panzer Division). NB. It will be remembered that Tactical Reconnaissance on 22 May reported 20 tanks and 15 Armoured Cars at U 6151.

Opinion
Everybody was sure that an attack was due to take place within a few days, and heavy punishments had been promised those who talked unduly – he was surprised that the 'panzerangriff' had not already commenced.

Chapter 1

25–27 May

7 Armoured Division Intelligence Summary No. 33

(Based on Information Received up to 2000 hrs 25 May 42)
This Summary will be destroyed within 48 hrs of receipt.

1. GENERAL.
Again an extremely quiet day over the whole of our front. Visibility steadily worsened all day, and the enemy was almost inactive . . .

Peter Vaux paused, pencil in hand. He wanted to add 'too damn quiet', but such phrases had no place in an intelligence report. He continued to write in the requisite prosaic, codified style, capitalising proper names and double-checking grid references. Every day he was more certain that an attack was imminent and that it would fall here in the south.

That 90 Light Division's headquarters had moved his way was particularly suspicious. So too was the presence of that engineering officer with the unusual name, Deutch-Meister, who they'd caught making gaps in the minefields opposite Bir

Hacheim. In Vaux's view, 90 Light would spearhead the attack as they had before. But his superiors at both Corps and Eighth Army headquarters were not convinced; they all thought that Rommel's main strike would come farther north, aimed straight at Tobruk. That's where the panzer divisions were marked in blue on the map mounted on the bulkhead behind Peter's driver's compartment. But would the German tanks stay there? Vaux thought not.

It was his job to see things from the enemy's point of view. If he were Rommel, he would certainly avoid the British mine-fields and defensive 'boxes' up north and try to sweep round the southern flank. This, after all, was what the German training manual recommended. Vaux had a copy in his desk drawer. Eighth Army command had allowed for this eventuality by placing 7 Armoured Division here in the south. Captain Peter Vaux, not yet twenty-six, was the intelligence officer for the division, respon-sible for placing the best possible information in the hands of General Frank Messervy, who commanded its 13,000 men and 227 tanks. Vaux glanced up at the scattered red flags on the map. The tanks were thinly spread, as if to reassure the infantry that they would not have to face the enemy alone.

Vaux had begun his career in the Royal Tank Regiment, where he had been taught that the strengths of the tank were mobility and armament, and that both must be used together. Armour should be employed in a mobile block that could react to any sudden changes on the battlefield. But right along the line, all the way north to Gazala on the coast, the British armour was split up for close infantry support, into units too small to resist a big offensive, and too far forward to escape.

He continued with his report.

ENEMY DISPOSITION
(i) A patrol to grid reference U 8078 on the night of May 22/23 reports a position, probably ITALIAN, 80 yards WEST, and much digging there during the night. The captured map on April 22

showed this area to be held by 155 Lorried Infantry Regiment, which had moved by 10 May and has apparently been relieved by ITALIANS . . .

A German battalion replaced by an Italian one; another sign that Rommel was massing his best units somewhere. But where? Over the last few weeks Vaux had been on reconnaissance behind the German lines and had visited the Long Range Desert Group at the Siwa oasis. He'd pored over air reconnaissance reports and radio intercepts and laboriously mapped out every detail he could discover of German and Italian positions. He'd sent out patrols and spies and interrogated prisoners. Only yesterday the Free French had brought in an Italian on a donkey posing as an Arab. By coincidence, John Bagot Glubb, the greatest English expert on Arab affairs, happened to be visiting. He cracked the Italian by making him undress and pointing out that his clean underwear gave the lie to his story of having travelled for three weeks. The man had then confessed that he had been sent to search for British positions. The Free French who had initially captured him had been suspicious, so they said, because he was young and handsome and the Arab woman accompanying him was old and ill favoured. Bravo for Gallic intuition. Vaux decided to include a spicy account of all this in the next intelligence report. But he sympathised with Colonel von Mellenthin, who would have been responsible for the unlucky Italian spy. Only last month Peter had almost sent someone the Germans' way with a box of Swan Vesta matches in his pocket.

He attached the appendices: the latest estimate of Italian strength; a German officer's impression of the progress of the war; and a long list of the locations and content of enemy store dumps. He marvelled at the detail. He sometimes wondered how they got some of this information. Surely the Long Range Desert Group couldn't come up with all of it?

Time of Signature 2330. P.A.L. Vaux, Capt.

Vaux swivelled the chair towards the door of ACV2, the great armour-plated monster that was his office, and reached for the phone to call for a clerk. The two radio operators were still on duty at the massive No. 9 sets at the back of the vehicle. He would check the typing tomorrow and then dispatch riders in jeeps would distribute copies throughout the division. He jumped down from the armoured command vehicle and made his way to the 'chateau', an untidy structure improvised from wireless aerials and Italian groundsheets, where he slept and kept his personal possessions. He stepped over the sleeping figure of his friend Donald Reid and rolled out his sleeping bag.

There were times when Peter Vaux thought he was fated to fight Erwin Rommel for ever. In May 1940, when Vaux had taken part in his first tank battle, Rommel had been the opponent. The general had almost died that day in northern France when fire from the British tanks killed his aide-de-camp standing next to him. If they had got him it would have saved everyone a lot of trouble. As it was, he gave them a first-hand demonstration of what German 88mm anti-aircraft guns could do when turned against tanks. Peter's colonel was killed that day, along with half of the Royal Tank Regiment men he'd trained with.

When he arrived in the desert in February 1941, Rommel was there to meet him. The British had just won a spectacular victory over the Italians but Rommel soon smashed his way through and surrounded the port of Tobruk. During the long siege, Vaux was promoted. He became an intelligence officer at 7 Armoured Division, trying to learn everything he could about his opponents and their habits, especially Herr Rommel's habits. In December 1941 Tobruk was relieved and on Christmas Eve the crew of ACV2 celebrated with liberated bottles of Chianti and a barbecued goat. But Rommel hadn't finished with him yet. The panzers rolled forward again in January 1942, driving everyone back to this new

Gazala line just short of Tobruk. In the meantime Vaux had been promoted again and was now the division's senior intelligence man.

They had just got a new general. Brave and personable, Frank Messervy was an old Etonian who had been a cavalry officer in the Great War. In the following years he had distinguished himself playing polo in India. His drawback as commander of an armoured division was that he had no training, and very little experience, with tanks. This was something that his junior officers, trained in mechanised warfare, sometimes found more than a little frustrating.

On the morning of 26 May, Peter Vaux's superiors at 30 Corps issued their response to his opinion that Rommel's main attack would come in the south. But their Operation Instruction No. 46 was a disappointment: 'It still appears probable that the main weight of the enemy offensive will be in the north.' They allowed that some part of 90 Light Division might make a feint attack in the south, along with the Italian Ariete Division that was already there, but that was it. Couldn't they see that if the headquarters of 90 Light was here, then the whole lot would almost certainly follow?

So we are to expect a small German feint and possibly an Italian armoured division, thought Vaux. Well, perhaps they're right. Perhaps they know something that I don't. Let's hope so.

At 1400 that afternoon, after a brief artillery bombardment, four divisions of Italian infantry attacked the northern sector of the Gazala line. In order to deceive the British, a small number of German tanks led the assault. Meanwhile the rest of the German army gathered in their assembly area near Segnali. In the early evening part of this force moved off north towards the point of the Italian attack. Rommel blessed his luck. A violent sandstorm that had raged for most of the day, cleared just in time for the regular British evening reconnaissance flight to witness this diversion. As soon as the planes had flown over, all the German tanks turned abruptly south.

At 2030 the shadow-boxing ended and Rommel ordered 'Operation Venezia' to begin in earnest. Four divisions with 560 tanks and 10,000 other vehicles headed exactly where Peter Vaux had predicted they would: south-east towards Bir Hacheim, the Well of Dogs, the strongpoint that marked the southern end of the Allied line.

Rommel's men were experienced, used to winning, and confident in their own ability. Before midnight the Luftwaffe began to drop flares to guide the advance columns forward.

Pat Bland opened the bidding: 'One club.'

The hurricane lamp threw dramatic shadows about B troop's signals truck, where Bland was teaching two friends from D troop how to play contract bridge. Battery Sergeant-Major Earnshaw was deep in thought, counting on his fingers like a five-year-old. He was the senior man present, and a leader his men had come to rely on through the siege of Tobruk. The captain had recommended him for a commission after that, but the Officers Training Unit had rejected him, just as Earnshaw had predicted they would. He didn't have the right accent for an officer.

'No bid, as usual,' he said.

Harold Harper studied his cards, trying to remember what Pat Bland had taught him about a replying hand. It was only his second lesson, and Bland was a demanding teacher. 'One heart. No, sorry, I meant diamonds.'

Earnshaw: 'Hey, that's cheating.'

Hewson: 'The red pointy ones, you mean?' Mack Hewson was taking the piss as usual. He did have the right voice, more or less. Hewson, like Bland, was a sergeant in B troop and both had been to Nottingham High School, the senior grammar school in town. But even they were not quite at ease with the public school boys in the officers' mess.

Harper: 'Yes, diamonds, sorry, got them mixed up.'

Hewson: 'OK, you're going one diamond. My partner Mr Earnshaw has his usual rubbish, so no sodding bid as well.'

Bland: 'Well, with a hand like this I have to do it, lads. Three no trumps. Try to watch how I play them, Harold.'

Bland played out the tricks as Harper looked on in bemused admiration, marvelling at the way his partner quickly worked out what everybody else had in their hands. No trumps was weird. Even with a handful of kings and queens, you could be completely powerless once a skilful opponent seized the initiative. 'Bring out your dead,' said Bland with a grin as he neared the end of the contract, laying down his winning twos and threes, and the rest of them threw away their useless aces and kings.

'Shit!' said Hewson. 'Blast!' muttered Earnshaw. Harper chuckled. Claude Earnshaw was the only soldier he'd ever met who never swore. 'Eh, Harold, how's Marion?' asked Bland. 'Haven't heard from her in weeks,' said Harper. He hadn't seen her for two years either. Boots of Nottingham, where Harper had been training to become a store manager, was in another world now, and so was Marion. He couldn't really blame her if she got fed up waiting. All his mates were still in England, mostly tradesmen with the RAF or other sensible things like that. But he'd had to listen to that sergeant-major in his dad's fish-and-chip shop: 'Why don't you join our lot?' And that had been it. And where had it got him? Tobruk! Sitting in a gun pit in Tobruk for nearly a year, and now here. He hardly remembered what anyone back home looked like. His mother had died in November, just as they were fighting their way out of the place. He hadn't seen her since that day on the station platform in 1940 when the South Nottinghamshire Hussars had all left town. He'd made a mistake on the gun director just after the padre had broken the news. The battery commander, Gerry Birkin, had just said, 'That's the first mistake I've ever seen you make, Harold.' He was a good officer, Gerry Birkin, public schoolboy or not.

'How's *your* family Pat?'

'My mum and dad won the county championship again.'

No wonder he was good.

Harper had passed his eleven-plus exam and gone to High Pavement: a grammar all right, but, in the finely graded system of English schools, an inferior establishment to Nottingham High in every respect. Nevertheless, among the coal miners who made up the bulk of his unit, Harper stood out as unusually literate and numerate. His dad had been a miner before he got his chip shop so Harold could mix with the men who taught him how to dig, but unlike them he also knew all about logarithms and how to use a slide rule. So Harper became a specialist. As assistant to Ivor Birkin, the battery commander's younger brother, he helped to work out the fire programme for his troop of four 25-pounder guns, one of two troops in the eight-gun battery. All the way through Tobruk, as the men matured into hardened veterans, in every barrage Harper had written down instructions for the guns. They were a fine team, 'The best bloody battery in the Pommy army', like that Australian had said.

Sometimes they would do 'OP' duty. He and Ivor Birkin would go forward to an observation post in the front line or else climb a tower just behind it, up fifty feet of rickety scaffolding with German shells flying around. From there they would get number-one gun to bracket the target, fire long, then short, then all four guns would hit halfway. For six months they had held the line against every attack that Rommel could throw at them. Then they had broken out. For a while there had been great relief, a massive party on looted Italian wine, even a few days' leave in Cairo. Now they were in the open desert and training for mobile warfare.

Harper and Birkin shared an armoured car, and they were supposed to move with the tanks of 22 Armoured Brigade, directing the fire of the guns to where the tank commanders needed it. It was a new kind of fighting, but they had trained hard. D troop could have all four guns in action within thirty seconds of getting a fire order. Earlier that evening Ivor Birkin had said, 'I do not know what else we can do to make this troop more efficient.'

'Do you think you're getting the hang of it now?' asked Pat Bland after another couple of contracts.

'Well, it'll take a bit more practice,' Harper said.

'In a few months we'll have you up to county standard.'

'Well, I don't know about that. Better get some shut-eye anyway. Early start in the morning.'

Harper was fascinated by the desert stars. There seemed to be more than ever shone over Nottingham. They'd long ago mastered the art of finding their direction from the position of the more obvious constellations. Tonight there was a beautiful full spread, except when a flare across the minefield towards Bir Hacheim slightly spoiled the view.

As Rommel's army rolled forward through the darkness, Winston Churchill was thinking about the Battle of Austerlitz. The Prime Minister wanted to send his commanders in the desert a cable outlining some of the lessons of Napoleon's most brilliant victory. General Alan Brooke was trying to persuade the Prime Minister that this was not the best moment.

In 1940 Brooke had supervised the British army's frantic preparation for the expected German invasion, impressing Churchill so much that in November 1941 he asked him to become Chief of the Imperial General Staff (CIGS), the most important soldier in the empire. As CIGS he directly commanded the army, had considerable influence over the navy and air force and was at Churchill's right hand as he made Britain's war strategy.

But the daily consultations with his political master were the hardest part of Alan Brooke's job. He nearly refused the post because he had seen how Churchill gradually undermined the former CIGS, his old friend John Dill. The Prime Minister's disastrous juggling of forces in early 1941 was the low point. When Hitler invaded the Balkans, hardened divisions that had been thrashing the Italians in North Africa were hastily shipped to

Greece. Arriving with minimal air support, they were quickly outmanoeuvred. Evacuated under a cloud of enemy aircraft, the British suffered heavy losses. This, the High Command agreed, was Churchill at his worst, the Churchill some remembered from the Great War: overconfident, endlessly interfering in military details, weakening a good strategic position to pursue a fantasy. From the moment he took over, Brooke was determined to prevent this kind of distraction and maintain a tight focus on the major strategic issues of the war.

Perhaps Churchill understood that he needed someone to contradict him. If so, then he could not have made a better choice. Strong willed and acid tongued, Alan Brooke was more than capable of standing up for himself. When faced with Churchill's eloquent bluster he would lean towards him, say 'I flatly disagree', and break a pencil. At times they seemed about to growl at each other.

Brooke believed in discipline and plain speaking. Churchill liked men with a touch of flamboyance. Brooke damned people with remarks like 'prima donna' and 'film star'. Churchill enjoyed being the centre of attention and would hold court in his crimson-and-gold dressing gown, suddenly burst into a popular song or prance around in an elderly man's version of bayonet drill. Brooke craved domestic tranquillity and daydreamed about chopping logs with his children, long country walks, fishing and bird-watching. Churchill liked to talk strategy and history, drinking and philosophising late into the night with expansive gusto. When General Marshall, Brooke's opposite number in Washington, complained that he only saw President Roosevelt once a month, Brooke – in a rare joke – groaned that it was *his* fate to see Winston at least every six hours.

Brooke regarded Churchill as a sixty-seven-year-old child, either bursting with a new enthusiasm or lost in an unfathomable rage; and he thought Churchill's drinking made him petulant and headstrong. Yet there were sides of the man he admired deeply: his political skill, his courage, the way he could take and give bad news without flinching and still communicate an unshakeable confidence in ultimate victory. Brooke had seen defeatism at work in France, and he knew how close Britain's leaders had come to the collapse of their *own* will to resist. For preventing this apparently inevitable end he would always respect his Prime Minister. But, as he mastered his job, he became ever more convinced that this dangerous child-man should be kept as far away from professional soldiers as was humanly possible.

> He knows no details, has only got half the pictures in his mind, talks absurdities and makes my blood boil to listen to his nonsense . . . It is far better that the world should never know, and never suspect the feet of clay of that otherwise superhuman being. Without him England was lost for a certainty . . . with him England has been on the verge of disaster time and again.

There were similarities between war in the desert and playing a tricky hand in no trumps. One small mistake and a position that looked very strong could quickly collapse. And once you started to lose, you lost a lot very quickly. Half a dozen well-placed 88s could destroy dozens of expensively produced tanks and their laboriously trained crews in minutes. A sudden outflanking panzer movement, one of Rommel's favourite tricks, could neutralise the best artillery or infantry. It had happened time and time again. Military aces and kings lay burnt out and ruined all over the Western Desert.

The attack that was developing on 26 May was the latest in a campaign that had already seen both sides advance and retreat thousands of miles. Rommel's plan, as Peter Vaux had guessed, was to round the Gazala line in the south, roll it up from the rear, take Tobruk at last, and then press deep into Egypt. The attacking force was even larger than Vaux had feared, consisting of Rommel's four best divisions: 90 Light, 15 Panzer, 21 Panzer and the Italian Ariete.

The advance was shadowed by South African armoured cars, whose reports were passed to Vaux's divisional headquarters and to his superiors at 30 Corps. But Corps remained convinced that what the armoured cars were reporting was exactly what they had anticipated: a diversionary move by, at the very most, an Italian division and a small German battle group. Peter Vaux was on duty for the first watch. When he went to bed at 0200, waking Donald Reid to take over from him, nothing at all alarming had been reported from Corps.

About 0300 on 27 May the enemy vanguard stopped to refuel just south of Bir Hacheim. More and more vehicles joined it, and the reports from the watching armoured cars took on a more urgent tone. In the middle of the night generals were woken and phone calls exchanged between 7 Armoured Division and 30 Corps, then between 30 Corps and Eighth Army HQ. The night-duty staff at Army and Corps wondered whether the South Africans might not, in the darkness, be exaggerating enemy numbers. Junior officers urged action but General Messervy and his superior at Corps, General Willoughby Norrie, remained calm. Norrie did ring General Lumsden, commander of the next nearest armoured division, to ask him to alert his tanks to be ready to support Messervy if necessary. Lumsden, who like Peter Vaux had a low opinion of Messervy's ability to handle tanks, argued against committing them prematurely. So Norrie relented, awaiting confirmation of the situation by air reconnaissance at first light.

The morning mist of 27 May was thinning out and the rising sun threw long purple shadows across the stony ground and desert scrub. Believe it or not, the birds were singing. Harold Harper was constantly surprised by the birdsong in the desert. Where did they all nest? And along the branches of the bushes that surrounded the little depression where they had spent the night were white snails, an amazing number of white snails crawling along the thick stalks of camel thorn. Harper stood up and stretched his arms and took in the beauty of the desert morning. Almost as far as he could see the vehicles of 520 battery, South Notts Hussars, were parked in a column ready for an early move. Their eight guns were drawn up in a line to the west of the trucks facing out over the minefields. The armoured car that Harper shared with Captain Ivor Birkin was parked near the front of the line so that they could speed off first in case of emergency. Other figures were rising around him and stretching and busying themselves. Birkin was still huddled in his blankets on the ground by the vehicle. It was Sergeant Harper's turn to make breakfast.

He shook out his blankets. 'Christ almighty!' An angry snake fell from them and coiled itself on the ground in front of him, rearing up and hissing. Harper reached behind for a shovel and slashed wildly. The snake retreated, winding rapidly across the ground, and disappeared into a hole behind a stone. Not the best start to the day.

Harper unhooked a battered petrol can from the side of the armoured car, half filled it with sand, soaked the sand in petrol and set it alight. As ever, the 'Benghazi burner' gave off an intense heat. He half filled another petrol can with water and put it on to boil. He poured the water very carefully. Supplies were good for the present, but the stuff was still scarce and old habits died hard. The armoured car was chock-full of luxuries they had brought down from Cairo. He extracted a tin of Carnation milk, some oatmeal and salt for the porridge from among the other precious tins and bottles. But first, a good brew.

Boomhmh. The distant rumble of artillery. It seemed to come from the south, and that was puzzling. Yesterday all the noise had come from the north.

I'd got the porridge going and we were just having breakfast when the battery commander Gerry Birkin came up in his armoured car. He drove right up to us and pointed out this cloud of dust on the horizon – it would have been about five miles away. We thought it must be some of our troops manoeuvring but he said, 'I think they're Germans.' We threw everything into the back of our armoured car and followed him.

The two armoured cars tore off to find the tanks that the South Notts battery was supposed to be supporting. The 25-pounders were designed to fight at a distance, but the acute shortage of decent British anti-tank guns meant that they were often pressed into providing close support for tanks. Harper was remembering his first close-up battle against panzers. It was at Tobruk, yelling the elevation angles at the gun crews through his megaphone, then firing over open sights at 3,000 yards at the fifteen or so tanks that had broken in. The men cheered every time they knocked one out. Two staff cars had stopped in full view and they had picked them both off with their ranging shots, with all the Australians cheering and one of them clapping the lieutenant right on the shoulder. Yes, he had fought tanks before, but that was from behind a prepared defence, not out in the open like this.

General Messervy's armour was in no position to resist Operation Venezia. Three regiments were dispersed across the desert, each with about sixty tanks. One was surprised and destroyed in its camp, the second was bypassed by the advancing panzers and the third deployed just in time to line up against the two hundred tanks of 15 Panzer Division. The British tank crews fought extremely fiercely and gave the enemy an unpleasant surprise. The Germans knew little about the new American Grant and its powerful 75mm gun. For a moment their attack stalled, the leading vehicles ablaze. But they sized up the threat, swept round the flanks and brought up their 88mm guns. Most of the Grants were soon burning. Meanwhile, Ariete Division attacked Bir Hacheim while 21 Panzer and 90 Light divisions drove on. Rommel's great offensive was going to plan, and still the British generals hadn't realised that this was no feint, but the real thing.

The next nearest tanks in the piecemeal British deployment were those of 22 Armoured Brigade, part of General Lumsden's 1 Armoured Division, which included the mobile artillery batteries of the South Notts Hussars. When it became apparent that there was a genuine threat in the south, Lumsden was ordered to help Messervy. He complained that his men were not ready and orders reached his units only slowly. Harold Harper and the rest of the signals truck bridge school were farthest south, astride the 'barrel track' from Bir Hacheim, up which 21 Panzer Division was advancing at top speed.

Harper was peering at the horizon, although the amount of dust in the air made it hard to see more than a hundred yards. He was in his armoured car with Ivor Birkin. Ahead, half obscured by the dust cloud, was Ivor's brother Gerry's car. They were both searching for the tanks that their gun battery was due to support. They were supposed to be near a barrel painted with the number 701, but they seemed to have disappeared.

Gerry Birkin's car stopped. Another three hundred yards ahead were tanks, but they didn't look like British ones. Birkin began to make calculations ready to radio back to the battery. If he was quick he could get fire down on these panzers before the Germans knew anything about it. He climbed down from the turret and asked his driver, Bobby Feakins, to check the figures. Feakins climbed up to the turret just as a shell landed behind them. 'Whoops!' said Birkin. They had not gone unnoticed after all. Feakins thought he saw a shape moving towards them in the dust. 'Sir, quick!' They swapped places again and Feakins quickly revved the engine and started to turn away from the danger.

He heard a noise, turned, and as he did so what was left of Gerry Birkin collapsed all over him. An armour-piercing shell had gone straight through his stomach. The same shell had beheaded two of the radio operators sitting behind. The third operator was screaming into his radio and, like Feakins, was covered in blood and worse. Feakins realised that some of the blood was his own. His first thought was that the armoured car was still a sitting duck. He slammed it into reverse gear and tried to press hard on the accelerator, feeling the strength draining from his leg as he did so. The car shot backward and with a great crash fell straight into a slit trench, where it stuck fast. Feakins pushed past Birkin's body and lowered himself from the vehicle. He found that he had inadvertently run over the surviving radio operator, who had jumped from the back of the vehicle just as he reversed. Both his legs were broken.

Harold Harper and Ivor Birkin were still edging forward through the dust:

> We were driving slowly, at about 10 mph, and we'd only gone about half a mile when we heard this very panicky garbled message on the radio. There was obviously something wrong ahead. Ivor and I climbed out of the turret, jumped down and ran over to Gerry Birkin's car.

As Harper approached he saw the signaller burst from the back of the vehicle, saw him run over and then saw Bobby Feakins climb out and hang on to the back door.

> We ran to the driver's door to find out what the trouble was. I'd never seen anything like it in my life. There was Gerry lying there, obviously dead. I ran round to the back to get the signallers out. When I opened the doors, there they were sitting with their microphones still in their hands but they hadn't got any heads. Their intestines and things were poking through what was left of their upper bodies and their heads were lying on the floor.

Ivor Birkin was utterly distraught and Harper couldn't make him leave his brother, despite the obvious danger. 'I said, "Come along, sir, you must come back." He said, "No, you get back."' Harper obeyed the order and ran back to fetch the other armoured car.

I had just ordered the driver to turn. I pressed on his right shoulder to make him turn right and out of this great cloud of sand came one of our own tanks, a bloody great Grant, and it hit us head on. By this stage the whole of the desert around us was one great cloud of dust. We bounced back and the engine burst into flames. So we had to jump out. We dashed over to where Ivor Birkin was and told him what had happened. There we all were, stranded.

21 Panzer Division was now headed straight for the rest of 520 battery.

The sergeants had been standing by B troop's signal truck, gathered round the radio. It appeared that 22 Armoured Brigade HQ had no idea what was going on. Then they heard a voice on the inter-battery frequency whimpering incoherently and another screaming, 'We've been hit! We've been hit!' Then they saw the panzers.

'Tanks alert! Take post! Independent gunfire! Open sights!' Tank shells were falling all around the wagon lines.

Pat Bland and Mack Hewson sprinted to B troop's guns. German tanks were coming over the ridge. Bland threw in his weight as they unhitched the gun from the limber and pushed it round. Drivers were digging all round, piling stones, frantically trying to create some cover for the gunners. Hewson, two hundred yards farther back, had his shoulder against the wheel of no. 4 gun.

'GF target. HE 119 cap on!'

B troop had no choice but to fight where they stood. They got one panzer at close range but then Pat Bland's gun took a direct hit and Bland was killed along with all his crew. At the last second Mack Hewson made a run for it. His crew bundled into a truck and weaved away through streams of tracer bullets. It was over very quickly. Fifteen men were killed outright. The troop that had defended Tobruk for nine long months barely lasted nine minutes of the mobile war for which it had trained so hard.

D troop was shielded from the oncoming tanks by B troop, which was directly in their line of fire. They wouldn't be able to hit anything even if they tried, but they might just escape. The captain climbed on top of his vehicle and hoisted a blue flag. Sergeant Claude Earnshaw reacted to the signal immediately. 'Get those guns moving! Go north!' Guns and lorries pulled away with machinegun bullets bouncing in the sand. Earnshaw chivvied them on.

The South Notts men pulled back to a position next to what was called the 'Knightsbridge box', and there eventually they were joined by the remnants of the tank units that they were supposed to be supporting. Instead of fighting as an integrated, mobile unit, each subsection of tanks and artillery had been confronted with an overwhelming number of German tanks. All they could do now was dig in and wait.

Alan Brooke knew how this war would be won: slowly and carefully. First there would be victory in the desert, then the conquest of North Africa. Next came command of the Mediterranean and perhaps a direct attack on Italy. But until the British army was better trained and substantial American forces were available, any bolder action was simply not practical. This meant no early invasion of occupied Europe.

Britain's military reputation had been buoyed up by the heroics of 1940, and during 1941 the brave and much-publicised defence of Tobruk balanced failure in Greece. But since Christmas it had been disaster all the way. Japanese aircraft sunk two battleships, *Prince of Wales* and *Repulse*. At Singapore, the great eastern fortress, 85,000 British and Australian troops surrendered without even putting up a fight, or so the world believed. In February three of the German navy's most powerful warships dashed through the English Channel, evading every attempt to intercept them. Foreign politicians and journalists wondered aloud whether the British had forgotten how to make war. For Churchill, with his keen sense of Britain's glorious military traditions, it was almost too much to bear.

Brooke, who had to deal with Churchill's outbursts against the High Command, always defended his subordinates in front of mere politicians, but in private he was angry and confused.

> Cannot work out why troops are not fighting better. If the army cannot fight better than it is doing at present we shall deserve to lose our Empire . . . We are going to lose this war unless we control it very differently and fight it with more determination.

The battle that was developing along the Gazala line on 27 May gave Brooke and the generals under him the chance to show that they could fight with 'control' and 'determination' after all.

Chapter 2

27 May

Peter Vaux had spent weeks trying to persuade his superiors that 90 Light Division would spearhead Rommel's attack. Now he was about to be proved right in a most unpleasant way.

Inside ACV1, dug into a pit and camouflaged with nets, General Messervy was trying to find out what was happening to the various brigades of 7 Armoured Division. At 0630 the Indian Motor Brigade had reported that an Italian armoured division was in front of them, and now they could not be contacted at all. It was not until the morning air reconnaissance report confirmed that over three hundred tanks were south of Bir Hacheim that the situation became clearer.

Donald Reid burst into the 'chateau' and woke Vaux with the news. He was soon listening in to the radio traffic in ACV2, trying to piece together enemy movements, and work out which units were involved. The Free French garrison at Bir Hacheim reported itself surrounded, but said it had repelled an attack by the Ariete Division. Around him orderlies were packing away tables and chairs, reeling in telephone lines, clearing the debris of a divisional headquarters into about forty lorries and the other ACVs responsible for signals, administration and cipher. The 'chateau' was being hastily dismantled and bundled into ACV1.

27

All the ACVs, distinctive with their armour plating, were now disguised as ordinary ten-ton lorries, their metal superstructures covered wtih sheets of rough hessian. ACV1, with General Messervy inside, ran up the blue flag, signalling an immediate move, and the other vehicles manoeuvred into column. But ACV1 was stuck, its wheels churning uselessly as it tried to reverse out of its pit. Precious minutes went by and nervous fingers drummed on steering wheels. None of the lorries had the power to haul it out. Half an hour passed before ACV5 succeeded in dragging ACV1's fourteen tons out of the hole. As the column finally moved westward shells began exploding among the vehicles, and some Grant tanks withdrew through and past them, their turrets turned to face backward over their engine covers. Peter Vaux looked around at the command column. Apart from a few light machineguns, it was unprotected.

As we steamed away at best speed the northerly breeze sent a wall of dust from our wheels billowing out to the right. I was sitting on the roof of the ACV while the others were below sorting out maps and radio headsets, when suddenly there was a rattling of machineguns and the thudding of cannon and a column of German armoured cars and half-tracks dashed through the concealing dust and were amongst us, firing in all directions. A number of vehicles stopped, clearly hit, and among these was ACV1, from which I saw some figures jump a moment before it burst into flames. It seemed that the general was being captured.

Before Vaux could see exactly what was happening to the people from ACV1, his attention was caught by a more immediate threat. A German armoured car drove alongside, dwarfed by the massive ACV, and the commander shouted up to him in English, 'Put your hands up and stop!' Vaux dived inside and slammed the hatch shut, calling for the Bren gun to be disinterred from the heap of bedding at the bottom of the vehicle.

As the expert on German equipment, his first instinct was to assess the enemy. 'A Kfz 222 – has a twenty-millimetre cannon with a hundred rounds of armour-piercing as well as its machinegun. Please God let him think we're a lorry.' He did. A rattle of bullets bounced harmlessly off the steel sides of the ACV. Inside the relative safety of his armoured truck, Vaux was pleasantly surprised to discover that the disguise had worked. It couldn't be long before the German realised his mistake and called for some armour-piercing cannon shells, but in the meantime there might be a few seconds for Vaux to get a few shots in himself.

When the machinegun fire stopped I climbed out again with the Bren loaded, but we seemed to have driven clear of the battle, for behind us I could see a lot of smoke and shooting. There were a number of vehicles with us, and it suddenly dawned on me that if anyone was commanding 7 Armoured Division at that moment it must be me, so I hoisted the blue flag and the other vehicles converged on me.

At a junction of two desert tracks, marked by a painted barrel numbered 711, Vaux stopped. He needed to get a grip of the situation. It was not every day that a captain found himself in command of an armoured division, and these were not the ideal circumstances in which to learn the job. The obvious and urgent necessity was to tell Corps what had happened and to get in touch with all the brigades. The problem was that ACV2 was geared to listening to radio signals, not to sending them. The transmitters were not switched on and, when they were, they had to be laboriously tuned in. The operators were having difficulty finding the frequency. On top of this, both ACV3, the signals vehicle, and ACV5, the cipher vehicle, were missing, along with all the communications specialists. The codes for the day had been in ACV1 and they did not know whether the Germans had captured it intact. He could hardly announce in clear language that the better part of the divisional headquarters had just been overrun and that General Messervy had been captured. Vaux found a liaison officer with a motorbike and told him to try to get through to Corps in person. Two of the brigades then did make contact, reporting themselves fighting and too busy to speak much further.

A radio message was sent to Corps, but there was no way of knowing whether it had been understood. At 1020 one of the brigades that Vaux now commanded reported that their position at Retma had been overrun and that they were moving back to reorganise. At 1030 another brigade, the 4 Armoured, reported that it was heavily engaged and had destroyed twenty German tanks. Better news. The Free French were also fighting well, holding the Italians outside Bir Hacheim. Perhaps something could be salvaged after all. Then he saw another ominous dust cloud in the distance and shells began to fall close to what remained of the command column: 90 Light strikes again, he thought bitterly. The only thing seemed to be to retreat farther, so he led his assorted vehicles back in the direction of Sidi Rezegh.

'We're to take that off again.' There were groans all round.

Since breakfast the crews of C squadron had been disguising their Crusader tanks as lorries. In the distance there was gunfire. Yesterday afternoon it had just been to the north; now it was mainly to the south and it sounded quite close. But for the tanks, laid out facing west, there had been no order to move. Now it looked as though they were preparing to get under way.

Sergeant-Major Neville Gillman was called over to the tank of Viscount Cranley, C squadron's leader, who gave his fifteen tank commanders their orders: 'We are to move now on a bearing of 270 degrees. This is it very briefly: a lot of Germans have come up from the south and appear to have taken every bugger by surprise. We are to come up on the right of the line here. A and B squadrons are going forward, and we lucky bastards in C get to watch the flank. Right, let's fucking well get to work.' If there were ever an inter-regimental swearing competition, Gillman thought to himself, and not for the first time, then Viscount Cranley would win it by a mile.

He walked back to the tanks, seeing crewmen tightening the tracks, checking the tension on the fan belts and tipping oil into the engines. His driver was already inside, revving up, watching the gauges as he made the V-12 Nuffield 'Liberty' engine roar. The Crusader was a notoriously unreliable machine and nobody wanted it to let him down over the next few hours. The gunner, stripped to the waist, was loosening the 2-pounder ammunition in the racks and checking the belt on the machinegun. The radio operator hummed into the microphone, testing for interference. They said little. Gillman repeated the orders, totted up the ready ammo, told the operator to get a few more shells unpacked. Already his throat felt dry. The troop commander's pennant fluttered over his head and the dust billowed behind the angular Crusader, as it moved slowly away into the open desert.

Neville Gillman had been something of a pacifist once. His family were all Congregationalist, Nonconformists with an independent streak who tended to be rather left wing. He was raised when memories of trench warfare were strong, and he'd sympathised with the students who had carried the notorious Oxford Union motion 'This House will not fight for King and Country'. In 1936 he began training as an articled clerk. One of his first colleagues, a good mate called Jenkins, was a fierce socialist with loud opinions about how the ruling classes always led the workers into war to benefit their own vested interests. But as Hitler's power grew, Gillman came to believe that war, if it came, would be in a good cause this time, and that he should be prepared to put himself in the firing line.

He decided to join the Territorial Army in 1939. He applied to the Medical Corps because he thought that he would be able to serve his country without killing but, somewhat comically, he was turned down on medical grounds. His own doctor could find nothing wrong with him except the perverse desire to join the military medics, and suggested he join a 'proper regiment' instead. A school-friend recommended the 'Sharpshooters'. The name sounded good, as did their full title, the County of London Yeomanry. But it still came as something of a shock when on 4 September 1939 trainee accountant Gillman theatrically downed his pen in mid-audit and set off for the Lex Motors garage in London's fashionable St John's Wood. There the Sharpshooters kept their three antique Rolls-Royce armoured cars.

The officers were an impressive bunch, expensively educated, many with shiny sports cars and jobs in the best City banks. Jenkins would definitely have called them 'the class enemy'. There was an Italian count, the son of an ambassador and even the assistant secretary to the MCC. When a big cricket match was called off in the panic that followed the declaration of war, the Sharpshooters were all invited to the members' enclosure at Lord's so as not to waste the luncheons.

By May 1940 they were a tank regiment without tanks, and at one point Gillman trained to repel invaders in a commandeered Fyffes banana lorry bristling with machineguns. Then he attended gunnery school at Lulworth Cove and was promoted sergeant. His squadron commander was Viscount Cranley, son of the Earl of Onslow, and he arranged that they might be based in late summer in the grounds of his father's home, Clandon Park. Despite his background, Cranley was completely unstuffy and informal, and obviously devoted to his men. They called him 'the Corsican Bandit' on account of his dark good looks, and they all enjoyed his creative use of common English obscenities.

For a happy interlude Gillman supervised the gunnery school from the viscount's stable block. There were embarrassing moments, such as the time when an impatient Lady Cranley had stopped Gillman on his way to see his squadron leader and said, 'Will you tell my husband that I've been waiting here for a quarter of an hour.' When Gillman mentioned this, Cranley replied, 'Go out and tell her she can bloody well wait to do her shopping until I'm ready.' He managed to convey the message to her ladyship in slightly more diplomatic terms.

When they sailed for Africa, Gillman's background in book-keeping determined his fate. Cranley made him quartermaster sergeant. During the first bloodbath in November 1941, when half the regiment was destroyed, his job had been to organise the supply of petrol, water, ammunition and food. More recently he'd commanded the forward support unit. Every day he drove a hundred miles across the desert with a column of lorries loaded with tank fuel. They had been dive-bombed by Stukas and lost in trackless wastes, but they had kept Cranley's squadron supplied and got it home every time. He had been code-named 'Squeaker' and, inevitably, this became his nickname. Gillman, who was only five foot four, had long ago learned to put up with such things. And it was not meant unkindly. Cranley had been impressed with Gillman's performance and promoted him to squadron sergeant-major with a troop of three tanks to command.

But before today Gillman had never taken a tank into battle. He fitted his earphones and crouched on the commander's seat, folding his legs beneath him because he was too small to sit comfortably. He scanned the shimmering horizon through his binoculars.

They soon ran into some Grants from the Gloucester Hussars. Enemy armour was near by, but impossible to locate in all the dust. Then an order came: all available tanks were to retire north-ward while an artillery screen held the enemy off. They fell back to a position just west of the 'Knightsbridge box'. Some panzers appeared out of the cloud about five hundred yards to the south and there, for the first time, Neville Gillman opened fire.

'Gunner, Panzer Mark III in front with the red pennant, range five hundred. Aim for the base of the turret. Got him? Two-pounder fire now.' Gillman followed the line of the shot. 'Just over. Down a tank height. Reload and try again.' The loader dragged the round from the bin and the breech clanged shut. 'Firing now.'

The instructors said that the best tank men stayed calm and

took things slowly. Try not to think of the other man shooting at you, and take your time to get your own aim right. Chances are the enemy is frightened too and will rush, panic and miss. All good advice, no doubt, but hard to put into effect with your head sticking out of a three-foot-by-six-foot metal box that might become a petrol-fuelled bonfire at any moment.

Cranley's voice was on the radio. 'OP, see if you can get your battery on to those guns.' There was a loud bang on the front of Gillman's tank and the engine stalled. The turret was suddenly full of dust. But no flames, not yet. 'Driver, are you all right?' 'I can't start the engine.' There was another hit and the gun turret shook and echoed with the reverberation. Whatever was firing had got their range, and it was only a matter of time before a round caught the front armour at the right angle to kill them all. 'It's no good. Engine won't start.' 'Right, get out.' Gillman called Cranley. 'We're hit, sir, all crew OK. Baling out.' Gillman switched back to the internal circuit to hear the panicky voice of the driver: 'I'm trapped down here unless you move the turret.' 'Sorry. Gunner, traverse forty right and for God's sake shoot at something, then jump.'

Gillman got behind the machinegun and searched for the flash that would betray the anti-tank gun. They would have a machinegun nearby, just waiting to pick off any escaping tank crews, an unpleasant new escalation in armoured warfare. Gillman had been told that it was sometimes safer to stay in an obviously crippled tank, one that would not attract further fire, rather than risk the machineguns. On the other hand, if the tank was burning, or about to burn, you had little choice. Gillman fired a wide burst anyway in an attempt to cover the driver, who scrambled out of the hatch and scampered safely round to the back of the Crusader. The gunner and operator followed. Then Gillman levered himself out of the turret. At which point the Germans noticed the escape and a clatter of bullets resulted. But from five hundred yards, he reckoned he stood a decent chance, and he made it safely around the back to join the others. The anti-tank crew would have seen him too. They could expect a round of high-explosive any minute, so they all ran for the cover of a nearby gully.

Some minutes later another Crusader approached and they all sprinted for it and clambered on to the back. It began very slowly to reverse. Gillman felt oddly happy. He'd faced the enemy, he'd fired a few shots and he was pretty sure that at least one of them had hit something. And he'd lived to fight for King and Country another day.

General Alan Brooke was well aware that his biggest problem was a lack of good generals.

> Half our Corps and Divisional commanders are totally unfit for their appointments, and yet if I were to sack them I could find no better. They lack character, imagination, drive and power of leadership.

The men who led Britain's desert army had all learned their trade in the Great War. In Flanders they had fought in great battles of attrition, and studied the correct synchronisation of artillery barrage and infantry attack, the importance of barbed wire and machineguns. This was not the ideal preparation for the armoured conflict of the open desert, this war of manoeuvre with combined arms that their enemy practised with such evident skill.

But one general knew something of desert warfare: Sir Claude Auchinleck, Britain's Commander-in-Chief, Middle East. During the Great War 'the Auk', as he was universally known, won victories over the Turks in the deserts and open plains of Egypt and Mesopotamia. In 1940 Auchinleck was a member of Alan Brooke's anti-invasion team and when Brooke became CIGS, he made him responsible for the vast Middle East theatre. From his bustling headquarters in Cairo, Auchinleck had to worry about Palestine, Syria, Mesopotamia and Persia as well as the war against Rommel.

Auchinleck inspired deep loyalty in those who served under him but, it was said in London, he did not always appoint the best men. His most important subordinate was the commander of Eighth Army. His first choice, Alan Cunningham, had fared so badly that Auchinleck had sacked him halfway through the campaign to relieve Tobruk in late 1941, and led Eighth Army to victory himself. As a stopgap he then appointed a friend and staff officer called Neil Ritchie. Over the past few months Ritchie had made confident noises but looked slightly out of his depth. By the end of May neither Auchinleck in Cairo nor Brooke in London was completely sure of him.

Although Brooke struggled to prevent Churchill from making direct contact with commanders in the field, the Prime Minister had been breathing down Auchinleck's neck for months, urging an attack because he was concerned about the number of rein- forcements reaching Rommel. Auchinleck had resisted what he called Churchill's 'prodding' because there had been a history of hastily and poorly planned offensives in the desert and he did not want to be responsible for yet another one.

Shortly before Rommel's attack at Gazala, Auchinleck had been called to London for urgent consultations. A politically sensitive general would have obediently flown home and spent an evening in Number 10. It would have begun with recriminations, no doubt, but ended with a long boozy conversation about Napoleon. Then he would have returned to Cairo to continue planning exactly as before. Churchill would have been satisfied that the right man was doing the best that he could and would have turned his attention elsewhere for a while. But Auchinleck had resisted the summons and, when Brooke all but ordered him on to a plane, insisted to the point of rudeness that his proper place was in Cairo.

It was an article of faith with Churchill that grand gestures and bold actions could turn the tide of history. He thought of Nelson at Trafalgar or his own ancestor Marlborough at Blenheim. He also, no doubt, thought of himself in 1940 resisting the logic of defeat while armed with little more than the English language. Since then his restless pursuit of 'the bold stroke' had cost his country dear at times, no more so than during the Greek adventure. And yet who could deny that those same qualities had kept the British people engaged in an apparently hopeless war through months of privation and failure?

The great leader steadying and revitalising the nation. The manboy playing soldiers. With Churchill the one came with the other. Although he dreamed of being a second Marlborough, Churchill was first and foremost a *political* genius. And it was as a politician that he pressed for his desert offensives. Aware of the poor state of home morale by the spring of 1942, he knew how much a victory in the desert would boost the British people. He also knew how it would reassure the Soviets, who were expecting another German offensive any day.

As the crisis of late May broke over Churchill, Brooke and Auchinleck, the Prime Minister's reaction would be affected by his irritation at the caution of the past few months. And by a general's refusal to come and dine at Number 10.

The survivors of the South Notts observation party, Harold Harper, Ivor Birkin, Bobby Feakins and the radio operator with the broken legs, were still lost in the desert. They couldn't see much because the movement and fighting all around had thrown up so much dust, but the panzers seemed to have swept past. Suddenly a lone Crusader tank came into view, firing backward as it went. It was moving very slowly and the men seized their chance. The others helped Feakins, whose thigh was still bleeding, up on to the tank. Harper forced Ivor Birkin to leave the body of his brother and together they lifted the radio operator up.

The tank started moving backwards again. Its commander had no idea we had climbed aboard and we had to keep dodging as the turret kept swinging round. High-explosive shells were bursting close by and we were all hit by shrapnel. Feakins fell off and we thought he'd been crushed to death. We kept hammering on the top and eventually they heard us and agreed to take us back to their own base, if they could find it.

Feakins was lucky enough to be picked up later by another stray British tank. The others reached a forward supply base. Harper asked a sergeant-major to take them to hospital. They had all been hit by little pieces of shrapnel, but he was particularly worried about the man with the broken legs.

The sergeant-major said, 'No, we're off.' But another young lad offered to drive us to a field dressing station near by. When we got there an ambulance was about to leave taking people all the way back to the rear areas and safety. We all piled on, but as we were just leaving a lad turned up who'd had his foot blown off by a mine. So I got off for him and said I'd catch the next one.

There wasn't going to be a next one. Harper could still see the ambulance disappearing into the distance when about a dozen German tanks and armoured cars arrived in the middle of the field hospital. He was now their prisoner, along with all the other wounded men lying around and those treating them.

I surrendered to the sergeant in charge of the nearest tank. He took my revolver but was quite friendly. He asked me to empty my pockets. I had about ten pounds in Egyptian currency, which was quite a lot of money. He laughed and told me to put it away. Then he pulled out a great wad of freshly printed stuff. He said he expected to be in Cairo by 10 June and he'd been given that to spend there. He gave me a bar of chocolate too.

The British colonel in charge of the dressing station heard me speaking in German and came over and asked me to be his interpreter. He had a wagon full of water and he was anxious to keep it. I'd been taught quite a bit of German at school, which was unusual in those days. German lorries began to pull up and ask for the doctor. I pointed out the operating theatre and they brought their wounded in.

In the fast-moving fighting of the desert war, locations often changed hands several times in a day. Field hospitals were generally left unmolested and would accept casualties from both sides. Whoever was in command of that piece of territory at the end of the day would then take prisoner the soldiers of the army that had departed. Some men went into the operating theatre thinking themselves POWs and awoke to find themselves free, and vice versa. But it looked as if Harold Harper was 'in the bag' for good.

An hour or so later this car drove up and an imposing figure stepped out and went over to the tanks. It was Rommel. I was standing with the commanding officer of the dressing station when he came over and thanked him for attending to the German wounded. At the height of the battle he took time to say that everything possible would be done to make we British prisoners comfortable, and that he was sorry he couldn't get any food through as yet, but his officers would try. I couldn't fail to be impressed.

It was late afternoon when Peter Vaux stopped again. The vehicles pulled up on the Capuzzo track, beneath the picturesque domed tomb of Sidi Rezegh on its hillside. While Corporal Williams got a brew on, Vaux sat on the steps to the ACV wearing radio headphones and tried to talk to the brigades of the division he now commanded. Earlier 7 Motor Brigade had reported being in combat but now he could not get any answer from them. He did get through to 4 Armoured Brigade, who reported that, after the morning's fighting, they had 80 'runners' left out of 180. He still had no orders from Corps, who could not have understood his earlier messages. He sent another liaison officer off to find them. Of General Messervy there was no news.

There was more dust in the distance, and once again they were under fire. Nothing very serious but armoured cars and half-tracks were more than a match for them. Vaux ordered the column to move again, heading for Gambut, where there was a big airfield and Eighth Army headquarters. If they were to find safety anywhere it should be there.

Just short of Gambut they stopped again and were met by the missing ACV3. The colonel in charge of signals banged angrily on Peter Vaux's door and asked where the hell he had been. Vaux's reply was rather brusque. He suggested that now the proper signallers had reappeared they might like to help him get through to Corps. Finally they got off a cipher message that was understood and acknowledged. Then, during the night, they received some orders at last. What was left of 4 Armoured Brigade was to fall back and come under the command of 30 Corps at first light. The next few hours were spent arranging to get fuel and ammunition through to them. By midnight there was, in truth, not much more for Vaux to do, and only the men around him remained his own responsibility. It would have been time to retire to his tent, had the tent not fallen into enemy hands at breakfast time.

'You get some sleep, sir. I'll watch the radio, but I don't think much more will come through tonight. We've found some blankets for you.'

'Thank you, Corporal.'

He took the blankets from Corporal Paxton and rolled up next to the ACV. For the third year in succession he had been caught up in a chaotic disaster, for the third year in succession he had almost been killed, and for the third year in succession he had lost all his personal possessions. It was barely credible. He thought back to May 1940 when he first made Rommel's acquaintance at the Battle of Arras. After the battle he had been cut off from his unit and his crew had gone into hiding, trying to escape to their own lines. On 27 May he had been captured by a German officer. He'd killed him and escaped, but in the process he had lost all his kit. In May 1941 they had been sent to recapture the Halfaya Pass. Vaux had survived the ensuing carnage but on 27 May his bag had been shot off the back of his tank and once again he had lost all his things. And now, 27 May 1942, it had happened all over again.

Forceful confidence followed by sullen despair was a rhythm familiar to those closest to Winston Churchill, but in 1942 the 'black dog' moments seemed deeper and longer lasting. The ebullience and good cheer never entirely went away, especially after a good dinner, but the Prime Minister had lost some of his sparkle.

One reason was the recent series of defeats, another the incessant Soviet demands for a Second Front in Europe. Stalin wanted to see an early Anglo-American invasion of France to draw German troops away from his hard-pressed forces. In the spring of 1942 the Red Army was confronting 178 German and 39 other Axis divisions, while the British in North Africa were having difficulty dealing with just three and a half German and six Italian divisions.

When faced with statistics like these Churchill always drew attention to the scale of the war he was trying to fight. In the six months prior to May 1942 British, imperial and dominion forces had been in action throughout the Mediterranean, in East and West Africa, in Madagascar, Syria and the Lebanon, and all over the Far East. They had launched commando raids on the French and Norwegian coast. They had parachuted agents, saboteurs and assassins into occupied Europe. In addition a vast naval effort was under way. Germany was being blockaded and hundreds of merchant ships a month were being convoyed across the Atlantic, through the Mediterranean to embattled Malta and across the Arctic to Russia. The RAF was also fully engaged, running fighter sweeps over northern France and building up the world's largest night-bomber force. Churchill and his ministers would patiently explain all these commitments to Soviet representatives, and claim that by their actions they were occupying almost as many Axis troops as were fighting in Russia. But the Soviet demand for a Second Front would not go away.

Molotov, Stalin's foreign minister, visited London in May to receive the unwelcome news that an invasion of France was extremely unlikely in 1942. He then travelled to Washington where President Roosevelt gave him the opposite impression. As May became June the question 'Who's in charge here?' was being asked in more places than the Western Desert.

Chapter 3

28–30 May

The American military attaché, Colonel Bonner F. Fellers, was one of the most charming men in Cairo. Energetic, informal, and a great source of wisecracks, Fellers was a regular guest at the British embassy, was on first-name terms with General Auchinleck and all his senior staff, and was even seen at some of Momo Marriott's rather louche cocktail parties at the Turf Club.

Hermione Knox, Countess of Ranfurly was a well-connected aristocratic lady whose husband was in the Eighth Army. She met Fellers on the luncheon circuit in 1941, describing him as 'an original and delightful person who seems to say exactly what he thinks to everyone regardless of nationality or rank'. He was generous too. When Ranfurly's husband was captured, Fellers spent weeks searching out information about him from American diplomats in Italy.

As one of the most important Americans in the Mediterranean, Fellers, a forty-six-year-old West Point graduate, could travel just about anywhere he liked and would frequently turn up with a welcome bottle of Scotch or two at Eighth Army's forward headquarters. Fellers was a great supporter of Lend Lease and, when America came into the war, he celebrated with his British friends with great gusto. After that he spent even more time with senior

British officers, driving around in what he called his 'hearse', a camouflaged van with a bunk in the back that he used for his trips into the desert.

Fellers was well aware of the Eighth Army's weaknesses. Over a lunch with Ranfurly in January 1942, he told her that he was in trouble with Washington for being a 'defeatist', but said he was only reporting what he had found:

> The trouble is your top brass are overconfident which they've no right to be: your gear is still inferior to the enemy's, and you are less well led – too many senior officers are sitting on their arses at GHQ.

Fellers kept himself informed about every aspect of British military equipment, tactics and performance, reporting what he learned back to Washington two or three times a week. The planners at the War Department were desperate for up-to-date information about what a modern armoured battle was like, and Fellers' cables included whatever he could garner for them about Eighth Army's order of battle, supply situation, tactical plans and appreciation of the enemy. Models of accuracy and insight, the reports helped Washington plan for America's own future battles. But, unfortunately, that was not all that they did. A great many British soldiers died in May and June 1942 as a result of what was contained in the pages Fellers cabled back to Washington, because most of his cables were placed in Erwin Rommel's hands within hours.

America was new to war, and to the intense concern about secure communication that war brings. No one in Washington had thought to overhaul the old cipher codes, and some of them had been badly compromised during the past few years of frantic Axis intelligence-gathering. The US diplomatic service's 'black' code was used by the State Department to communicate with America's embassies, and also by military attachés reporting back from abroad. In 1941 Italian agents broke into the US embassy in Rome, stole a 'black' codebook from the safe, copied it and returned it before anyone realised it was missing. From that moment they could read US diplomatic traffic, and they passed some of their intelligence to Rommel. By autumn 1941, in a separate breakthrough, the 'black code' was analysed and deciphered by the German Cipher Branch, OKW/Chi, who picked up the messages from their listening station near Nuremberg. The deciphering of the Fellers' cables was one of the greatest Axis intelligence coups of the war.

Fellers' accounts of the situation and plans of the Eighth Army gave Rommel invaluable help in his January 1942 offensive. One cable of 8 January 1942 provided a precise breakdown of the British tank strength:

> Estimates (Cairo) on equipment (British army) serviceable tanks in Libya: 328; repairable tanks in Libya: 521. Tanks destroyed [last campaign] 374.

Some of the information contained in Fellers' intercepted cables, such as '2 Armoured Brigade of British 1 Armoured Division now west of Haseiat . . .', was of obvious use to the enemy. Other, smaller details, such as 'Malta air forces report two [Axis] merchantmen . . .', alerted the Germans and Italians to imminent attacks on their supply ships.

As he planned Operation Venezia, Rommel received more inadvertent help from the Allies because, by April, Fellers was being invited to Auchinleck's daily staff conferences in Cairo, which included all details of British army, naval and air operations in the Mediterranean. This produced such messages to Washington as:

> To oppose Rommel in the desert the British have: 1st Armored Division whose combat strength at best is fair; 50th British Division; Polish Brigade deficient in transport; Guards Brigade whose combat efficiency is good; 1st South African Division which

lost a complete brigade in November; 2nd South African Division which is without transport and is holding the frontier posts. Part of the 10th Armored Division, tankless, is now enroute to the desert. All of these units combined could not stop Rommel were he reinforced as indicated above.

The same document also explained that an Australian corps had gone to the Far East, and gave a complete breakdown of the RAF's latest strength. Another made it clear that

It will be the end of March before the 10th and 7th Armored divisions can be fitted with tanks ready for battle. If present flow of tanks is maintained, British will not have battleworthy armored division ready until June 30.

Knowing which units were under strength and which had transport problems allowed Rommel to target his attacks with great precision. It was a little like playing cards with an exact knowledge of your opponents' hands.

Other intercepted cables from Fellers contained a complete run-down of British armour and the latest British efficiency ratings of their armoured and mechanised units at the front. One detailed Eighth Army's knowledge of Rommel's own forward positions, telling him which of his units was in danger with information such as 'his outposts on the Tmimi–Mechili line are near to strong British forces'. Finally, there was a detailed description of where the British thought the key German units were located in the days before Operation Venezia commenced, down to the level of individual regiments.

According to one member of his intelligence staff

Rommel used to wait for the dispatches every evening [before deciding his orders for the next day] . . . we just knew them as 'the good source'.

The German High Command was so proud of the intelligence breakthrough that it informed Hitler of it. He announced to his dinner companions one night in June that

> It was only to be hoped that the American Minister in Cairo [*sic*] continues to inform us so well over the English military planning through his badly enciphered cables.

The British were given some early indications of the security breach. On 13 April German intelligence sent an urgent warning to the desert to the effect that the British had discovered the location of the Luftwaffe desert headquarters and might attack it at any moment. This warning was in turn decrypted by Britain's own code-breakers at Bletchley Park (who had cracked the Luftwaffe 'Enigma') and handed to Churchill as part of his daily Ultra papers.

Churchill wrote immediately to the head of the intelligence service, Sir Stewart Menzies, known as 'C':

> Please report on this. How did they [German intelligence] know that we had told the Army in Egypt where it [German air HQ] was?

'C' replied that he had asked Cairo to investigate.

A troubling reference to information obtained by the Germans from 'a good source' was sent to Churchill on 24 April. A German intelligence report had been decrypted, saying – based on 'the good source' – that the British were not strong enough to attack before 1 June and that the situation on Malta was reaching crisis point. Then, on 26 April, a very detailed German account of the British positions was decrypted – a long list of place and unit names, with troop nationalities and battalion numbers. Such detail could only come from a senior officer. Was there a spy in Cairo?

On 2 May the British discovered another reference to 'the good source' in a German intelligence report. This one included more details of newly arrived British units, and an account of the poor serviceability of their equipment, adding that it would be some weeks before it was battleworthy.

'C' now knew that he had a major security problem on his hands. Attention focused on a possible traitor in London or Cairo, but no one for the moment considered that the Americans might be responsible for the leak.

The sight that greeted Peter Vaux when he reached 30 Corps headquarters left him with mixed feelings. There was Donald Reid, right as rain, smiling his toothy smile in his best white cravat, and there standing next to him, in equally good form, was General Messervy. Vaux was delighted to see Reid again, but the presumed loss of his general had not been absolutely unwelcome. For a moment there had been a ray of hope that General Ritchie or General Auchinleck or General Brooke or whoever really decided these things (Winston Churchill, he suspected) might give 7 Armoured Division to someone familiar with tanks.

Reid explained what had happened. Their driver had been killed by cannon fire and the engine destroyed. Reid, himself slightly wounded, edged open the door and told the general that vehicles all around were on fire and that an armoured car had its guns trained on them. They set light to the codes with their own incendiaries, Messervy tore off his badges of rank, and they all piled out with their hands up. A German doctor attending to Reid's shrapnel wounds remarked that the man next to him seemed rather old to be fighting, to which Reid answered that he was his batman. The Germans had been fooled by the disguised command vehicles and had not realised that they had captured anything more significant than a few supply lorries.

The prisoners were put into captured British trucks and driven east in one of the advancing German columns. They had discussed whether they might overpower the driver, but didn't need to. Before long they came under shellfire from the British lines. The driver leapt out of the cab and threw himself flat on the ground while the prisoners simply scattered. They hid in a little depression until nightfall and then walked on eastward. In the morning they were approached by some vehicles that turned out to be British.

Given his own recent experiences, Vaux was surprised to find a generally optimistic attitude at Corps and Eighth Army headquarters. And the news from the battle was far from all bad. Because Bir Hacheim was still being held, the Germans were being forced to take their supplies on a huge southern detour, along a route that was being constantly attacked by the RAF and the French. Vaux and his assistant, Corporal Paxton, interviewed a stream of German and Italian prisoners who told them of unexpectedly stiff resistance and of problems getting fuel, ammunition and water to their lead units.

The 'khamsin' was a wind straight from hell. Sweeping across the Sahara, it reached the north with the heat of a blowtorch. The local Arabs said that after four days of it Allah would excuse even murder. Today, 29 May, a khamsin had gathered all the loose sand and grit dislodged by the tracks, wheels and shells of the last days' fighting and was flinging it into the faces of the tank commanders. The scarves wrapped over their mouths did not prevent them being simultaneously burned, blinded and choked.

Neville Gillman had another reason to feel subdued. In the morning he had buried a good friend.

We came across one of our tanks. I knew the commander, Freddie Mason. He was a really nice man. He had just his head out of the turret and a bit of shrapnel had gone straight through his neck. It must have been shortly after it had happened. I was the senior man there and not sure what to do. And I was pretty shaken by it all to be honest. It was the first time I'd seen the body of someone I knew. I was just mumbling the Lord's Prayer when the Medical Officer came by and he read out a short burial service for us.

In a new Crusader tank, Gillman and the rest of C squadron were now searching for the enemy's latest positions near Bir Harmat. He tried to clear his mind of Freddie Mason, and his eyes of the blistering hot sand.

General Lumsden's Order of the Day read: 'This is the most important battle of the war so far.' But there was no battle to speak of, only sand and confusion. Visibility was so wretched they had to be directed by bearings to numbered barrels. Hundreds of these barrels with map references painted on them had been placed around the desert to make navigation possible. But the sun compass did not work in storms and the prismatic compass was unreliable unless you stopped and dismounted to check the bearing. In the featureless landscape it was only too easy to get lost, searching for a painted barrel in the sand which the course of the war might depend on your finding.

The commanders of 15 Panzer Division were having the same problem, and the fighting, when it did commence, soon became hopelessly confused as friends and enemies slipped in and out of vision. Gillman exchanged fire with tanks he could hardly see. But at least for the Crusaders, with their small 2-pounder guns, the sand-storm made it easier to get within range. After a while the Sharpshooters seemed to be under fire from all directions. The order to withdraw was a relief for the men sweating and swearing inside the baking-hot Crusaders. Gillman reversed, turned to what he thought was the right direction and had his narrowest escape yet.

Suddenly the storm lifted and there a couple of hundred yards away was an eighty-eight-millimetre gun that was pointing straight

at us. Point blank, couldn't miss. And then, just as suddenly, the
sand gathered around us again and we drove on past it.

They fell back to Barrel 230 but were heavily shelled, so they
pulled back half a mile farther. Viscount Cranley led them with
a running commentary over the radio. It turned out that Ariete
Division had joined their mêlée from the west and that 21 Panzer
had come down from the north, and so they had been caught
up between three Axis divisions. Rommel was drawing in his
horns, pulling his armour together.

With the exception of the new 'long-barrelled' Panzer IIIs, the
German tanks were not much better armed than the British ones,
and most Italian tanks were considered by their own crews to be
more dangerous to themselves than the enemy. But both the
Italians and the Germans had quite deadly anti-tank guns. Britain's
tank crews had come to fear them more than any panzer.

The long-barrelled 50mm Pak 38 lay so low to the ground
that it was almost invisible when dug in and camouflaged. It fired
a shell that was twice the weight of its British equivalent, the 2-
pounder, and 150 per cent more penetrative. At a range of 1,500
yards, it could cut through the frontal armour of any British tank
except the Valentine. Unlike the British gun, it could switch
between armour-piercing and high-explosive shells, so that it
could hurt gun crews, infantry or lorries as well as tanks.

The 50mm was bad enough, but infinitely preferable to the
88. Seeing one of *those* generally meant that your tank was
doomed. But you rarely got close enough to see it; a nearby tank
suddenly becoming a blazing inferno was generally your first clue
that an 88 was around. It didn't flash when it fired either, and it
had an intricate telescopic sight and even coloured lenses to help
the gunlayers peer through the midday haze. It could fire high-
explosive or a massive 23-pound armour-piercing shell. The
British army had nothing even close.

They said you could see it coming: a greeny-white line snaking
low over the ground, accelerating like hell as it approached, the

vortex of the shell cutting a little furrow into the sand. And when it hit, it felt as if a giant had swung a sledgehammer. It sounded like it too as, with a terrible clanging sound, it cut a perfect four-inch circle in the metal and filled the inside with red-hot shards. If it went into the petrol tank, the whole thing burned like a torch. In their sardonic way they called it 'brewing up'. But it was a brew that left behind evil-smelling black stumps that had once been men.

On 30 May Peter Vaux wrote up the results of the battles in the sandstorm. He was pretty sure he knew what was going on now.

> *The enemy armour was frustrated in its object by the action of our armour to his EAST, WEST and SOUTH, and by mobile columns including tanks attacking him from the NORTH. A confused battle consequently went on in the area NORTH of BIR HARMAT all day, and it is apparent from the move of 500 Motorised Transport from the area WEST of BIR GUBI that the bulk of 90 Light Division has been sent across to the assistance of the enemy armour in order to keep the gap open between HARMAT and KNIGHTSBRIDGE, and to bring pressure to bear on EL ADEM.*
>
> *It is considered that the enemy was surprised to find our armour in such strength in the HARMAT area, and that this has considerably upset his plans.*

And it would upset his plans even more, Vaux thought, if we did something decisive about it quickly. The Free French stand at Bir Hacheim was now causing the enemy severe problems, as the intelligence flowing in confirmed. Having failed in his first thrust at the coast, Rommel was concentrating his forces around the centre of the Gazala line at Bir el Harmat. He was hoping to open up a new, shorter, supply route through the British minefields. But, unlike

Peter Vaux, he did not know that the British 150 Brigade with its supporting tanks was in the way and that he faced being caught like a rat in a trap. A very bold plan formed in Vaux's mind.

> Now was the time to attack in force. 150 Brigade was blocking Rommel's retreat through the minefield so it was possible to attack southwards like he had, around Bir Hacheim.

Such an advance could sweep away Rommel's lightly defended supply units and take the unprotected Italian infantry in the rear, leaving all the panzers high and dry and completely stuck. This was surely the moment to 'gerommel Rommel'.

> Horden, the intelligence officer at Corps, was recommending that this should be done. I was very keen and Donald Reid wanted it too. We nagged on about it. But General Messervy wasn't interested. He said, 'Peter, you don't understand. It's not as easy as that.'

Everybody at Eighth Army HQ agreed that they had Rommel pinned down, and that this was a golden opportunity to destroy his army. But how were they going to do it? The generals came and went from Ritchie's yellow wooden caravan. While they conferred, Peter Vaux wondered when Rommel would perceive the danger he was in and how long it would take him to react.

Harold Harper was still at the field hospital with its mixed bag of British and German patients. He'd broken some ribs in the crash with the Grant tank and had shrapnel in his knee from his escape on the Crusader, which the captured British doctor treated. While he was there he watched what the Germans were doing, as he had been told that a prisoner should. He noticed that they used purple smoke to signal they were friends to their own aircraft. He memorised how many tanks there were and what markings they had on their sides. Gradually there were fewer of them. The Germans seemed to have pulled back and the fighting died down. He thought it might be possible to slip away. A Welsh infantryman agreed to go with him.

There was moon and starlight to walk by and the few remaining Germans did not seem very bothered about guarding them. If people were fool enough to wander off into the desert it was their responsibility. In just a pair of shorts and a bandage the night was chilly, even in late May. It was also strangely quiet.

My theory was that if we went due south-east we would be edging out into the desert where there was less likelihood of anyone being around.

After a while a dark shape loomed ahead of them and they could hear low voices and laughter. 'It's a lorry-load of Germans. What shall we do?' 'Just keep walking. I'll speak. Ready? *So, Hans, so hab'ich gesagt . . .*' But the Germans were playing cards and did not hear them pass.

The Nottinghamshire lads had spent many nights in Tobruk watching the stars and getting their bearings from them. Now Harper used them to guide his escape. They moved through sand and over hard rock and through patches where the camel thorn threw ghostly patterns over the moonlit ground, constantly on the alert for danger. The desert nights were short in the spring and, just as the sky began to lighten, they were alarmed to see the shapes of more vehicles ahead. 'Are they theirs or ours?' 'Ours, I think.' They crept closer. But the vehicles were derelict, one burnt out, another with a broken engine. 'What's on it? Is it water?' 'Bloody ammunition.' 'Sod it. No food anywhere?' There was a tin of Meat and Veg in the driver's compartment but no tin opener. In the end the best they could do was to swill their mouths out with what was left in the radiator. Then they crawled underneath to hide from the sun.

We had the sense not to appear in the daytime. When the sun was belting down we just got under a vehicle. We never slept to any great extent, kept awake all the time because you daren't sleep.

Once, in the far distance, Harper thought he saw a column of vehicles. When he looked again the lorries were up in the sky. A trick of the heat haze or a friendly column? There was no way of reaching them even if they were British.

Once it got dark they set off again, the Welshman walking a few yards ahead through an area of soft sand. Suddenly there was an explosion and he'd gone. Harper called but there was no answer. What do you do in a minefield? He crawled forward, feeling in the sand with his hands. He didn't know whether his next movement would be his last, but he found nothing and nothing happened. When he reached the body it was a mess. A big mine, anti-tank for sure. There was nothing he could do, so he just crawled on. After a hundred yards of crawling without being blown up he felt stupid and decided to take his chance on his feet. Perhaps it was a stray mine, there were plenty of those about. Anyway, if this was the end, then so be it. He'd now gone almost twenty-four hours without a drink. He cupped his hands and pissed into them. He was just going to swill his mouth out, but he forced himself to swallow.

He walked on, feeling lonely, lost and confused. He was at Nottingham station again saying goodbye to all his mates. In the chip shop helping his dad. Why had he listened to that sergeant? By dawn he was beginning to stagger, but then he saw vehicles. 'If they're German, I don't care,' he muttered through cracked lips. But as he got closer he recognised an armoured car like his own. And those were definitely Bren carriers.

He paused, thinking, it would be just my luck to get shot now. He put his hands up and staggered boldly forward, shouting in English as loud as he possibly could. The sentry on duty was only mildly surprised to see a bedraggled and half-demented figure come in from the desert. But he tried to shout a warning to him. Harper waved his hands enthusiastically and came on. The guardsman waited impassively, smiling slightly, until Harper arrived. Then he said, 'You were bloody lucky, chum. You just walked through our minefield.'

In the months before Operation Venezia began, someone in Cairo had realised that Bonner Fellers might pose a security problem. Since he was now turning up at staff conferences, and at brigade and divisional headquarters, it was decided that there should be an official directive describing what he could, and could not, be told.

It was clear that the first priority of those writing the paper was to preserve American goodwill. On 25 April the first draft of the liaison document stated:

> It is essential to avoid giving offence to Colonel Bonner Fellers or to give the impression that information to which he is entitled is being withheld . . . He is entitled to seek the most secret information on any subject connected with the war effort.

Several drafts and redrafts followed as the paper circulated within Middle East HQ. On 26 April the Director of Military Intelligence wrote:

> I am glad this list is being reconsidered . . . he should receive nothing the leakage of which might have serious consequences.

That there was a certain unease about Fellers is evident from the correspondence attached to the draft liaison document. On 27 April a note by Lt Col. A.T. Cornwall Jones, the secretary of the Commanders-in-Chief Committee, explained that the Commanders-in-Chief should note that Fellers was in Egypt to gather more than information on the enemy. He was to gather information on the British situation too. The note suggested that someone should

> ask Colonel Fellers to give us an assurance in writing to the effect that information transferred to Washington will be sent by safe means. We shall discuss with him what these means are and satisfy ourselves that they are secure.

The final directive on how Fellers should be treated was distributed inside Middle East headquarters and senior levels of Eighth Army on 12 May. Issued by the Commanders-in-Chief for air, land and sea, it made clear that Fellers was to be allowed access to Joint Intelligence Committee papers and memos and was to be told the General Staff's latest information on the enemy position.

> The Joint Planning Staff are authorised to discuss frankly with Colonel Fellers the strategical situation. This will include discussion of future strategic plans.

The directive also stated that Fellers was to be allowed to visit units in the field and

> [he] will be given every facility to see and study the following:
>
> a) British tactical doctrine.
> b) The handling and behaviour of the war equipment with the troops, particularly American equipment.

He was also given permission to see Eighth Army's daily and weekly intelligence summaries, and the RAF's own intelligence summaries. However, and quite confusingly, all of this access was hedged by a paragraph written in a very different tone of voice, stating that

> highly secret information of an operational nature (e.g. dates of operations, precise strength and location of our forces) is restricted.

Unless therefore American forces are actually participating in an operation, information of this nature must be withheld from Colonel Bonner Fellers.

Given the fluidity of the situation, the amount of socialising that Fellers did with high- and middle-ranking officers, his brief to roam the desert talking to brigade and divisional staff, and his presence at many of Auchinleck's staff conferences, there was a dangerous contradiction at the heart of this working arrangement. He was to be involved in key intelligence and strategic conversations, but somehow once talk turned to 'operational' matters he was to leave the room or be told not to listen. It's evident from the detail contained in his reports that Fellers was, in fact, told almost everything all the time.

Peter Vaux was an important operational intelligence officer. He met Fellers many times, liked him very much and has no memory of any concern about security. He would show him the maps on the wall of his ACV and discuss the way the battle had been going, but if Fellers wanted any details of upcoming operations Peter always referred him to the general in ACV1.

Point 12 of the liaison directive stated that

Colonel Fellers has agreed to show and obtain the approval of the Branch or Officers concerned, before despatch to Washington, any appreciation of the situation or similar studies which represent official M.E. opinion.

It does not appear that this happened in practice. Fellers' cables were encoded and transmitted not on British equipment, which would have been a more secure route to Washington, but at the US embassy, using the compromised 'black code'. Asking to scrutinise secret State Department communications would have been a gross insult to a new ally, but it might have saved many lives.

Chapter 4

30 May–4 June

Edith Heap had never thought of her herself as an officer, so she was surprised when Wing Commander Churchill suggested she apply for a commission. Actually there was no need to apply, he said – a short interview in his office would suffice. 'But you're definitely too wild and woolly to be anything but Intelligence, Edith.' 'Wild and woolly?' How dare he! Actually it made her smile. She'd always had problems with RAF discipline, especially discipline she could not see the point of. But she was well organised, thank you very much, and capable of being quite fierce when she felt like it. Or so the boys all said when they got to know her a bit. It was the way she looked at them sometimes, apparently.

In 1940 Edith had been a plotter at RAF Debden in Essex, one of the young women in the Fighter Command operations rooms helping to guide the pilots into battle during the Battle of Britain. She was on duty the day that her fiancé Denis Wissler was shot down and killed. After that everything was a blur. She took some compassionate leave, cancelled the wedding plans, moved his ring from her left to her right hand and tried to stop thinking about him so much. She took what comfort she could in the company of her friends, and threw herself into her work.

Her best friend Fay Swaine was wonderful, and so was the rest of the gang. Leaving her alone when she needed the space, but always trying to include her in the parties and the dances that were part of life on a busy station. But she hung back from most of the fun. Denis's best friend, 'Birdy' Bird-Wilson, tried to help. He invited her down to his new base on the River Avon for a flip in a Miles Magister trainer. Edith adored flying and cadged trips off every pilot she knew; the more aerobatics they performed the better. Birdy flew her right under a suspension bridge, against all the rules, of course, the pair of them yipping and yahooing like a couple of maniacs.

By the middle of 1941 she was feeling a little better. Summer was warm and beautiful and the girls had lovely billets in Debden's old manor house. Fay and Edith took their beds up to the roof, using the fire-escape ladders to add a few extra minutes to their evening passes. They lay in the dark, listening to owls hooting in the woods and the roar of returning night fighters, and woke fresh as daisies with dew on their beds. They picked figs from the trees in the garden, until the owners complained about the disappearing produce.

There were songs on her lips again. She and Fay were always caterwauling together as they walked down the country lanes or drove along in her car, a smart little Jaguar covered in camouflage paint. They sang 'Amapola' or Fay's favourite, 'Deep Is the Night'. The newsreel people came by and filmed her driving a fuel bowser, along with Fay kneeling right in front of a pilot and helping him put on his parachute. It was all a bit embarrassing and rather suggestive and completely hysterical, and nothing like what usually happened at all. A relation saw her in the Ilkley flicks and shouted out, 'Good God, it's our Edith!'

Denis was still part of her life. She saw his family more often than her own. Every time she had leave she went to stay with his parents at their lovely big flat in London's Dolphin Square, down by the river. It was where they had announced the engagement and it felt like a second home now. The Wisslers were such great fun and they really appreciated her company, too. It made it easier for all of them. She would walk from King's Cross Station through the bomb damage, with rubble everywhere but people always seeming busy and chatty, then across Russell Square and down to Piccadilly, where the loitering men would wolf-whistle and ask her out on dates. Edith gave them frosty answers and her best hard stare. Then through the park, past Westminster and along the river.

Fay got engaged, but her fiancé died in a training accident. Edith did what she could to support her, knowing better than most how hard that was to do. A friend suggested they go to a medium. Edith was sceptical but found it surprisingly comforting. The large, mysterious-looking woman said she had visions of submarines going under the water. She thought this meant that Denis had drowned, which is what she had always imagined because he'd been having trouble with the release pin on his harness. The woman said that pilots who had already passed over would sometimes come to the aid of living crews. It was an odd thing to say, but in the months that followed she'd have cause to remember it.

They both passed the officer course. Fay went into administration, which was very funny considering how many rules they had broken together. Edith, as the Wing Commander had predicted, was selected for Intelligence and posted to Pocklington, a new bomber station in East Yorkshire. After six months as an acting section officer her rank was confirmed. She had a very responsible job in Operations, helping to look after 405 Squadron, Canadians flying Wellington bombers. 'Pock' was one of the first RAF bases to use WAAFs in this demanding role. Edith managed the preparation of the planes and the crews, and had to debrief the men on their return. She was half authority figure, half friend and confessor. Most important she was back on 'ops', at the centre of the action again.

Our ops room was always busy. With anything between twenty-five and thirty planes and their crews to look after, and raids every couple of days, there was always someone coming in, or some new information to process from Group. It was one of those places that seemed to hum with energy. We had to be cool and collected with no panic stations, making sure the right information got to the right people at the right time. It was good to have that kind of responsibility, and quite rare for women at that time.

Every week some of the high-spirited young men she helped send off to Germany and occupied Europe failed to return. 'Ops' would call through to the mess so that their kit could go into storage and their room be made ready for a new man.

Fighter and bomber boys were very different. The [bomber] crews were a bit older, not quite so madcap, but they had the same disdain for stuffiness and some of the sillier rules and regs as I had. There was a lot of clowning on all sides. But we all knew it was covering up churning stomachs and jangling nerves.

We were the first to see them after an op, before they had time to get their masks on. And we knew, we could tell just by looking, what it had been like.

The stupid accidental deaths were the worst. In April Squadron Leader McCormack and Flight Lieutenant Fetherstone had just finished their tour of duty but were killed having a final flip in a Miles Magister trainer.

They stalled after a tight turn and were too close to the deck to recover in time. Both really nice men.

It was harrowing to the last degree, slow-marching with the band to the village cemetery, the 'Last Post' and rifle fire and, worst of all, each officer had to march to the foot of the grave and salute. I for one was always apprehensive of taking one step too many and falling in.

'I wondered how long it would take *them* to get here,' said Peter Vaux to his driver as from the dust cloud emerged the unmistakable figures of a number of old acquaintances, the representatives of the world's press. Several had adopted the casual dress that old desert hands were supposed to wear, corduroy trousers and silk cravats, and they all looked faintly ridiculous. He adjusted his own cravat, jumped down from his jeep and walked over to greet them.

Vaux had been about to visit the division's tanks, but he had instructions to be nice to the press so he steered them towards ACV2. There were several people he recognised: Alex Clifford of the *Daily Mail*, Alan Moorehead of the *Express* and American Chester Morrison of the *Chicago Sun*. There were photographers too. As they came by with their cameras, Corporal Williams smirked. Vaux knew he was remembering the visit of that society photographer fellow, Cecil Beaton, who for some unaccountable reason was travelling around the desert disguised as an RAF officer. 'He smells nice, don't he, sir?' Williams had commented.

Vaux showed the journalists his big map with the enemy's positions in detail and the new British ones sketched out. No harm in that – everything they sent out was censored. They were chiefly interested in the Free French at Bir Hacheim, whose stand against Rommel was big news all over the world. But Vaux explained that it was difficult and dangerous to get there. They then asked whether it might be possible to visit one of the tank units that had fought the Germans on the first day. 'Funnily enough,' said Vaux, 'I was just going there myself. I'll guide you.'

All of 7 Armoured Division's remaining armour had now combined into a single makeshift unit of about sixty tanks, twenty-eight of which were Grants and the rest fragile Stuarts and slow Valentines. The Americans in particular were eager to meet 'Pip' Roberts, a young colonel who had led the first batch of their Grant tanks to fight the panzers, and had accounted for twenty of them. But before convening a mini press conference, Vaux wanted to talk to Roberts himself.

Vaux trusted Roberts and was anxious to get his informed opinion about what had really happened in the recent fighting. Away from the scrutiny of senior officers, the two tank men spoke frankly. Roberts had long admired the dexterity with which the Germans combined their forces. When the British attacked, the Germans would retreat through a screen of dug-in anti-tank guns. These were both difficult to see and very powerful. When the British were stopped by the anti-tank guns, the panzers would creep round their flanks. It was the basic Panzerarmee tactic, and it seemed to work every time.

The British had a new weapon that might give them the chance to imitate German tactics. New 6-pounder anti-tank guns were being delivered even as Vaux and Roberts spoke. These would help in defence, but they wouldn't solve the problem of going forward against the enemy guns. Most British weapons could fire only a solid armour-piercing shot, when what was needed to kill gun crews and infantry was the shrapnel from high-explosive shells. The latest attempt to deal with this problem was to attach 25-pounder field guns, like those of the South Notts Hussars, to the armoured brigades. These could fire both kinds of shell. Vaux asked how this was working out. 'Not too well,' was Roberts' answer, owing, he said, to poor coordination and lack of practice.

Vaux asked how the Grants had performed. They were a big improvement because their 75mm gun matched the best German weapons and could fire high-explosive as well as armour-piercing. But there were problems: they couldn't carry enough 75mm ammunition and the main gun was mounted too low while the other, smaller one just got in the way. The gun sight was poor; even at close range the gunner had to adjust his aim according to the commander's observation of where the previous shot had fallen. Nevertheless, Roberts was confident that he had dented Rommel's tank strength with it. Vaux left energised and refreshed. So long as there were commanders like Roberts around, then all was not lost. Then he let the journalists loose on him.

High above the desert a man named Chink was flying back to Cairo. His mission was particularly sensitive: to report to General Auchinleck on how General Ritchie was handling the Eighth Army.

Eric Dorman-Smith had received his nickname in his first regimental mess. An older officer said the new boy reminded him of the Chinkara antelopes that skipped around the Indian plains. The description stuck. Light on his feet, with a quick mind and bursting with nervous energy, 'Chink' Dorman-Smith, like his animal namesake, was twitchy and permanently on the lookout for danger.

He was an unconventional officer within an institution that placed an unusually high value on convention. Brilliant but nervy, brave but neurotic, he had trouble fitting in from the start. Chink had loved the life at Sandhurst military college: the uniforms, the exercises, the ragtime guitars and colourful blazers. But he'd instantly disliked most of his fellow cadets. Feeling superior in every department, he hadn't much bothered to obscure the fact. He hated their slowness, their lack of imagination and their rampant bullying.

Chink graduated as one of the best in his year and, in the Great War, displayed both courage and a capacity for thinking for himself, winning the Military Cross on the Western Front. He ended the war in Italy where, lounging in a bar one evening, he began one of the most important relationships of his life. His new friend was another unconventional figure, the American writer Ernest Hemingway. Hemingway was fascinated by military history and saw Chink as a hero straight out of Kipling. Chink thought the American was wonderfully open minded and plain speaking. Together the two talked and drank together, climbed mountains, skied, rode horses and set the world to rights.

A career soldier with bohemian friends was never going to fit naturally into the world of the regiment and the colonial club. This social isolation wasn't helped by the sense of cold superiority that others sensed in him. Slower, duller rivals out-climbed him on the career ladder and Chink found it difficult to find a place where his skills could best be deployed. In the late 1920s he attended the army's staff college and was unimpressed with the formulaic techniques on offer. One instructor particularly irritated him – Bernard Montgomery, a man whose ability to take offence was almost as well developed as Chink's. During a tactical exercise Chink accused Montgomery of 'using a sledgehammer to crack a nut'. When he offered his own more adventurous ideas, Montgomery announced to the class that 'Dorman-Smith allows cleverness to precede thoroughness'. After this Chink treated Montgomery with open disdain, mocked him behind his back and cut his classes. Their feud reached a high point when Chink wrote a sketch lampooning him for the 1928 college pantomime. Such flamboyant gestures stored up trouble for the future. Nevertheless, Chink passed out near the top of his class.

By the late 1930s Chink was a brigadier, but the sight of faster-rising contemporaries caused him intense pangs of jealousy. Then, when working as Director of Training for the Indian army, Chink finally met a senior officer who was enthusiastic about him: Claude Auchinleck. He and the Auk possessed what Chink called 'a shared horror of military backwardness'. By the outbreak of war Chink was Auchinleck's deputy and the two had become very close friends. Most days would begin with early-morning walks into the hills where they would talk and plan. In India Chink moved in highbrow political and cultural circles. He befriended Muhammad Ali Jinnah and other nationalists. He read modern novels and political theory, and he dreamed of escape from his marriage. In 1940 he met Eve Nott, the wife of a junior officer. The openness of their love affair created much scandal in the army. Chink's contemporaries now had another reason to hate him.

By May 1942 Chink was in Cairo as Auchinleck's Deputy Chief of General Staff, with the temporary rank of general. Just before Rommel's latest attack, he had made an accurate and prescient assessment of the weakness of the British position on the Gazala line and warned Auchinleck to concentrate his armour urgently. He was already very dismissive of the men commanding it, writing to Eve:

> Brains? We just haven't damn well got any. We have personalities and prejudices and pomposities and politics.

Despite what they said in Moscow, Britain had already launched her 'Second Front'. During 1941 the production of heavy bombers had been rapidly expanded. Small daylight raids on factories and airfields achieved some spectacular results, but larger attacks by day proved very costly once they went beyond the limit of fighter escort, which was well short of the German border. So the new force was designed to fly by night. 'Concentration' was the key. The RAF's scientists developed new methods of navigation and target marking to get as many planes as possible together over the target at the same time. Bomber Command's doctrine was called 'area bombing'. The targets were towns and cities, and the intention was to destroy as much industrial and residential property as possible, thus disrupting economic activity, creating a homelessness crisis and spreading terror among the population. The chief architect was Air Marshal Sir Arthur 'Bomber' Harris.

At the height of the London Blitz, Britain's capital had received 500 tons of bombs a night. It had stood firm, despite pre-war predictions of overwhelming casualties and mass panic. Harris believed that much larger attacks, consistently applied to the smaller enemy cities, could knock Germany out of the war, or at the very least fatally weaken her capacity to fight.

From RAF Pocklington's operations room, Edith Heap and

her colleagues sent Wellington bombers to raid Essen, Hamburg, Dortmund, Bremen and Stuttgart. Big raids were accompanied by strafing attacks on the German night-fighter bases en route, and smaller diversion attacks intended to divide the defence. Bomber Command's 'boffins' experimented, searching for the right mixture of incendiaries and high-explosive for each task. The attacks on Rostock and Lübeck were particularly successful. Both were beautiful medieval cities with wooden town centres; both received showers of incendiaries followed by high explosive to knock down buildings weakened by fire. At Pocklington Edith debriefed the crews of 405 Squadron.

> Four of the aircraft carrying 4,000-pounders achieved very satisfactory results . . . [crews] observed surges of burning debris and flames, the whole mass closing over the scene . . . Fires were seen over a hundred miles away and were spread over the whole island, and gutted roofs were visible in the light of the flames.

Hitler ordered retaliation against the oldest and most beautiful cities in Britain, the 'Baedeker raids' on Exeter, Norwich, Canterbury, Bath and York. The centre of Exeter was totally destroyed. Pocklington was near York, and Edith visited the city shortly after the raids to find that it had escaped with little damage to its ancient heart. Fighting now on several fronts, the Luftwaffe could only spare between fifty and a hundred two-engine bombers to hit Britain, whereas the RAF was regularly putting four hundred aircraft over German cities. And the British planes were getting bigger. The two-engine Wellington was the workhorse of the fleet with a 4,500-pound bomb load, about the same as the largest German bombers. But hundreds of new four-engine bombers were in service by early 1942, Halifaxes and Stirlings that could carry between 12,000 and 14,000 pounds. A new bomber called the Lancaster was also being introduced, capable of lifting 15,000 pounds to the farthest regions of Germany, and over 20,000 pounds on shorter missions.

405 Squadron were switching from Wellingtons to Halifaxes. On 25 May the operation log recorded:

All leave cancelled and men on leave recalled to unit. All squadron personnel are working with fury. Maintenance personnel have worked long into the night to get our new Halifaxes ready for operations as soon as possible.

Edith Heap sensed that something big was coming. On 28 May they were told to get the maximum number of aircraft ready, and some new ones flew in. Then all training was cancelled for a week. At group headquarters they were secretly calculating how many planes could be put over a target in a single ten-minute 'slot' without them colliding or dropping bombs on one another.

At 0900 on 30 May Edith was the first person at Pocklington to discover what all the fuss was about. She listened in on the regular morning 'tie line' for the broadcast from Group, as the WAAF watch-keeper copied the orders into the book. The target always came in a code that changed regularly – names like 'Swallow' for Mainz or 'Whitebait' for Berlin. She walked over to the safe and took out the book. It was Cologne, and it needed every bomber on the base. Every bomber on every base, it sounded like. The figures coming through were fantastic. Even training units were involved.

The ops team took down the route; the bomb loads; the take-off times; the times on target; the pathfinder methods; the colours of flares and marker bombs and details of the diversion attacks. This was going to be easily twice the size of the biggest raid Edith had ever been involved with. Everything would have to be coordinated to perfection.

At 1000 she informed the station CO, the navigation section, the armourers, Signals, Meteorology, Intelligence and the Flying Control boys in the tower. Pocklington was then 'shut down'; no one involved in the operation was allowed out and all personal telephones were cut. A stream of section leaders came into the ops room to check on the details. There was constant communication with Group, as some details had to be amended to accommodate the number of planes that were going to be in- and outbound at the same time.

Edith distributed the day's call signs to the section leaders on 'flimsies' made of rice paper. Elsewhere route maps were prepared along with bombing cameras and the escape kits. Late that morning she filled in the ops board with the name of each captain, chalking up the take-off times and times over the target. Lunchtime brought the watch change. Edith was supposed to get some rest now, as she would be on duty all night to follow 'her' operation right the way through. But she was far too apprehensive. She talked to David Harris, the station intelligence officer, instead.

She'd never seen the camp so busy. Riggers and fitters applied de-icing paste to wings and propellers, checked batteries and hydraulics and turned engines over searching for oil leaks. Armourers aligned the guns, loaded rolls of ammunition into the bins and drew bombs from the underground store, towing them out on the long carriages towards the waiting aircraft.

It was a very tense day. We were really on our toes. The RAF had been building up to something like this for years, and we wanted it to work. We felt strong, capable and strong, and we knew that the whole country wanted us really to hit back hard after years of taking it.

Those bombs would explode in Cologne tonight. It would look like the parts of London that she'd walked through. There would be bodies too, like those she'd seen at Debden when the WAAF slit trench took a direct hit.

At 1800 she attended the briefing. The room was packed and the crews gasped when the full details were read out: a thousand bombers, one target. The commanding officer read a message from Air Marshal Harris:

... the force of which you form a part tonight is at least twice the size and has more than four times the carrying capacity of the largest air force ever before concentrated on one objective. You have an opportunity, therefore, to strike a blow at the enemy which will resound not only through Germany but throughout the world.

The section leaders spoke too, as did the Met man. Groans and catcalls normally greeted him, but today everyone was concentrating hard. 'Good luck to you all,' said the CO, and Edith issued the escape kits and maps. The crews went for their pre-op meal: bacon, eggs and beans. 'Not the best thing for a happy stomach in a bomber,' but what they always wanted.

She was back in her chair in the ops room at 1900. There was an unusually long wait until take-off at just before midnight; 405 would be one of the last squadrons over the target. Outside, as they did their final checks, the ground crews could hear the rumble of bombers leaving from the stations near by. Those not on duty stayed up and went to the watch office to wave the planes off from the balcony. Edith was told by Flying Control as each aircraft left. She filled in the details on the board and told Group. They all felt part of history tonight. At forty other airfields the same scenes were taking place, the same thoughts running through the minds of the men and women left behind to face the anxious wait. Warsaw, Rotterdam, London, Coventry – everyone knew the list. Well, tonight a new name was going on it.

Two thousand tons of bombs fell on Cologne; 602 Wellingtons took part, along with 131 Halifaxes, 88 Stirlings, 79 Hampdens, 73 Lancasters, 46 Manchesters and 28 Whitleys. The pilots reported an excellent navigation track, clear visibility and near-perfect concentration. There was only one collision. Thirty-nine other bombers were lost to fighters and flak, a relatively modest loss rate of 3.9 per cent in all, at a time when over 5 per cent was usual. As Harris had hoped, the defences were overwhelmed by the unexpected weight of the onslaught.

At Pocklington they waited for planes that they knew were coming home damaged and for those that were missing. Flying Control announced each landing and Edith told Group. Sergeant Wadman's 'K' never returned. Then she and the other debriefing officers interviewed every crew, extracting the reports while memories were fresh. Where was the flak? The searchlights? From which direction did the night fighters come? Where were the decoy fires? What bombing pattern did you see? Any detail might make the next mission that little bit better, that much safer. She wrote the details up and teleprinted them to Group.

The men who had flown over the stricken city told Edith that it looked like a saucer of fire; 405's crews

> aimed at areas not already ablaze . . . fires were seen for over a
> hundred miles; no one could see bomb bursts owing to the extent
> of the fires. There were fewer searchlights and less flak than usual.

There was coffee, rum and biscuits. The photo section processed the bombing photos. David Harris checked them against target maps. The best ones were put up on a board for all to see, and copies sent to Group.

Churchill sat up all night to hear the news, and made sure that President Roosevelt received details. Roosevelt's envoy and confidant Harry Hopkins cabled Churchill from the White House to say, 'You have no idea of the thrill and encouragement which the RAF bombing has given to all of us here.'

Smoke made accurate aerial photography impossible for almost a week. It cleared to reveal a sight that no one in the world had ever seen before: 300 acres at the heart of a great modern city reduced to piles of rubble. Factories, houses, apartment blocks, roads, stations, churches and bridges, all blasted and burned to ash – 13,000 buildings were destroyed, including over 300 factories; 500 civilians were dead and 45,000 made homeless.

The British, American and Soviet press rejoiced, and for months Cologne's fate was rammed home in propaganda broadcasts to occupied Europe. No attempt was made to obscure the number of civilian casualties. Leaflets dropped over Nazi-occupied Czechoslovakia revelled in the carnage, describing Germany as a land where 'at night the sirens wail and bombs teach the Germans the meaning of terror . . . the air of their cities smells of death . . .' Pictures of Halifaxes and Stirlings leaving a factory were set alongside 'before and after' photographs of Lübeck and Cologne, as examples of 'the first instalment of the retribution to be meted out'. In the desert, intelligence officers like Peter Vaux were instructed to circulate accounts of Cologne's fate to boost the morale of the troops. It was vengeance, it was hope, and 'Bomber' Harris announced that it was only the start. On the radio he declared that the German people would soon look back at his attack on Cologne 'as men lost in a raging typhoon remember the gentle zephyrs of a past summer'.

After each night shift in Pocklington, Edith Heap had the next day off, followed by a day of the relatively easy 1300–1900 shift, although that was often extended if they were short handed. Then she made herself ready for another early-morning start, 0900 on the dot, and the long vigil began all over again. Wind, whirlwind. Cologne for Coventry, Lübeck for London: the zephyrs were gathering speed.

The news from Cologne came as a welcome boost at Eighth Army HQ, where the generals were now convinced that Rommel was attempting to withdraw and were discussing what to do to exploit his supply problems. General Ritchie was conscious of his inexperience in the field, conscious too that his two corps commanders, William 'Strafer' Gott and Willoughby Norrie, were older, more experienced men who might have expected to get his job. He felt he needed their approval on any big decision. Then there were the South Africans, who regarded themselves as semi-independent and whose views also had to be considered. Ritchie and his corps and divisional generals spent days discussing the various plans that were being pressed on him from all quarters. The one favoured by Peter Vaux and his seniors in the intelligence staffs, to go round the south with all the armour, was quickly discarded as too risky. It alarmed the infantry generals, who felt that to send the armour away left them exposed to Rommel's tanks, which might be refuelled and suddenly attack them.

The more urgent problem was how to help 150 Brigade, which was blocking Rommel's escape through the minefield. Unfortunately, the limited attacks launched for this purpose failed. A regiment of Lumsden's 1 Armoured Division went up against the German anti-tank screen on the Aslagh ridge and lost three-quarters of its tanks. A second attempt fared no better. Lumsden became convinced that ground troops were needed and, on the evening of 30 May, Ritchie decided that infantry assaults should be mounted the next night.

Meanwhile Rommel had discovered 150 Brigade for himself, and realised that it stood between him and easy access to his supply dumps. For a day the brigade defended itself obstinately, but by nightfall on 31 May it had lost ground and was running out of ammunition. Everything hinged on Ritchie's relieving infantry attacks scheduled for that night. But, at the last minute, these were postponed for twenty-four hours because the corps commanders discovered that the troops required could not be got ready in time. It was twenty-four hours that 150 Brigade did not have. On 1 June Rommel threw all his weight at it, destroying it as a fighting force in less than twelve hours and taking three thousand prisoners. Now that he had a clear line back through to his supplies, the chance of cutting him off had disappeared, but Ritchie still believed that his enemy was in retreat.

'I am much distressed over the loss of 150 Brigade after so gallant a fight, but still consider the situation favourable to us and getting better daily,' Ritchie cabled to Auchinleck. Then he reconvened the staff conferences. An attack by the South Africans in the north was rejected as impracticably bold at short notice. The only uncommitted formation was 5 Indian Division, which had just arrived at the front. The generals debated using it for an outflanking attack round the south but rejected that idea as too hazardous as well. Then General Messervy suggested a frontal attack on the 'Cauldron', as Rommel's position had come to be called. Gott thought this too reminiscent of the infantry attacks of the First World War and refused to participate. Responsibility for the attack passed to Norrie, and he in turn passed it back to Messervy.

As Messervy went off to plan the operation, Ritchie received Auchinleck's reply to his earlier message. 'I am glad you think the situation is still favourable to us and that it is improving daily,' Auchinleck wrote. 'At the same time I view the destruction of 150 Brigade and the consolidation by the enemy of a broad and deep wedge in the middle of your position with some misgiving.'

Colonel Bonner Fellers continued to send home his admirably detailed reports. On 1 June the 'good source' appeared again in a German intelligence document. This one revealed to Rommel that the Free French were still in control of the area north of Bir Hacheim, and that the British were convinced that the Axis forces were now withdrawing from the battle: '[They] seem firmly to believe in the withdrawal of the Axis forces.' The message also contained details of the various British armoured units now in the southern sector, including their current number of 'runners'. All of this was, no doubt, of great use to Rommel as he eliminated 150 Brigade and planned his defence of the 'Cauldron'.

On 4 June, referring once again to the 'good source', German intelligence described a visit to the headquarters of 30 Corps and a conversation with the staff of 7 Armoured Division, which is likely to have involved Peter Vaux. According to the Germans, the 'good source' said that 'British training [was] very inferior according to American ideas', that British troops lacked armour-piercing ammunition and that there was currently poor coordination with the RAF. The 'source' also reported details of the latest British tank replacement plans and their general level of supplies.

From his many reports to Washington, it is evident that Fellers had by now become disillusioned with the performance of the British army. He'd also reached a conclusion about the future.

> The U.S. must absolutely have its own separate theaters of operation, separate bases, separate lines of communication. British methods are lax, and follow-up lacking, and attitude casual, and sense of coordination faulty. They are unable to attune their army attitude with the tempo of mechanical warfare. An observer of 15 months of which a considerable time was spent observing actual combat reports that our forces can never work in harmony in the same theaters with the British.

General Messervy established his own separate tactical headquarters from which to run the attack on the 'Cauldron', leaving the divisional staff to look after the other units of 7 Armoured Division without him. On the evening of 4 June, Peter Vaux drove over to report on the day's events and to offer any help he could give the general. Messervy had just completed a conference, and the map was still laid out on the table. Vaux enquired what the plan was for the next day. Messervy was brusque and confident. He explained that the Indians supported by tanks would clear the Aslagh ridge; 22 Armoured Brigade, reinforced to full strength and with the support of four artillery regiments, would then pass through and assault the Sidra ridge. This would also be attacked from the north by another tank brigade, while more Indian infantry would exploit the armoured breakthrough. The 'whole cortège', explained Messervy, would then break through the enemy lines, dealing Rommel a crushing blow.

Vaux looked down at the map. Yes, Cauldron was a good name for it. But he was instantly worried. The whole battle would take place in an area rimmed by ridges. He warned Messervy that the enemy would dig in their anti-tank guns there and try to lure the British armour on to them. It was just what he had been discussing with Pip Roberts the day before. Messervy listened politely and wished him a cheery goodnight. 'Good luck!' said Peter. It was clear that they would need it. He was full of foreboding. It was that word, 'cortège'.

Neville Gillman and the rest of C squadron were to be the cutting edge of 22 Armoured Brigade. Supported by artillery from the South Notts Hussars, they would spearhead Messervy's main strike into the Cauldron. But as he drove to the assembly area on the evening of 4 June, Gillman came upon

> one of our tanks which had been hit a few days before. The crew had not managed to get out and they were burned, really badly burned, and they'd probably been there two days. One was half out of the turret. And they were like Michelin tyre men, all blown up. Terrible. And there was a ghastly smell. We got some petrol and poured it all over them and set light to it.

Gillman's squadron had been reinforced with new tanks and new crews, although on closer inspection the tanks proved to be hurriedly repaired casualties, some of which looked as if they might not last a day's fighting. So they worked on them quietly behind the lines, trying not to think too much about what lay ahead. Even so, Gillman found it hard to clear his mind of those bloated, charred figures wearing the same uniform as him.

Chapter 5

5–6 June

'Take post!'

It was 0300 on 5 June. Under the stars and the moonlight D troop tensed by the side of their 25-pounder guns. Everything was very still. Sergeant-Major Claude Earnshaw could hear the second hand of his watch ticking. He spoke into the megaphone. 'Zero minus five, four, three, two, one. Fire!' There was a shuddering roar as all one hundred guns on the artillery line kicked back into the dark, stony ground. The South Notts Hussars had just announced the beginning of Operation Aberdeen, General Messervy's battle for the Cauldron.

Then it was over to the fire programme. Earnshaw checked his sergeants. They were all following the instructions on the pieces of paper in their hands, shouting directions to the gunlayers while they went through their old routine. Take the fire orders, set the angle on the sight clinometer, bring the graticule in line with the gun aiming point, report 'Ready' and then pull back the firing lever and hear this terrific crack. Then choke on the smoke.

For three-quarters of an hour the guns leapt about and the men fed them with shells. 'Cease firing!' Earnshaw cried. For a moment there was silence, or what seemed like silence after all the noise. Then 'Rear limber up!' The crews closed down the guns, clamped them and hooked them on to their limbers. The 'quad' transporters came forward and they attached the guns to them and drove off to the rendezvous with the tanks of 22 Armoured Brigade at Barrel 230, leaving a litter of empty shell cases and ammunition boxes strewn over the desert floor.

Neville Gillman was woken by the barrage. For an hour the shadowy, sleepy tank crews packed their bedding and brewed tea. They tried not to let their nerves show, but some sat silently brooding while others chattered, shivering in the pre-dawn chill. The infantry would be attacking the Aslagh ridge around now, he thought. At 0400 Gillman's Crusaders, and about 150 other assorted tanks, set off for a rendezvous with the supporting South Notts artillery at Barrel 230. From there they were to advance on the Aslagh ridge and then on towards Bir el Scerab, before swinging north. The tanks were to keep moving at all costs. Infantrymen following up close behind would rescue any crews that baled out. These were brisk, confident orders.

> We were told this would be the decisive battle of the desert campaign. That Rommel was stuck and we were going to knock out his armour then drive the whole Axis army back to Tripoli.

Gillman drove across the start line at 0616. There the Sharpshooters paused to allow other units to catch them up, and the whole of 22 Armoured Brigade moved on. Fifteen enemy tanks were reported to the right front. C squadron was told to take care of them.

The South Notts Hussars were moving forward just behind the tanks. This was another chance to put all that coordination training into action. Claude Earnshaw looked around him at the men in the lorry. They were scared, obviously scared. Some of them looked very young too, real raw recruits, just arrived to replace the men who'd gone ten days before. Earnshaw had seen it all before, but it didn't get any easier, this bit before the battle started when you were just waiting for the action to begin. He thought of Pat Bland; no bridge lessons for a while now. He would try to make someone pay today for what they'd done to Pat.

The observers in their armoured cars were up ahead with the tanks. They would radio instructions back when the tanks needed supporting fire. Then they would drop into action, get the guns off the quads and the fun would start. It would be better then.

'Roger Three to Arthur. Eight hundred yards on the left. I'm sure they're Italians, sir.'

'OK. Engage,' said Viscount Cranley. 'All stations, Arthur here. Let's have a fucking good shoot at the buggers.'

It was difficult to make out the Italians through the mist. Gillman estimated the range. 'Gunner, tank in the middle by the bush, six hundred yards. Fire now.' Gillman watched the shot through his binoculars. It was just low. 'They're moving back. Raise two tank heights and try again.' 'Firing now.' The Crusader rocked back as the shell left the barrel.

The Italian tanks fell back as C squadron advanced. And the Sharpshooters were living up to their name, hitting their targets time and time again. It was working, the plan was working. They were moving forward faster now, pausing to shoot, then moving on again. 'Four hundred yards right. Fire now. Good shot. OK, reload and on we go.'

Suddenly shells of every kind were tearing into them. Flashes of fire showed where the anti-tank guns were, and there were more than Gillman had ever seen before. Just sitting there, waiting until the whole brigade had driven right up to them. 'Go right through, go right through,' said Cranley over the radio. 'No stopping now, keep going and keep shooting. Where's that artillery support? I want high-explosive on those bastard anti-tank guns now!'

Tanks accelerated, twisted and swerved. The Italian tanks had disappeared: it was 22 Armoured Brigade versus the anti-tank guns now, on ground that the enemy had chosen. The handful of close-support tanks with their howitzers fired high-explosive at the guns while Cranley continued to yell into his radio. 'Artillery observer, artillery observer, can you get your guns ranged in on these and give us some fucking support?'

Claude Earnshaw's truck came over the slightest of rises and suddenly they could see in the distance a big arc defined by little bursts of fire. They were moving gently downhill when the radio began to babble with demands for immediate artillery support. The captain stopped the truck, waving his arms at the men behind. They moved off to either side and the 25-pounders were pulled down ready for action as shells began to fall among them.

Earnshaw climbed out and ran towards the nearest gun. 'Dig them in as best you can,' he shouted. 'It's rock hard,' replied a gunner wielding a pick. They were on the far left of a ragged line with the other South Notts batteries out to the right and slightly forward, all now trying to respond to the frantic calls for assistance coming from the tanks.

'Sergeant-Major!' 'Yes, sir!' 'Range one thousand, right ranging. Might as well go on the zero line. There's plenty to choose from.' 'Yes, sir.' Earnshaw raised the megaphone. 'High-explosive 117. Right ranging, range one thousand. Fire!'

This was the battle that the British tanks and their supporting gun crews had trained for. The problem was that they were deploying seventy guns and facing over two hundred, while 22 Armoured Brigade had driven right into one of the best executed tank traps of the desert war. As the Grants and Crusaders burst into flame or slewed to a halt, Neville Gillman realised that the charge was faltering. The 88s were doing most damage as usual. More tanks stopped, and the men who abandoned them fell to the machinegunners. New orders came over the radio to attack to the north, where another body of Italian tanks had appeared. These, too, soon proved to be covered by concealed guns.

A thump on the front. 'Everyone all right?' 'We got donked, Sarge, but no harm done.' Gillman could see the strain on the face of the radio operator. He was gripping the mouthpiece and shaking. They moved off again, gathering speed, weaving to make themselves as difficult a target as possible. The Crusader's only chance was to use its speed and try to get in close.

Suddenly we were going very left. I shouted, 'Driver right!' and he replied, 'I can't.' I looked round. The left-hand track had been shot right off and was lying in the sand behind us. Now we were going straight for some more guns, all on our own. So I said, 'Right, bale out.' We climbed out and got on the lee side of the tank. The firing continued, so we just sat there, leaning against the four-foot-high wheels of the Crusader. Then there was a big clanging noise. A solid shot of armour-piercing had gone right through the tank and come out about a foot above my head. We decided it was time to move, so we made a run for it.

They ran through the inevitable machinegun fire in the direction of some rough scrub. It was still very misty, and that helped to conceal them as they flitted from clump of thorn to heap of rock. After only a couple of hundred yards they seemed to be out of immediate danger, but shells were still screaming overhead, aimed, no doubt, at targets farther back. They paused, breathless, for a moment. There was no sign of the infantry that were supposed to be following up and rescuing tank crews. The battle was going on all around with noises and flashes in every direction. Then ahead of them they saw one of the brigade's tanks. The driver was trying to restart the engine and, to their joy, as they approached it sputtered into life.

The survivors of 22 Armoured Brigade pulled back, with tanks towing others, nursing damaged engines or carrying tankless crews. Gillman arrived in the area where they rallied north of Bir el Tamar on the back of the tank with the faulty engine. They had already lost more than a third of their tanks and a lot of the surviving crews had been taken prisoner. No one had seen any sign of the supporting infantry, and the 25-pounders that were meant to cover them had made little discernible impression on the well-prepared defences. It was a savage disappointment, although, in fact, they had fared better than the other tank brigade that had attacked that morning.

Ordered forward towards the Sidra ridge from the north, 32 Army Tank Brigade first ran on to an unmarked minefield laid by British infantry, and then found itself trapped in front of the guns of 21 Panzer Division, dug in along the ridge. The brigade lost fifty of its seventy tanks in half an hour. It was the no-trumps problem all over again. High-quality men and machines, appropriate training and good intentions, all rendered useless by tactical naivety and lousy communications. Rommel's chief intelligence officer, Colonel von Mellenthin, was watching from the ridge and felt sorry for the brave men below who had been sent on this, 'one of the most ridiculous attacks of the campaign'.

With both armoured brigades defeated, the German counter-attack fell upon the exposed infantry and artillerymen, who had little time to prepare defensive positions of their own. The infantry in the centre were practically wiped out, some of them almost in sight of tanks that did nothing to intervene. Furious messages and frantic pleas passed back through brigade headquarters to the battle headquarters of General Messervy, where staff struggled to stem the increasing rancour and confusion.

Late in the afternoon Rommel launched a larger counter-attack, a pincer movement by both panzer divisions: 21 Panzer advanced from the Sidra ridge, hooking round the Cauldron from the north; 15 Panzer, which was farther south than anybody in the British army knew, emerged through unknown gaps in the minefield and drove into the rear of the British infantry reserves. Next in Rommel's line of attack was the headquarters of 7 Armoured Division and Messervy's nearby battle HQ.

At Sandhurst Peter Vaux had been taught that an officer might sometimes find it necessary to run. And at other times he might find it necessary to shout. But an officer should never, at any time, allow himself to both run and shout at the same time. It had the most unsettling effect upon the men. The lesson crossed his mind as he saw a lieutenant sprinting towards ACV2 and yelling frantically. But as Operation Aberdeen unravelled, that sort of thing was happening all over the place. Vehicles hurtled past as they tried to make their second escape in a week. There had been more warning this time of the enemy column that was approaching from the south-west. They coordinated their retreat with the reserve of tanks and were able to pull out to the east in safety. Nevertheless it was deeply embarrassing, and Vaux was furious with himself because he had not known that it was possible for the Germans to approach from that direction. It was the final blow in a sad shambles of a day. Messervy's battle headquarters would have to move as well, he thought, and God help whoever was still stuck in the Cauldron then.

Claude Earnshaw peered into the smoke and dust. There seemed to be panzers moving round both flanks now. The South Notts Hussars had been fighting for hours. Recently they had been shooting at tanks and there were Italian infantry digging in within rifle range. Some of the gunners were taking pots at them. All day British tanks had pulled back through their gun positions to refuel or repair, and almost every one of them had been covered with wounded men clinging on for their lives. Then, in the evening, just about all that remained of 22 Armoured Brigade had come through, some towing others, littered with more wounded. The gunners had shouted to them, 'Bugger off and leave us, won't you?' or 'See you in the morning, we hope!' Earnshaw assumed that they would be coming back, because it looked as if his guns were staying where they were.

As night fell the fighting died down and the only noise was the crackle of burning vehicles. There was nothing much more to be done. They had dug in as best they could but, as the battery's many ex-miners had discovered, the ground was mostly solid rock. Earnshaw had studied it during the day. It was a very beautiful pinkish colour, with weird patterns in it like Arabic writing. It almost looked man-made, like the floor of some vast palace.

Twenty-five-pounders were not designed to be attacked at short range. They needed any cover they could get because their flimsy gun shields were not up to much. So they piled stones, empty ammunition boxes and anything else they could find in front of the guns. They sorted what shells they had left, putting aside the small amount of armour-piercing ready for the first tanks of the morning. Then they wrapped themselves in their blankets and slept by the guns.

Earnshaw met the gun position officer before it was light and they made their morning tour together. 'We've been ordered to fight to the last man,' he said. 'Last man, last round. Apparently the brigadier was quite insistent. It's going to be a right bastard of a day.' The first rays of dawn were glinting over the lip of the saucer-shaped depression in which they were trapped. There were no sunrises like the sunrises in the desert, he thought, wondering how many of them would ever see another.

The fifty remaining tanks of 22 Armoured Brigade had pulled out just in time to avoid encirclement by the advancing panzers, and camped overnight to the west of the 'Knightsbridge box'. In the darkness the leading tanks ran on to the minefield that guarded it. Throughout the night fitters worked to replace damaged water pumps and filters clogged with sand. In the early hours of 6 June the brigade received new fuel and ammunition and was ordered to move east to fend off a threatened attack. As they did so, 88mm guns picked off several tanks at long range. But when they arrived, no attack materialised.

While the tanks with which they were supposed to fight drove ten miles to wait for an attack that did not take place, the South Notts Hussars could see the enemy making leisurely preparations for their extermination. Just after dawn a supply column got

Looking from the 'Knightsbridge box' towards the 'Cauldron', 1 June 1942

(*Left*) Peter Vaux in 1942

(*Below*) Members of Vaux's team. Left to right: driver, Corporal Williams with 88mm shell, Peter Ashworth, Jim Marshall, Kenneth Paxton, Corporal Finch

(*Right*) The interior of ACV2 drawn by Corporal Barrett

(*Below*) Peter Vaux's Armoured Command Vehicle (ACV2) disguised as a lorry

Harold Harper enjoys a brew at dawn

A 25-pounder gun in action

Arthur Onslow, Viscount Cranley   Neville Gillman

Three Crusader tanks of 4 County of London Yeomanry
(the Sharpshooters), summer 1942

Don Bruce

115 Squadron's armourers prepare for a mission. A Wellington bomber waits for its bomb load in the background, spring 1942

Edith Heap in RAF Pocklington's ops room

Flak over Brest in 1942, similar to that encountered by
Don Bruce's Wellington

Ariete Division postcard:
'Every day of battle brings us closer to our destination'

through in a flurry of dust, shells and machinegun bullets. It brought ammunition, fuel, water and food. Earnshaw thought that it was good to know they were not entirely cut off, but the lorries were badly shot up as they came in and one of the petrol trucks was set ablaze.

They beat off the first attack by tanks and motorised Italian infantry, watching through the sights until the target's nose moved on to the little cross, yelling, 'On! On! On! Fire!' Shells exploded around Earnshaw and bullets spat in the sand and clattered against the gun shields. One by one gunners fell and were carried away. Earnshaw was hit by a splinter from the beautiful pink rock. They had come to hate it now, hate the fact that you couldn't dig into it, hate the way that it shattered and spat fragments every time a shell landed. He limped back to the first-aid point, which the doctor and his orderly, Harry Day, had set up around a three-ton truck in a shallow depression. Day's shorts were covered in blood and he was shaking violently. He said that he had just been sitting in the truck, supporting a man's head while the doctor replaced a splint on his leg, and a shell had come straight through, taking the man's head off right between his hands, and missing everything else. 'Lucky escape, eh?' he said with a weak smile. More casualties arrived. Earnshaw saw men missing legs and arms. Day gave the worst ones a lethal dose of morphine.

Around midday they tried to get another ammunition column through, but this time it turned back. Unless some relief came in the form of armoured support then it could only be a matter of time. Where had all the British tanks gone?

In the afternoon 22 Armoured Brigade was ordered to go back to the other, westward side of the Knightsbridge box, to form up with two other brigades and break through into the Cauldron from the north. But when they arrived there was no sign of the other brigades. So nothing happened.

The Sharpshooters' war diary recorded the battle with restrained phrases such as 'a really bad day', 'again something went wrong', 'again a good looking plan for combined action fizzled out'. But the diarist's frustration was obvious. Tank men were now openly admitting to 'a nagging, aching doubt about the functioning and competence of our commanders' and were baffled and infuriated by 'our own lamentable and inexplicable inability to bring the enemy to battle with a numerical superiority to our advantage'.

Meanwhile, inside their own particular pink rock cauldron, the abandoned South Notts Hussars were almost done. Earnshaw saw the gun nearest to him take a direct hit. The blast blew the gun sergeant ten feet into the air and threw him towards Earnshaw. He ran over and was surprised when, a moment later, the man sat up, rubbed his head and just looked dazed. Another had fallen on top of the twisted metal and was obviously dead. A third, trapped beneath the wreckage of the gun, was screaming continuously. Earnshaw and the gun sergeant ran over and tried to drag the heavy metal off him. His leg was a sickening mess. Earnshaw pulled out his field dressing and pushed it into the hole, but it was no more than a gesture. As the stretcher-bearers ran to Earnshaw's call one of them took a bullet in the stomach and pitched over sideways. Earnshaw ran and grabbed the other end of the stretcher. They bundled the injured gunner on and ran back towards the first-aid post. A shell burst close by and they all fell, but they got up and stumbled on as fast as Earnshaw's wounded knee allowed. Harry Day took one look at the man when they got there, and told them to put him in the pile with the other bodies.

As he limped and crouched back towards the remaining guns, feeling wretched, Earnshaw saw the colonel's armoured car on fire. The driver dragged out the adjutant but the colonel and his wireless operator burned to death inside. An officer was machine-gunned as he stood on his truck. Some of the guns were being moved back and turned to face the other way against panzers approaching from the rear. Some vehicles tried to make a run for it. Most burst into flame after a few yards. The odd gun was still firing but one by one they were silenced until the moment came when German tanks drove right into the position. Their machineguns blazed and then stopped. The dirty, ragged, bleeding survivors slumped down where they were until they were rounded up.

Earnshaw was very thirsty. His knee hurt. He saw the body of Bill Lake, an old friend who'd been in the regiment from the beginning, lying a few yards away, and he limped over to it. What was his wife's name again? He must remember one day to tell her that he'd looked very peaceful at the end. And that he'd been very brave, very brave, in a way that whichever general had been responsible for this damned shambles didn't deserve. There was still some water in Lake's bottle so Earnshaw drank it and sat there, surveying the debris all around. Harry Day and the doctor were still treating the wounded and the Germans left them to it. He felt very light-headed now and odd details caught his eye. He recognized the signals truck where they had played cards only a week before. A German came over and told him very cheerfully, in the way that they were all supposed to, that, for him, the war was over.

With no firm control at any level and a near complete lack of coordination between units that were meant to fight together, the battle for the Cauldron marked a new low point. Rommel was referring to it when he wrote of his enemies:

In a moment so decisive they should have thrown in all the strength they could muster. What is the use of having overall superiority if one allows one's formations to be smashed piece by piece by an enemy who, in each separate action, is able to concentrate superior strength at the decisive point?

Chapter 6

6–14 June

As they looked across the Atlantic, America's strategic planners could see only problems. War Minister Henry Stimson and Chief of Staff General George Marshall jointly told Roosevelt that keeping the Russian army in the war should be America's main priority for 1942. The Russians had already lost four million men, 8,000 aircraft and 17,000 tanks. In the view of these two powerful Americans, Churchill's reluctance to invade France exposed the anti-Nazi alliance to a terrible risk, making Stalin susceptible to a German offer of a separate peace.

The American military was suspicious about Britain's motives for resisting the Second Front. Did Churchill prefer to let Hitler and Stalin exhaust themselves while he looked after Britain's imperial interests in the Middle East?

Other criticisms were being voiced. In London ex-minister Harold Nicolson met Roosevelt's envoy, Harry Hopkins. Hopkins told him that Americans were saying Britain was yellow. CBS reporter Ed Murrow gave General Alan Brooke a similar account of 'intense' anti-British sentiment in the US. Murrow said that the capitulation at Singapore had fuelled the feeling that the fighting spirit of 1940 had somehow ebbed away. *Time* magazine printed an article highly critical of 'oft-burned, defensive-minded' Britain.

Churchill was aware of the accusation that his country had gone soft, and it was one that he secretly shared. He told Violet Bonham Carter that

> Our men cannot stand up to punishment. We are not fighting well. That is the sadness in my heart. There is something wrong with the whole morale of our army.

The planners had already drafted several ideas for an early Anglo-American invasion of France. 'Operation Sledgehammer' was a plan for an attack in the late autumn of 1942. If Churchill had ever been tempted by it, Brooke would have broken every pencil in the Cabinet Room to stop him. He was worried enough about the fighting qualities of his own troops, let alone the untried GIs. Thus far no American unit had faced the German army and, from what he had seen of them, Brooke thought that when they did they would be in for a most unpleasant shock. For the moment, he wanted to see the Americans training, not fighting, and building up their strength in Britain.

The attitudes of both sides were affected by popular stereotypes. America: brash and overconfident, liable to charge headlong into military disaster, unappreciative of British sacrifice. Britain: cagey, deceptive, keen to win the war with American dollars and Soviet blood. Roosevelt agreed with some of the criticism of Britain that he heard around his cabinet table, and accepted that America's priority must be support for Stalin. He told Treasury Secretary Henry Morgenthau that

> The English promised the Russians two divisions. They failed. They promised them help in the Caucasus. They failed. Every promise the English have made to the Russians, they have fallen down on ... Nothing would be worse than to have the Russians collapse ... I would rather lose New Zealand, Australia or anything else than have the Russians collapse.

Churchill, who received regular reports about the currents of opinion in Washington, announced that he and Brooke must go there soon to sort out the question of the Second Front.

After the devastation at Cologne, the Germans poured resources into protecting the Reich from the new threat. New anti-aircraft gun batteries ringed German cities, along with clusters of new searchlight and radar towers. The night-fighter force was expanded by 50 per cent.

At RAF Marham in Norfolk, Pupil-Sergeant Don Bruce shared his room with an observer who was already flying ops. The man usually talked to a picture of his wife before he flew, saying goodbye. It was rather touching. But when he returned from the great raid on Cologne he laid the photograph on his chest and whispered to it about the terrors of the night. 'Those fires, those poor people, those poor people.' Bruce pretended to be asleep but the man just wouldn't shut up.

Bruce's pupil status ended a week later. After breakfast on 6 June the crews wandered over to inspect the blackboard in the main hangar. Chalked up there were the daily ground crew instructions, including one to fill Wellington KO-A with 600 gallons of petrol and a standard high-explosive bomb load. The petrol was a clue. Old hands hoped for 450 gallons, indicating a 'cushy' to the factories near Paris. But 600 usually meant a trip to 'Happy Valley', the heavily defended industrial cities strung out along the River Ruhr.

The target was revealed at the teatime briefing: not the Ruhr valley but Emden on the German North Sea coast. Bruce worked on his flight plan and was handed the weather reports and flight rations: chocolate, oranges, raisins and chewing gum; thermos flasks of coffee, tea and Bovril. Then the five-man crew of KO-A changed into their flying kit and parachutes and boarded a lorry for the short journey to their plane, now loaded with 4,000 pounds of high explosive.

The WAAF driver smiled and soft Norfolk light streamed across the fields from a sun now low in the western sky. As each crew dropped out of the lorry the others wished them luck. Bruce stood by his bomber and looked over a hedge to where a farmer was working. He desperately wanted to swap places. The men took turns to piss against the wheels for luck. The Air Ministry discouraged the practice to protect its struts from corrosion, but no one took any notice. Bruce climbed in first. It was the observer's job to set the detonators and the navigation equipment before take-off. It was warm inside the big aircraft.

> For a second I looked around the observer's compartment and wondered what it would be like with a hail of cannon shells from a night fighter ripping through the cabin.

The others clambered aboard. As the engines coughed into life, Bruce was busy with his plots and charts. Wellington KO-A taxied through the gathering twilight along the perimeter track and, on a green signal from an Aldis lamp, rumbled down the main runway and climbed away into darkening eastern skies. Don Bruce lifted his hands from the navigation table to write down the take-off time. They left a damp stain.

He'd always wanted to fly, but for most aeroplane-mad teenagers in the 1930s even getting *inside* a plane belonged to another world.

> I remember once we walked to Croydon airfield from my home in Woolwich. There was me and Jack Wills, the son of the local barber, and some others. We tried to get a tour of the aerodrome but hadn't got enough money. So the guide agreed to take us round for half-price.
>
> We looked over one of the Imperial Airways Hercules. They had red plush seats inside, and there was a parachute under each passenger's seat. It was so exciting. We spent ages watching the planes landing and taking off. We'd spent all our lunch money

on the tour so we had to walk home hungry. By the time we got back our parents had called the police.

In 1938 Bruce applied to join the RAF. He passed all the relevant flying tests, but was rejected for the pilot course. Instead he was offered training as an observer. But his father didn't approve and wouldn't sign the papers necessary for a seventeen-year-old to join up. In 1940, anxious to do something for the war effort, Bruce joined the Local Defence Volunteers and got a close-up view of the London Blitz.

It was in an air-raid shelter that I first felt that fear. One man panicked and tried to get out. Some of the men near the door rushed out to drag him back in and they had to sit on him to hold him down. The shelter rocked and jumped as though it were floating on water.

Bruce still had the letter accepting him as an observer, and so, without telling his parents, he went back to the recruiting centre. Soon he was training to become one of the specialist observers, known in the mess as the 'Flying Arseholes' from the winged 'O' pinned on their chests on qualification.

He was sent to Canada for basic flying training, where he was discovered to have above-average night vision and qualified as an 'astro-navigator' for the new night-bomber squadrons. Next came bomb training. Bruce lay on his stomach over the sight and called 'Left, left; steady; left; steady' until the moment came. He spoke to the cockpit through a 'Gosport' tube. The pilots' reactions were so slow that Bruce's friend Len Clough reckoned that most of the time they had *their* end of the tube plugged somewhere other than their ears.

Then came live bombing practice at an Operational Training Unit (OTU) in Scotland. The place was heaving with young airmen, working day and night to get them through their courses in time for the summer offensive. The main hangar had a huge slogan painted on the walls: 'BOMBER COMMAND RISES OR FALLS BY THE SUCCESS OR OTHERWISE OF ITS OTUs'.

Slowly, they were introduced to death.

I was sharing a room in an outside billet with Len Clough and another observer called Harry. One night I was coming back from Elgin. I'd got off the bus down by the harbour and was coming up towards the billet, and I could see a fire over on the hillside – obviously it was one of our kites that had gone into the hillside. I went back to bed and next morning I noticed that Harry's bed hadn't been slept in. It turned out he'd been in the burning plane and died.

Len Clough was forced to admit to his friends that he needed an operation for haemorrhoids, giving rise to more arsehole jokes. It was set for the final week of their time at the OTU, and when he came out of hospital Bruce was on leave.

Len was divorced, his mother dead and his father a sea captain, so he had no real home life. I'd given him my home address. He came down to London from Newcastle. I said he was always welcome at my home.

Clough suggested that they go up to town to find 'a bag'. Bruce – whose experience with women lagged some way behind his friend's – thought the idea immoral and said no.

I remember one evening he'd got a bit sloshed at the pub, we'd come back and my Mum was talking about one thing and another, and he said to her, 'You know, Mrs Bruce, I don't think you need to worry. I think Don will be spared.' And she said, 'Yes, but what about you, Len?' Len went quiet and shrugged his shoulders and said, 'Oh, well, does it really matter?'

There were posters on the wall of Bruce's mess: 'Notify the crew before attempting aerobatics', 'Beware of the Hun in the sun', 'Stragglers from formation invite attack'. Just before they were all posted to their operational squadrons Bruce and Clough took the bus into Elgin to see *Gone with the Wind*. In the newsreel they saw Bomber Command boys waving to the camera, climbing up into their Wellingtons and setting off for Germany.

And now he was too. They had both been posted to 115 Squadron at RAF Marham. It had twenty operational 'Wimpies', as the crews called them, and they were all being used on this, his first mission. As he wiped his hands dry, the pilot was managing to evade the first hazard of the night: trigger-happy British convoys that had put a number of holes into 115's Wellingtons in recent weeks. They climbed towards Holland and the two air gunners practised firing their Brownings. Bruce unfolded and locked the cockpit armour plate into position. It was meant to protect the pilot. The rest of the crew had to trust to luck.

KO-A reached the Dutch coast. The wireless operator was in the 'astrodome' up top, assisting the gunner as he scanned the cloudless sky for fighters. They weaved gently back and forth so that the rear gunner could check the blind spot directly underneath the bomber. They were at 10,000 feet now. It was colder but not unpleasant, and Bruce relaxed a little. His course was set correctly, and there was comfort to be found in the sound and sight of nearby Wellingtons, Manchesters and Halifaxes in the bomber stream.

The crew switched to oxygen and the pilot turned on the engine superchargers. Then the rear turret hydraulics failed, leaving the gunner with only slow manual controls, not what was needed if a night fighter flashed past. This was a reason to turn back, but such things were frowned upon by the intelligence officers at base, suspicious of the number of abandoned missions. After a brief discussion, KO-A flew on.

Bruce was still well inside Dutch airspace when he saw the fires. From 12,000 feet, Emden stood out like a lantern. The

Wellington lurched to avoid nearby pockets of flak and Bruce was called forward to take up the bomb aimer's position.

I lay prone over the bombing hatch and for the first time I could see what it had all been for. It was like a running red sore across the black earth and the sky. For a moment I felt sick with horror and I thought of the shelters in London and all the people below me now.

He set the rotor arm that spaced the sticks of bombs and removed the 'bomb release' cable that automatically fused them. Then he lined the target up in the bomb-sight. The flak was bursting closer, the Wimpy weaving more dramatically now. Pressure waves from the exploding shells lifted the plane up and pushed it from side to side, as if it were no longer flying but floating on a dark, choppy ocean.

Red balls climbed up lazily from the ground and then accelerated as they streaked past us like bolts of lightning. One was coming straight for my stomach. I could see it. I sucked my breath in and held it and clenched my muscles as hard as I could, as if they would somehow better withstand burning metal like that.

The gunners are yelling, 'Drop the bombs, Don. Let's go! Let's go!' It's all noise, a lurching aircraft, exploding light on my face, the searchlight beams waving all around. 'Over to port,' I call, 'get over to port.' Then the target is in the wires. 'Hold it, hold it.' Then the moment, 'Bombs gone.'

Free of its black burden, the Wellington rose like an elevator. Bruce scrambled back to the main cabin as they went into a shallow dive to gain speed and came around to set a course for home. Everyone relaxed. Soon they were over Holland again with Emden a fading glimmer in the rear turret windows. With no sign of any fighters, they poured out coffee and passed empty milk bottles around, a method they all preferred to the cramped, unstable chemical toilet in the back of the plane. Once over the North Sea they faced little danger. Bruce felt relief and pride. He was not a pupil any more.

Over Marham they lowered their wheels but the cockpit light indicated that they would not lock into place. They fired a distress flare and the station got the 'blood wagon' and fire tender ready. They made a perfect landing and the wheels held firm. The cockpit warning light had been out of order. Bruce climbed out and felt the weight of the parachute on his weak legs. He was more tired than he could ever remember being. After a quick conversation with the intelligence officer he went back to smooth sheets and the deepest sleep of his life.

On 7 June, after crushing General Ritchie's attack on the Cauldron, Rommel took his troops south to deal with the Free French at Bir Hacheim. But the garrison continued to hold out, refusing to surrender and beating back attack after attack. A tremendous air battle developed overhead as the Germans tried to pulverise their enemies with Stukas and the RAF made every effort to protect them. Rommel was infuriated by the delay.

Ritchie appeared powerless to intervene. French courage bought him time but he spent it reorganising his defensive boxes. On 8 June, Chink Dorman-Smith wrote:

> There are so few men in our army who make war their profession; such as there are, are rebels, and rebels aren't employed till orthodoxy is emptied . . . I'm sorry for the Auk. He has stuck to Neil Ritchie and Neil Ritchie hasn't the divine spark.

On the afternoon of 10 June Rommel launched his strongest attack yet on Bir Hacheim. At 7 Armoured Division HQ Peter Vaux listened anxiously to news of its progress. At lunch-time a hundred planes attacked. As they pulled away, the ground attack went in. At 1600 Vaux heard reports that the enemy had broken through the northern minefield. In the evening there was a further mass air raid. The French decided to evacuate that night and, in the middle of all this, the division lost its general again. Messervy was hiding at the bottom of a dry well, having been cut off by the Germans while returning from a visit to his last few tanks.

At brigade and regimental level officers gritted their teeth and, cursing the lack of coherent orders, did their best for their own units. The tank crews were bitter about being sent repeatedly in small numbers against lines of concealed guns. The infantry and artillery were bitter about being left without tank support. Ritchie, however, offered more reassuring words. Auchinleck visited his headquarters on the evening of 12 June and then cabled London: 'Atmosphere here good. No undue optimism and realities of situation are being faced calmly and resolutely. Morale of troops appears excellent.' Churchill cabled Auchinleck back: 'Retreat would be fatal. This is a business not only of armour but of will power.' Chink had already made his diagnosis: Eighth Army suffered from an 'embarras de Ritchies'.

After two weeks of fighting Rommel was finally able to cut north out of the Cauldron and up towards the coast. Ritchie ordered a general retreat and the panzer columns were soon closing on Tobruk.

On 10 June another intelligence decrypt came to Churchill, with a note from 'C':

> another long report to German Army in AFRICA from 'good source' concerning British morale, training, supplies and intentions, evidently based on the good source's visits to British units.

The German document was the one from 4 June that had referred to the 'good source', his visits to British units, and his unflattering comparisons with American methods. *American* methods: this was the final piece of the jigsaw. On a note attached to the decrypt 'C' had written in his habitual green ink:

> Prime Minister, I am satisfied that the American cyphers in Cairo are compromised. I am taking action.

On 11 June Churchill, in his own emphatic red ink, wrote back to his intelligence chief:

> Say what action? And let me know what happens.

Previous material on the security leak was urgently checked and cross-referenced, and on 12 June documents were laid before Churchill concerning an old argument about the RAF's servicing of American planes.

An intercepted German cable had talked of British problems with American aircraft, going into details about the poor servicing skill of RAF technicians and a shortage of the correct spares. Someone in Cairo had now spotted that these complaints echoed almost exactly the language used in a note that had come in from Washington, detailing complaints by US mechanics. It was clear now: someone was reading traffic in *and* out of the US embassy.

'C' told Churchill on 12 June that the Americans had been informed and were investigating.

Auchinleck and Chink Dorman-Smith still started every morning with the 'dawn patrols' they had enjoyed in India. Chink urged his boss to remove Ritchie and fight the battle himself. He identified four problems: leadership; the dispersal of artillery; the dispersal of armour; and the reliance on defensive boxes that could be bypassed and isolated by a fast-moving enemy. But would Auchinleck listen? Chink wasn't sure, as he confided to Eve:

Here I am with a head running wild with ideas for reshaping this Army, because we have got to reshuffle it and its weapons before we find the right tactical combination ... the business now is to rectify this in the hot heart of a war in which the enemy still has the initiative.

Back in the desert Ritchie was methodically evacuating the infantry who had become trapped in their boxes while his dispersed armour tried to hold off the enemy.

Neville Gillman also started each day with a dawn patrol. The Sharpshooters would be woken before dawn at 0500, start their tanks and drive to their battle positions before first light. The blackout would not allow them to make a hot drink before they started. The day would then be spent waiting, patrolling, preparing an attack, or expecting an attack. The tension was exhausting. The commander had to stand all the time, alert for danger. Their seats were built too low for them to sit while scanning the horizon. Inside, the engine would be running; there was noise, vibration and fumes, and they wore headphones all day. If there was no immediate danger it might be possible occasionally to get out and brew up, stretch the legs, have a pee, even cook some food. But on dangerous days the crew could spend the whole time shut inside in the sweltering, stifling heat. Three hours in the morning or the late afternoon might be spent fighting. The middle of the day, when visibility was too bad to fight, was the least dangerous time, but by then the tank would have heated up so much that touching the metal would burn your hand. Sunstroke was common.

After fifteen hours in the field, the opposing tanks would draw apart and seek the shelter of their leaguers for the night. This might mean two or three hours of night driving to get close to where they had to fight next day. Then, for another hour or two, they had to refuel, load and stow new ammunition, carry out maintenance on the tank and pick up rations. As in the morning, the blackout stopped them making hot food or drink. Sometimes the supply column brought up packages of food that had once been hot, but it was often so unappetising that by this stage the crews preferred to sleep. They rarely got to wrap up in their blankets before 0100. And then they took turns to mount a guard until they woke again at 0500. Unless the enemy made a night attack, in which case they might not sleep at all.

'Fatigue in tanks has been one of the major problems of the present campaign,' reported the Medical Research Section of GHQ Cairo in July.

This is attributed to the longer hours of daylight than in previous campaigns, and to the more intense and prolonged fighting . . . It is a generally accepted opinion among the senior regimental officers interviewed that, under the conditions outlined above, it is impossible for men to go on fighting with any degree of efficiency for more than a week.

By 12 June Viscount Cranley's C squadron had been in constant action for seventeen days:

such was the fatigue of everyone that if the men had not been ordered to get out and walk about at intervals they would have slumped into a hopeless coma, the heat of the tanks adding to their natural exhaustion.

Neville Gillman found that the need for sleep would sometimes overcome that for security.

It's impossible to describe how tired you could get, so much so that you'd take any opportunity for sleep. It was like a force of nature, like gravity weighing you down. On guard duty in the leaguers you had to shake the next man to wake him up before lying down yourself, and some of them took some real shaking. From time to time one would grunt and roll over and not actually wake up and meanwhile you'd fallen asleep yourself and the whole place was unguarded for a while.

On the morning of 13 June the panzers struck in force again, moving right round to attack their position from the east. There was fighting in the morning and again in the evening. Some of the other tank units took very heavy casualties, and they only just clung on to the Belafaa ridge. C squadron was ordered to camp in battle positions on the ridge. The Guards Brigade was still evacuating their Knightsbridge box and the tanks had to safeguard their retreat. The fact that there were German infantry only half a mile away made the Sharpshooters distinctly jumpy. At 0130 the lookouts spotted them approaching. Everyone was dragged from their sleeping bags once again and they received an immediate order to mount. They moved three-quarters of a mile in the dark. During one pause Gillman walked over to Cranley's tank to discover his commanding officer and the entire crew asleep in their seats. Very lights were going off all over the place, illuminating the desert in the strangest patterns, and as they crawled along Gillman thought he could see a German tank three or four hundred yards away.

> It seemed to move when we moved. When we stopped it stopped. In the end I reported it to Cranley. He said, 'Well, you'd better get out and take a look.' So I got my tommy gun and went over, very carefully. When I got there it was very knocked out. Thank God.

After some more nervous progress through the darkness, the Sharpshooters' Colonel Frank Arkwright fired a red Very light and C squadron found his headquarters. The Germans had seen the light too, and continued to light up the area with their own white Very lights, so the tanks moved on a further half-mile. One Crusader was picked off by a long-distance shot, but they managed to rescue the crew. At 0300 they heard the clank of tank tracks. A cautious scout reported that they were British. New orders came to retire over the escarpment. They had been a small part of a much larger armoured body holding the ridge to allow the

Guards to escape from Knightsbridge, and they had succeeded. Now they were free to follow.

Some of their tanks were sent back into the battle to join the forces that were keeping the line of retreat open. But Gillman was relieved to find himself among the rest, loaded into lorries and sent east along the coast road. Relieved, but vaguely guilty: when Arkwright had told him he was going back, the colonel had looked quite dreadful himself, with bloodshot eyes and a week's stubble on his face. If anyone needed a rest it was him. They drove all night, hardly woken by the bumps, and at 1500 the next afternoon arrived at Sollum. They all raced across the bright white sand beach and threw themselves into the turquoise sea.

Chapter 7

14–17 June

Mtarfa hospital's nurses' mess was on the top of a small hill overlooking ta Qali aerodrome. From its garden Mimi Cortis could see almost the whole of Malta: south to the Dingli cliffs poised hundreds of feet above the sea; west to the beach at St Paul's Bay; east to her home town of Sliema with the capital Valletta just beyond. With the aid of the matron's binoculars she could also peer northward and glimpse the coast of Sicily, sixty miles away through the heat haze.

As a girl Mimi had read all about Edith Cavell and Florence Nightingale. She enrolled as a Volunteer Aid Detachment (VAD) nurse in 1939, shortly after her nineteenth birthday. It was the first time she had lived away from a home she shared with her father and eight brothers and sisters. Her sixteen shillings a week brought her independence, of a sort.

We were woken each morning by the domestic staff, who took our uniforms once a week for laundering and starched the aprons and caps. I felt like I was in boarding school. We were not allowed to come for breakfast in dressing gowns but had to be properly dressed in our uniforms. I hated the caps as they got in the way when you were bathing or lifting patients.

At first she would often eat her lunch outside the mess, taking off her hat, removing her itchy regulation stockings and stretching out in the sun. One of the girls had strung a hammock between two trees. From here you could look down at ta Qali and see the planes coming and going. But no one spent much time in the hammock now. Ta Qali was a prime target for the German and Italian bombers that swept in from Sicily three or four times a day. The hospital was only a few hundred yards away down the other side of the hill. The caretaker had painted large red crosses all over the roof and the grounds, but stray bombs hit them nevertheless.

Enemy airmen were sometimes brought on to the wards. They said their orders were to avoid civilians. But Malta was such a crowded little place, with so many air and naval bases, harbours and anti-aircraft batteries, that the most punctilious bomb aimer would have difficulty avoiding the houses, hospitals and churches. So it had been possible to forgive for a while. But not now. The intense bombing this spring suggested new orders: bomb Malta flat. By late May only 20 per cent of the homes in Valletta still had their roofs, and all but two thousand of the people who'd once lived there had been evacuated to outlying villages, mostly to stay with relations. Everyone slept four or five to a room. This meant that entire families would be wiped out in one explosion. It also meant that even kind-hearted nurses now felt little sympathy for wounded Axis airmen.

The Mediterranean had become a fascist lake. Italy was Germany's closest ally, Franco's Spain was sympathetic to Hitler, southern France and much of North Africa was run by the government in Vichy, whose collaboration with the Nazis was ever more open, and the Balkan States had all been occupied in 1941. Apart from Malta, the Royal Navy had bases only in Gibraltar and Alexandria, two thousand miles apart. Admiral Cunningham's fleet had done great damage to Mussolini's navy but German and Italian aircraft commanded the air and were a permanent menace to all British shipping. As a result, supplies to Egypt now travelled 'the long way' around Africa and back up through the Suez Canal.

Malta lay between Sicily and the principal Italian ports in North Africa, Tripoli and Benghazi. Much of the equipment and supplies destined for Rommel passed within easy reach of the island and, during 1941, Malta's bombers and submarines had taken a steady toll. Some Axis convoys had lost three-quarters of their ships.

Malta had endured bombing throughout 1940 and 1941, but the offensive that began in early 1942 was the most concentrated Axis air attack of the war. By late April more bombs had fallen on the island than London received during its Blitz, a prelude, everyone assumed, to an invasion. The navy performed miracles to defend and supply Malta. In March a bold attack by destroyers scared off a larger Italian force and allowed a small convoy to get through. The oil tanker *Breconshire* was hit and rolled over on to her side in shallow waters. Sailors went out to cut holes in her side and, night after dangerous night, tiny lighters full of salvaged oil were towed back into the relative safety of Valletta's Grand Harbour.

Breconshire was carrying clothes as well, including some badly needed uniforms for the hospital. 'Well, there go your new aprons!' said the matron. But though the uniforms got dowdier the routine went on:

> Every day we would clean the dressing room, prepare trolleys for the rounds, carefully laying out the medicine and the dressings. Then we cleaned gloves, washed bandages, packed drums with rolls of cotton wool and gauze ready for sterilisation and made ready for the matron's round. Proper 'hospital corners' on all the bed sheets or we'd be in trouble.

Maltese was Mimi's first language but she had always been good at English, and over the last few months she'd mastered a lot of new accents. One day she announced to her ward that she now considered herself fluent in Geordie, Cockney, Irish, Welsh and even Scottish if spoken slowly. She loved to chat away to the men, although the matron didn't like it when she used the patients' first names.

We always tried to be cheerful. It's important. I used to walk around singing 'It's a Lovely Day Tomorrow' and other songs by Judy Garland or Vera Lynn. The patients called me 'Sunshine' and 'Smiler'.

But keeping smiling wasn't always easy. One night Mimi was in Valletta on her way back to the hospital. Then the siren went.

I was near one of the best shelters, the basement of the Auberge d'Aragon, a fortress first built by the Knights of Malta. Inside I felt a truly huge blast. Everyone was shaken and toppling on to one another with the force of it. My friend's coat was ripped at the shoulder and we were all covered in dust. We came out to see debris everywhere, and we had to clamber over the piles of rubble that were all that was left of people's homes.

As they went round the corner there was another raid. They ran for another underground shelter.

The bombing got heavier again, we heard the whistling of bombs and knew they were close by, sounding louder and stronger. At last we heard the all-clear siren. When we came out our first sight was the Royal Opera House, a lovely theatre that we had considered our very own Covent Garden. Now it was just a heap of masonry.

Malta desperately needed fighters. On 20 April Mimi had watched forty-six Spitfires fly in to ta Qali after a 450-mile journey from the aircraft carrier *Wasp*. The Germans watched them too and launched a series of raids that shook the hospital for two days, at the end of which there were only seven Spitfires left. A hospital building took a direct hit. Some sisters ran out to help but didn't notice that a veranda had disappeared. They fell twenty feet on to the rubble. One had a fractured arm and another a broken spine.

There was no point risking an aircraft carrier to get fighters all the way to Malta if they were going to be destroyed on the ground. So steps were taken to ensure their safety. At ta Qali and the other aerodromes men filled empty fuel containers with earth and piled them up twenty feet high to create individual blast-proof pens. On 10 May another sixty-one Spitfires arrived. All were safely in their pens and refuelled for action within ten minutes.

In their attempts to destroy the Spitfire pens the Luftwaffe and the Italian air force turned the aerodrome into a cratered ruin. There was a layer of concrete near the hospital end of the base, next to some abandoned excavations. The enemy air commanders were convinced that this was the roof of a vast underground hangar and dropped special bombs designed to burrow into the ground before exploding. These shattered windows half a mile away and shook the fillings in the nurses' teeth.

The new fighters allowed the RAF to hit back at the bombers, but the raids continued. The Italian navy filled the narrow approaches to the island with mines and torpedo-firing patrol boats, driving the British submarines from their Malta base. During May three-quarters of Axis shipping reached North Africa unscathed, delivering the reinforcements that had allowed the Panzerarmee to sweep forward against the Gazala line with such force.

The Canadians at RAF Marham were loud and funny and refreshingly undisciplined. After two more missions in KO-A, Don Bruce, to his great delight, was switched to the crew of a Canadian pilot called Delmer 'Del' Mooney.

We were all briefed and were coming away from the hut when Del and another Canadian chap heard the station warrant officer tearing a strip off 'Knocker' Knowles for having his hands in his pockets. And Del started shouting back at the warrant officer, who defended himself by saying he'd been sent to smarten up the aircrew. Del said, 'Well, you've picked on the wrong bunch here, mate!'

Crews tended to be superstitious about who they flew with and Bruce instinctively felt relaxed about Mooney. Of Irish descent, he was broad faced with a cheerful smile and a calm demeanour. Their first mission was a small raid on the U-boat pens at St Nazaire. Joe Richardson was the front gunner, Jack Goad, another Canadian, was the wireless operator and Bill Margerison manned the rear gun.

It seemed as though everybody had turned out to see us off. The padre roared up on his motorbike and started handing out caffeine pills to the gunners and words of comfort to us all, so we were getting the full treatment. We all knew how well these U-boats were defended, so in a way this special attention was a bit unsettling. The CO gave us a final briefing. He wanted us to come down to seven thousand feet to get a good photo, but when we got inside we decided to ignore this: after all, it was our first operational flight together and we wanted to take all possible precautions. Damn the better photo, we'd stay at ten thousand feet!

As they approached the target, Bruce's compass began to give peculiar readings. He plotted a course to what he thought was St Nazaire. There was no flak, and the night was uncannily quiet. The two gunners were getting jumpy, straining into the darkness for night fighters. When they reached the target it was covered with haze and they couldn't find a single landmark.

If it had been Germany we could have just dropped the bombs anyway, but as we were over France we had to identify the target. We turned for home. I gave Del the course and asked the front gunner to look out for the coastline ahead and give me a shout when he could see it.

They flew over Brittany searching for its northern coast. After fifteen minutes the sea should have appeared, but the Wellington was still tracking over land. Bruce kept calling up to Richardson,

'Can you see the coastline yet?' but he couldn't. Bruce checked his compass again and realised that he had based the homeward course on the faulty reading from near St Nazaire. They weren't flying north after all, but west.

I nearly had a baby on the spot. We were way off track. I had to do a lot of calculating as quickly as I could, and I'd just got my pinpoint worked out on the chart and it came out smack over Brest. I shouted over the intercom, 'Christ, we're over Brest!' and a few seconds later the searchlights snapped on all around us.

They were 'coned', caught between searchlights. Mooney weaved crazily through the sky, but already the flak was bursting close. It felt as if every gun in France was firing at them. The harbour at Brest was one of the most heavily defended targets in Europe, and they were sitting inside a lone aircraft at the mercy of the defences.

Del was good at weaving and diving, climbing five hundred feet then dropping five hundred. It was sickening inside, especially because when the engines cut out in a dive only Del knew if *this* time it was because we'd really been hit or not.

With my table going up and down I couldn't plot a thing. There were some more heavy bursts of flak, and Del was throwing the plane about all over the place. It was all deafening noise, vibration, lurching, and a sense that at any moment you could be burnt alive. The gunners were shouting and yelling for Del to get out of it but I was silent with fear.

Mooney snarled down the intercom: 'Give them a fucking stick, Don.' Eight 250-pounders whistled away into the night. As they exploded, all the searchlights immediately went out.

Had we hit a generator? We would never know.

By now the port engine that ran the hydraulics and the radio was out of action. We turned and limped away from Brest heading north, surrounded by the smell and taste of fuel, dust, sweat and hydraulic fluid.

They steadily lost height and were still descending as they crossed the English Channel. Bruce jettisoned the other bombs into the sea and then the crew threw out flares, smoke floats and anything heavy that would slide down the flare chute. Jack Goad managed to get the transmitter working from battery power and sent out a mayday call. They discussed whether to throw the machineguns out, but decided to keep them just in case. The plane wallowed through cloud and mist as Mooney struggled to maintain height. Bruce couldn't decide whether to blame himself or the broken compass, and 'got so dejected that I swore I would never fly again'.

They were at 2,000 feet and considering baling out when they finally saw the English coast. Bruce located an aerodrome near Exeter and Mooney put the nose down and built up speed for landing. He was worried that the wings may have been holed by flak and didn't want the Wellington to stall. They hit the ground far too fast for comfort.

I felt the wheels start to fold and I thought, Christ, this is going to be unpleasant. The Wellington went right down on its belly, and great streaks of sparks shot back from the fuselage. I could see the plane disintegrating as it rubbed along the ground. We slewed off the concrete and on to the grass. Now damn great clods of grass flew through the air, into a window and settled down the back of my neck. I could see the front of the aircraft crumbling, it was folding in, and I thought, Poor old Del, he's going to be crushed.

They swung around in a 180-degree arc. Bruce looked towards Mooney, wondering how he was getting on, and saw his feet disappear through the pilot's escape hatch below him.

I was still in a bit of a daze and there was a lot of dust around and noise. Someone shouted down from the astrodome: 'Is there anybody else in there?' and I said, 'Yes, I am!' 'Well, get out bloody quick, then!' So I nipped across and there was a head and shoulders and arms reaching down and I was yanked out. We were piled into a transport and taken off for breakfast. While we were sitting there a fighter pilot came in off patrol and said he'd just seen a Wellington near Brest taking an awful pounding.

The average human being requires 2,200 calories a day to maintain basic health and energy levels. A man performing manual work needs nearer 3,500. By late June the Malta daily ration was a little over 1,500 calories. The Royal Navy launched operations Vigorous and Harpoon to get some merchant ships through.

The Harpoon convoy left Gibraltar with six merchant ships protected by two aircraft carriers, *Eagle* and *Argus*, a battleship, *Malaya*, three cruisers and eight destroyers. Vigorous left Port Said at the same time, with eleven merchantmen, eight cruisers and twenty-six assorted destroyers, minesweepers and corvettes. A great plan was hatched to protect the convoys by attacking Axis airfields with air raids and commando landings. This, it was hoped, would create a distraction and allow the merchant ships to slip through to Malta. Few in Cairo knew about the plans, but one who did was Bonner Fellers because the convoys included several American freighters.

On 11 June, only a day before Washington learned of the security problem in Cairo, Fellers drafted his message No. 11119:

Nights of June 12th June 13th British sabotage units plan simultaneous sticker bomb attacks against aircraft on 9 Axis aerodromes. Plans to reach objectives by parachutes and long range desert patrol. This method of attack offers tremendous possibility for destruction, risk is slight compared with possible gains.

Fellers' message was intercepted at 0800 on 12 June and was

decoded by 1000. By 1130 it was with Rommel. When the commandos arrived that night, the Italians were waiting for them.

Four of the merchant ships of the Harpoon convoy were sunk in well-coordinated air and underwater attacks. Bombers, E-boats and submarines harried the Vigorous convoy and, when news came that the main Italian battle fleet was at sea, it was ordered back to Egypt. Only two supply ships out of the seventeen dispatched arrived in Valletta's Grand Harbour, and the navy lost a cruiser and five destroyers to get them there. Malta had never felt so isolated. Italian radio stations taunted the islanders, saying that they lived in Europe's most cost-effective prisoner-of-war camp.

'We're not giving you a flight now, Lee, because you'll find the terrain is entirely different and you'll need time to get used to it. I'm going to post you as a supernumerary flight commander to 112 Squadron instead. They're up at Gambut near Tobruk flying Kittyhawks. American plane, rather complicated. See how you get on with it. You know the squadron leader, I think. Billy Drake, just taken command. You have a few days before going up there. I suggest you make the most of the comforts of Cairo while you have the chance. Bit primitive up the blue, I'm afraid. You'll find that RAF officers are honorary members of the Gezira Sporting Club. Nice swimming pool. Show yourself out.'

Ken Lee's interview was over. He shut the door behind him, smiling at the WAAF secretary behind the desk. 'I think you'll need these, sir,' she said, handing him a pile of passes and chits and a copy of the *Services Guide to Cairo*. 'You might find the maps useful.' Lee paused on the steps to survey the scene. Things were definitely looking up. The sun was shining, it was hot but not too hot, Cairo lay before him in all its ancient, squalid splendour and, best of all, his new squadron was commanded by Billy Drake. Before the war at Tangmere, Drake's 1 Squadron and Lee's 43 had shared the aerodrome. Drake had been fun: purposeful, a fine flyer and a man who did things his own way without too much regard for form. Lee respected him as a fighter and liked him as a man. In the tight-knit environment of a squadron, that was crucial. Yes, things were definitely looking up.

Lee, twenty-five years old, had been one of the first RAF fighter pilots to see action. Over France and later in the Battle of Britain he'd destroyed four enemy aircraft and been awarded the Distinguished Flying Cross. But 'Hawkeye', as he was called, had not been on active service since being shot down and wounded in August 1940. When he got out of hospital he was sent to pass on his experience of air fighting to the hundreds of new men being pushed through the system. Then he was posted to the Middle East. On the way he looked after a bunch of novices – Australians, Kiwis and Canadians mostly. At Freetown in West Africa they waited for some crated Hurricanes and then, once they had been assembled, flew them across Africa, over hundreds of miles of jungle and desert all the way to the Sudan. From there the fighters went to the maintenance units in the delta and were distributed to squadrons 'up the blue', as the Wing Commander had called it.

He spread the map of Cairo out. All around the city centre huge areas were marked 'out of bounds' in red. He'd deal with those later. For the moment Gezira and its Sporting Club looked distinctly inviting. He set off through crowded streets where hand-carts and donkey traps jostled with dilapidated trams and shiny new Wolseleys. Arabs in long-sleeved djellabas mixed with Sikhs in turbans, Australians in bush hats, and the occasional WAAF or nurse. Over the next few days Lee got to know the layout of the city. He visited the Citadel and the Blue Mosque, the zoo, the Pyramids and the archaeological museum to inspect the mummies. He discovered the Musqi, an amazing rabbit warren of little streets and alleys, packed with craftsmen working on plates, pottery, baskets and rugs. 'Sir, sir, you buy amber grease,' a man said, tugging on his arm. 'Will make you powerful lover.' He drove over the Kasr el Nil bridge, which was guarded by two great lions which were, according to the taxi-driver, supposed to smile when a virgin crossed the river.

The Gezira was more like a town than a sports club, set on an island in the Nile with an eighteen-hole golf course, a horse-racing track, cricket pitches and innumerable tennis courts. Lee swam in the pool and watched the cricket. There were wicker armchairs by the scoreboard with a slot to put your drink in. It was all very exclusive, packed with senior officers, diplomats and the more well-favoured locals. As a sop to democracy, there was an area by the boundary where other ranks could drink beer and watch the game.

Lee read the English papers at Shepheard's Hotel, the after-hours HQ for Auchinleck's staff officers and the newspapermen, and the hub of all the best gossip. Groups of very attractive Levantine women lingered over coffee on the terrace, and some of them looked distinctly approachable. Most English-speaking people in Cairo were under thirty, and lived their lives with a tangible nervous urgency brought on by their involvement in the serious business of war. If you could wangle an invite, there were gala balls and parties most Saturday nights, in aid of the various war charities. Groppi's Jardin, an elegant café-bar in the Malika Farida, was the place to be seen at lunch, although it was a magical place at any time, with little tables and chairs on the sand and scented flowering plants all over the walls. Lee enjoyed coffee and cream cakes there in the afternoons, highballs and whisky sours in the warm evenings. Strings of coloured lights, suspended in the overhanging trees, illuminated the garden after dark. At Groppi's dance hall near by there was a little stage with amateur dancing girls. The show wasn't up to much but the girls were and the whole atmosphere was marvellous. Lee also liked Joe's Bar, just across the road from the Turf Club, which was all very sophisticated with waiters in immaculate white djellabas and bright red fezzes on their heads.

But it couldn't last. The 'blue' beckoned, and all too soon the day came when Lee had to climb into a small truck with four other officers for the four-hundred-mile trip to Tobruk. They drove up the desert road towards Alexandria and branched left along the coast road, on and on through scenery that was at first sandy, then stony, then nothing very much but dark flat earth. And hot, a lot hotter than Cairo. Occasionally there were patches of arid cultivation with stunted wheat and, very occasionally, little oases with huts clustered around a well and picture-perfect palm trees that looked as if they belonged on the cover of a packet of dates. He soon got used to the sight of camels and flocks of sheep tended by small boys. On the second day they crossed the frontier with its impressive wall of rock, winding up the steep escarpment through the notorious 'Hellfire' pass and camping near the ruins of the Italian Fort Capuzzo. On 12 June Lee and the other new pilots joined 112 Squadron at Gambut, the principal British desert airbase, about thirty miles east of Tobruk. And there, just as promised, was a smiling Billy Drake.

There was a map of Europe on the wall of the Pocklington ops room, next to the blackboards for the names of the crews. As she wrote up the names, Edith Heap would sometimes have a feeling that a particular crew wouldn't return. Fated men had an aura. 'We lived hand in glove with death so we knew, it's not something you can explain.' There was a story that a bomber had landed at Pocklington with only a tail gunner on board and no sign of the rest of the crew. He had not heard the bale-out call. Edith thought of the medium and the help from pilots on the other side.

Everyone was aware that they lived on borrowed time. They were all liable to blow their tops and apologise later, nerves stretched by fatigue, anxiety and grief. She rarely listened to the war news or read a paper. What mattered was her base, her job, her boys.

Debriefing was difficult if they'd had a bad trip. Cold and grey, hungry and tired, they wanted bacon, eggs and bed, not a cross-examination. She was on duty when a crew came back after an hour in the air. Early returns like that were always treated with suspicion and the WAAFs were told to look for signs of 'twitch'.

This crew mooched about nervously and told their story of engine trouble. The young sergeant-gunner quietly sagged against the wall as the others spoke. Edith asked him whether he wanted to lie down and requested another WAAF to keep an eye on him. They talked some more, but when the time came to wake the sergeant he couldn't be roused. The doctor came and called for orderlies. He was carried out stiff, literally stiff from the neck down. 'Petrified with fright,' the doctor said. They never saw him again. His life had been saved by cowardice, which is how some of them saw it, but there wasn't much you could do with cases like that. Some got a bit flak happy and developed odd tics and twitches and funny mannerisms. Those you could send away for a rest and they'd come back fine. But not him, he'd be a liability to any crew. Afterwards the men he'd flown with were very friendly to Edith and no more was ever said about that night. It looked as if the gunner, a novice on his first trip, had had a panic attack and they'd brought him home but not wanted to tell the truth. Such nice boys, such brave boys, and all of them killed a few months later.

From time to time the sadness would take her by surprise. The latest killed or missing at Pock, the older feelings about Denis and that November morning in 1940. But she didn't inflict it on others, preferring to walk in the woods by herself or a couple of miles down the road to Allerthorpe.

But life was oddly light-hearted. There was an excellent dance band and each mess took turns to throw parties, making a big effort to get food and flowers. There were some great pubs near by, and the brewery town of Tadcaster just down the road. Betty's Bar in York was where the crews wrote their names on the mirror and picked up the local good-time girls.

Edith flew whenever possible. A few WAAFs were smuggled on ops, or so the story went. Rumour had it that a handful had been killed. Wimpies were her favourites, a great aircraft with wings that appeared to move gently up and down just like a bird's. She'd have liked to have gone on just one op, to understand it all, to see them making a difference.

Gambut, when Ken Lee reached it, turned out to be a very busy place. On one side of the main road was General Ritchie's headquarters, with generals and journalists tearing in and out in jeeps. On the other were the Desert Air Force's two principal fighter fields with Air Vice Marshal Coningham's HQ. All day planes droned overhead, coming in to land supplies on the vast, tussocky plain. It wasn't exactly an aerodrome, more a huge expanse of flat firm ground from which the biggest rocks and other obstacles had been cleared. The planes of 112 Squadron proved to be easily recognisable, though. Lee had already been told that Billy Drake's boys were well known for painting sharks' mouths on the undersides of the engine cowlings of their American-built Kittyhawks, a move that had attracted the press photographers and War Office publicity men. He also knew that 112 had been the first squadron to convert to a fighter-bomber role and that the pilots were being retrained for close air support. This sounded scary enough, and the reason for it – that the lumbering old light bombers had been suffering unacceptable losses – was hardly reassuring.

Lee reported to Drake in the squadron office, a truck parked a little way from the Kittyhawks. Drake was as delighted as Lee to renew their acquaintance, but he was busy and looked tired. 'Been doing our best to keep them out of Bir Hacheim for the last few days. We gave up yesterday. They're on the move again today so we're a bit busy trying to make it hot for them. We've been having quite a bit of fun shooting up transport. You'd better go and find yourself a spot to put up a tent. Then you might like to go and meet a plane. I'm afraid you'll find it's not quite like a Hurricane. You'll need to practise a bit before you can fly in combat. I'll see you tonight. The mess is that table over there, and that marquee. Did you bring any whisky? Good. I hoped you might.'

The old hands showed Lee how to dig a slit trench and put his tent up over it so that if the Luftwaffe raided in the night he could roll off his camp bed into the hole and keep sleeping. At least, they said he could. Outside his tent there was a canvas washbasin on wooden props. Everything was temporary and moveable: the mess consisted of foldable wooden tables and a couple of benches. He changed into the new safari jacket and desert boots he'd bought in Cairo. On the advice of someone in the Musqi, he'd also bought a rather natty-looking fly whisk. As he brushed the flies off the lip of his first cup of 112 Squadron tea, he discovered just how useful this was. He glanced in the mirror and decided that he looked a bit too smart. What he'd seen so far was not quite the desert air force of popular carica- ture − suede boots, baggy cords, cricket jumpers and leather flying jackets − but the dress code round here was definitely more relaxed than back home. He opened up his collar and rolled up his sleeves.

That night they all had a good drink under the stars, making the most of what the new pilots had brought up from Cairo. Lee immediately made friends with Jim Walker, the burly Canadian who commanded A flight, and with a Rhodesian named Edwards. They told Lee about the stupid order they had received recently, banning them from referring to the Germans collectively as 'Rommel'. It made Rommel sound like a superman, they had been told, and was bad for morale. Towards the end, when Billy Drake had gone to bed, his men tuned the radio to a German wavelength to catch 'Lili Marlene', the evening signing-off theme. 'He doesn't like us doing it,' they told Lee, 'but it's such a great song.' Then those who were still up, those who did not have to be 'at readiness' at first light, stumbled back to their tents.

Next morning, Lee's first impression of his American-built Kittyhawk was most favourable:

I was delighted with the look of the thing. And it was comfort- able. You had a huge cockpit. You sat there as though you were in a greenhouse.

But a few conversations with the ground crew and a spin or two in the air soon revealed the defects. The Allison engine was decidedly under-powered and the controls were all electric rather than hydraulic and were prone to going wrong when the sand got to work on them. They were also very complicated.

There were something like thirty-six different switches you had to put on before you were operational. Sure, you could fire two guns instead of all six, which was useful, but it was all too fussy.

Lee quickly came to appreciate the particular problems of working in the desert. Engine filters had to be changed constantly and the guns would frequently jam. He tried to learn the landmarks, sandstorms permitting. He discovered that it was easy to spot the sudden sort of sandstorm – the little *ghiblis* – and track their movements from the air, timing his landings to avoid the worst part. Navigation was simplified enormously by having the sea to one side. All the aerodromes were near the coast. If you reached water then you had gone too far north and you simply had to turn right for east or left for west.

There were other hazards more pressing than sand and navigation. He would be unlikely to escape a Messerschmitt 109 in a Kittyhawk, but the real danger was to be found closer to the ground. Lee had never tried dive-bombing before. Practising was fun, but the other pilots told him that the real thing was pretty hairy. German flak was good. The Rhodesian that Lee had been drinking with the night before was killed by some of it during Lee's first day in the air, and two more pilots went missing on 16 June.

That day he didn't need the noise to tell him that the fighting was very close. The squadron was escorting Boston bombers, and it took them just five minutes to reach the bomb line. Coningham stayed very cool and, in a last defiant gesture, on 17 June he sent four squadrons to raid the recently captured airfield at Gazala. They caught the German planes on the ground and, as the Kittyhawks swooped in, found there was only light flak. They shot up at least fifteen Messerschmitt 109s and left petrol bowsers blazing everywhere; 112 Squadron came back cock-a-hoop. Lee, who had not been allowed on the mission, never got to fly a single proper sortie from Gambut.

With German armoured cars closing in, all the planes took off hurriedly for the old Italian aerodrome at Sidi Azeiz, about sixty miles back nearer the frontier. Lee followed in a lorry with a few more spare pilots. It crossed his mind that what was happening was all a bit like his first campaign in France in 1940, only without the champagne.

The Americans were investigating the security leak, but doing it rather slowly. On 14 June 'C' wrote to Churchill in exasperation:

> There are at least three American cyphers in use between Cairo and Washington, and until the Americans inform me which cypher was used for the messages in question, it is impossible to determine whether the Germans have broken a cypher, or whether there is a traitor who is betraying information and transmitting it to the enemy by a secret channel.

The pressure mounted. On 16 June 'C' wrote:

> PM directed me to wire Washington on 15th that unless I received a report on the leakage within 24 hours, he proposed to write to the President.

Later that day a cable went to Cairo:

> Please inform General Auchinleck that Washington now accepts that American military attaché's cypher is compromised. A new cypher is being introduced. We have suggested that no reason should be given for change.

Chapter 8

18–20 June

The midshipman was only eighteen or nineteen, badly burned and badly shell-shocked too. In a moment of clarity he grabbed Mimi Cortis's hand and said, 'I'd rather die than go through it again. Don't make me, don't make me.' She gave him her best Edith Cavell smile and said, 'You're *my* hero, you know that.' Later, in the kitchen, she sat quietly and said, 'The poor boy, the poor boy' over and over again.

Geordie or Cockney, Irish or Welsh, talking to the patients was important. Some, in their distress, would confuse the girl at their bedside with their wife or their mother. It was best not to correct them. Often there was little the nurses could do but inject more morphine and offer what a dying man needed more than anything: a female hand to hold. Mimi hoped that the real wives and mothers would find out that someone had been with them at the end, that they died among friendly faces. The nurses kept a Union Jack in the store cupboard, to cover the bodies on the way down to the morgue. This midshipman would not need it, but would he ever recover his mind?

It was the end of her shift. Mimi walked outside for a few minutes to take in some fresh air before returning to her billet. All was warm and calm and, in the last still hour before dawn, she could see a glow brightening in the east. Soon the church bells would be ringing. After some sleep she would go and pray for the man and the woman he had been calling for.

High overhead she heard an aircraft engine, a night fighter returning to ta Qali. From the aerodrome came the chugging of a bulldozer and the shouts of men clearing up from yesterday's raid. Perhaps she would go for a swim in Golden Bay after church, or else walk in Buskett Gardens, watch the butterflies and doze beneath the shade of the orange trees. It was still full of people at the weekends, even if their picnic baskets contained only handfuls of apples or a meagre sandwich.

Suffering and death had always been part of her job. But nursing the sick and elderly in a normal hospital ward had not prepared Mimi Cortis for the injuries of war.

The RAF men often had terrible burns. We put them in a sort of sling and I would spray them with gentian violet to soothe the pain and kill germs. I'd have to change their dressings every few hours to give the flesh a chance to breathe. I remember a wounded pilot officer with horrible deep burns between his legs from all the aviation fuel. I had to wrap and unwrap his penis ever so delicately.

After a sinking, men would arrive black and purple with burns and coated with the thick fuel oil, which had to be removed quickly from exposed flesh. Mimi spent hours carefully cleaning nostrils, mouths and tongues with cotton wool and Acriflavin liquid. Edwin Gaffiero was a childhood friend serving in an anti-aircraft battery. He got both legs badly cut up.

He was on the verge of having them amputated, but slowly we nursed him back from the brink, spending hours making sure the circulation was OK, spraying him with antiseptics and moving him about to stop sores or gangrene developing. Eventually he was able to stand and then he learnt how to walk on crutches. I will never forget how he thanked us all when he left to rejoin his unit. But a week later he was dead.

So much had been destroyed so quickly, and the smallest details were the saddest. Mimi picked her way through the narrow Sliema streets remembering how hard her neighbours had worked to keep up appearances. Cleaning days began with the brass door knockers: huge shiny elephant's heads, Maltese crosses or leaping dolphins, all polished to dazzle visitors with a show of domestic pride. But now a street could be gone in a second, broken brass lying alongside pieces of charred green wood from the window shutters and the remains of the flowers that once grew on every balcony.

Alan Brooke thought that a soldier should always look smart. Washington was uncomfortably humid in June and he had ordered some lightweight suits and a new warm-weather uniform. Then Churchill, typically, had brought the trip forward at the last minute. Even the Chief of the Imperial General Staff was subject to rationing, and Brooke had invested several months' worth of precious clothing coupons. Fortunately the tailor met him at Euston Station with two nearly finished thin suits.

Brooke travelled up to Scotland in Churchill's private train, discussing how they would handle Roosevelt and the American High Command. Late at night on 17 June they were ferried by motor boat to a Boeing Clipper lying at anchor in Loch Ryan off Stranraer. Brooke had been looking forward to his first experience of this, the very latest way to travel, and he was not disappointed. Inside were comfortable bunks, a spacious dining saloon, bathrooms and stewards to fuss over Churchill and the nine other members of the delegation.

All slept soundly as the Clipper headed west over Ireland, and woke to the sight of an Atlantic convoy. At this Churchill, for no particular reason, burst into a jaunty chorus of 'We're here, because we're here, because we're here . . .' Above Newfoundland the sky was clear and bright, and they enjoyed epic views over the expanse of the Canadian maritime states. Turning south from Nova Scotia, they tracked along the coast of New England and down over Cape Cod, passing New York and turning south-west towards Chesapeake Bay. At nine in the evening local time they circled over Washington and made a smooth landing on the river near the Lincoln Memorial. From a loch in Scotland to the Potomac in a single twenty-six-hour leap! Brooke marvelled at the idea.

Awaiting the British party were men who were extremely anxious about Britain's strategic policy. Brooke met Henry Stimson, Roosevelt's Secretary of War, and ran into problems straight away. He identified him as another 'strong adherent of breaking our heads in too early operations across the Channel'.

Leaving Brooke to argue the case in Washington, Churchill travelled north to visit Roosevelt at his family estate of Hyde Park in New York State.

Corporal Kenneth Paxton was in his element. He'd found a German private who came from a little village not very far from where he had spent a year as a language student, and now they were discussing their old haunts, mountain beauty spots, the merits of different *Wirtshäuser* and *Weinkeller*. Peter Vaux listened and smiled. '*Schön*,' he heard. '*Aber Ihre Schwester war auch in Köln?* Was it badly bombed? How dreadful! I hope she was all right . . .' It was Paxton's favourite method, apparently charming, inconsequential, harmlessly eccentric. '. . . Such an unhealthy place, the desert. And was your battery commander . . . I've forgotten his name.' 'Müller.' 'Yes, Müller, that's right, was he *very* ill with dysentery?' Vaux caught Paxton's eye, smiled, and made a note of the name Müller. He knew that before long Paxton would have discovered the names and social background of half the men in the German's company, whether they were homesick and what they thought of the war.

Of course, they did not always talk like this one, but Paxton was a genius and Vaux felt jolly lucky to have him. He owed his luck to a security officer who had come along and said, 'As far as I can tell he's absolutely useless. See if you can do anything with him. I'd be glad to see the back of him.' With the gangly build of an emaciated scarecrow, Paxton certainly hadn't looked promising as he peered down anxiously through his crooked steel-rimmed spectacles. He was angular and clumsy and his cap fitted so badly that it fell off when he failed miserably to pinpoint some units on the map in response to Vaux's first question. But other little tests revealed distinct promise. Paxton had a degree in modern languages from Oxford and had studied for a year in Berlin and a year in Padua. He also spoke ancient and modern Greek and enough Arabic to bargain with a Senussi herdsman over the goat that became last year's Christmas dinner.

Vaux was very happy with all of his intelligence team. The driver and the chief radio operator were sound regular soldiers, Royal Signals corporals both, while his junior radio operators were bright and promising public schoolboys. The three operators manned the two big wireless sets throughout the twenty-four hours and maintained an accurate log. His assistant, Captain 'Tony' Viney, was a Cambridge-educated South African and a Royal Tank man like himself. A good practical soldier, he was learning fast. But Paxton was the star. The prisoner was now offering a vivid description of what he had seen of General Rommel's headquarters, and the shorthand clerk was scribbling furiously. Apparently it consisted of two armoured cars, two staff cars, three lorries mounted with anti-aircraft guns and a couple of captured British ACVs known as 'Max' and 'Moritz', each towing a 25-pounder gun. Rommel, he said, always rode standing up in a staff car.

When the interrogation had ended, Vaux started work on his latest intelligence summary. He put in the account of an escaped British prisoner, alleging mistreatment by Italian guards. They had fired over their POWs' heads with machineguns to get them moving, and when one man moved to avoid the fire he stood on a mine and lost a foot. Guards had been trading water for personal effects too, and a lame sergeant-major was shot dead when he couldn't keep up.

Vaux was just completing his report when there was a knock on the door and General Messervy looked in, as he had done so often. Vaux put on his beret, jumped out on to the sand and saluted.

I've come to say goodbye, Peter, and to thank you for all you and your chaps in there have done for me. The army commander says that he has lost confidence in me. I've got to leave you.

Messervy was such a decent and brave man that it was not hard to find words of sympathy, even though it should have been blindingly obvious that he was unsuitable for this job in the first place. His instinct to lead from the front was a good one, and it was partly bad luck that enemy action had kept him from headquarters at crucial times. But it was not a surprise that he was going. Two days earlier, the division's tanks had been sent charging into action once again, coming off worst in another attempt to halt the whole of 15 and 21 Panzer.

The enemy was steamrollering on. General Ritchie's headquarters had made a hurried withdrawal to the frontier, while the air force had pulled back beyond Mersa Matruh. Now the division had orders to harass only, to buy time for the retreat. With so little armour left, it could do little more and was waiting for the code word, 'Cocoa', to tell it to fall back into Egypt too.

In the last few days they'd had 'Carrots', 'Sprouts' and 'Donald Duck'. The British army, Vaux thought, badly needed to find some words that sounded just a little bit more warlike.

As he prepared for his meeting with President Roosevelt, Churchill was thinking hard about the future. He had devoted his life to the cause of Great Britain and her empire, but that empire appeared to be dissolving in front of him. India had rallied to the British cause for the second time in thirty years, but pressure was growing for this display of loyalty to be rewarded with the promise of dominion status after the war, as a step towards full independence. Churchill had sent Stafford Cripps, a prominent Labour politician, to work out a deal with the Indian Congress Party. Most London politicians thought that Indian independence was inevitable, but Churchill, who had been raised in an era of imperial self-confidence, hesitated. He did not wish to be responsible for losing the 'jewel in the crown' and wouldn't give the guarantees demanded by Congress's leader, Mahatma Gandhi. Cripps returned empty-handed.

At the moment, military calamity made it appear unlikely that anyone in London would be required to rule on the question of India ever again. Burma had fallen to the Japanese and Ceylon, Calcutta and the whole of eastern India were threatened. Tokyo politicians appealed to Indian nationalists to join them and rid the sub-continent of its European masters. Few were tempted, but the desperate state of affairs gave Congress enormous leverage over the imperial authorities. Gandhi was known to be planning a nationwide 'Quit India' campaign of civil disobedience.

Churchill had an unshakeable belief in the political, economic and moral superiority of what he liked to call 'the English-speaking world'. Aware of the growing power of the United States, he had long sought a way to integrate it with the British Empire. He saw a perfect fit: Britain's tradition of maritime trade and talent for colonial administration, America's vigorous new democracy and vast economic resources. During the rancorous 1930s, when trade disputes between London and Washington sparked a series of tariff wars, Churchill had urged both nations to take the longer view. At the time he had little influence. But he had plenty now.

To sustain its empire, Britain needed two things that were in short supply in London but abundant across the Atlantic: money and moral force. The anaemic British economy could no longer pay for the world's largest navy as well as the education, health and social security demanded by its own people. If America shared the burden then perhaps the books could still be balanced. But the empire's *moral* deficit was even more important. Britain had fought the Great War to protect smaller nations from the hegemony of Berlin, Vienna and Istanbul. Having witnessed this, those who graduated from university after the war were less sure than their parents had been that colonial administration was right. Such ethical qualms were reinforced by the massacre of protesting Indians by British troops in Amritsar in 1919, and a series of bloody colonial wars in Iraq and on the Afghan border.

Compared to this, America had moral force to spare. The outside world had long seen it as the place where the common man could get a decent break. When Roosevelt's envoy Harry Hopkins met Joseph Stalin in 1941, he was surprised to hear the dictator say that, whatever the benefits of communism, it was American democracy which could do most to rally the undecided against fascism.

It was obvious that, if the Allies won, America's would be the loudest voice at any conference called to reorder the post-war world. Churchill wanted to persuade Roosevelt to use that power to underwrite his vision of a redefined British Empire. He frequently spoke of the benefits of imperialism; the education and economic development that would allow Britain's subject peoples, one day, to take their independent places in the world. The timing of this happy moment was always left vague. But it would ideally take place within a world policed by the two great English-speaking nations. This would be Churchill's greatest political achievement: winning a final, glorious lease of life for enlightened British imperialism, underwritten by American decency and American dollars.

The explosions were getting closer and Mimi Cortis was still two hundred yards away from the shelter. Why had she stayed for that last cocktail? 'Tonight we'll introduce you to Tom Collins,' her friends had said, as they'd shared out their black-market gin.

Dare she leave the doorway and sprint for the shelter entrance? The stone arch offered some security, but there was nothing to protect her from a blast direct from the street. From somewhere behind the ruined house, there was a loud screech followed by a thud she felt reverberate inside her chest. Half a second later she heard the blast, slightly muted. About three streets away. She crouched down and wrapped her arms around her legs. Then another explosion, closer now, and she could feel a warm gust of dusty air on the side of her head as her ears echoed painfully with the metallic crack.

'You die if you worry. You die if you don't worry. So why worry?' Mimi had said that often enough. Cheering people up as usual. 'Hello, Smiler', 'Morning, Sunshine'. The sailor with the burnt-off face whose eyes she cleaned every morning called her 'Snow White'. And, yes, she whistled as she worked. Sang too. 'Just forget your cares and troubles, for tomorrow is a lovely day.'

'Oh God, this is it.' Mimi felt sadness more than fear. Sadness that she would never have the chance to marry and have children and tell them all about the war and what she'd seen and done. She wanted tomorrow now, lovely or not, wanted to see her sister and talk about her wedding again. She prayed to Santa Maria for a simple life. To grow old and wear a black dress and sit outside in the sun and gossip with the widows and spinsters.

Faces swam before her. Burnt ones, dying ones, faces disappearing under the Union Jack. Edwin Gaffiero in the ward kitchen. How hard they'd worked to save his legs. 'You're being discharged soon.' Touching his hand. 'Do take care.' He was scared behind his smile. A really nice boy, with a little sister that he doted on. And three days later he was dead.

Even nearer now, blasting the corner off a house at the end of the street and sending lumps of masonry flying past her head.

More clouds of dust swirled around and she coughed frantically to clear the bitter taste of explosive from the back of her throat. The next one would be it. It had to be. Here we go.

The bombing stopped, but it was some time before Mimi Cortis uncurled herself and went looking for another bus.

'First we're going to relieve Bir Hacheim, then we're not. Next we're going to hold a box at Knightsbridge, and then we're not. Next we're going to defend Tobruk, and then we're not. Now I reckon we've come round in a bleeding great circle and we're very nearly back where we started. It makes no sense to me.'

Dougie Waller chucked a handful of sand over the oil that he'd splashed on to the gun shield of the 6-pounder and studied the result with satisfaction. It was the best they were able to do by way of camouflage, and it was actually quite effective. He wiped his hands on his lucky German shorts, and went on. 'Anyway, I'm glad to be out of Tobruk. I didn't fancy it last year and I fancy it even less now. The last thing you want is to get stuck in that cockroach-infested shithole for six months.' He sat down on the stones piled round the edge of the shallow pit they had just scraped out for the gun. Alf Reeves nodded in tolerant agreement. He had his eyes fixed on the horizon to the north and, conscious of his corporal's stripes, knew that his job was to concentrate on what might be coming over the hill. Mind you, you couldn't make much out for certain through the heat haze. And half the time these days the enemy turned up driving captured British vehicles.

Bill Ash was totally absorbed in pulling apart some colour-coded German ammunition to see what sort it was, and George Moggeridge had gone off to park the 'portee' a hundred yards away back across the stony ground. The portee was their gun transporter. 'The latest thing in flexibility and mobility', the officer that delivered it had said. And it was. It went bloody quick, you

A Kittyhawk of Billy Drake's 112 'Shark' Squadron takes off in a cloud
of sand, loaded with a 250-pound bomb

Ken Lee relaxes at the Gazira Sporting Club, Cairo

Ken Lee's photograph of 112 Squadron pilots enjoying the 'pilots' mess' at Landing Ground 91. Billy Drake is on the left

Erwin Rommel (*right*) and his superior, Albert Kesselring

Churchill and Alan Brooke visiting Egypt, August 1942

'It was like being caged with a gorilla'. Churchill speaks
to Claude Auchinleck; Eric 'Chink' Dorman-Smith stands at
the back of the group, 5 August 1942

Churchill and Harry Hopkins aboard *Prince of Wales* in 1941

Other than air attacks, Rommel is the immediate threat to the Middle East. His tank strength is now the equal of the British. Due to intense and continous pressure on Malta by the German Air Force, 85 to 90 per cent of Axis supplies and reinforcements from Italy enroute Tripoli are arriving. Benghazi is being used by light vessels as an Axis port. British Intelligence estimates that Rommel's Panzer Divisions may be brought up to full tank strength and that an Italian Armored Division may be sent to him as a reinforcement. These armored units, an additional small motorized force, together with the forces now in Cyrenaica, make possible the invasion of Egypt.

A second threat to Middle East exists. There is increased air activity against British shipping in the Mediterranean. Some 200 long range bombers in Greece are available to strike at the Naval Base in Alexandria, what remains of the British Eastern Mediterranean Fleet, shipping in the Canal and upper Red Sea areas. RAF Intelligence estimates that by 1 April German will have 1000 combat aircraft in the Eastern Mediterranean area. This force will be as strong as that which captured Crete last year and which defeated the British battle fleet off Kythera Straits.

The possibility of an overseas expedition is a third threat. The German is building concrete barges in Greece, has improved his airdromes, built new ones. Should his air force close the Eastern Mediterranean, it would then be free to attack the British Fleet. Consequently, the Italian Fleet might easily dominate this area. As a result an overseas expedition from the Aegean and Southern Greece into Syria or Palestine must be considered a possibility.

To oppose Rommel in the desert the British have: 1st Armored Division whose combat strength at best is fair; 50th British Division; Polish Brigade deficient in transport; Guards Brigade whose combat efficiency is good; 1st South African Division which lost a complete brigade in November; 2nd South African Division which is without transport and is holding the frontier posts. Part of the 10th Armored Division, tankless, is now enroute to the desert. All of these units combined could not stop Rommel were he reinforced as indicated above.

The Australian Corps which was in Syria has left for the Far East. In all Syria and Palestine the British have only the New Zealand Division and a small portion of the 10th Armored Division, tankless.

Throughout the British offensive which started 18 November, the RAF had an average of 782 serviceable aircraft. That of the German was 220 and the Italian 584. Italian aircraft seldom ventured over British positions and the RAF justly claims air superiority. The Nazi Air Force in the Mediterranean area, exclusive of Libya, is 520 strong. Obviously, therefore, if the German concentrates this air in Libya he will have superiority over the RAF.

Demands made by the war in the Far East legislate heavily against the strength of Middle East. Less shipping is available for this theatre; equipment, personnel, destined for here are being diverted; troops and equipment are being taken from this theatre. The minimum

One of the messages sent to Washington by Colonel Bonner Fellers

January 12, 1942.

    Malfaya Pass area still in Axis hands and still under heavy
bombardment.

    ▲ London cable gives an estimate of 16,500 German soldiers
now in the vicinity of Agheila.

    British troops: 1th and 1st Brigade of British 1st Armored Division
now west of Hasciat. Force on Coastal Road El Agheila – Agedabia
contact Axis forces from Mersa Brega along a line 5 miles to Southeast.
British run into prepared infantry and artillery positions along Bir
es Suera––Beleleibat – Ma'aten Giofer.

    West of Burmaei a British Armored Car unit is in contact with a large
number of Axis motor transport moving westward.

    Location of Axis tanks unknown.

    R.A.F. bomb Catania and Tripoli Harbor night of 12th.

    Axis Air Force continue bombing of Malta. (Bombings on the increase)

January 13, 1942.

    Malta RAF reconnaissance planes report 6 motor vessels escorted by
3 destroyers 12 miles SSE of Keliba, course south.

    Axis bombed Benghazi. Bombing of Malta by Axis continues unabated.

More cables from Egypt sent to America using the insecure 'black code'

RG 226   COI/OSS Files
Box 102   9457

COORDINATOR OF INFORMATION
—————
INTEROFFICE MEMO

FROM: Lt. Colonel Ulius L. Amoss   DATE   July 20, 1942
TO: Major David Bruce
SUBJECT: Colonel Bonner Fellers

        I am informed that the brilliant and thoroughly
informed Colonel Fellers is returning here from Cairo.
Every report from every source is lyrical in praise of
this officer, some going so far as to say that he should
be C in C in Egypt. In view of his profound knowledge
of everything in the Middle East, I suggest the possibility that you and Colonel Donovan may wish to see him.

                        U. L. A.

Fellers returned to a medal and a hero's welcome

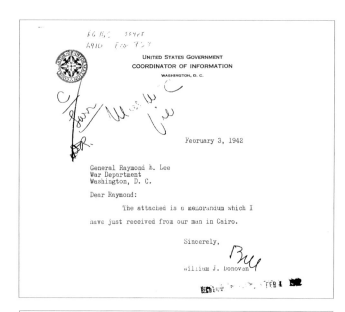

UNITED STATES GOVERNMENT
COORDINATOR OF INFORMATION
WASHINGTON, D. C.

February 3, 1942

General Raymond E. Lee
War Department
Washington, D. C.

Dear Raymond:

The attached is a memorandum which I
have just received from our man in Cairo.

Sincerely,

William J. Donovan

FEB 4

One of the questions in Washington was how the British
and the Colonials got along. Since Crete the feeling of the
Colonials against the British has run quite high. The
British on the other hand do not seem to be excited about
it, and are willing to admit many mistakes in their handling.
The Australians are the main cause of most of the trouble.
They had no discipline individually or collectively. Their
officers have little control over the men, and make no
attempt to get things under control. If the British are
at fault in asking them to do too much, (which I doubt)

The Australians make up their own mind as to when they
have had enough regardless of the circumstances. (The
relief of Australians at Tobruck). They rob and steal and
sell their arms to the natives when they run out of money.
The South Africans and New Zealanders seem able to get on
with everyone, and my guess is that the anti-British feeling
among them is not of serious proportions. The British
have great respect for them. Our own associations with
the Australians may turn out to be disillusioning in many
respects.

Fellers' reports went to the most senior intelligence men in America.
In this case, William Donovan, future founder of the OSS, is informed of
Fellers' insights into the quality of Britain's dominion troops

could fire the gun from it on the move, or wind down the runners and have it off the vehicle and properly dug in within minutes, then back on and away again in a few minutes more.

Sid the Bren gunner sat a few yards away on his own. The rest of them preferred it that way. The flies liked Sid because of his desert sores, and if he drew them off it gave everyone else some peace. 'Sid the walking fly trap', they called him.

The last few weeks had been typical of their experience in the desert so far. The Tower Hamlets Rifles, a territorial battalion of the Rifle Brigade, had arrived in Egypt on the last day of 1940 and they had been unlucky ever since. Their initial battle had been the Germans' first attack. They lost 350 men out of a thousand, mostly 'into the bag'. Then they'd spent a time defending Tobruk before being withdrawn to Alexandria by destroyer.

They were an anti-tank gun crew, the British army's answer to all those 50mm and 88mm German guns. But, for a long time, all they had been armed with was a ridiculous little Boys anti-tank rifle stuck on the front of a Bren carrier. The rifle was pretty effective against lorries, or camels, but near useless against anything with a bit of armour, and so they had quickly learned to avoid enemy tanks whenever possible.

But things had improved recently. First they got a 2-pounder gun which they had practised firing with great success at a group of knocked-out Italian M13s just outside Tobruk. They'd only shot it for real once, before being sent back in the middle of this latest battle to swap it for a brand-new 6-pounder. They'd had no chance to test this new gun because they were dispatched to Bir Hacheim to relieve the Free French. This did not sound like a promising assignment, but they never got to carry it out anyway. Bir Hacheim was cut off and under siege. They were bombed and attacked by tanks, infantry and artillery and were very grateful for a sandstorm that allowed them to pull out in something of a hurry.

Since then they had been sent here and there until finally they were put under command of the South Africans in Tobruk. Their platoon of four 6-pounders had moved through the minefield by night, losing the odd portee to mines. Nobody seemed to know where the minefields were any more. In fact nobody seemed to know what was going on anywhere any more. Tobruk was seething in total confusion. They had just found themselves a nice head-quarters and were beginning to unpack when they had got the order to move out again. They had fought their way through the jams of lorries trying to leave the town by the frontier road, only to have to head off back into the battle. Now they were under 7 Armoured Division, digging in and presumably waiting for an attack. In the three weeks since 27 May they had been under the command of seven different brigades.

While Alf Reeves kept up his nervous watch, Waller broke out some biscuits and tins of fish and bully beef and Bill Ash got his radio down from the portee's driver's cabin. They listened to the BBC evening news, which was full of the usual sunshine talk and some guff about cheery desert soldiers frying eggs on the bonnets of lorries. They never mentioned the scorpions or the shit beetles, or the fact that if anyone ever actually tried to fry an egg on a lorry it would turn into a fly omelette in seconds flat. Alf searched for the German music station, which always played more of the latest stuff than the BBC. It looked like they were going to be here for the night, so they might as well have some decent music with their supper. It had to be better than Sid's rendition of every known verse of 'Eskimo Nell'.

Cairo and Alexandria had long welcomed non-Egyptians. Turkish, French, Lebanese, Jewish, Italian and Greek families all added to the colour and economic vitality of the great cosmopolitan cities. A British soldier on a weekend pass may easily have got the impression that the Egyptian Arabs themselves only carried drinks, drove taxis and tried to sell them carpets. In fact plenty of them owned shops and small manufacturing businesses, had jobs in banks and insurance companies, and were well placed in the civil service and the police. Tens of thousands more studied in the country's universities, widely thought to be the best in the Arab world. Relations between Egyptians and the British had once been held up as an example of the empire at its benign best. But now things were very tense.

Britain had run Egypt for years without ever really admitting it. Long before 1914, Egyptian ministers did what their British advisers told them, while the men in khaki in the garrisons, and the warships at anchor in the naval bases, reminded everyone where the real power lay. During the Great War, Cairo was the base for a series of victorious campaigns against the Turks, and there was much talk of self-government to follow. By 1922 Egypt had a king, a male-franchise parliament and its own seat at the League of Nations. But this independence was limited by an 'understanding' that allowed Britain to keep military forces there and to take responsibility for defence and foreign relations. In 1936 a treaty formalised the relationship.

War with Mussolini brought direct British military control of transport, press, police, gas, electricity and just about every other aspect of life. The treaty allowed for this, but most Arabs thought it humiliating. Vast tented bases sprung up throughout the Nile Delta, along with workshops, foundries, airfields, hospitals and supply dumps. Alexandria teemed with sailors and yet more British and Commonwealth soldiers. Egyptians unhappy at this display of imperial power came to regard the outcome of the war with indifference. The young King Farouk leaned towards the Italians. He appointed a pro-fascist prime minister who did little to prevent anti-British demonstrations. By the end of 1941 students were chanting 'We are Rommel's soldiers' in the streets, praising Hitler and calling for attacks on Jews. The members of the underground 'Muslim Brotherhood' were discovered to be planning anti-British sabotage. Despite intense pressure from London, the King refused to remove his prime minister and so the British military authorities delivered an ultimatum. In February the King refused to budge and one morning, only three months before Rommel attacked at Gazala, the residents of Cairo woke to the sight of tanks surrounding the Abdin Palace, while inside armed British officers handed King Farouk his abdication papers.

Farouk backed down and appointed the prime minister that the British wanted. But in the weeks since then animosity between the two communities had grown. Egyptians resigned from the British-dominated social clubs in protest; the students still marched and chanted; and a young Egyptian army officer called Anwar Sadat was working with German spies in Cairo. With the well-publicised defeats of the Eighth Army in June, soldiers on leave began to notice a new edge to the gharry-driver's joke: 'Today, I take you to Groppi's. Next month, you take me!'

The rump of 112 Squadron arrived at Sidi Azeiz in the small hours of 18 June, having driven across the desert in the gathering gloom. In the morning they looked around. Gambut had been flat and featureless, but this was an open, arid expanse of absolute nothing. A few bombed-out ruins of old Italian buildings were all that marked it as an airfield. Away off in the distance Ken Lee could just see the low, domed tomb after which Sidi Azeiz was named. While some of the pilots flew a 'recce' back to Gambut, Lee drove over in a jeep to take a look. Inside was the mummified body of the holy man, wrapped in shrouds, and around were a few Bedouin graves, with some more recent additions. The ground near by was littered with shell cases and mortar bombs from some earlier skirmish.

When the pilots returned they reported that their old aerodrome was already in enemy hands. At ten the next morning new orders arrived instructing the squadron to abandon their new home as soon as possible. The pilots flew all the planes east over the Egyptian frontier towards another base, Landing Ground 75, a rough strip just south of Mersa Matruh. Once again, Lee followed on in a lorry, picking up the railway line near Fort Capuzzo and following it south of the great rock wall that was the border escarpment, until the cliffs finally petered out and subsided into the desert. There, next to the cairn that supported a board marked 'PICCADILLY MR610339', some joker had erected a statue of Eros made out of petrol cans with a bit of aerial twisted into a bow. The signpost next to it pointed the way to various destinations across the emptiness. They drove on in the direction indicated by the sign to 'CHARING CROSS' and then into Matruh to find out where the airstrip was. Lee got out his camera and snapped the other pilots sitting on the jetty in the harbour. By nine that night everyone had arrived and they began again to dig slit trenches and put up tents before it got completely dark.

The next day he flew his first sortie. He set off in his Kittyhawk, one of a flight of six under Flight Lieutenant Leu, Billy Drake's right-hand man. Their orders were to 'recce' the frontier. It had been reported, although they could barely believe it, that German columns were already nearing Egypt. Sure enough, there they were, pushing on towards Fort Capuzzo. Lee saw with a slight shock that they were already close to the tomb of Sidi Azeiz he'd visited two days ago. Only a little way ahead of them the coast road was clogged with retreating British troops, mile upon mile of lorries, motorcycles and jeeps. Things looked bleak for the troops left behind in Tobruk, now clearly cut off. As he looked towards the city on its peninsula in the far distance a great black cloud began to rise from it. Soon it was towering in the sky. Lee had seen sights like this before. In France all the oil stores had been burned as the Germans approached.

7 Armoured Division Intelligence Summary No. 52, 20 June 1942

Today the enemy has pushed down the CAPUZZO TRACK as far as the Fort, and while containing our forces in that area, has made a determined attack against TOBRUK. He penetrated the defences in the South East Sector, and advanced elements have reached the harbour.

Peter Vaux had hoped he would never have to write this, the account of the fall of Tobruk. To an intelligence officer used to dealing with the press, the significance to morale was clear. For days all the men had been asking, 'Are we going to be holding Tobruk again, sir?' It had not yet surrendered, but with Rommel through the inner perimeter and in possession of the harbour, it did not seem likely that the garrison, 35,000 strong though it might be, was going to be in much of a position to fight.

If the soldiers would be shocked at the loss of Tobruk, what was the rest of the world going to think? It was a symbol of British stubbornness, trumpeted throughout most of last year. His own regiment, 4 Royal Tanks, was part of the garrison, and as soon as he could he asked after them. Apparently they had been given no warning of the attack, but in the morning, after the Germans had already broken through the outer perimeter, they had been ordered to stop them. At the minefield gaps, their thirty-five old Valentines had taken on the panzer divisions, with the Germans using purple smoke to direct the Stukas on to the defenders. The British tank men had fought from 1000 until 1630, when their last five tanks were finally silenced. Apparently everyone had been either killed or captured. Vaux wondered what on earth General Klopper, the South African in charge of the defence of Tobruk, could have been doing to allow the place to disintegrate into such chaos. Here again, the British had had enough men but, when it mattered, they were all in the wrong place. There was nothing wrong with the individuals – most of them were as brave as his old friends in 4 Royal Tanks. But again and again, they were being asked to fight at a disadvantage in numbers, fire-power and location. Good men were dying thanks to bad general-ship and bad staff work – that was what the majors and colonels in the field were telling him. But you couldn't write that in an intelligence report. He scribbled on, resignedly, about how the enemy had taken the airfields at Gambut and Sidi Azeiz as well as the railhead at Capuzzo. Whatever the situation, one had to be precise and informative.

And they had been so close. He had just been reading the diary of a captured staff officer from 15 Panzer Division, which described Operation Venezia from the German point of view. How they had rounded Bir Hacheim full of confidence. How costly the fighting had been for them, with one mechanised infantry battalion completely destroyed by the British. How they had almost run out of petrol and all begun to worry about where Rommel was leading them. We stopped them, Vaux thought, we stopped them and we had them on the back foot and then we messed it up. Now it was difficult to see how they could be stopped again.

Chapter 9

20–25 June

The Hyde Park estate is a few miles down from the Vanderbilt mansion on a stretch of the Hudson long favoured by New York's élite. From the grounds there are open views of the valley, and thickly wooded hills plunge down to the river. This had been the young Franklin Roosevelt's playground. Half a mile wide though it is, the Hudson freezes in the winter and he had spent many happy hours skating and sailing ice boats on it.

Roosevelt, crippled by polio, drove Churchill around in his modified Ford Phaeton, with specially adapted hand-clutch and brakes. The two men toured the area, shared extravagant dinners and talked privately in Roosevelt's study. There was a good reason for privacy. One of the things they had to discuss was the future of atomic research. In 1941 Churchill had handed the Americans the results of a British investigation into the possibility of creating an atomic bomb. It was known that the Germans were also pursuing the idea. The sums of money required to continue the work were immense. At Hyde Park they decided that it should carry on in America and be paid for by America, but with all scientific information shared. In addition Churchill tried to wean his host away from the idea of a Second Front in 1942 and instead offered Alan Brooke's vision of progress in Africa and the Mediterranean.

They travelled down to Washington together in the President's train and, on 21 June, were talking with Brooke and Harry Hopkins in the White House when General Marshall brought in a message. It read, 'Tobruk has surrendered, with twenty-five thousand men taken prisoner.' Churchill wouldn't believe it and rang London for confirmation. The full story was even worse. He was told that the defence of Tobruk had lasted barely a day, and that 33,000 men, along with their vehicles, equipment and fuel, had fallen into Rommel's hands. The fleet at Alexandria was expecting to be bombed at any moment. According to Brooke, 'neither Winston nor I had contemplated such an eventuality and it was a staggering blow'. Churchill had come to discuss offensives and wonder-weapons. Instead, here was Britain's greatest humiliation. 'Defeat is one thing; disgrace is another,' he whispered, and turned his face away. Roosevelt broke the silence that followed with 'What can we do to help?'

In London the news struck 'like a thunderclap' according to Harold Nicolson, whose sleep was interrupted by a call from the *Chicago Sun* asking whether Churchill would survive the week.

The disaster was proof, if more were needed, that the German army was fearsomely tough, and that the idea of an early invasion of France was foolish in the extreme. With the American papers full of the fall of Tobruk, and with several taking the *Chicago Sun's* line on the imminent fall of Churchill, talk turned to shoring up the collapsing British position. That night, after Roosevelt had gone to bed, Churchill sat up late with Harry Hopkins. They talked strategy, history and politics, as they often had before, but mostly they talked supplies. On 23 June fifty-seven Mitchell medium bombers flew from California on the first stage of a long journey to Cairo. Within a week another eighty Kittyhawks and sixty bombers were flown to Africa, the bombers flown by American crews in American Air Corps squadrons. This was a turning point in the Anglo-American relationship. Previously, the idea of sending Americans to fight in Egypt had been rejected because it would embroil them in British imperial policy, always a touchy subject in Congress.

The Sherman was the latest American tank, only just going into full production. Roosevelt promised Churchill that 300 of them would be sent to the Eighth Army along with 100 new self-propelled 105mm howitzers. Hopkins said that the 400 vehicles would be dispatched as soon as he could get them on to merchant ships. Some of the Shermans had already been issued to American units that would now have to relinquish them, a gesture that particularly touched Alan Brooke:

> Anybody knowing what it entails withdrawing long-expected weapons from fighting troops just after they have received them will understand the depth of kindness that lay behind this gesture.

It was kindness blended with desperation. The Japanese were poised to invade India. Cairo and Alexandria were threatened. Malta had not received any supplies for weeks. It looked as if the Axis powers were about to take control of the entire Mediterranean, the Suez Canal, the Persian oil fields and the Indian sub-continent. Such a shock might force Stalin into the separate peace that remained Washington's principal fear, allowing the Germans to pack western Europe with their finest troops and leaving America allied to a thoroughly demoralised Britain.

On the morning of 21 June, as the South Africans raised the white flag in Tobruk, Ken Lee took off with seven other planes under Flight Lieutenant Leu to raid their recent home at Sidi Azeiz, now occupied by the Germans.

'Hawkeye', they'd called him before, because he always spotted them first. He'd excelled at that deadly aerial ballet, curving round for the kill, sweating and panting with the tearing cacophony of the Brownings burning in his ears. Until that moment when he suddenly felt like he'd stepped into a stream, but it wasn't water in his boot, and he'd fought to get out of the burning Hurricane 16,000 feet above Sussex. Now he tensed himself for a new kind of war, knowing that you couldn't swerve out of the way of a cannon shell, remembering all those ground-attack boys in France who'd taken on the German flak and never made it home.

They came in from the east out of the early-morning sun, and swooped low over the airstrip.

The idea was to place your nose down below the target, and then at about a thousand feet you suddenly levelled off and as your nose crossed the target you pulled on a piece of wire and the bomb fell away.

It didn't sound very scientific, but it worked pretty well. Lee released his single 250-pound bomb on a collection of lorries and climbed away, too focused on controlling the unwieldy Kittyhawk to look back and see what had happened. He was disappointed to discover that the plane handled much the same without the bomb as with it. So much for that Yank engine. He did a quick circuit and ran straight into the more dangerous aspect of his new role.

All these brightly coloured lights were suddenly coming up and flying past, great long streams of tracer shells.

It seemed certain that he would be blown out of the sky, and at this height there'd be no question of a parachute. He pulled quickly away from the source of the ground fire but others were not as lucky. 'Red Three down, Red Three down.' He looked round and saw a plane streaming smoke. Crichton, who had ridden with him in the truck during the latest retreat, came on the R/T to say that he was hit but would try to make the frontier.

Lee switched on all six machineguns and, in a turning dive, roared in to attack the anti-aircraft positions that were throwing up all those lines of tracer. He came in from the west, hoping that other Kittyhawks still making their bombing run would distract the gun crews. About 500 yards ahead and below he could see the lines of explosions in the sand and banked hard right to direct them towards a mobile flak gun. Men leapt from it as his bullet track approached and swept over them.

But someone was still firing back. Leu, the flight leader, reported that he was hit and would try to make an emergency landing. One of the good things about desert flying was that you could land a plane just about anywhere if you had to. From above, the circling pilots could see German infantry in trenches no more than half a mile away from where Leu's smoking Kittyhawk came to rest. They watched him climb out of his plane, run, and then dive into a trench. It looked as if he was under fire. Suddenly, one of the other planes left the formation and turned to land near by. 'Blue Four, Blue Four, what the hell are you doing?' said Lee. As the senior officer, he was now in command. 'It's Johnson, he's his best friend,' explained Knoll, the New Zealander. 'He owes him fifteen quid, you mean,' someone else volunteered. 'OK, everyone calm down,' said Lee. 'Circle round and give them some cover. Machinegun anything that moves towards them. And keep your eyes open for bandits. If there are any around they'll be on their way here soon enough.'

Johnson landed and sat in the open desert with his engine running. Leu tried to climb out of the trench but fell back. They could see the sand spurting as bullets hit close to him. He crawled to the other end of the trench and tried again. 'If Johnson waits there any longer, they'll have him too.' Johnson took off again, leaving his friend behind.

They found their own landing ground, circled round once to check that everything was OK, and landed. The ground crew moved in to refuel and rearm. There was no sign of Crichton, who had evidently not made it home. As the other pilots trudged towards the mess, Johnson went over to plead with Billy Drake to allow him to go back to make another attempt at a rescue.

Drake and Lee exchanged glances. 'All right, we'll come with you.'

Half an hour later the three flew back to Sidi Azeiz and circled low over the airfield looking for the lost flight leader. His plane was there but there was no sign of its pilot. The whole area was dotted with German armoured cars and half-tracks now. 'We'd better go back,' said Drake, 'but we'll let them know we've been.' He dropped from between the other two and dived towards two armoured cars and released his bomb. By the time it hit the ground they were too far ahead to see whether he'd done any damage, but they all felt better for the gesture.

That evening the others told Johnson that he had done his best. That said, they were sure Leu was still alive. 'He didn't stand a chance with just a pistol. He won't have tried to fight it out. He'll be in the bag.' But Johnson just sat silent, head bowed. Lee had not been with the squadron long enough to make firm friendships, except with Drake, but he remembered how it had been, before their hearts had hardened and they had refused to allow themselves to get too close to anyone. Just as they were all getting thoroughly maudlin, a lorry pulled up in a flurry of dust and Crichton jumped out. He'd made it over the escarpment with only a few hundred feet to spare and landed on the beach near Sollum. He'd even had time for a quick swim before hitching a lift to Matruh.

On 21 June, Chink Dorman-Smith gave a press conference in Cairo. Faced with a clamour of questions from a highly aggressive group of journalists, he was forced to make the best of the fall of Tobruk. He talked of the seesaw nature of the desert war. He said that the port had been indefensible in the present circumstances. 'Our commanders,' reported *The Times* on 22 June, '. . . are not despondent . . . They are convinced that the next time the pendulum swings it will go in our favour.'

Privately, Chink agreed with many of the criticisms voiced by writers like Alex Clifford and Alan Moorehead. The journalists had spoken to men who had recently seen action at the front. They also knew that there were soldiers in Cairo who were taking rather longer to return to their units than they should have, and that the Military Police were carrying out sweeps of the bars, bazaars and souks searching for those absent without leave. Few knew that the problem was so serious that Auchinleck had requested permission from London to shoot deserters. It was refused.

German and Italian agents were in Cairo seeking out Arab allies to lead a new administration. In Alexandria troops scanned the skies for parachutists, and the Royal Navy filled up the fuel tanks of its warships in case they needed to make a hasty departure. And yet the Commander-in-Chief still supported Ritchie. On 22 June Auchinleck flew to Eighth Army's new headquarters at Sidi Barrani. En route Chink again tried to persuade him to take charge. They arrived to discover that Ritchie was now preparing to stake everything on a defensive battle at the town of Mersa Matruh. Chink thought Ritchie's plan was 'fatuously numb'. Chink had studied the ground at Matruh himself and knew it was ripe for another of Rommel's favourite outflanking manoeuvres, the last one he would need to execute before reaching the delta. In Chink's opinion there was only one place worth making a stand in the whole Egyptian desert, at a line running south from the railway halt of el Alamein. This lay a tantalising sixty miles short of Alexandria but, squeezed in between the sea and the impenetrable Qattara depression, it at least offered a narrow, cramped position with little room for Rommel's tricks.

Ken Lee was getting ready to move home once again. The Germans had crossed the frontier and were closing in on Matruh.

At first light on 23 June he flew a recce to establish the enemy positions, and then escorted bombers to blast the coast road in the afternoon. It felt a lot safer than ground attack.

From 12,000 feet Rommel's supply train resembled a gigantic black snake, one that was irritated rather than stunned by the bombs dropped on it. When he came back, the ground crew reported that the Luftwaffe had repaid them for the ground attack of two days before, bombing and strafing near 112 Squadron's own camp. They were ordered to leave next morning and by midday were at Landing Ground 102, another improvised strip on flat ground a little inland from the coast, about halfway between Matruh and Fuka. This time they didn't even bother to unpack the trucks.

'I want you to tell me what Rommel is going to do next, Peter,' said the new general of 7 Armoured Division, 'and how he will attack Matruh.' 'Wingy' Renton had previously been in charge of one of the division's brigades and, like his predecessor, had little direct experience of fighting with tanks. He was a rather short-tempered man, entirely lacking in Messervy's charm. And, where Messervy had been all for glorious charges and leading from the front, Renton, having been 'winged' in the Great War, seemed determined to keep his remaining arm.

So that morning of 24 June, as ACV2 rumbled through the desert, weaving between the worst of the stones, Vaux began his 'Written appreciation by the German commander, 1200 24 June 1942'. He knew that the German spearheads were well into Egypt as he wrote, having crossed the frontier the night before; 7 Armoured Division was the rearguard now, and their armoured cars and mobile infantry were falling back just in front of, or sometimes just behind, the lead panzers.

General Ritchie had decided to make his stand at Matruh, reinforcing the relatively unscathed divisions of 13 Corps with some well-rested, tough New Zealanders, once rated by Rommel as the best troops in the desert. These, in theory, would have substantial armoured support from all the regrouped and re-equipped tank units and, even though the RAF had also been forced into a precipitate retreat, they would probably be able to muster some decent air cover too.

Vaux imagined himself in Rommel's desert boots once again. Presumably he would pause to size up the new obstacle and wait for his air force and tank replacements to come up and join him. When last in action the enemy was down to an estimated 150 front-line tanks. Before they attacked Matruh they would be rein-forced with captured tanks and repairs. Perhaps 180 German and 200 Italian tanks, then. He would assault Matruh with three Italian divisions, land commandos by sea to seize the station and support them with a panzer battle group. Meanwhile Vaux would draw the British tanks on to an anti-tank screen on the escarpment. He presented his plan to Renton.

On 23 June, while he was still digesting the fall of Tobruk, Churchill found his White House breakfast spoiled by another Ultra decrypt, this one detailing continued German use of their 'good source'. He wrote immediately: '"C", is this still going on?'

'C' replied to Churchill: 'Cyphers now changed.'

They had been. A German memo dated 29 June was later found in Berlin:

we will not be able to count on these intercepts for a long time to come, which is unfortunate as they told us all we needed to know, immediately, about virtually every enemy action.

Within a month, Bonner Fellers was back in Washington, to some-thing of a hero's welcome.

From: Lt Colonel Ulius L. Amoss
To: Major David Bruce
Subject: Colonel Bonner Fellers

I am informed that the brilliant and thoroughly informed Colonel Fellers is returning here from Cairo. Every report from every source is lyrical in praise of this officer, some going so far as to say that he should be C in C in Egypt. In view of his profound knowledge of everything in the Middle East, I suggest the possibility that you and Colonel Donovan may wish to see him.

Later that year Fellers was awarded the Distinguished Service Medal for his work in Cairo which, in the words of his citation,

> contributed materially to the tactical and technical development of our Armed forces . . . his reports to the War Department were models of clarity and accuracy.

Peter Vaux's ACV was at the front of 7 Armoured Division as it pulled back into Egypt. The Tower Hamlets Rifles were at the back, acting as rearguard for the division. And the anti-tank platoon was the rearguard of the Tower Hamlets Rifles. All of which meant that if the panzers caught up with them again, the first British soldier they would reach would be Rifleman Douglas Waller.

Darling Dougie,
It's two years since we got engaged! I wonder how you are my darling and what you look like now. In his last letter Arthur said you're almost black because in the desert you never wear a shirt. Things are better than they were and we haven't been bombed much since the autumn. There wasn't very much to celebrate our

anniversary with. You have to buy everything with points now. The latest thing is they've even rationed soap! Of course I would love to meet Arthur and Bill. They are welcome any time if they ever allow you to come home.

Love, Laurie

Waller took out his photograph with the message in green ink: 'To you darling from your own Laurie XXX'. It had been taken in August 1940 just before he was called up. It had a few tears around the edges now, but she still smiled back at him. He had been walking with a friend in the navy when she'd first come out of the crowd and touched him on the collar for luck. Lots of girls did that with sailors. Not that it had done the *sailor* any good: he'd transferred to submarines and that was the last they'd heard of him. But Dougie's luck was in, all right. He'd got chatting and found out where she worked and soon enough they were at the pictures together. Laurie Richmond was her name, and she was gorgeous. Her dad was a pitman from up north who'd come down to London for a job in the coke works. He'd been a sailor in the Great War and done Arctic convoys to Russia, so they were a bit of a naval family. All through that first year she'd seemed in more danger than him, what with all the bombs dropping on London and the City in flames. He found it hard to imagine what it must look like now. And his lot had been on holiday in Egypt, everyone said at home. Well, the holiday had ended soon enough when Mr Rommel turned up.

The bulk of the column had disappeared over the horizon a few minutes ago. Waller, Alf Reeves and Bill Ash crouched by the gun. Sid lay on his own a few yards away with his Bren gun and his flies.

'What's the betting we never hear from them again?'

'Can you see anything yet?'

Alf Reeves was scanning the horizon behind them. They were ready to shoot at the first sign of a half-track or an armoured car. It had been like this since early morning. They seemed to be in an eastward race with another column which, despite its largely British equipment, did not seem to consist of friends. And they were only just winning. Every few hours the 6-pounders were dropped off as rearguard. The portee had just backed up behind a rocky hummock. Once they caught sight of the first Germans they would fire off a few rounds to pin them down and buy some time. Then they would hare off as fast as possible after their mates.

They kept moving after it got dark, hoping that the enemy wouldn't do the same. Moggeridge followed the dimmed tail light of the vehicle in front. The others cursed him when they hit a bump, fearful of a puncture, staring wide-eyed into the darkness behind for any sign of their pursuers. During the night they found the railway and crossed it, still moving east. Eventually they reached the latest defensive positions south of Matruh, where they were able to rest for a time. They were not far from divisional head-quarters and, in the evening, when all they really wanted to do was listen to the radio and sleep, they all had to line up to meet the top brass. That old fart 'Wingy' Renton came over in his jeep to thank them all for their good work

Neville Gillman had spent three blissful days by the sea. The Sharpshooters swam, got clean and slept in the sun. They wrote letters and ate fresh food and there was even a generous supply of bottled beer. But it was not to last. As the enemy began to draw uncomfortably close to their beach, they were pulled out. They had hoped that, like other weary survivors of the tank battles, they were being sent back to the delta. But instead they were in search of replacement tanks. They drove south through the desert to Sofafi and then, crossing the railway, arrived at the big ordnance depot at Bir Enba, just inside Egypt. There they waited a day, and there they learned, to everyone's dismay, that Tobruk had fallen. Because of this the tanks would no longer be coming up this far. Instead, they were sent farther back, in more lorries through more desert to Fuka, where the main ordnance depot was now supposed to be. They got there on 22 June. Still there were no new tanks. A squadron went off to take over some Grants from another division while B and Gillman's C squadron kicked their heels and Viscount Cranley shouted down the telephone about bloody incompetence and piss-ups in breweries. Finally they were sent towards Matruh to take over some Stuart light tanks from the Scots Greys, who had just arrived in the desert and been rushed to the front. The army decided at the last minute to give the precious tanks to battle-hardened crews instead, so Cranley's men took them south to take up position near the New Zealanders on the escarpment overlooking Matruh.

Harry Hopkins did not simply owe Franklin Roosevelt his political career. He owed him his life. In 1939 Hopkins lost three-quarters of his stomach to cancer and was expected to die within weeks. Roosevelt summoned America's best oncologists and nutritionists and ordered them to keep his friend alive. Months of blood transfusions and experimental drug therapy followed, as Hopkins clung on. Eventually he was allowed home to convalesce, at which point Roosevelt installed him in the room at the White House that he still occupied in June 1942.

Hopkins could barely digest normal food. His days began with Alutropin, amino-acid powder, 'Hepavex compound', 'V-Caps', 'Halivir oil' and vitamin D. These were followed later by regular doses of calcium, liver extract and 'Appell powder'. Looking gaunt and exhausted most of the time, he was prone to sudden vomiting and intense attacks of diarrhoea, and had to make embarrassing changes of clothing as a result.

Yet Hopkins remained full of life. Hunched over his desk one moment, his pallid face bent over a pile of papers, next moment he would sit up and deliver a wisecrack or a profanity that would command the attention of the room. Pamela Churchill, the Prime Minister's vivacious daughter-in-law, thought him fascinating company. And, despite repeated lectures from doctors and friends, he was rarely seen without a glass in his hand. A three-to-four-pack-a-day smoker, he continued to enjoy good whisky, fast cars, high-stakes poker and jazz clubs. He also loved the game of American politics. Less than a year after his operation he had been sent by Roosevelt to fix the President's 'spontaneous' nomination for re-election in 1940.

Hopkins' friends could never quite determine which was more important to him: the game or the cause. He had always blended opportunism with idealism, as might have been expected from a man whose mother was a Methodist schoolteacher and whose father was a gambler and gold prospector. Raised in an atmosphere of Christian compassion, Hopkins had been interested in social work from his early teens. But, although his days may have been spent doing good, in the evening basketball games his college nickname had been 'Dirty Hopkins' because of his liberal use of the elbow.

Hopkins became a ten-dollar-a-week social worker in the poverty-stricken Lower East Side of Manhattan. By the early 1920s he was director of the city's Tuberculosis Association and, when the Great Depression struck, he was hired by state governor Franklin Roosevelt to help create a pioneering relief programme for the unemployed. This was a test run for the ambitious welfare projects that Roosevelt applied to the nation when elected President in 1932. By then Hopkins was one of his most trusted aides, and received some of the most important jobs in the first 'New Deal' administration.

In Washington Hopkins was widely admired and equally widely feared, seen by some as 'Roosevelt's Rasputin', or 'the intriguer from Iowa'. The key to his success was that he and the President were genuinely very close friends. The notoriously secretive Roosevelt preferred to delegate many of the most important functions of government to a series of close aides like Hopkins, rather than work through his cabinet in the normal way. Summoning up resources, cutting corners, haranguing juniors, Hopkins was a man who made things happen.

His second wife died of cancer in 1937, two years before his own brush with the disease. Their daughter Diana was frequently in the care of nannies and boarding schools. By the outbreak of war Hopkins was the de facto Deputy President of the USA and very close to another of Roosevelt's key aides, the envoy Averell Harriman, one of Pamela Churchill's lovers. Together Hopkins and Harriman outflanked and outranked the State Department and both developed excellent relations with Churchill.

In London he would frequently 'escape' to bars at the top hotels, and attend late-night parties with Pamela Churchill and the other 'Dorchester girls', as she called them. And he was drawn into the network of friendships around Churchill, growing close to Brendan Bracken and Lord Beaverbrook. One note to him from Bracken catches the mood:

> My Dear Harry, Be kind to the bearer of this letter, Major Rex Benson. He is a grand fellow and no teetotaller, and he hates the Huns more than you do!

Hopkins described himself as a catalyst between the two war leaders he called his friends – Roosevelt the subtle strategist, calm and charming and often away from his desk; Churchill always shouting for assistance, generating ideas and memos and appearing to relish being at the heart of the action. In 1941 Hopkins had crossed the Atlantic with Churchill on the *Prince of Wales*, playing hours of backgammon and even teaching the great man gin rummy, the latest craze in Washington. Hopkins observed that Churchill played games as he made war, doubling and redoubling with reckless gusto.

Like Roosevelt, who had also survived a debilitating illness, Hopkins admired courage. He defined it as the ability to cope with disaster and carry on without making too much fuss, a characteristic that he, Roosevelt and Churchill all had in common, and never more so than in mid-June 1942.

As a reward for taking Tobruk, Hitler made Rommel a field marshal. The following day Auchinleck offered Brooke his resignation, but received no reply. Then, from the Bletchley Park decrypters, came the news that the Panzerarmee Afrika had been instructed to drive east again as soon as possible. By 25 June, its leading elements were outside Mersa Matruh.

Hitler cabled the Italian army with the message 'Eighth Army practically destroyed ... the historic hour draws near', and Mussolini flew to the desert ready for a triumphant entrance into Cairo. With him he brought a military band and a mighty white horse on which to ride into the city. In a cable to Auchinleck from Washington, Churchill called for all the reserve and clerical staff to be thrown into battle. For days he had been complaining to Brooke that Auchinleck was not using anything like his full strength. Brooke pointed out that the Commander-in-Chief, Middle East, was also responsible for the defence of Persia, Palestine and Syria. At moments like this Churchill was apt to reply, 'Rommel, Rommel, what matters but beating Rommel?' Certainly it had come to mean everything to the mood in Parliament. On the day before Churchill flew home a motion was tabled in the House of Commons stating that 'This house, while paying tribute to the heroism and endurance of the Armed Forces of the Crown in circumstances of exceptional difficulty, has no confidence in the central direction of the war'.

Churchill and his Labour coalition partners dominated the House of Commons, but a strong current of anti-government opinion was running through the country, as was demonstrated at a by-election in Maldon, Essex. The pro-Churchill Conservative candidate saw his large majority overturned in favour of an anti-government campaigner running explicitly against the incompetent management of the war and the supposed deadening influence of 'Colonel Blimp', an upper-class, red-faced cartoon soldier who appeared to sum up the British High Command. Normally loyal newspapers were printing letters and columns calling for a new sense of leadership and 'grip'. They commented angrily about amateurism at the highest levels of the army and urged a sweeping-away of the 'Blimpish' dead wood.

Churchill said goodbye to Hopkins and Roosevelt with 'Now for England, home, and a beautiful row'. Alan Brooke was feeling sentimental as he flew back, remembering scenes from his childhood and longing for peace. And once again he was amazed at the power and the comfort of the big Boeing aircraft that, this time, made the trip in under twenty-four hours. As the Clipper descended into Stranraer Loch, other Boeings were leaving airfields in Bakersfield, California, and heading for the Middle East, and Harry Hopkins' men were on the telephone bullying shipping companies to get transport ready for the Sherman tanks.

But Rommel was fifty miles inside Egypt when they landed.

Chink had been trying to get to sleep for hours, but the standing offence to musical good taste that called itself the Continental Hotel Dance Band was still going strong, fighting with the poorly oiled electric fan for the privilege of disturbing his rest. It was late at night on 24 June, and he had spent most of another frustrating day trying to make some sense of what was happening out in the desert, all the time being eaten away with anxiety at the likely result of the next German attack.

He wasn't the only one. The whole city was twitchy now. The wives of senior officers and colonial civil servants were quietly packing their bags, and even the waiters in the clubs had been overheard making jokes about the need to acquire German phrase books. Unlike some, Chink had not yet lost confidence in Auchinleck, but if the general didn't do something dramatic then that hopeless, blundering Neil Ritchie was going to let Rommel drive right up into the Nile delta, of that he was absolutely convinced.

As he lay in his noisy sweat-box of a room, Chink's mind ran over the many unfairnesses and stupidities of this war and this army. The endless rewarding of mediocrity. All those stupid garden parties. He remembered coming out to Egypt in 1937 to take command of a battalion. He discovered that the training programme was designed around preparations for an inter-regimental polo tournament and its associated social scene. He'd cancelled the whole thing. As a result his well-trained men performed brilliantly in the opening months of the war, and the officers to a man had hated him for it. What was the point?

On the other side of the room was a half-finished letter to Eve containing all his bitter feelings. Then, just as the men downstairs were finally packing away their instruments and he was drifting off to sleep, the telephone rang. Thirty seconds later Chink put down the receiver, smiled and picked up his pen again.

> 11.30 pm. Just been told guardedly on the open that I must go to the WD [Western Desert] tomorrow and be prepared to stay there for several days. Worse situations have been retrieved by bold and courageous action. We'll see what can be done, but it won't be very orthodox!

After a career being unorthodox, and arrogant and annoying, the British army was finally going to give Chink his chance. He was dressed, shaved and packed by 0600 the following morning. Before he put the letter into an envelope and left the room he wrote a final line at the bottom of it: 'One hot helter skelter!'

Chapter 10

25–30 June

On 25 June, after an excellent 'last meal' at the Muhammad Ali Club, Auchinleck and Chink flew up to Eighth Army headquarters. As they sweated inside the Boston bomber Chink urged central artillery control; abandoning the defensive boxes; a co-ordinated retreat to a better position; grouping the remaining sixty or so Grants into a single decent armoured unit and hitting the vulnerable Italians whenever possible. Most of all he recommended, once again, the immediate replacement of Neil Ritchie.

A staff car met them at the Maatan Baggush airfield. Auchinleck went straight to Ritchie's caravan and dismissed him, then all the staff officers gathered in the underground operations room to listen to Auchinleck's address and hear their new instructions. Chink's voluble optimism instantly jarred with tired men who had been struggling at the sharp end for weeks. Nevertheless, his tactical advice was quickly put into effect.

I had the strangest feeling of certainty about all I did or advised. The certainty that I could see what the enemy was about to do and how one could damage him. It seemed as if all I'd read or thought about war came to my aid.

Auchinleck and Chink planned to draw Rommel on and break him on the low ridges around Alamein. For this they needed a delaying action at Mersa Matruh that would buy as much time as possible to prepare defences farther east. The army was ordered to hold Matruh for as long as possible, but then to fall back to Alamein in good order. Auchinleck wrote a memo to his senior commanders:

> At all costs and even if ground has to be given up, I intend to keep Eighth Army in being and to give no hostages to fortune in the shape of immobile troops holding localities which can easily be isolated.

Cables flew from Churchill insisting that every spare man in the Middle East be thrown into the battle. On 26 June Auk replied, 'Your instructions regarding fighting manpower will be carried out . . . We will do our best.' But Auchinleck had no intention of taking the Prime Minister's advice. He'd come to believe that one of the problems facing the British army in the desert was the presence of too *many* men, or rather too many infantrymen sitting in boxes, consuming water and food and in need of protection from Rommel's roving panzers. The last thing he needed was more of them. Better, at last, to copy the German model, something Chink had been arguing for weeks. This meant a flexible, fully mobile army of integrated tank and artillery units, backed up by close air support.

Auchinleck tried to clear his mind of all his other responsibilities, but he couldn't ignore the reports from the Soviet Union. The Germans had just begun a drive towards the Caucasus Mountains and Persian border. There was a possibility that the Middle East would be caught in a vast pincer. Although he appeared cool, he found the burden of command at this moment painfully hard to bear, but he shared his fears only with Chink, who was constantly at his side. The two slept together in a tent next to the command caravan, and at night sometimes held hands for comfort. Auchinleck later told him that

I think what sticks most clearly and vividly in my head is that drive back along the dark and deserted road after we had taken over from Ritchie, and the next morning when we were very much alone in the desert. Also I remember often our tent at our HQ and our bedding rolls in the sand ... I do not think I could have stuck it out anywhere else, or without you to advise and plan ahead.

Ken Lee was amazed at how smoothly the RAF continued to function even during such a calamitous retreat. The army might be in chaos, the entire Middle Eastern position might be about to collapse; for all he knew, the whole war might be coming to a cataclysmic end. But every time 112 Squadron pulled back to a new stretch of desert that passed for an aerodrome, the fuel bowsers and the ammunition lorries were waiting. The ground crews kept up an amazing rate of serviceability, 80 per cent most days, better than the average back home, and the maintenance units continued to turn around damaged planes with impressive speed. Nobody needed to be told to do anything. The rigger would be up on the wing before you reached the cockpit ladder. The fitters worked all night under tarpaulins by the light of a hurricane lamp. Armourers and pilots climbed up on trestles together to align the guns. In such an atmosphere of easy comradeship, there was no need for old-school discipline. 'Would you do this please?' was about as strong as an order got.

Drake, Lee and four others flew another bomber escort mission from Landing Ground 102. They were bombed themselves that night but watched from their tents as the gunners around the field trapped a Heinkel in their searchlights and shot it down. The pilots cheered and went back to sleep. Lee flew two bombing runs the next day, aiming at airfields and the 'Charing Cross' road junction. That day they got some more Kittyhawks, new ones with American radios and more sophisticated bomb racks.

On 26 June, the RAF threw everything it had into Auchinleck's effort to slow down Rommel's advance; 112 Squadron flew sixty-nine sorties, with one flight taking off as another came in to land. Lee's own contribution was four. He led three raids in the morning on the German forces gathering south of Matruh, taking on the anti-aircraft guns again to get his bombs down on to the supply columns. They were so close now that each trip lasted less than three-quarters of an hour. In the afternoon he flew a bomber escort mission. From the air it was clear that it was all having an effect. Late that day the main enemy supply train halted forty miles short of Matruh. For dozens of miles back towards Tobruk German and Italian drivers were cowering by the side of the road, only crawling forward again as dusk put a stop to the bombing.

But Rommel was still coming on. Once again his skirmishers were little more than a dozen miles away from Ken Lee's airfield and, while a screen of RAF armoured cars went forward to hold them off, the squadron began to leave Landing Ground 102 at 2200 that night. Six planes flew out just after dark, but through poor visibility or exhaustion one crashed on take-off. The small group that was left behind slept on through the anti-aircraft fire, until the Air Officer Commanding, 'Mary' Coningham, unexpectedly flew in. He'd come to congratulate them for seizing the Western Desert record for the number of sorties flown by one squadron in a single day. After a very short celebration they tried to get back to sleep.

Sleep was not something that Rommel's men were enjoying much of, thanks to a moment's inspiration by someone in the Fleet Air Arm. The Albacore was the all-metal version of the old wood-and-canvas Swordfish. It was a biplane, slow but very manoeuvrable, and able to deliver bombs with unusual accuracy. Unfortunately Albacores were so slow that, when faced with a decent anti-aircraft gun, they became deathtraps. But there were times when a low speed could be an advantage. Beginning on the night of 26 June, Albacores were used to drop flares over enemy encampments as their occupants slept. Squadrons of

Wellington bombers then used the flares as targets. The results were irritating rather than devastating, but all added to the exhaustion of Rommel's army.

On 27 June 112 Squadron regrouped at its latest base, Landing Ground 106 near Sidi Abd el Rahman. Once again Lee dug himself a trench and a tent emplacement. Then they threw themselves back into action near Matruh. Lee's friend Jim Walker, the Canadian leader of A flight, was shot down that morning but survived. On 28 June they attacked enemy vehicles on the escarpment overlooking their previous airfield, and that night they moved again, right back to Landing Ground 91, just south of Alexandria on the desert road to Cairo. This time they were told that they were behind the shelter of a firm defensive position at last, something called the Alamein line.

After his terror over Brest, the squadron leader challenged Don Bruce about the mistake with the compass, but Del Mooney said that he was more than happy with his observer and his navigation.

Spring was turning into an unusually warm summer, and life at RAF Marham settled into a pattern. A raid every three or four days, interspersed with sleeping, drinking, games of football and trips to Hunstanton or Brancaster on the north Norfolk coast. Swimming and sunbathing one day, the next that early-morning walk to the hangar, the briefing, the drive along the perimeter track and the long, cold eastward flight. There was a plague of 'June bugs', brown beetles that were strong flyers. The airmen bunged up their chimneys with newspaper but they still got down. One night high over Germany, Don Bruce found one buzzing around his head as he lay over his bomb-sight.

Death was a close acquaintance now. Bruce had only been on the station for six weeks and he had already seen half a dozen crews disappear from the mess.

There was a very attractive blonde WAAF who was always around in the mess when the bombers were coming back; her boyfriend had been killed recently and she just hung around. It was very sad.

Actually, the boys could be quite cruel about this. If a girl had more than one boyfriend killed they called her a 'chop girl' behind her back and avoided her.

Thirty missions was the target, at which point crews were taken off operations and sent to train others. But the consensus was that surviving half that number was good going. One night an operation was cancelled by last-minute bad weather. The men tore off their flight kits and headed straight to the mess, where they celebrated this unexpected deliverance, drinking themselves stupid, singing and playing raucous games until three in the morning.

The local pubs were good too. The Ostrich at Castle Acre, or the Crown at Downham Market. On the way they might wave at a landgirl driving a gyrotiller, clearing heathland or marsh for cultivation. The girls, all conscripts into the war effort, would sometimes turn up at the pubs too. Even the local farmers had been known to stand Mooney's crew a round or two of Bullards or their favourite beer, Elgood's. The countrymen talked about changes on the land, about fen reclamation and the new dykes and concrete roads. How to grow new crops like sugar beet and use the monstrous new machines that were coming in from Canada and Australia. The airmen discussed searchlights and bomb-sights and how to jump if you had to.

One baking-hot, still afternoon they hijacked a lorry and drove it to the lake in the grounds of a nearby country house. Some WAAFs in their swimsuits came along. They picnicked and lazed around in the sun watching the dragonflies hovering over the water. Then they threw themselves in. The boys had brought an escape dinghy from one of the bombers and they paddled out into the middle of the lake. Some fool threw out the marker dye and turned the water bright yellow.

From out of the shrubbery appeared an army major, armed to the teeth, berserk with rage because this was his troops' drinking water. The adjutant, smooth as a roll of silk, said, 'Don't worry, old boy, it's quite safe to drink,' without a clue whether it really was or not.

The squadron leader came over to talk to them all one afternoon as they were lounging on the grass outside the dispersal hut. He said there was a special new squadron to mark targets in advance of the main force. They would wear a gold albatross emblem on one side of their tunic and do sixty operations instead of the usual thirty. He asked for volunteers and all the men were issued with a piece of paper with their names written on it. Next to his, Don Bruce wrote 'No'.

On 26 June he took part in his biggest raid yet, his first thousand-bomber job, aimed at Bremen this time. The weather may have been blissful in Norfolk but over the North Sea they flew into a summer storm and struggled to keep in formation. But they made it to the target on time, in the middle of what appeared to be an endless line of two- and four-engine bombers. Underneath were the most intense fires Bruce had seen. They hit the vast Focke-Wulf aircraft factory hard that night, and left much of the city centre in ruins. But Bomber Command lost 44 planes and a further 65 flew back damaged. Of the 6,000 airmen over the city, 291 failed to return. The RAF's casualties were mounting as the Germans got better at dealing with these mass attacks. Mooney's Wellington saw little flak and no night fighters, but the pressures of the night were beginning to tell on them all.

The exhilaration of returning safely from a raid obscures the mind. You have no thought of the future, just the bodily demand for a bed and the deep sleep of exhaustion. I no longer expected to reach the unattainable thirty completed raids. On a base like Marham after fifteen operational flights you were an old hand. Few of us ever lasted beyond that number, and many fell before they'd done five. As an alternative to death I hoped to survive as a prisoner of war. There seemed like no other choice.

Other weary young men were dropping bombs on Malta. Thirty-three civilians died in an old people's home, twenty-eight in a church crypt, sixteen in an air-raid shelter. Around Valletta there was hardly a house left standing, and every one of the old narrow streets was clogged with wreckage. St John's Cathedral, the great hospital of the Knights of Malta, the ancient university, fine baroque churches: all were hit. At Mtarfa hospital Mimi Cortis became even busier when the naval hospital had to transfer most of its patients.

The hardest thing was breaking the news to someone coming round from anaesthetic that they were now blind or had lost a limb. I hated doing that. What do you say? There just aren't the words.

An Australian pilot who had been a great favourite at our Monday night dances went missing. We asked for news every day and after about a week heard that he had been found dead near Dingli cliffs. He still had his life jacket on. He must have floated around for days, but no one came for him.

A church in Sliema was hit during a mass, killing a family and two priests. Two policemen leading people to the shelters were also killed. One was a relative of Mimi's who left six children including a baby of six months. The other was a friend who left a wife and three daughters under seven.

Once in Sliema creek we saw bombs splashing in the sea only a few yards away from us. In the distance we could see clouds of smoke and dust and the blaze of a fire. All the Karrozini, the beautiful horses and carriages waiting at Fort Manoel bridge, were blown to pieces: horses, carriages and men.

Nearly all my brothers' friends were in uniform. Every day their numbers diminished as you heard that someone else had gone. Some people used to pray for it to end, but I never once heard anyone say we should surrender. It was just a case of gritting our teeth and dealing with the next day and praying to Our Lady, Star of the Sea, to save us from invasion.

Transport was now very difficult. Buses ran only two or three times a day because petrol was so short.

I would get a lift with someone or walk, or borrow a bike from the nursing sister. My sisters were always overjoyed to see me, especially as I always brought 'eats'. The hospital was in the country and we made friends with the farmers, they let us go into the fields and pick vegetables and fruit. If I was on leave for more than a day there was a problem because of the extra food needed. The Victory Kitchens [government canteens that now fed most of the civilian population] only provided enough for the number of people in the household. The food wasn't very good anyway: 'minestra', supposedly a vegetable stew, but mostly water! It was tough for my sisters, tougher still for families with children.

They tried to continue nursing as normal during the raids. Sometimes they just lay on the floor of the wards when they heard the bombs but, if there was enough warning, they would wheel beds and chairs down ramps to the shelters.

I felt sorry for a bashful flight lieutenant who had dysentery and was in great pain. But there was no privacy for him in the shelter, not even a screen in the corner.

Mimi was on night duty in the isolation ward as the bombers aimed for ta Qali's Spitfire pens once again.

We were very busy. A lot of infectious diseases spread because of hunger and overcrowding: diphtheria and scabies in particular. And – on the seriously ill list – there was an eighteen-month-old baby girl with nasty bronchial pneumonia. She was in a separate room under an oxygen tent. I had a resuscitation tray laid near by on a locker to use in an emergency.

It was impossible to use the shelter because there wasn't enough room. And the raids were coming so close together that we didn't have time to move anyone. Suddenly very close there was an explosion, with red flames near the building like a fire. I heard glass smashing and immediately came out of the office to see if the baby was all right. Before I got to her room I heard the whizzing of another bomb. I tucked myself down into a corner and suddenly felt a hard blow on my arm. When the spluttering was finished I went into the baby's room and found she was all right. Then I looked down and saw a hole in my overall where I had felt the impact; some shrapnel had gone right into my arm.

An auxiliary male nurse ran from the isolation unit to the general hospital to get help. Mimi was put on a stretcher and carried to the Family Hospital half a mile away.

I tried to insist that I was all right and could walk but they wouldn't hear of it. Lying there in the open I could see the lovely moonlit sky. And the raid just stopped. I was taken straight into the operating theatre.

I had lots of visitors. A girl who'd taken over from me remarked that my shrapnel was not too big: 'The ones I saw lying around were as big as your head!' It was true. The corridor where I'd been hit was peppered with it. I *had* been very lucky.

Signs were put up all over Malta: 'Blitzed, but unbeaten'. Families spent all day in the deep underground shelters cut into the sandstone, living by candlelight. And still, everyone waited for the invasion.

A German and an Italian parachute division were waiting for

the same thing. But in the days following the fall of Tobruk, Rommel and his immediate superior, Field Marshal Albert Kesselring, had a fierce argument about it. Kesselring said that Rommel should follow the agreed plan and wait while he conquered the island, thus securing a smooth flow of supplies to Africa. But Rommel went direct to Hitler and persuaded him that, with his newly captured equipment and with his troops' morale so high, the parachutists and planes would be better deployed in an immediate push for the Nile.

7 Armoured Division was pulled out of the defence of Matruh and ordered to move by the desert route back towards Alamein. Peter Vaux and the other headquarters staff once again packed up their lorries and ACVs and headed east. As they rumbled along slowly, at first following a line of telegraph poles and then swerving to avoid the bigger rocks, they listened to incoming news on their radio sets. The enemy had already cut the main road east of Matruh and with a strong force was attacking the division's rearguard.

'Keep your head down' – that was Dougie Waller's motto. The trouble was that some sodding general kept putting Waller's head right back in front of the enemy. Here they were again, manning a roadblock with a single company, while the rest of the bloody division got clear. Stuck outside a place apparently already infested with Eyeties, called, of all gloriously appropriate names, Fuka.

The name fascinated Sid. He was lying there with his Bren gun, flies buzzing over his head, reciting it in every possible variation. 'Fuka off, you filthy Fuka, I wanna Fuka your sister . . .'

'Shut up, Sid. Give us a moment's peace.'

'I give you Fuka peace, you Fuka.'

There was a noise overhead. 'Hold on, it's a shufti kite,' said Alf Reeves.

Having had its 'shufti', the reconnaissance plane sped off westward. Waller went over to the portee to check on the state of their 'boodle', recently supplemented with supplies picked up from one of the dumps, tins of stuff and some milk and lots of cigarettes. 'Quite a shindy going on about two miles away,' said Reeves, looking through his binoculars. 'Won't be long now. Get that ammo ready.' To kill time Waller brought out the dodgy phrase book he'd found in a burnt-out lorry. The most-thumbed pages contained all the essentials for a great night in Cairo. 'I have an appointment with a beautiful girl – *ana andi mee-ad way-ya bent gameelah*. His girl flirts with me – *el bent di betghazelni*. This woman is my harlot – *el set di khaleelty*.'

They took turns to practise the Arabic and laughed. Yes, they could do with a spot of leave right about now. Or a few hours with Rita Hayworth.

Italians coming, keep your head down. Keep everything you value as low to the ground as possible. That's what Waller wanted to do, but instead he sat at the 6-pounder on the back of the portee with his eye glued to the sight, putting on the range to stick a shell through the radiator of the armoured car that was bearing down on them. 'Five hundred, four hundred, three hundred. Ready, Bill.' He pulled his head away. 'Firing.' 'Got it! Nice shot!' Smoke poured from the armoured car and men leapt from its turret. 'See that, Sid, you great Fuka? See that shooting?' Firing off a few rounds himself, Sid added his own compliments. Waller leaned forward over the eyepiece as they swung the barrel round to find a new target. 'Right, who's next for a right lacing? Three hundred and fifty, three hundred . . . oh, you bastard!'

He fell backward, clutching his eye. It was streaming with blood. 'I told you to let me know when you fired the thing.'

'I didn't fire it. You've been hit, you stupid bugger.'

'What was it, then?'

'I don't know but it was close.'

The officers evidently agreed. They were being waved away. Moggeridge started the engine. In the back Alf Reeves and Bill Ash tended to Waller's head wound. 'Your eye's all right, but you've got a nasty big gash over the top of it. There's nothing I can do until we catch up with the medics. I'll stick a couple of safety pins through it for now, and a bandage on top. That's all we've got.' Ash's attempts at doctoring hurt a lot more than the injury, but the safety pins did the trick, holding the loose flap of flesh in place.

As they tore away Sid was shouting to the desert: '*Bent gameelah! Bent gameelah!* Me Fuka *bent gameelah!*'

Shortly after Dougie Waller's anti-tank company fell back, Neville Gillman's Sharpshooters reached the same escarpment over-looking the same road. All afternoon they waited in their new Stuart tanks to ambush the enemy, also making jokes about the place name. In the evening, having seen no sign of anyone, they moved south to leaguer down for the night.

They woke suddenly in the middle of the night to the sound of shooting. Their own refuelling party was being shot up five miles away from their camp. One of the tanks drove into a well in the chaos and had to be abandoned. On 30 June there was more of the same, but with a happier ending. The Italians who had been causing all the trouble during the night had leaguered just a few hundred yards away and were clearly not planning on an early start. The Sharpshooters took fifteen lorries and 150 pris-oners without a struggle. Then another Italian column arrived with an escort of M13 tanks, ten of which were soon burning after a well-executed ambush by the British tank men.

With so many enemy units blundering around, it struck Cranley that they had been overtaken. The problem was that, having lost their fuel lorries the night before, they might not make the remaining forty miles to Alamein. Fuel gauges were checked and maps consulted. They soon passed their burnt-out petrol tankers and everything went fine until Gillman's troop spotted a large concentration of German vehicles and guns directly in their path. A sandstorm was blowing up and this helped them make a wide detour round, and they eventually crossed the Alamein track at dusk, down to the last pint of petrol.

When he arrived at the Alamein line, it was clear to Peter Vaux that the new army commander already had some defences organised, and that control from above was firmer and clearer than it had been. But it was equally clear that there was not much with which to stop the Germans. The defences looked nothing like as strong as those at Gazala, and it would take something to motivate the retreating soldiers to turn about and fight. Contingency instructions had already been issued for the division's retreat in case of yet more disaster, along the track that led direct across the desert towards Cairo.

Vaux was puzzled by the enemy's amazing confidence. He'd not paused at Matruh for even half a day. It was as if he knew that the British were planning to pull back and fight it out elsewhere. Or was he just gambling? It was disturbing, and it was clear that at army level they were as worried as he was and a big security flap was on. Vaux had just received a firm instruction to circulate a 'careless talk costs lives' message throughout the division.

> It is again emphasised that THE ENEMY LISTENS TO EVERY WORD WE SPEAK ON THE WIRELESS. We know that he can understand when we use Hindustani and military Hindustani at that. All ranks should be warned of the great danger of employing INDIAN dialects under the impression that they are speaking in code.

Eighth Army seemed to be putting it down to radio intercepts. Vaux knew that the German listening stations were good and it might very well be that one of them had overheard something important. Evidently Auchinleck suspected all these Indian-trained officers jabbering away in Hindustani. What it was to have an empire!

About the time that the remnants of Eighth Army fell back to the Alamein line, Harold Harper discharged himself from hospital and rejoined what was left of the South Notts Hussars. After his escape he had been sent back to Tobruk in an ambulance. He was taken to the docks and put on to a flat-bottomed boat that weaved its way between the many wrecks in the harbour to the waiting hospital ship, and he was hoisted on board. Then he was taken by sea to a hospital and then to a convalescent depot next to it.

Someone told me that one of our officers was in the officers' part of the hospital and took me to see him. It was Ivor Birkin. He said, 'I never expected to see you again. How did you get out?' And I told him my story.

One day towards the end of June, Harper spotted the red, blue and yellow flash of a South Notts lorry. He walked over and introduced himself to the driver, who said, 'You know the regiment's gone. They were all killed or captured in the Cauldron.' Harper was stunned.

I discharged myself and went with this lorry back to rejoin the remnant at Gaza. I was glad to see anybody I knew. There were one or two there who were friends. But for ages we were asking after people.

My father and sister got news after Knightsbridge that I was missing presumed dead. Then they got a message saying I was wounded in the left lung instead of leg. My girlfriend gave up on me about then.

The remnant of the South Notts Hussars at Almaza camp outside Cairo was re-formed as a battery of medium artillery. They were armed with new 5.5-inch guns and put into the 7 Medium Regiment. The 5.5-inch was the biggest gun that the Eighth Army had ever had. Harper found himself in charge of one.

> I have to say I was ready to put my feet up when I finally got back to the battery, but they said, this is your gun, seven and a half tons of it. I didn't sleep much that night. I was supposed to have a crew of nine but I never had above seven. My gunlayer had had a bit of a nervous breakdown and they asked me to look after him.

There was very little time to practise before the new guns were sent forward into action. Every available weapon was needed to stem the tide. Very soon the gunners were put on a train and sent to join the rest of their new regiment, just behind el Alamein.

On 30 June, Auchinleck issued a call to arms.

> The enemy is stretched to the limit and thinks we are a broken army . . . He hopes to take Egypt by bluff. Show him where he gets off.

But the Royal Navy was taking no chances. It evacuated Alexandria on 29 and 30 June.

Eighth Army's new tactical HQ was twenty sand-covered vehicles tucked behind Ruweisat ridge at the centre of the Alamein position. Chink was usually at Auchinleck's side in the operational caravan, its walls covered by talc-faced maps for the grease pencils. He wrote long letters to Eve several times a day. He told her that 'we are still sorting ourselves out prior to giving battle again under more advantageous conditions which will cramp his armour and give our better artillery a chance'.

But the time for sorting out was over.

Chapter 11

30 June–11 July

'We want "Might" in our propaganda here, Mr Beaton,' the Minister had said. 'Especially for the Egyptians. Don't photograph one aeroplane, photograph sixty at a time. Never four tanks, but a hundred. Go for "Might".'

Cecil Beaton, the famous society photographer, was working in the public relations office of the British embassy. He was surrounded by photographs of tanks and planes, some of which had been taken during a visit to Peter Vaux's command vehicle. But the confident tone of the draft articles that lay on his desk had been rendered ludicrous by the events of the past week.

More effective propaganda fluttered down from the sky. The Germans were dropping facsimiles of pound notes, with a message in Arabic explaining that it was no longer worth even a beggar's time to pick one of these useless items up. Beaton was staying at Shepheard's Hotel, its bar home to the 'Short Range Shepheard's Group' of HQ officers, journalists and assorted hangers-on. The front line was so close now that the reporters drove up for the day. On their return they told Beaton and anyone else who would listen that Eighth Army was 'badly shaken, tired and discouraged'.

Until recently thousands of troops had thronged the markets, spilled in and out of the cinemas and bars and fought to get on to the buses and trams, pestered all the time by an army of hawkers offering to sell them fly whisks and teapots, coloured spectacles and scarabs, sand-proof watches and dirty postcards. But, with all leave cancelled, the streets were half empty now, and the only crowds were to be found in queues outside banks and railway stations. Rumours abounded. On 30 June the BBC war correspondent noted in his diary, 'Navy gone . . . Rumour in Cairo today that Alex is lost already.' Telephone calls came in to the hotel manager from Alexandria claiming that it was surrounded and that German parachutists were landing at the coast.

At Shepheard's a BBC announcer told Beaton that Auchinleck was bound to lose again and that British shells always bounced off German tanks while German shells had special metal in them which meant they could destroy anything. Another BBC man disagreed and said that there were some new American planes around that could knock out German tanks with a secret gun. An Egyptian woman arrived at the bar to say that Alexandria hadn't fallen after all but that it was like a dead city, with empty roads, silent but for the ringing of unanswered telephones.

The BBC presented the Alamein line as a strongly fortified barrier, a Maginot Line for the desert, but the soldiers who were to defend it found it indistinguishable from the miles of sand to east and west. To the north was the sea; to the south steep cliffs that dropped down to the Qattara depression where the surface was too soft for armoured movement. In the thirty-five miles of open desert in between the Eighth Army occupied four defensive positions, ringed by minefields. They were like the old boxes, but with fewer men inside and more transport. The principal position, at Alamein itself, was held by South Africans and covered the coast road and the railway. The second, near Deir el Shein, held by Indians, covered the approach to the commanding Ruweisat ridge. New Zealanders defended rocky broken ground at Qaret el Abd and the final position in the far south was held again by Indians. The open spaces were patrolled by what was left of the armoured and motorised troops.

The dawn reconnaissance flight on Wednesday, 1 July reported a thousand enemy vehicles fifteen miles away and moving eastward towards Alamein. Another three hundred were refuelling about twenty miles away, opposite Deir el Shein. Peter Vaux got the news at 7 Armoured Division's new HQ, camped at the foot of Mount Himeimat, a conspicuous twin-peaked crag, almost due south of Alamein. This provided a viewpoint from which to survey the division's positions. Once again they were responsible for covering attacks in the southern sector. But for the present the enemy appeared to be well to the north.

The RAF struck the first blow, hitting the panzer divisions just as they approached their assembly area at dawn. Ken Lee was at his aerodrome on the desert road near Alexandria. The pilots were standing around in the grey misty light drinking hot mugs of sweet tea as they were briefed. Lee was to lead seven planes to escort Boston bombers in an attack on the smaller of the two enemy concentrations. Despite poor flying conditions, the approach went like clockwork. He had hoped that the war might have moved too fast for the Luftwaffe, and it did indeed look as if the Messerschmitt 109s had not yet caught up with their comrades on the ground. A good omen.

As the bombers turned for home, Lee caught the eye of each of his two section leaders and pointed down. They waved their acknowledgement and the seven Kittyhawks swooped down to add their own bombs to those dropped by the Bostons. It would have been quite a party if it had not been for the quality of enemy anti-aircraft gunnery. Even the Italians were not bad gunners. They flew into intense and accurate fire:

Believe you me, this was far more dangerous than anything I had done in the Battle of Britain.

Then they turned for home, quickly catching their slower charges.

With Rommel at the end of long supply lines and the British close to their bases, the position in the air had changed dramatically. Taking into account serviceability, which was much better on the British side, in the first week in July the Germans could put up at most 55 fighters and 40 dive-bombers. The British could fly 235 fighters and dive-bombers, 62 light bombers and 67 medium bombers.

Yet, as the men of the Panzerarmee made their first probing attacks towards el Alamein and Deir el Shein, they were confident of a swift victory. They planned to drive to the sea east of Alamein, trapping the British divisions guarding the northern sector. Auchinleck and Chink had expected this, and had positioned their artillery and armour to the south and east of Alamein. To get up to the coast the German armoured columns would have either to take these positions or drive between them in open ground, exposing themselves to the British guns.

Auchinleck was using the bulk of his artillery in a single mass under central direction from Army HQ. Harold Harper's new medium regiment was part of this force. The new 6-pounder guns were also being used effectively. Some, like Dougie Waller's, were up with the front-line infantry, trying to sap the strength from the German advance. The doctor had seen to Waller's eye when they arrived at the Alamein line the night before and he had a big bandage round his head now. Then they'd been sent up late in the evening to dig in between two South African positions. They'd exchanged a few pleasantries as they'd passed. Everyone said it was the South Africans who'd failed to fight at Tobruk, and so having them on each shoulder wasn't too reassuring. But Bill Ash's taunts of 'Hope you lot are going to stay and fight this time!' as they struggled through the soft sand past a battery of South African 25-pounders may not have been the best way to guarantee supporting fire if they got into trouble. They dug in, thinking they might soon be moving back again.

'Don't take that portee too far away, Moggeridge, or your balls will have more than one scar on 'em.'

As it turned out, they did retreat twice during the day, but not before sending an impressive burst of fire into the Germans and Italians and really slowing their progress. British bombers came over, too. Waller could hardly remember seeing the RAF in action before, but they were here today. Whenever a half-track emerged through the smoke they took a shot at it. This gun was bloody good. Once or twice Stukas came close, but mostly they dived on the gun batteries behind them. At least the soft sand would dull the impact, Waller thought. He was warming to the South Africans, who were fighting like tigers. 'Got any more cigarettes, Bill?'

90 Light Division attacked between the Alamein position and the Ruweisat ridge and was caught by the anti-tank guns, Dougie Waller's among them, the massed artillery, and yet more RAF raids. Its advance was soon halted; something had gone wrong. Rommel came forward to motivate his men in person and urge them forward. It had worked before. But once again they ran into unexpectedly well-organised resistance.

British shells came screaming in from three directions . . . tracer streaked through our force. Under this tremendous weight of fire, our attack came to a standstill . . . For two hours Bayerlein and I had to lie out in the open. Suddenly, to add to our troubles, a powerful British bomber force came flying up towards us.

That day saw the first use of the word 'panic' in the German official war diary, as men recoiled in shock at the weight of fire descending upon them.

In the evening, 21 and 15 Panzer divisions threw their whole weight against the Indian position at Deir el Shein. The British armoured reserve was ordered to intervene. The Sharpshooters, including Neville Gillman, approached the area with less than twenty tanks and lined up against fifty-five. More British tanks arrived just in time to save them from one flank attack, but as the Indians pulled back the Germans moved against the other flank. Then Colonel Frank Arkwright's tank was knocked out and he was killed while standing on the back of another, trying to get new orders. They withdrew to their leaguer. That night in the moonlight Viscount Cranley and the other squadron leaders carried the colonel's body to its desert grave. Cranley described the scene:

> On a brilliant starlit night we were able with great sadness to give Colonel Frank the only real burial service I saw on active service, culminating in his little soldier servant, Kirkby, who in civil life was a hunt servant, blowing the most perfect 'Gone Away' on a hunting horn that any hunt servant could have blown in the peaceful countryside at home. I am sure that, could he have known it, Frank, who was a great horseman, would have appreciated this.

The Deir el Shein position was lost, and two thousand men of the Indian Division were prisoners, but the armoured reserve had held out long enough to prevent a major breakthrough. After the first day's fighting Auchinleck felt satisfied that his new methods were making a difference. It had been touch and go for a while but the line had held and the policy of concentrating artillery was undoubtedly working. All night British flares and British bombs robbed the Germans of their sleep.

Rommel had sent a series of confident messages to Berlin on 30 June and these were duly written up into an official communiqué that was released the next day. As their field marshal was cowering in a shell hole under RAF bombs, German radio was claiming that the British were retreating in disarray from el Alamein and preparing to abandon the delta. Although London issued an immediate denial, this caused panic in Cairo. Charred paper drifted down from the ministry chimneys as officials burned anything valuable or secret. 'Ash Wednesday', everyone immediately called it. Anyone with the money for a ticket or a bribe was at the station, or pouring out of the city with their possessions piled on the roofs of cars, risking bandit attacks on roads suddenly devoid of policemen. A curfew was ordered in Alexandria but the abandoned naval stores were soon looted. Clerks with revolvers replaced local police, many of whom had already fled or were no longer willing to be seen wearing the uniform of the British. Hundreds of British and Commonwealth troops with no desire to go back 'up the blue' to take part in Auchinleck's last stand were hiding from the military police. Sirens and gunshots punctuated the evening hum of Cairo.

The German Arab radio service, slick and very popular in the delta, dubbed Mussolini 'the saviour and protector of Islam', and announced that he and Rommel were coming in person to liberate Egypt from the British. Hitler was cleverly presented as an ordinary man from a once humiliated nation, who understood how the Egyptians felt. He had crushed French and British imperialists in Europe and would now deliver Egypt. He would also save the wider Arab world from an international 'plot' to impose a Jewish homeland in Palestine. Such messages found ready listeners. The Muslim Brotherhood urged its members to prepare Molotov cocktails and be ready to take to the streets as soon as the first panzers neared Alexandria. A German spy signalled to Berlin:

> The Mohammedan leaders are in continued conference and wish to prepare a reception for Rommel which will surpass that of Napoleon.

In Alexandria shopkeepers had their Hitler and Mussolini pictures ready in their frames, and some already had red-and-black Axis bunting hanging outside their shops on the evening of 1 July. The clerks with revolvers noted their names for punishment later. Anwar Sadat helped draft a treaty intended to seal a deal between Germany and a group of nationalist officers in the Egyptian army.

In return for independence Sadat's men offered full support in a drive to rid the Middle East of the British for ever. The document, plus some helpful intelligence on British positions, was put in an aircraft and flown west by another anti-British nationalist. Sadly for them, Rommel's men shot it down.

Journalists trying to find out what was happening for themselves couldn't reach Alamein, and in the vacuum of real information the rumours spiralled. Despairing of getting a seat on a plane out of Egypt, Cecil Beaton drifted away from his work and mournfully toured the streets, walking through alleyways surrounded by the habitual swirl of gold, richly coloured carpets and spice. He was thinking about the death of empire. This was one of the many beautiful, exotic places that Britain had ruled for so long. But it felt as if all that was coming to an end. Caught up in 'the waste and despair of an evacuation', Beaton concluded that the British had lost confidence in their ability to govern and to fight. At a more personal level he feared that his own diaries – as likely to contain remarks about naked soldiers swimming in the sea as about Cairo's beautiful minarets – would be captured and read out over the radio by Lord Haw-Haw.

Rommel resumed his attack on 2 July. Six hundred vehicles from 90 Light Division advanced before dawn, but they were soon halted again by concentrated artillery fire. Rommel planned to send 21 and 15 Panzer to the aid of 90 Light. They started late, thanks to the disorganisation caused by shelling and bombing, and ran straight into the British armour. What happened next troubled the Germans a great deal. Instead of charging as normal, the British tanks, with Cranley and Gillman among them, merely halted and exchanged fire at long range. The Sharpshooters had some mobile 6-pounders attached to them now, which meant they could shoot it out on something like even terms. Their war diary noted that 'the 6-pounder guns appeared to have a very steadying effect on the enemy'. The Germans also noted with concern that batteries of field artillery stationed well behind were contributing coordinated supporting fire.

The House of Commons confidence debate took place on 1 and 2 July. As Eighth Army halted Rommel's advance, speaker after speaker condemned the direction of the war and the poor performance of the army. Churchill had the leadership of both major parties behind him, and was going to win whatever happened. But if he won by an unconvincing margin then convention dictated that he must offer his resignation to the King, as Chamberlain had done in 1940.

Some Conservatives argued that Churchill was interfering in the military effort, others that he had not interfered enough. Left-wing firebrand Aneurin Bevan claimed that

> the Prime Minister wins debate after debate and loses battle after battle. The country is beginning to say that he fights debates like a war, and the war like a debate.

Bevan said that the army was 'ridden by class prejudice' and badly led. Former Secretary of State for War Leslie Hore-Belisha asked the House how it could possibly place any faith 'in judgements that have so repeatedly turned out to be misguided'. He cited the disasters at Greece, Singapore and Tobruk.

It came down to the word they were all using in Cairo: professionalism. Among people who called themselves progressive, the belief that there was something inherently old-fashioned, mediocre and amateurish about the military had become well entrenched. And Churchill had to do something about it.

Not all of this was fair. In 1942 the RAF was probably the best-managed fighting force in the world, full of bright grammar school and technical college boys and bursting with new ideas. But the army made an easier target for class warriors like Bevan. They echoed the complaints of ordinary soldiers about the senior ranks, complaints that had escaped the censors and were being freely discussed inside homes and on factory floors.

After two days of listening, the Prime Minister got up to speak. He laid out the recent military disasters in frank detail. He gave an account of the paper strength of the desert army and offered no excuses for their failures. But then he turned to the political impact of the debate itself, speaking of the pleasure that his fall would give to Britain's enemies, and the despair it would generate in all who looked to London for their hope of freedom. If he won the vote, he said, 'the knell of disappointment will ring in the ears of the tyrants we are striving to overthrow'.

He won by 475 votes to 25, but the victory was not as clear cut as it appeared. Over a hundred MPs did not vote, putting the Prime Minister on notice that he could no longer rely on their support. If things continued to get worse, that block of votes would be enough to remove him from power. Harold Nicolson believed that the House was 'anxious and dissatisfied' and predicted more trouble to come.

From Washington came a supportive telegram from Harry Hopkins:

> These have been some of the bad days. No doubt there will be others. Those who run for cover with every reverse, the timid and the faint of heart, will have no part in winning the war . . . I know you are in good heart for your military defeats and ours, and our certain victories to come, will be shared together.

Churchill replied with 'Thank you so much my friend. I knew you and the President would be glad of this domestic victory. I hope one day I shall have something more solid to report.' Then he cabled Middle East HQ, stressing the value of the Nile delta canals as obstacles to Rommel's tanks and urging that 'Egypt should be defended just as drastically as if it were Kent or Sussex'.

Rommel staked everything on one last attack near the Ruweisat ridge. The two panzer divisions sent out their twenty-six remaining working tanks and their rather stronger force of supporting artillery. Against them were Auchinleck's last thirty-eight Grants, plus sixty Stuart light tanks and twelve old Valentines, with their accompanying 6-pounders. The German attack stalled, as did a simultaneous one launched by 90 Light Division. The Ariete Division was also moving forward, but Auchinleck and Chink had something special in store for it. As the Italians' advance stalled under shellfire, it was hit by a bayonet charge from an entire battalion of New Zealanders. The enemy reeled back and was promptly taken in the flank by part of the British tank force. 'The total bag', as Peter Vaux wrote the next day, 'was 360 prisoners (all from Ariete), seven 105mm guns, five 150mm guns, 11 German 88mm guns (manned by Italians), sixteen 75mm guns and five (British) 25-pounders of which four were intact.'

In the afternoon and evening the Germans made two further attempts to break through and both failed. Auchinleck now had a clear advantage, and there were very few German tanks left in fighting condition. There seemed to be a chance to break Rommel once and for all. The chosen, if somewhat unlikely, instruments of his destruction were the Stuart light tanks, one of which was commanded by Neville Gillman. They were ordered to charge under cover of fire from the bigger guns. The Sharpshooters were not enthusiastic. They had come to like this new defensive warfare. Attack, as they had discovered time and time again, was a great deal more dangerous. There might be few German tanks un-brewed, but their anti-tank screen with its 50mm and 88mm guns was still intact. The British crews had seen too much death and knew that their little Stuarts provided practically no protection.

The Sharpshooters' new commander, Major Scott, put the idea to Viscount Cranley over the radio: 'I think we should do a bloody great charge, don't you?' Gillman heard Cranley reply, 'No I fucking well don't. I think it's a bloody stupid idea.' A frank and voluble exchange of views followed, during which Scott explained that he had already argued the case with the brigadier and had been ordered forward. Cranley said, 'Well, if we've got to do it, let's fucking well get on with it.'

Gillman's radio operator looked horrified. Gillman had watched him becoming increasingly jittery over the last few days. But he was not the only one:

> I was bloody scared. The Stuart didn't have a lot of armour and it ran on high-octane fuel. So we went down into this great wadi in a charge and up the other side and started shooting it out with the Germans. The operator was very twitchy. Suddenly he yelled, 'We've got to withdraw!' I said, 'Right, driver, reverse.' The driver shot backwards at top speed. There was this shout over the radio. It was Cranley. 'When I say "withdraw" I don't mean "get the fuck out of it". Behave like a bloody soldier!'

The Germans pulled back under the cover of smoke, and after an inconclusive encounter the rest of the Stuarts did likewise. But all in all, the last three days had been a major success, the first for months. Rommel was forced on to the defensive and began to send a series of demands to Berlin for immediate reinforcement. The Alexandria shopkeepers took down their bunting.

On 4 July, Chink Dorman-Smith enjoyed one of the best mornings of his life. Although he had not had the time to shave since leaving Cairo eleven days before, and felt more tired than he'd ever been, having the entire army at his disposal at last had been exhilarating. From the intelligence decrypts he knew that Rommel had given the order to dig in and defend. They had done it. For Eve he wrote a description of the desert dawn:

> Quiet with a low whispering desert wind and the Eastern sky one great streak of gold and crimson . . . The sky deepening from

light blue to sepia at the zenith and two glorious day stars. Like one clear high note of music.

That day Auchinleck received another telegram from Churchill: 'I cannot help liking very much the way things seem to be going. If fortune turns I am sure you will press your advance as you say RELENTLESSLY.' He tried, but neither the infantry nor the tanks could make the aggressive moves that Auchinleck now demanded. They had neither the confidence nor the energy. They had already been asked to pounce too often on an enemy who proved not to be on his last legs but at his fiercest and most agile when cornered. That evening General Lumsden of 1 Armoured Division argued with his corps commander Norrie about why the attack had not gone farther. Lumsden explained in terms that were 'almost insultingly insubordinate' that his men were exhausted. The next morning Gillman's Sharpshooters were taken out of the line for a rest and were sent back to Alexandria to get new tanks.

Ken Lee, too, fell out of the line. He had not been feeling well for days. By 5 July he was lying wrapped in a blanket on the floor of his tent, shivering and not knowing where he was. He was convinced that the squadron was retreating again and that they were about to abandon him. The others could not convince him otherwise so they took him to the nearest field hospital. The doctor diagnosed sandfly fever and sent him to Cairo.

In this first week of July, Eighth Army was showing signs of change. Unable to break through anywhere and manoeuvre, Rommel's own armour became concentrated and so made a perfect target for the RAF bombers that swarmed overhead. High-level bombing like this rarely scored direct hits on tanks, but it damaged unarmoured vehicles and demoralised the accompanying infantrymen, who had to leap for slit trenches with every raid. It imposed great difficulties on commanders attempting to coordinate forward movement, meet up with supply vehicles or organise the refuelling of tanks.

Auchinleck was disappointed that he had not crushed the Germans while they were off balance, but with his next moves he aimed further kicks at his enemy's legs. Ariete had been the best of the Italian divisions and yet on 3 July they had collapsed. If their morale was faltering it should be a good moment to test that of the other Italians. This would have several benefits, not least being the beneficial effect on the morale of their own men. He and Chink planned a night attack on the Pavia Division. On 7 July armoured cars from 7 Armoured Division broke right through it and raided the airfield and petrol dumps at Fuka.

New strength was arriving all the time – 9 Australian Division, fresh from Syria and Palestine and keen for action, came into the line on 9 July. Chink and Auchinleck withdrew some New Zealand troops from the southern sector in the hope that it would encourage Rommel to move his best forces down south and once again expose the Italians. It did exactly that. Then, on 10 July, the Australians were ordered forward in the north, all but wiping out two battalions of Italian troops and causing Rommel to rush back up north at top speed to save his headquarters, which had been exposed. Intelligence chief von Mellenthin succeeded in forming a defensive line around the HQ, but not before he had lost his wireless intercept experts, whose grasp of military Hindustani had given Rommel an extra edge in the intelligence war. The Desert Fox had surrendered the initiative.

But Churchill was far from happy. During the cabinet meeting of 10 July he turned to Brooke, and said:

Pray explain, Chief of the Imperial General Staff, how it is that in the Middle East 750,000 men always turn up for their pay and rations, but when it comes to fighting only 100,000 turn up? Explain to us now exactly how the remaining 650,000 are occupied.

Brooke tried to keep his temper:

> He could never understand, or at any rate refused to do so, that
> the Middle East was a vast base for operations in various theatres
> besides the Western Desert.

Churchill had agreed to see a young officer just back from Cairo
called Julian Amery, the son of the Secretary of State for India.
In front of a quietly seething Brooke, who strongly disapproved
of politicians basing policy on the opinions of junior officers,
Amery repeated what Churchill had heard time and again in the
House of Commons: that there was a low level of confidence in
the High Command among the troops. Then Amery said something that all but made Brooke explode, urging Churchill to pay
a personal visit to the front. Brooke had been trying to prevent
such a thing for weeks. He cross-examined Amery about the
source of his knowledge of the state of the army. It turned out
that most of it had been gathered in Cairo. When Amery left,
Brooke dismissed him as a 'bar lounger' and a 'most objection-
able young pup', but Churchill took quite a different view. His
men needed him, and he must go to them. He and Brooke would
fly out together soon and settle the whole business of the
command once and for all.

Chapter 12

12–24 July

Harry Hopkins arrived in London with General Marshall and Admiral King to discuss the Second Front again. Keeping Stalin in the war had suddenly become an urgent concern in Washington once more because, on 1 July, the Germans had smashed a hole in the Russian line in the Ukraine and surged forward. By mid-July more than a million Axis troops were on the move, spearheaded by three panzer armies. The threat now was not to Moscow, but to the southern cities of Stalingrad and Rostov, in the direction that the Americans and British feared most. Rostov was the fortress that stood between the Germans and the oil fields of Persia and Iraq. By mid-July the Germans were bearing down on it. The British military attaché in Russia warned that the whole of the Caucasus was expected to fall within a month, bringing Hitler's armies to the lightly defended borders of Persia.

At the first Anglo-American meeting Churchill raised the possibility that American troops might soon be needed to shore up southern Russia. Then talk turned to an invasion of France. Alan Brooke thought that Roosevelt had already been squared, but from Washington the former CIGS John Dill had warned him that the fantasy of an early landing in France was proving hard to kill. Marshall in particular was still all for it. For three days they argued. Could a force of six divisions – all they could real-istically assemble – make enough of an impression to draw some of the pressure off the Russian front and then withdraw in good order? Or would it be isolated and overwhelmed? From the start there was a split within the American camp, with Hopkins more sympathetic to the British. In order to help smooth things over, Brooke was prevented from meeting Hopkins one on one in case Marshall and King felt they were being outmanoeuvred.

He had performed a most notable feat of navigation, of which anyone might be justifiably proud, in bringing the ship straight here after eleven weeks without sighting land. But he felt no elation about it. It was Hornblower's nature to find no pleasure in achieving things he could do; his ambition was always yearning after the impossible, to appear a strong silent capable man, unmoved by emotion.

Lonnie Dales could not help thinking of his great fictional hero as, through his binoculars, he watched the little corvette circling. She was dropping depth charges again. The escorts had been hunting like this for hours now. The coast of Ireland was in sight and still they'd had no success. But the convoy was intact and not far from Belfast, where he had cousins he had never met. His first ocean crossing was almost over.

Dales had always loved the sea. From his earliest childhood he'd spent every vacation at his Uncle Cliff's holiday home on the South Georgia coast. The first time he took a canoe up the creek, Cliff shouted after him, 'Look out for 'gators!' as he pulled away from the jetty at the end of the lawn. After that he paddled and glided through the slow muddy waters of the brackish marshes every summer, half hoping for an alligator that he never saw, plagued by mosquitoes and every other insect that could bite. He remembered the moment when Uncle Cliff had let him take the helm of their little dinghy, and the feeling as the warm breeze filled the sail and blew the scent of the Georgia pines over the river and a mockingbird squawked its raucous taunts. And that other time in Augusta when his other uncle, Reggie Dales, stood behind him as he took the wheel of his steamship and guided her down the wide Savannah river loaded high with timber and cotton.

Cadet-Midshipman Francis 'Lonnie' Dales was still a trainee, and his assignment to the Grace Lines company was his work experience, part of the US Merchant Marine Academy's ship's officer course.

Dales joined the Merchant Marine at a grim time. America was in the war but its coastal trade was on nothing like a war footing. Convinced that the British system of convoys made merchant ships more vulnerable, the authorities advised them to travel alone. Most still showed navigation lights and followed their old peacetime routes. The U-boats quickly grasped the opportunity. Operating in their favourite manner, on the surface and at night, they picked off the merchant ships as they were silhouetted against the lights from the shoreline. Off the neon-lit coast of Florida in the winter holiday season, the result was mayhem. The authorities attempted to disguise the losses and pretended that they were sinking enemy submarines. In reality the U-boats escaped practically undamaged. Huge explosions lit up the sky offshore, windows broke, and bodies washed ashore in the middle of oil slicks. Some 400 ships and 5,000 sailors were lost between late December and the end of June.

So it was with some trepidation that Lonnie Dales and the crew of the *Santa Elisa* left Long Island Sound for Boston, steaming on to Halifax to join a convoy bound for Britain. Dales' anxiety was only increased when he noticed that all the ships were sailing with their lifeboats cranked over the sides, so as to be ready for a quick escape.

The crewmen talked very little about their previous ships, but I know that five of them had been torpedoed prior to coming to the *Santa Elisa*.

The first night was disturbed when the escorts began hunting for a submarine after torpedo tracks had been sighted. But if there was a U-boat, they lost it. The Germans had been enjoying such easy pickings off the southern coastline that they left the well-guarded Atlantic convoys temporarily unmolested. The main enemy proved to be the treacherous Atlantic weather:

> During heavy fog all the ships in the convoy streamed paravane floats, which the lookouts on the bow and the bridge were supposed to watch for to keep us from running into a ship ahead. This did not prove too satisfactory in bad weather, believe me. None of the ships ran at the same speed and so we were constantly increasing or decreasing the revolutions one or two RPMs just to maintain position.
>
> I can remember on one occasion walking out on the starboard side of the bridge on the 12 to 4 a.m. watch and there was a ship alongside of us, and one of her lifeboats was caught up in between two of ours. It was a ticklish situation trying to get untangled without hitting.

This was not something he'd ever read about in Hornblower.

Eighth Army hit the Italians once again on 14 July. Rommel was now dangerously short of fuel and on 17 July had to tell Berlin that he could not hope to progress farther unless large quantities of supplies and dozens of new tanks arrived quickly.

Dougie Waller had spent the last few days on the Ruweisat ridge. There had been fighting around here for weeks now. Nobody had won and nobody had lost, except for the dead. If hell really was full of flies, this must be it; open your mouth for a brew and they'd be all over your lips in a second. There was a dead German tank about a hundred yards away, and whatever was inside it was generating more flies every day. They'd even given Sid a holiday. The doctor had sent him back to Cairo for a rest when the sores and their attendant insects got beyond a joke.

There were too many unburied bodies, but it was difficult to do anything about it because neither side held the whole ridge. Someone had tried to organise a clearing party the other day, but the snipers had opened up on them. You would have thought the bastards would lay off for a bit. It must smell just as bad to them.

The previous day there had been some Italians nosing around. A couple of shells from Waller's 6-pounder had sent them scampering back to their own trenches. But, apart from that, everything was very quiet. Today's highlight was a visit from the army's mobile barber, snipping and chatting away to the lads as if he were in a shop on Tottenham Court Road rather than in the middle of the stinking desert. Bill Ash kept himself busy. Today he was making a bomb by packing some spare cordite into a mess tin, trying to see whether he could blow up a derelict lorry with it. Waller wrote to Laurie again. Having time to write was one of the few benefits of being stuck up on the ridge. Every day Arthur Cox, an old mate who used to drive a London bus, would come up with supplies. Occasionally he would bring letters from home and he always took Dougie's letters away to post. Cox didn't have a girlfriend of his own and, after reading Laurie's letters to Dougie, he'd started writing to her himself. Waller didn't mind. They all planned to get together in London and go to see Spurs play and spend the rest of the day in a pub, if they ever got away from Egypt.

Neville Gillman's Sharpshooters were away for a while, spending ten days camped by the railway at Amiriya, resting and re-forming. They had leave to visit Alexandria during the day and for a week they relaxed while they waited for new tanks.

One day, as Gillman was checking the other two tanks of his troop, the adjutant, Captain Brown, came over. 'Congratulations,

Squeaker,' he said, 'your commission's come through. Come over to the mess and have a drink.' 'Thanks, sir,' said Gillman. 'Don't call me sir now, call me Robert,' Brown replied. Obediently, Neville followed Robert to the large tent that the Sharpshooters had erected as the officers' mess. Outside the entrance stood a pair of parasols borrowed from certain Alexandrian cafés. There was a full bar, with every mixer that could be obtained in the town. Viscount Cranley, who had recommended him for the promotion, was there to greet him with a smile on his face. 'What will you have, Squeaker?' he asked. 'Scotch all right? Dash of ginger? They want us to send you to be trained as an officer, but I told them you knew everything there was to know about it already. Anyway, we need you here. Can't afford to lose anyone who knows what they're doing.' Cranley had a couple of pips ready and Major Scott himself came over to present them along with his drink, which clinked with delicious ice. 'RHP,' the men said – 'Rank Has Privileges', in this case ice for the whisky driven up in an insulated bucket from Alex.

'I'm an officer now,' Second Lieutenant Gillman told his crew when he got back to his tank. They didn't seem to mind. In the tanks they all called each other by their Christian names anyway, and used the word 'sir' only on formal occasions like parade.

On the last day of their rest period the officers made a trip to the bar of the Cecil Hotel. Tall and white and topped with triangular castellations, it overlooked the sea front of Aboukir Bay. Palm trees ringed the square in front of it and smaller potted palms stood outside the hotel where Arabs touted carriage rides. The Cecil might have been a little piece of Venice. It was unbelievable luxury after the desert. A modern lift carried the officers up to the bar, which had recently been decorated in the fashionable Egyptian-classical style. They sipped gin and tonic and watched the waves breaking as the sea breeze played on their faces.

Gillman told Cranley about his radio operator, and how exhaustion had got to him. He was a nice chap but quite genuinely his nerve had gone. People got bomb happy sometimes, and when they did you had to get rid of them. Otherwise it was bad for the rest of the crew, too much of a risk to the team to carry someone who was too frightened to do their job properly. Of course, everyone was afraid. It was just a question of how much you could take. Cranley said that he would send the man away for a rest.

Grants were as usual in short supply and there were arguments about who would get them first. Cranley was heard shouting down the telephone a lot but, despite his entreaties, C squadron drew Crusaders again and moved off. Gillman and the other twenty or so crews drove the tanks on to the back of some tank transporters and headed back west along the coast road. Then they drove across the desert to Brigade Headquarters. Six of the new Crusaders broke down during the ten-mile trip.

In between negotiating with his American visitors, Churchill was demanding more attacks in the desert. Given the situation in Russia and the threat to Persia, it was imperative to defeat Rommel immediately. On 15 July, Auchinleck wrote to him in scarcely concealed exasperation.

> I quite understand the situation and will, as I think you know, do my utmost to defeat the enemy in the WEST or drive them back sufficiently far to lessen the threat to Egypt.

Chink protested that breaking through the German defences was beyond the army at present, but an attack code-named Operation Splendour was scheduled for 22 July. Auchinleck's staff had just four days to plan it.

The infantry, mostly New Zealander and Indian, made some progress but the tanks arrived late in support, leaving the men exposed; 23 Armoured Brigade, which had just arrived in Egypt and had never fought a battle, was thrown into the attack. Thanks to inexperience and poor staff work, it got caught in a minefield and then set off on a death-or-glory charge. The result was far from glorious. Within two hours it lost 93 of its 104 tanks. It was the Cauldron all over again.

When Auchinleck sought to renew the offensive on 24 July, the Australian General Morshead questioned his orders, explaining that his men had done enough attacking and had no faith that they would receive armoured support. He insisted on appealing to his government, as was his right, before agreeing to the plan. His corps commander told Auchinleck that the Australian infantry had lost all confidence in British armour. The attack was delayed. Chink pressed Auchinleck to abandon the offensive altogether, but the Commander-in-Chief was under the most intense pressure from London. Rostov fell on 24 July and Germans were pouring into the Caucasus, closing on Persia by the hour.

On the evening of 26 July Eighth Army attacked again. The infantry made some progress but the tanks were bogged down in another minefield and failed to keep up. By dawn, with all tactical surprise lost, Auchinleck decided to abandon Operation Splendour. It had demonstrated that whatever it had learned about defence, Eighth Army still could not coordinate armour and infantry when moving forward.

Despite Brooke's efforts to tone down and check the correspondence that flowed from Number 10, Auchinleck was assailed by more cables. Churchill had learned that a large consignment of new German tanks was on the way to Africa, and he demanded another attack before they arrived. After the failure of Splendour, Chink and Auchinleck were convinced that the army needed comprehensive retraining before it was capable of winning an offensive battle. Communications on this question flew back and forth until Churchill announced that he would make the trip recommended to him by Julian Amery and come out to the desert in person. 'Blast the PM,' was Auchinleck's comment to Chink.

Chink wrote to Eve at the end of the month, saying in exasperation, 'We do lead a queer life. Tiny battles and the highest policy all muddled up as only Lewis Carroll could imagine it.' Chink feared for his friend and commander's future. To Eve he complained about backbiting and malice. He accused men who had squandered their own opportunities of command of blaming him and Auchinleck for the fiasco of Operation Splendour. He was right, for in true Alice in Wonderland style both he and Auchinleck *were* being blamed for the failure of an attack neither had wanted to make.

It was not immediately clear why Splendour failed so comprehensively. Exhaustion, illness, fear of the enemy, poor staff work, distrust among subordinate commanders of orders from on high, all sapped the ability of Eighth Army when asked to go in for the kill. Auchinleck was now convinced that Gott, the commander of 13 Corps, had lost confidence and energy. Ritchie had gone back to London and had had his case heard sympathetically by Brooke. Norrie had also returned to London and saw Brooke on 21 July. Meanwhile, the divisional commanders – New Zealander, South African and Australian – were truculent and resentful, blaming each other, and especially the British armour, when things went wrong. Lumsden, now the senior armoured commander, was unimpressed equally by the infantry leaders and the High Command, and increasingly insubordinate. Renton just appeared to want to keep his head down. The whole army needed a sense that it could move forward as a unit and actually win.

Advised by his team in London that the British were still resolute, Roosevelt agreed to kill Operation Sledgehammer once and for all on 23 July. There would be no landings in France in 1942 and all attention was switched to Operation Torch, an Anglo-American invasion of north-west Africa scheduled for the autumn.

Marshall, King, Hopkins and Harriman were all invited to a celebratory dinner at Chequers. Behind the smiles and the toasts a serious political game was being played out. Churchill now understood why these emissaries had been sent to trouble him. Although he thought that Roosevelt had seen the logic of the British position during their Hyde Park conversations, Moscow had been bringing huge pressure to bear, pressure that was welcomed by those in the American military who doubted Britain's resolve. Behind this was the Americans' constant fear that, unless fully supported, Stalin might be tempted or forced into a separate peace.

It was important to put all the haggling behind them. Churchill decided to tell Stalin face to face that there could be no Second Front this year, and extended his planned trip to the desert to take in a visit to Russia. With him he would take a senior envoy from Washington, to prove to the Soviets that they could no longer play one Western ally off against the other.

Lonnie Dales had every right to be proud when the *Santa Elisa* finally nudged into Belfast Lough. He seized the opportunity for five days of tourism.

> I looked up Mr Stuart Ward, a distant cousin, who had four daughters, two of whom lived in Belfast. They immediately took me under their wing to show me Ireland. We even went to Killarney Castle, and I was able to visit and kiss the Blarney Stone.

The *Santa Elisa* sailed for Newport, South Wales, and awaited further instruction. Dales and the other officers played cribbage and visited the local beauty spots, while the crew played poker, raised hell and chased women. On 4 July a group of them celebrated the American national day in a dockside pub. By closing time they were full of patriotic fervour and Welsh beer. A British destroyer that had once belonged to the US Navy was moored near by. The Americans decided it would be a good idea to board it and replace the White Ensign with the Stars and Stripes. The

British sailors took exception to this and a fight broke out along the quayside. The police arrested the better part of the crew of the *Santa Elisa,* and Dales was sent into town to bale them out.

He took a train to London and toured the historic sites. Ruins surrounded St Paul's Cathedral and the Tower of London. The House of Commons had been bombed too, but Westminster Abbey and Buckingham Palace still looked OK. The ship's officers toured around in a taxi and were vaguely embarrassed by the money they had to spend. There were not many Americans in London, but there were loads of Canadians, Australians and New Zealanders, all in uniform and most eager to be friendly.

> We met some Australian pilots who were flying Sunderland flying boats on patrol out of Plymouth. We invited them back to visit us one weekend in Wales, and they came. They enjoyed good food from us because we had plenty. They asked us to visit them and took us out on patrol. They had depth charges rigged on each wing, and upon sighting a submarine on the surface, would cut the engines, turn on the searchlight, light up the sub and try to drop the depth charges.

The *Santa Elisa* loaded ballast for a trip back across the Atlantic but was told to unload it again. There had been a change of plan. A few days later certain ominous developments took place:

> Our machineguns were removed and replaced with new 20mm Oerlikon cannons and 40mm Bofors guns. Temporary quarters were built behind the stack, and a Royal Artillery gun crew arrived. This was all in addition to the US Navy Armed Guard crew which we already had.

The Americans and the British regulars were taken to an army camp and taught how to tear down, repair and fire the new weapons. They were also given instructions on enemy aircraft and ship identification. Dales still had no idea where he was bound for but it was clear that it was somewhere where he would not be welcome. Then they started loading. To his considerable alarm, hundreds of five-gallon cans of high-octane aviation fuel were lowered into the main hold. On top of each hatch sacks of coal were piled to protect the fuel from bullets or shrapnel. The rest of the cargo was a mixture of food, more ammunition and medical supplies. The crew tried to work out where they were going. Russia was the obvious destination, but why load food and petrol? Everyone knew that the Arctic convoys all carried tanks and other heavy weapons.

They took their cargo out into the Bristol Channel and joined up with twenty-three other merchant ships and three British escorts to sail north in convoy to Scotland, arriving at Greenock, where extra fire-fighting equipment was loaded. Most of the freighters that were destined to form their convoy were already at anchor in the Clyde. Dales recognised a big new American vessel. It was the SS *Ohio*, the largest tanker ever built; 485 feet long, she could carry 170,000 barrels of oil. And, like the *Santa Elisa*, she was fast.

The fate of recent attempts to reinforce Russia was on everyone's mind. The PQ17 convoy had suffered catastrophic losses in June. Of its 37 merchant ships, two turned back and 24 were sunk by a combination of air attacks and U-boats; 210 aircraft, 430 tanks and 3,350 other vehicles had been lost. The rumour was that when the going got tough the Royal Navy had sailed away. In reality the Admiralty had discovered that a powerful German battle group, including the battleship *Tirpitz*, was at sea. In these circumstances the normal procedure was to scatter the convoy and send off the escorts in search of the enemy. Unfortunately, the *Tirpitz* group failed to materialise, and the undefended merchant ships became easy targets for the bombers and the submarines.

It was an intelligence error, not cowardice, which had sealed the convoy's fate, but that hardly made the saga any more edifying. Feelings about PQ17 ran particularly strong in Scotland, home to many of the men who had sailed in it. Dales heard stories of pub brawls between Royal and Merchant Navy sailors on the Clyde.

Peter Vaux was writing up his latest intelligence summary. He decided to circulate another document with it, a translation of a diary taken from a German captured up on the Ruweisat ridge. Things had been tough for Eighth Army over the past few months, but this little account showed that the Germans were under tremendous strain as well:

Diary of a soldier from 11 Company, 104 Lorried Infantry Regiment, 21 Panzer division

17 July: In the morning another attack. Heavy losses. We attacked with 2 Company with 40 men and 3 tanks. Are under heavy fire. At midday were once more in full flight. It was terrible. Very heavy losses in our 3 Battalion. Hauptmann Reissmann is finished and can't get through. My platoon consists of 5 men. At 1000 we are ordered to advance again. It's all the same to us; we only long to be put out of our misery. During the night 20 reinforcements arrived. When everyone rushed back at midday the police put pistols at our breasts to force us to go back into the line. This was the most terrible moment.

18 July: We remained in the old position under artillery fire. The Tommies attacked. We went back 3 kms, suffering losses. In the evening we attacked again; only 8 men in my company, and occupied the old holes.

19 July: In the old position 100 metres from the Tommies – a very dangerous situation. I can see myself captured. The 3rd Battalion has always got to be right up. Let's hope we soon get relieved.

20 July: Back in the line. Real trench warfare. One can't raise one's head. Our Hauptmann Kraus has just been granted the German Cross in Gold.

21 July: Still in the line. The Tommies have fixed Machine Guns on our positions. We are to be relieved tonight. In any case we are virtually surrounded. Have not had a bite to eat for three days and still am not hungry – only suffer from the heat and thirst. At 1930 the Tommies attacked [this was the first attack of Operation Splendour]. *They surrounded us and covered us with artillery fire. During the night the infantry attacked but we were the victors. We held our ground and took 500 prisoners. Dead niggers* [*sic*, i.e. Indians] *are lying around all over the place.*

22 July: In the old position. We had to surrender at 1030 hrs. It was either death or capture; we were quite alone and were surrounded. The tanks took us over, and so we entered imprisonment together with our Company Command.

23 July: On the way to the prison camp in Alexandria. So we got there after all, but without our weapons!

They were tough buggers, thought Vaux, but they were not invincible. Put enough fire on them and they cracked just like anyone else.

All sorts of prisoners had been brought to 7 Armoured Division headquarters in the aftermath of Operation Splendour, and most of them were uninteresting. As usual Vaux had Paxton do the interrogations while he went though the captured materials – diaries, letters, photographs – with one ear on what was being said on the other side of the room. And that was how he heard about the women. The man in question was just an ordinary soldier, one of a group. Paxton was doing the talking and Vaux was studying their possessions.

The photograph showed an ordinary street, somewhere in central or eastern Europe to judge from the houses either side of the road. What was unusual was that there were naked women running along the pavement. The camera had focused on one, quite attractive, quite young. She was obviously both frightened and embarrassed and was holding her hands between her legs. And the soldiers in the picture were laughing. Vaux interrupted Paxton's routine interrogation with a question of his own in English. 'Who are these?' He struggled to contain the surging anger in his voice. The soldier was quite startled. 'Who? Them? Oh, only Jews.'

Chapter 13

Mid-point

Peter Vaux was looking at a snapshot of occupation, and the absolute power of one human being over another that occupation meant. Most British people knew nothing of this. Most, but not all.

Only twenty-five miles from the coast of Normandy, the islands of Jersey, Guernsey and Alderney were indefensible. Churchill ordered the evacuation of all military personnel in June 1940 and the Germans landed a few days later. Hitler, delighted to have acquired a tiny piece of the British homeland, had the islands heavily fortified.

On Guernsey, ten-year-old Kaye le Cheminant's mother told her that the Germans were bad people who took over other people's countries and that she shouldn't speak to them. Her father said they were mostly just ordinary men who would rather be at home with their own families.

On a sunny Saturday morning in the fields near my home, I was playing with my friends. The branches of the large trees hung low enough to be used as swings. Paddy and I hoisted the two younger children up, then followed ourselves, setting the branches swinging. 'There's a German officer watching us,' said Paddy.

It was a doctor from the nearby military hospital. He held out his hand and called out that he had sweets for the children. The younger ones went to him and Kaye followed, but at a distance. 'Come on,' said Paddy, as he showed her his sweets: little pink and mauve shapes that smelt magical.

As the other three were sucking their sweets the doctor came to me, very tall, I remember, and slim in his uniform and knee-high boots. He wore steel-framed spectacles. 'Your parents have forbidden you to accept anything from a German?' I nodded. He said that refusing the sweets would make no difference to the war but, as a parent himself, it would please him if I had some sweets.

Kaye said thank you as she had been taught and took her share. The doctor said goodbye and returned to the hospital. 'I knew better than to mention the encounter at home, though I felt sure that Dad would not have minded.'

Most German soldiers on Guernsey had little else to do but feed sweets to British children. They were free to roam the cafés, cinemas and shops. They tended market gardens, wrote long letters home or sunbathed on the cliff-tops, leaving ample evidence of their homesickness and boredom: a wooden bowl with a message carved around the edge, 'For my darling wife on her birthday', doll's houses made from painted cigar boxes, thousands of tiny pieces of oak and beech dyed and polished and formed into a mural of the distant Rhineland. Protest at their presence generally amounted to little more than the occasional 'V for Victory' sign chalked up on a wall, or the whirr of a forbidden printing press.

Anyone who may have wanted to take part in more active resistance faced overwhelming problems. Almost all men of military age had been evacuated, there were no inaccessible mountains or teeming cities in which to hide a guerrilla army, and there were 37,000 occupying troops, almost as many as the remaining islanders.

So most people did as they were told and tried to live as normally as possible. As they did, Kaye le Cheminant was one of many surprised to find that the enemy could be quite pleasant.

But there were other newcomers on the island. The Organisation Todt (OT) was responsible for building the new fortifications, using slave labourers imported from Poland, Russia and other occupied countries.

A Methodist minister, the Reverend Douglas Ord, tried to help them. 'Many are now in a most repulsive condition,' he wrote in May 1942. 'All are treated like cattle by their German taskmasters.' The islanders were told to avoid the workers, who were described as murderers, rapists and child molesters – desperate men of the worst kind. One day a little girl saw a group of Russians singing beautifully but mournfully as they marched along. Most had no shoes and they were all obviously starving.

Although some islanders offered food and water, most were reluctant to become involved with frightening-looking people calling out to them in strange languages. On the occasions that men escaped and were found cringing in barns or grubbing in fields for food, they were generally turned in to the Germans.

After the war, survivors and captured guards described what happened behind the barbed-wire fences: exhausted men beaten to death, crucified on fences, hanged, drowned, beheaded with shovels and stoned to death. Such scenes would be horrifying anywhere, but on Guernsey, an Enid Blyton island of summer holidays with nice mummies and daddies, of picnics by the rock pools, they seemed peculiarly out of place. But, like the German soldier's photograph, they demonstrated something very important about Nazi occupation: you received a sweet or a shovel depending entirely on your race.

Kaye le Cheminant remembered that her family's doctor had been in a hurry to leave in 1940. Her mother had shaken his hand

and asked, 'Do you really have to go?' He'd smiled and said, 'Just look at my nose!' But some Jews were unable to escape. Therese Steiner had been born in Austria in 1916. She travelled to England to flee the persecution of Jews in the months after Germany and Austria united in 1938. Trained in dental nursing and childcare, she found a job with a dentist in Kent, becoming nanny to his two children. In the summer of 1939 the family was on holiday in Guernsey. For three weeks Therese led expeditions to the beach and singalongs around the piano. Then war was declared. The family went back to England, but they were not allowed to take her with them. No one with an Austrian passport could enter the mainland without special permission. In the panic, this was impossible to obtain, and so Steiner was forced to say goodbye. Soon afterwards she was arrested by the Channel Island police, imprisoned as an 'enemy alien', and freed only as the Germans approached. After that she managed to get a job as a nurse in Castel hospital.

Douglas Ord was a frequent visitor. He described Steiner as 'bright and universally respected', a well-educated young woman who was popular with the patients and could talk to anyone. Nurse Barbara Newman worked with Steiner and thought her very sophisticated.

> Therese was full of life, very intelligent, and she could talk on all sorts of things. She'd come from the Continent to a little place like Guernsey, which was quite something. She was a very good pianist. We used to have musical evenings every so often at the hospital, and she used to play to entertain the staff.

Those responsible for what Hitler called the 'New Europe' enforced his racial policies with great care, even in a tiny outpost like Guernsey. The first race laws came shortly after the occupation, and were incorporated into local statute by the pre-war civilian authorities. An announcement appeared in the *Guernsey Evening Post* instructing all Jews to register with the police.

Approved by their own representatives and backed by their familiar police and courts, the order seemed inoffensive. Some whose racial status was ambiguous decided to register.

Following this, a stream of anti-Jewish legislation passed into island law. Jews were barred from public buildings, lost their businesses and were prevented from seeking employment. The laws were administered by the officials of Victor Carey, the senior local official, known as the Bailiff. The German civilian administrator, the Feldkommandant, asked Carey to provide a list of all Jews living on the island. He complied:

Feldkommandantur 515, Guernsey
re: card-indexing of Jews

Sir,
I have the honour to acknowledge your communication of the 17th instant on the above subject, and in accordance with the instructions contained therein, I enclose copies of a letter which I have received from the Inspector of Police, together with the lists referred to in that letter, and which I hope will satisfy your requirements.

I have the honour to be, Sir, Your obedient servant,

Victor G. Carey, Bailiff

Once it became clear that registration was going to lead to some form of persecution, there was considerable debate about who was Jewish and who was not. Some islanders went to great lengths to prove that they were less than 50 per cent Jewish so as to escape the new laws. In this they had the active support of Carey and his officials. Hundreds of letters went back and forth, and two Guernsey people were removed from the list. To clarify matters, an order arrived from Germany in May 1942 stating:

Any person having at least three grandparents of pure Jewish blood shall be deemed a Jew. A grandparent having been a member of the Jewish religious community shall ipso jure be deemed to be of pure Jewish blood.

Detailed inventories were made of the businesses taken from Jewish ownership: a grocer with ten pounds of stock, a milliner with a hundred. The Bailiff let it be known that it was his intention to refund the money with interest once the war was over. Jews lost their wireless sets, then they were ordered to wear the yellow star in public. Pressure was brought on the local press. The *Jersey Evening Post*'s headline of 27 April 1942 was 'Jewish–Bolshevist Danger'. The propaganda film *Jew Süss* was shown in local cinemas with English subtitles. In the film's final scene a German woman tries to resist a Jewish rapist while an Aryan hero races to her aid. A member of the audience remembers the reaction:

This part of the film elicited cries of admiration from the German audience and their local female companions. The film ended in thunderous applause, when the Jew met his end.

Therese Steiner had not been overly concerned when she was first instructed to register and had gone down to the office of the Inspector of Police. There, a polite British clerk took her identity card, smiled, and gave it back to her marked with a red letter 'J'. He looked slightly embarrassed, his expression seeming to say, 'This is all so silly, but what can we do?'

As the months passed, Steiner became anxious. What she feared most was being taken away to work as a forced labourer. This, it was rumoured, was happening to Jews in France. Her disquiet increased in the early months of 1942 when, on the instructions of the Feldkommandant, the Guernsey authorities investigated her financial affairs. They determined that she had no savings and an income from the hospital of forty-eight pounds a year plus board and lodging.

Therese's employers wrote to the Feldkommandant's office to say that, as a hospital nurse, she was a 'key person' and should be protected from being drafted to work for the Germans. Therese's friend Elizabeth Duquemin, another native of Vienna, was engaged in a protracted bureaucratic struggle to free herself from the anti-Jewish laws. Although registered as a Jew, she was married to a British non-Jew and hoped that this might win her exemption.

> Every day I lived in fear and terror. I was in trauma all the time. Every day I was frightened, and did not know if they would take me away, or my baby daughter, or my husband.

Anonymous letters arrived on the Feldkommandant's desk. One woman who had married an islander was reported for being a 'bad-tongued Jew . . . who had just married for a business affair to escape your jurisdiction'. Steiner spent hours playing the piano to try to ease the tension. But the pressure was too much for some. On Jersey one Jewish man hanged himself, another went mad and died in the island asylum of 'maniacal exhaustion'.

The Bailiff was told to round up all registered Jews for deportation. He instructed the police to carry out the order. In late April Therese was told to report to police headquarters again. The duty clerk told her that she had to pack a bag and prepare herself to leave the island under the care of the German police.

> I do remember – well – Therese coming into the office, where I conveyed to her the instructions given to the Guernsey police by the German military authorities. Therese became extremely distressed, bursting into tears, and exclaiming that I would never see her again.

Two other Jewish women were to be deported with her, but not Elizabeth Duquemin who had been saved by her husband's

British nationality. The night before the deportation Therese went to her friend's house, where she borrowed a large suitcase for her belongings. According to Duquemin she 'had to report the next morning to be taken away to France and [she was] in a terrible state of anxiety'. Douglas Ord saw her that night too:

> She was in great distress and seemed to feel that her feet were now set upon her Via Dolorosa. I did what I could to comfort her but what can you say or do?

Therese went back to the hospital to play the piano. The next day Barbara Newman, her nurse friend, helped her with her case along the steep cobbled road down to the harbour at St Peter Port.

> We got down there at half past seven, which gave us half an hour to chat and say goodbye and so on. We met the other two women. We were laughing and joking as though she was going on a day trip to Herm Island or somewhere. Because what else could you do? You had to make as light of it as you could. There was a wire fence all across the entrance to the harbour, with a little doorway through, and an armed guard with a tin hat on standing there, and someone came from behind and called them and off they went. That was it.

There are palm trees down by the harbour and a statue of Prince Albert. Barbara Newman still watches the day-trippers sail off to Herm Island to look at the famous shell beach. The road she and Therese Steiner took that morning has steep grey granite walls grown over with ivy, and bright green ferns in the cracks. There are quaint little blue postboxes with Queen Victoria's name on them.

'This is all so silly, but what can we do?'

Those in authority could have refused to obey the order, resigned, organised a demonstration, tried to hide the Jews. It would have been very frightening to defy the armed men who had taken over their island, but such things were tried elsewhere. Not often, but sometimes. In Denmark, opposition of this kind did reduce the amount of human suffering.

After all, Guernsey was not Poland or the Ukraine. At this stage in the war, when they were still winning it, the Nazis were reluctant to punish civilians deemed – like the Aryans of the British Isles – to be fellow members of the master race. Obstruction and protest might have led to local compromise, and the worst the Bailiff and his officials could have expected was the loss of their jobs rather than their lives. Ambrose Sherwill, the island's Attorney General, admitted later that 'I still feel ashamed that I did not do something by way of protest to the Germans: a vital principle was at stake.'

However he rationalised it, Bailiff Victor Carey presumably considered the following question: is it worth risking trouble for 40,000 of his own people to prevent the rough treatment of a handful of foreigners?

Across Poland and thousands of miles into the Soviet Union, Hitler's armies were followed by the Einsatzgruppen, the 'cleansing squads', with orders to clear designated areas of the race enemy. Jews were rounded up and either shipped to the nearest ghetto to await employment as slave labour, or taken into the forests and shot.

The first experiments with gas began in the autumn of 1941, using vans with the exhaust fumes directed into a sealed passenger section. The drivers were told to drive around until the screaming stopped. The first specially built gas chamber opened at Chelmno in Poland shortly before Christmas. And by now the Nazis had found something more potent and reliable than engine exhaust: Zyklon B.

At the Wannsee Conference on 20 January 1942, a decision was taken to solve Europe's 'Jewish problem' within three years. The architects of the new plan set themselves a logistical challenge: the discreet murder of between eight and ten million people. Simply transporting the victims would require a substantial proportion of the available transport in the east. By the end of March new camps had been set up on main rail lines in Poland.

'Special treatment' and 'resettlement' were the favoured expressions. Jews were told that they were being sent to areas where there was room for them. But already the Allies knew more than Hitler realised. In their initial enthusiasm, the Einsatzgruppen had made detailed weekly reports, listing the numbers of Jews killed, messages that had been intercepted and decoded by British Intelligence. But, as yet, no one in London or Washington knew about Belzec, Treblinka, Sobibor or Auschwitz; all of which were busy by the spring of 1942 with facilities for gassing large numbers of people and disposing of their bodies. By June tens of thousands of Jews a week, mostly from the newly conquered lands in the east, were being transported in cattle trucks to their deaths.

Jews from France were also sent to the camps. For administrative purposes, France included the small part of Britain that was held by the German armed forces. The Guernsey Jews were being treated with formal politeness at every stage. But the pursuit of them was to be as remorseless as that carried out by any Einsatzgruppen.

On 13 July the Marham briefing room was hot and crowded. Don Bruce was thinking of the huge 4,000-pound ugly dustbin of a bomb that his Wellington would carry that night. The products of ingenious cruelty, these bombs were dropped half an hour after a raid and were designed to create maximum blast damage over a wide area. The intention was to kill rescue parties digging for the injured, firemen trying to douse the incendiaries and dazed

survivors venturing out of their shelters. The force of their explosion would burst lungs at several hundred feet. Crews hated carrying them, partly because of their evil purpose, but mostly because of the extra threat they posed to the aircraft. Their size required the removal of the bomb doors, which meant that if the plane went into the sea it would sink more quickly. Their thin skin meant they were vulnerable to flak, and might suddenly explode inside the bomber. And arriving so late over the target meant that you would be the final, isolated straggler on the journey home, with all nearby fighters on full alert.

Duisberg was the target tonight. Front gunner Bill Margerison would have to drop the bomb, while Bruce operated the GEE navigation equipment to make sure they hit exactly the right mark. The weather expert arrived to conclude the briefing and met with the usual derisory cheers. Bruce collected the maps and his radio codes, printed on rice paper so that he could eat them if he landed on enemy soil. He checked in his pocket for the lucky 'Blue Top' keyring he had picked up the previous year from the Canadian beer company of the same name.

I was walking back across the room when one of the WAAFs called out, 'I hope you have a pleasant trip, Sergeant.' I came out of my reverie, turned round and said, 'Yes, so do I, thank you very much.' She smiled sweetly and I made a mental note to look her up when I got back.

The thought of the trip acted as a laxative to most people. Before climbing into my flying gear I'd always visit the latrines. A bird had built its nest up on the pipes near the ceiling. It used to fly in and out and it had raised a family of chicks there; I always looked on this as a good omen. But on this day the painters had been in, they'd painted the pipes and chucked the bird's nest out.

Bruce and the rest of Mooney's crew waited for the WAAF to come along with the transport. Then they were taken round to dispersal. The others all took off, at two-minute intervals, while they sat there with the 4,000-pounder sticking out from the belly of the plane.

The outward flight was uneventful. They were all old hands by now. They found the target, the GEE led Bruce to his aiming point over the burning city, and the bomb was released right on time and right on target. But as they turned to escape they were 'coned' once again. The first blue searchlight landed on the rear turret, from where Ron Esling shouted, 'For Christ's sake, Del, get us out of these beams.' They had very little time before their height was calculated and all Duisberg's guns were trained upon them.

Mooney threw the plane into the normal series of evasive manoeuvres as the gunners screamed for him to get them out of the light. Bruce heard the sound of a stick rattling on corrugated iron and thought, That's shrapnel hitting the sides and wings. So this is what it feels like to be hit. The port engine began to burn; Bruce could see the flames through a side window. Mooney closed the engine down and, in desperation, tried something new, suddenly pulling the bomber up into a drastic stall turn. As equipment fell around the cabin, the Wellington quickly slowed until it stood on its tail. Bruce felt a moment of sickening inertia and then, with a sudden wrench on his control column and a boot on his rudder, Mooney had them in a dive back in the opposite direction. Searchlights flailed all around and they were free, but free only to tear down towards the ground at dangerously high speed.

We plunged down from about 14,000 to 10,000 feet, then 9,000, 8,000. The crew were floating in space inside the aircraft; only the navigation table held me down where it pinned my knees. Accumulators, maps, nuts and bolts, pencils, all floated past my face. My eyes were glued to my airspeed indicator: it read 320, 330, 340, 350 mph. I found myself thinking of the red warning plate on the pilot's control panel: 'THIS AIRCRAFT MUST NOT BE DIVED AT SPEEDS IN EXCESS OF 300 MPH'.

Gravitational force pinned Bruce down; his arms felt like lead, his eyelids were closing. As he hung on to his navigation table, the wireless operator crashed about inside the cabin and Mooney, his arm muscles bulging with effort, yelled, 'Come on, you big ugly bastard' as he struggled to pull up.

Slowly they started to level out. Over the intercom, Bruce could hear Mooney panting between his curses at the plane, their stupid bomb, the German searchlights, the entire 'RA Fucking F'. And then it was over. The floor was littered with debris. Bruce looked down at his table.

We'd dropped six thousand feet, virtually in a straight dive. The case containing our rations had burst open and the raisins had formed a little pile on the desk; as I looked bleakly and weakly at them an earwig suddenly crawled out of the sticky heap. Thank God I didn't eat any of those.

Mooney continued to fight with his aircraft to prevent further loss of height. But chunks were missing from the port wing and that engine was gone altogether. Then the starboard one began to overheat. Mooney had to throttle back to prevent a fire on his one good wing. Slowly the bomber sank back towards the ground as power seeped away from the battered, leaking engine.

We'd come back on one engine before so we thought we might make it. It's not that far back from the Ruhr. But as we travelled on we realised we were losing far more height than we should be. Del said he couldn't climb because of the state of the starboard engine. He said to me, 'Do you think we can make the sea and ditch?' I did some pretty quick calculations. I reckoned we were making a ground speed of seventy to eighty mph, but I worked out we would still be well inland by the time we reached zero feet. We couldn't crash-land on land at night, so after a little discussion Del said, 'I think we'd better bale out.'

Mooney gave the command, 'Jump. Jump.' The rear and front gunners were the first to go. Bruce remembered the drill: he removed his intercom leads from his helmet in case they strangled him, took off his tie and crawled towards the front escape hatch.

As I passed Del he grinned and gave me the thumbs-up. And then I was at the opening. Four thousand feet below, the ground appeared to be moving slowly past. It looked dull, grey and uninviting. As I hesitated I heard the instructor at OTU saying, 'If you have time, you will probably lower yourself by your hands.' That's the way for me: better than diving out head first. I faced the rear of the aircraft, hands on either side of the hatch. Gingerly I lowered my feet and legs. The slipstream caught them, and like a straw I was swept along the underside of the fuselage. For a second my parachute pack caught against the hatch. I wriggled and then was free, wrenched away into the night.

It was so quiet after the noise of the engine. I could hear the air rustling past my face. My stomach felt a bit strange, like being in a fast lift, but I thought, I've heard about this parachute lark and it's not so bad really. It was pitch black and I wasn't sure if I was looking at the ground or the sky. I suddenly realised my knees were bending towards my chest, I must be falling on my back head down towards the ground. It was quite pleasant really. Then I thought, Christ, the ripcord, pull the ripcord.

High above Bruce, Del Mooney was trying to save his own life. To buy time he'd applied full power to the starboard engine, which was now in flames. Having held the aircraft straight for the rest to get out, he struggled with his own parachute pack then let go of the controls and pulled himself down to the escape hatch under his seat. The plane immediately began to circle as it fell burning towards the ground. When he got to the hatch he was held in for an agonising moment by the G-force. He fought to push himself clear.

What possible purpose could be served by transporting three women? Yet it was obviously a matter of great importance: over five thousand documents relating to the Jews in the Channel Islands have been found, a staggering amount of paperwork considering that there were twelve on Jersey and ten on Guernsey.

Therese Steiner was now in occupied France, where local officials had been helping the Germans round up Jews for months. She was sent to the town of Laval. Although forced to wear the yellow star, she was allowed to seek work and for a couple of weeks found employment as a nurse, and a place to live. But when the orders came through from Paris for a quota of Jews to be sent east, 'stateless Jews' such as Therese were extremely vulnerable. She was arrested by French police on 19 July and taken to Angers. There she was locked up with a group of other Jews, who were told that they would be sent for resettlement to Poland, where there was room for people like them. Dr André Lettich was one of those who were

> herded together in the small rooms of a seminary, twenty-five to thirty to a room; the doors were locked with keys. The following day we were . . . put in lorries by our guards and taken to the railway station.

So far the men enforcing the rules had all worn the same 'what can I do?' expression as the Guernsey clerks. But as Steiner moved farther and farther from the island, the level of politeness declined. Now, as she prepared to board the train, there was no politeness at all. Rude, loud, angry guards who smelled of brandy waved leather whips. They seized her rings and her watch. She was allowed to keep one small suitcase. Some of the Jews started to weep, others quietly swallowed their jewellery or tried to hide rings inside their bodies. They were marched out on to the platform but there were no carriages for them, just old trucks used for animals. They were pushed in, seventy-five to eighty per wagon, and then the windows and the doors were sealed.

Rail convoy no. 8, carrying 824 Jews, crossed the German border near Trier late on 20 July. According to Franz Novak, the man who arranged the eastward transportation of all western European Jews, the deportees were loaded on to trains in broad daylight. In no surviving instruction is there mention of the need to do this at a quiet time of day. Those who scheduled the trains made no effort to separate them from normal railway traffic. A Jewish woman who was transported from Poitiers to Auschwitz in July 1942 recalled stopping at stations and calling out to passengers on the platforms for water. Every now and then a trainload of commuters or French children on a school trip would come to a halt at a red light next to a thousand people in cattle trucks. No one on Novak's staff thought mixing up the desperate and the ordinary like this would cause any serious problems.

André Lettich remembered that 'During the journey, crammed one against another, we suffered terribly from thirst, and we were obliged to sacrifice a small corner of the cattle car for calls of nature.' People put their mouths to knot-holes in the wooden walls for fresh air, or stood on each other's shoulders to reach the tiny windows high up, which were criss-crossed with barbed wire. There was no food and no water. Children were soon crying and asking unanswerable questions. Where are we going? Why can't I have a drink?

Therese knew about childcare, knew that children needed security, routine, regular sleep, someone to keep them clean and get them a drink of water. One of the purposes of this train journey was to remove all such props to ordinary life. To take doctors and piano teachers and professors and nurses and nice mummies and daddies and turn them into something resembling the normal occupants of these wagons; weak and unyielding and half ready for death.

Don Bruce and Del Mooney hung under their parachutes over Holland. They saw the Wellington spinning into the darkness below them, like a giant Catherine wheel throwing out spouts of burning petrol as it turned.

I suddenly thought, I'm going to live, I'm going to live. Because I really did think that was it for me in that plane. Then I saw some trees coming up fast and I pulled off a pretty decent landing in a field.

We'd always been told to hide the parachute so the Germans wouldn't know how many had come down. So I dragged the chute down with some effort, it was a huge mass of silk, God knows how you were supposed to bury it or hide it. I looked around and thought maybe I could just bung it under a hedge. I couldn't see any hedges, though, and I thought, If I muck around here much longer there's going to be a German patrol along. I left the parachute in a tangled heap under the tree, threw my 'Mae West' on top, and made off across the field away from the aircraft to look for a road.

Bill Hancock had injured himself on landing and was calling out to attract attention. He was near a German post, and soldiers soon came out to get him. Mooney was close by and was picked up too.

Some villagers were coming out of a church. I approached them and they took me to the village baker's house. I spent four hours there. People came from miles around to see me, to see a person from the country in which all their hopes for freedom were vested. I hope I was suitably impressive!

The baker asked the burgomaster what to do. The burgomaster said he had no choice but to hand me over – so many had seen me. In fact, people had come in and shaken me by the hand. The baker's wife asked how old I was. I drew on the table, '21'. When she saw this she threw up her hands and started howling. I felt like howling myself, I was so all in.

After a couple of hours they said a friend of mine was there: it was Bill Margerison. I was so pleased to see someone who spoke English. We were handed over to the Feldgendarmerie and taken to the Luftwaffe airfield at Eindhoven. There was an unpleasant guard, lantern jawed. He sneered, 'Tommies, eh!' and propelled us none too gently to the cells. There was no mattress, but I was so tired I was out like a light. We spent one night there, then were taken by train to a prison in Amsterdam.

A German officer came in and chatted amiably in English about places he'd visited in Britain before the war. Then he suddenly asked whether the RAF had concrete runways at Marham. Bruce, half expecting the thumbscrew, said he couldn't tell him that. The officer came back to the question two or three times without success. Next came a trick the aircrew had been warned about: a fake Red Cross form was produced supposedly to help the Germans notify the captives' families that they were safe and well. It asked for all kinds of technical details about their base, their raid and their aircraft.

I felt as if I was a minor actor playing a role in a play! I filled in the parts we were allowed to fill in, and signed it. Then the mood changed and he asked sarcastically, 'What church or hospital were you aiming for?' I, equally sarcastically, said, 'We were given the whole city to pick from.'

Bruce and the others were put on a train for a prison camp in Germany. They had to change at Cologne, just recovering from its battering by the RAF. The station was crowded with evacuees, and every carriage was soon packed, with more grim-looking people standing along the corridors clutching luggage. They stared at Don Bruce, sitting with his guard in a comfortable reserved compartment.

I was looking out at the platform. An old German came up and stood right in front of me on the other side of the glass, and though I couldn't hear him he was obviously swearing away at me, then he spat straight at me. It slowly dribbled down the pane.

He went off and fetched an officer and had a word with our escort to get us moved out of our compartment. Our officer told him to get lost. Then he went away and returned with someone with lots of gold braid on his uniform, who clearly outranked our officer. We had to go and stand packed in the corridor with all the German evacuees. A German sailor cracked me on the back as I walked past and everyone cheered. It was frightening.

Don Bruce's train left Cologne on 16 July, four days before Therese Steiner's cattle truck passed close to the city on its slow journey to Poland.

Refugees from Cologne with British 'terror bombers' in their midst, Jews travelling to Auschwitz, rolling over the same rails on the darkened fringe of a ruined city. For the rest of his life Don Bruce would feel guilty about the old man spitting, and all the good people he'd killed with his terrible ugly bombs. But when he discovered about the cattle trucks, he wished with all the force of an outraged decency that some of his bombs had fallen on *those* men, that he could have seen *those* men plainly through his bomb-sight as he'd clenched his stomach. That it could have been clear and straightforward.

They would sometimes stop for hours. At times people approached them. Some offered water, for free or in exchange for a ring or two. After three days in the trucks they reached Auschwitz and looked out, bewildered, at people with shaved heads and striped uniforms. Is this some kind of asylum? Surely we're not meant to be coming here? Men shouted, '*Raus, Raus.*' People jumped or fell from the wagons. Most were sick, weak. It was raining.

Dr André Lettich was there. 'They ordered us to stand in ranks of five. We were up to our knees in mud.' He remembered that 'anyone who tried to put on his waterproof or hat to protect him from the rain learnt by blows to the head that this was forbidden'. The women were given numbers. Three SS officers stepped forward. One raised a white-gloved hand, and with a small gesture indicated where each person was to go: '*Links; links; rechts; links.*' Right was for those young, fit and able to work. Therese Steiner might have survived the initial selection; no one knows.

The people in striped uniforms were not meant to talk to the new arrivals, but some muttered in Yiddish under their breath, 'You have a trade, tell them, now.' This is what saved Lettich. Some mothers were passed fit to work, but they did not want to be separated from their children. When they followed them they were not stopped. They began to walk towards the build-ings, the old and sick helped along by the others. They were told they had to shower, then they would get food and water and be put to work. They had to undress and be shaved. The shaving was painful, carried out by barbers in striped uniforms with razors blunt from use. They were herded into a long, narrow room with shower heads in the roof; the room was sealed. They stood crowded together waiting, hands between legs because they were embar-rassed to be naked.

Outside, a man in a mask climbed a ladder, and emptied a tin through a hole at the top of the wall. Inside, something was wrong. There was no water coming from the showers; they were not showers. They screamed and clawed at the door and walls. Their bodies convulsed and heaved, trying to expel the poison, and soon they lay thickly on the floor.

An SS man looked through a peephole. The room was venti-lated, and more men in striped uniforms were sent in, stepping on the bodies, checking orifices for hidden jewellery, removing gold teeth. These men too would be killed. They dragged the bodies out to a pit to be burned. Therese Steiner's clothes, shoes and hair were sent to Germany. Her ash was used as fertiliser.

Like a lot of men who don't see as much of their children as they should, Harry Hopkins felt surges of protective love at a distance. His ten-year-old daughter Diana had mostly been cared for in private boarding schools since her mother died in 1937, but he would frequently write her sweet little notes from his travels, promising to bring her with him one day and that they would share exciting adventures together. On the occasions that he could spend time with her, Hopkins gave Diana generous gifts and fancy parties at the White House attended by 'Uncle Franklin'.

'New Dealers' like Hopkins talked about children a lot. Although as steeped in the political game as any other Washington operators, they were driven too by a rare idealism. Some shared Hopkins' Christian socialist background, others were from groups that had rarely tasted power before, like the Jewish Treasury Secretary Henry Morgenthau. Taking their cue from Roosevelt, they liked to claim that their way of doing things was about winning a better deal for the ordinary people, about building a better future for the children.

Roosevelt's men talked about the 'Four Freedoms'. The freedom from want, the freedom of conscience, the freedom to worship and then the one that always resonated most strongly: the freedom from fear. The artist Norman Rockwell illustrated it for a wartime propaganda poster. A father and mother from an average home look down at their sleeping children, in their hand a newspaper reporting some horror in Europe. That's what this is all about, the picture says, we're fighting to create a world where children can sleep safe and clean and have all the bad things kissed away. It was sentimental, of course. America was fighting for a lot of reasons, as was Britain, and some of them were far from altruistic. But in 1942 the leaders of both countries were beginning to understand that this was a war unlike any other, against an enemy unlike any other.

Therese Steiner's train passed near Cologne on 20 July 1942, the mid-point of a war that Adolf Hilter was still winning. On that day, with the panzer armies advancing deeper into southern Russia, Heinrich Himmler ordered the final 'cleansing' of all remaining Jews in the Polish ghettos.

The men who sent Don Bruce to Duisberg had no more idea about Auschwitz than he had, or had the police clerks in Guernsey. But they did have a vision that was clear and straightforward: doing dreadful things, and sometimes doing dreadful things to civilians, was the only way they could see to set a world free from fear.

Chapter 14

25 July–9 August

'Them? Only Jews.'

For the first time Peter Vaux felt inclined to shoot a prisoner. But he regained his composure. The man evidently had experience of some of the more sinister things that were happening in the east and might be of great interest to the intelligence section in Cairo. He carefully put aside the photograph and wrote a note describing the circumstances of the German's capture, before passing him on to the higher authorities.

Alex Szima looked back at the Manhattan skyline as the *Queen Mary* slipped past Ellis Island. He imagined his mother and father's arrival in New York some thirty years before, looking at the same wondrous sights. They must have been nervous and excited, anticipating new lives and new adventures. And now he felt exactly the same.

Szima had grown up in the place where his parents had settled, the industrial city of Dayton, Ohio. At thirteen he'd translated the American constitution into Hungarian to help them with their citizenship tests. His father worked in a foundry and his mother in a cigar factory. During the long summer vacation they sent their son to the country.

> I hoed corn and picked strawberries on my godfather's farm. Living on the land taught me about two things: horse shit and weaponry. In return for cleaning out the stables, I was permitted to have, at first, a 'Buzz Barton' air rifle and then later a .22 rifle.

There were guns on the streets of Dayton too. One of Szima's school-friends, caught breaking into a grocery store, was shot dead by a policeman. He was fifteen years old.

A cycling accident left Szima with a deep, vivid scar on the left-hand side of his face and a reason to skip school. While convalescing, he began to read books by the dozen. The short stories of Guy de Maupassant were his first favourite, like 'Bel Ami', the adventures of a roguish old soldier in turn-of-the-century Paris. It was a window on to another world. He discovered other writers too – John Steinbeck, Ernest Hemingway and John Dos Passos.

He left school at sixteen to work in a bowling alley setting up the pins. He had a passion for baseball, and they had just begun playing games under floodlights in Cincinnati, about fifty miles away. He and a friend would jump on the back of one of the passenger cars of the New York Central Railroad, leap off when the train stopped at Sharonville, and hitch a lift on the rear step of the trolley to Crossley Field. The engineers and conductors rarely challenged them. At the ballpark they stood on top of boxcars by the fence, with dozens of others who couldn't afford a ticket.

In 1938 the local police recommended him for the Civil Conservation Corps, recently established to give young people a taste of discipline and the outdoor life. Szima soon found himself living in the mountains of Montana. He loved everything about it: the fresh air, the manual labour, the new friends and the chance to earn money. In a couple of months he went from a skinny 145 to a muscular 170 pounds, the result of food that was more nourishing than anything he'd received at home. By his eighteenth birthday he was tall and strong and popular.

He returned to Dayton because his parents had opened a bar and could offer him a job there. Szima was soon pouring drinks, a quick-talking, smart-looking barman who could tell a good joke and pay a good compliment.

Give me fifteen minutes and I could persuade you to do just about anything I wanted.

It was 1940 and, from time to time, the bar would fall silent when CBS radio carried Ed Murrow's reports on the London Blitz.

In spite of having a job that most of my friends envied, I longed to wear an army uniform and live the life that went with it. I'd read Hemingway and Dos Passos, both ambulance drivers in the Great War, and that had created a great curiosity in me to do something abroad. I wanted to explore the world, and explore myself.

One day Szima walked to the army recruiting centre and offered his services. Initially he was refused because of the scar, but eventually the US army proved susceptible to his powers of persuasion, although he was issued with a 'no overseas service' waiver.

Szima rose quickly through the ranks, showing a rare ability to organise. Within nine months he was a sergeant in administration, most unusual for a twenty-year-old, responsible for the rations and training routines of eight hundred men. Although most were considerably older than him, Szima was popular with the enlisted men, not least because he took every opportunity to pull 'strokes'. The sergeant was the man to see if you wanted to iron out a problem with your service record, or if you could use a little help with a tricky letter home. The men soon had a phrase for the way he operated: 'Szima logic'.

He was on manoeuvres near New Orleans when the news of

Pearl Harbor broke. War meant travel and danger and excitement and the chance, in true Hemingway style, to measure himself as a man. Like many Americans, Szima's real fear was not that he might be killed or injured, but that the fighting would be over too soon, just as it had been in the Great War, and he'd miss out on all the action. There was also the problem of the 'no overseas service' waiver sitting on his file. When the unit was finally ordered to embark for Europe and he needed a new identity card, Szima delayed having his photograph taken until the last minute.

> It was a couple of days before the *Queen Mary* sailed from New York. We were at Fort Dix waiting. I procrastinated as best I could because, with knowing the system, I could not afford the scrutiny into my record to discover the waiver, thus withdrawing me from overseas duty.

And so, with impeccable Szima logic, he made it on to the great ocean liner, a soldier in one of the first American divisions to be shipped across the Atlantic.

The Tower Hamlets Rifles pulled out of the front line on 4 August and were sent to Mena camp near Cairo. For Dougie Waller, it was a relief to be away from the battle and a great pleasure to be clean. Despite having been in the desert for nearly two years, it was the unit's first visit to Cairo, but it soon became clear that they would be lucky to get much of a chance to have any fun. Training was the order of the day. But they did get to see the Pyramids, which were very close to the camp. On a practice shoot, Waller's crew hit one of them with a shell from the 6-pounder.

They went to Shaftoe's, a big cinema on the camp. It didn't cost very much but the troops soon worked out that you could dig a tunnel under the corrugated-iron fence round it and get in that way for nothing. Known as 'Shufti's', it had only one projector. It would stop at the end of the reel and, while the projectionist changed the film, Arab boys would come round selling beer. If you stayed there long enough you could get very drunk.

But this was the only distraction, and Waller and Bill Ash got very bored. One day Waller discovered, to his horror, that Ash had volunteered them both for the Long Range Desert Group. He was most relieved when their application was refused because riflemen were not allowed to transfer. Then he discovered that Ash had signed them both up to be batmen to new officers. This also sounded like a very bad idea, as new officers were usually sticklers for 'red tape' and polish. But it turned out quite well. The riflemen duly appeared at seven in the morning with mugs of tea and bowls of water. They fetched the officers' breakfasts from the cookhouse and hung out their blankets to air. Then the white-kneed enthusiasts were off to the desert to supervise training, and Waller and Ash could put their feet up until NAAFI time. They discovered a back door to the NAAFI that got them out of the camp without having to pass the guards. From then on, when the officers were away, they slipped out of the back door and hitched a lift to Cairo. After over a year 'up the blue' they were rich with back pay. They had eaten practically nothing but bully beef for months so, at the first restaurant they found, they ordered half a chicken, chips and peas. Then they had another half-chicken. Then they had a whole chicken. After this, and the sixth whisky John Collins, they opted for a little tourism – first the Blue Mosque, then the Berka.

The Berka was a crowded ancient street with white houses two or three floors high with flat roofs. All the houses were brothels, with girls walking around in their knickers and nothing else. There were Greek women, Egyptian women, Cypriot women. Some sat and fanned themselves on the little balconies that lined the narrow street, or leaned over to call to the men below. The British soldiers wandered around with their eyes popping out of their heads. They began to feel thirsty again and pulled into a bar. 'Got any akkers, Dougie?' They sat back with ice-cold lagers and watched the street life. Bill whistled. 'Shufti bint!' Other soldiers joined them. Boys crowded round with necklaces of jasmine and cheap fountain pens. 'Yallah! Yallah!' they said, brushing the hawkers away. A photographer came over with a camera and they had their photograph taken to record the occasion. Empty bottles of Stella and McEwan's Red Label soon stacked up around them.

There were seven VD centres in Cairo by the summer of 1942. Orderlies were sent into the Berka tenements every night, where men queued on the stairs for the best girls, and handed out ointments and condoms. Drunken troops liked to compete at knocking off the gharry drivers' tarboosh headdresses, or hijacking cars and trams and racing them around the main streets. But it wasn't all brothels and boozing. There were clubs like the Aggie Weston, created to give sailors wholesome shore activities, which offered tea and cakes and magazines and rest. There were ENSA shows too, and showers, baths, reading rooms, barbers and classical concerts.

But Dougie and Bill saved that sort of thing for later. After leaving the bar they made their way to the Sweet Melody, a giant dance hall with a moat around the floor. You had to cross little bridges over it to dance. Given the number of fights, the proprietor had invested in the cheapest, most disposable furniture he could find, and wire mesh protected the band from flying bottles.

When me and Bill were there a Maori walked up to the bar and a South African turned to him and said, 'Bugger off, Kaffir.' There was a deathly silence from the Kiwis, Aussies and Tommies all sitting around. Then the fight started. Redcaps came in firing their guns into the ceiling. They ended up almost setting fire to the place.

Although German propaganda fulminated against RAF 'war

criminals', in 1942 most captured British aircrew were treated in accordance with the Geneva Convention. British captives, unlike Russians, Jews, homosexuals, Gypsies and political prisoners, were rarely used as forced labour and were allowed to receive parcels from the International Red Cross. In late July Don Bruce arrived at Stalag 8B on the outskirts of Lamsdorf. 'I wouldn't mind finding where the bog is,' he said to Ron Esling.

> Not only was the stench frightening, but when we looked in we saw this place with forty holes cut into a long wooden top on a brick support. The holes had wooden lids that you had to remove. When you lifted the lid you looked straight down and could see rats scurrying about. There was a small parapet just under the hole, just about where your privates hung when you sat on it, and the rats ran right along it.
>
> The sewage was taken out to the fields to use as fertiliser, so there was a perpetual stench over the camp.

Inside the gate of the compound was a hump of high ground on which grew a solitary tree. The huts were long single-storey buildings made of brick, each holding 120 men. There were wooden shutters over the windows. Between each half of the hut was a cold-water washroom and a stone boiler for hot water. There was a concrete floor and ten to twelve tables spaced out along one side, where the prisoners ate sitting on wooden forms. The other side was full of bunk beds.

> It was filthy, the walls dirty, the beds uninviting. The Germans gave us nothing to keep the place clean. They did once give us some 'soap' but it was more like pumice. We weren't given brooms, we made our own from pieces of wood from Red Cross packing cases and Red Cross string.

The beds were two-tier, with wooden boards forming the base and a palliasse on top, a coarse sack filled with dried leaves and brushwood. There was a large tiled stove in the hut. Each table had a table leader to see that rations were distributed as fairly as possible. When there was no Red Cross food to share, bickering would soon break out.

In good times we used to get one black rye loaf shared between five. We sometimes got a potato boiled in its jacket too. And we usually got a small square of what we called 'axle grease', some sort of white fat. We also got a spoonful of what they called jam – it was mashed swedes coloured red with saccharine added. Soup would come served in old tins, about a pint of very watery soup with inch cubes of swede floating in it.

Bruce had never been fat, but soon he could count every protruding rib. And yet, although he felt hungry all the time, he couldn't face everything that was put in front of him.

Sometimes we got 'fish cheese', which was made from compressed fish offal. It came on a board and in the summer was runny and horrible smelling. I've seen it black with flies. I could never eat the stuff, no matter how hungry I was. But people did eat it and would ask me for my ration eagerly.

Swede jam came in big circular tins. One day they dished it out and the hungry types had spread theirs on bread and were eating it by the time we got to the bottom of the tin. Lying there was a dead mouse. But even then some people said, 'Oh I'll have yours if you don't want it.'

One chap said, 'There's nothing wrong with this jam,' and another bet him he wouldn't lick it off the mouse. He said, 'What'll you bet?' and the other said, 'My wristwatch.' So he picked the mouse up by the tail and licked the jam off it.

At night we'd often hear the mice squeaking and running about. Occasionally we'd have a mouse hunt, but they always came back again.

Mice were irritating, but the really troublesome vermin were smaller. The huts were crawling with bedbugs. Bruce was bitten like the rest, but one man was allergic and his body became a mass of sores.

Then there were the fleas. One bloke reckoned that fleas knew their owners. We laughed at this and he said, 'You watch' and he dived into his vest and pulled out a flea and put it on the sand in the middle of us all. It hopped about a bit and finally made straight for him.

Transport aircraft could ferry people in and out, and bring urgent medical supplies or ammunition, but Malta had not seen a ship full of food since the two surviving merchantmen from the 'Harpoon' convoy in mid-June. Then Air Vice Marshal Keith Park arrived, one of the heroes of the Battle of Britain. The Spitfire force was still growing, allowing Park to launch a 'forward inter-ception policy' with attacks on the Axis bases in Sicily. This grad-ually blunted the bombing but it didn't bring any merchant ships.

Many of the troops had another problem to contend with: a persistent form of dysentery that they called the 'Malta Dog'. It recurred every four weeks or so, leaving hungry men even weaker. Troops were not allowed to mention the food shortages in their letters home because the information would encourage the enemy. The gun crews at ta Qali sang a song:

> Get them in your sights
> And shoot the buggers down
> Shoot the buggers up
> Shoot the buggers down
> As overhead they pass
> Just shoot them up the arse
> And – shoot – the – buggers – down.

Mimi Cortis fantasised about food, remembering hot Maltese bread, rich and brown, with salty goat's cheese. She was thinking about eggs too. Her sister Mary was due to get married in August and Mimi was determined she should have a wedding cake.

Before the war eggs were a halfpenny each. But I paid fifteen shillings on the black market to get six to make this cake.

Unless new supplies reached the island soon, starvation was going to force surrender some time in the autumn. And every day Italian radio said that the Royal Navy would never reach Malta again.

But it was trying. Fourteen merchant ships, including the *Santa Elisa* and the *Ohio*, set out from the Clyde on Sunday, 2 August, and, as they formed up, they were joined by more and more warships. The escort was simply astonishing. There were two huge battleships, *Rodney* and *Nelson*, three aircraft carriers, *Eagle*, *Indomitable* and *Victorious*, seven cruisers and twenty-four destroyers, together with some smaller corvettes. Yet another carrier, *Furious*, with her own escort of eight destroyers, soon joined them. To Lonnie Dales, no possible doubt remained – their mission was both highly important and highly dangerous. It appeared certain that they were PQ18, bound for Russia and a mission to erase the shame of PQ17.

On board the *Santa Elisa* the voice of Captain Thomson came over the Tannoy. It wasn't Russia after all, it was Malta; they were part of a very important operation called 'Pedestal' that would break the siege that was threatening to starve the Mediterranean island into submission.

There was great relief all round. We thought, We're going to make it.

Shouldering such a great burden of responsibility was exciting. Dales took his duties very seriously and busied himself in making the ship's performance as perfect as it could be. He kept his eye on his friend Fred Larsen, the third mate, and tried to behave as he was behaving.

> We constantly zigzagged and practised closing from four columns to two columns and back to four. We also had extensive gunnery practice. I at no time doubted that we would make Malta. When you see the largest naval escort ever put together, you feel that you can go anywhere.

Here was Hornblower's navy in action. Dales watched the great ships at work through binoculars. He gave little credence to the stories he had heard about how the Royal Navy had run away from PQ17. But, as the sailors learned more about the recent history of convoys to Malta, their feelings of relief began to subside. Pessimists muttered that heading south rather than north just meant that their watery grave would be warm rather than cold. Even as they steered way out into the Atlantic, to avoid the submarine-infested waters of the Bay of Biscay, there was a U-boat scare. Anxious eyes followed a destroyer as it peeled off to port and dropped three depth charges.

On board the escorts, the mood was sombre too. The *Furious* was only going part of the way to fly off its thirty-eight Spitfires to reinforce Malta's fighter force. The other aircraft carriers could put seventy-two fighters in the air, but southern Italy, Sicily and Sardinia were packed with aerodromes, so they could expect to face hundreds of bombers. And the narrow passages they would have to navigate near the island would attract every U-boat and E-boat in the Mediterranean. It was going to be a hell of a voyage.

Churchill and Brooke arrived in Cairo on 3 August. Brooke had already heard Ritchie and Norrie's accounts of recent events.

Now he talked to Messervy, Gott and others. He heard a lot about Auchinleck's poor judgement of character and particularly about the arrogant and meddling Chink Dorman-Smith, who, he was told, shared Auchinleck's tent and was responsible for a good deal of trouble and bad feeling. Auchinleck found that Churchill and Brooke were more inclined to blame him for the shame of losing Tobruk than praise him for saving Egypt.

Churchill unveiled the plan for Operation Torch. He explained that, before its launch, a spectacular victory of British arms in Egypt was imperative. This would encourage Vichy troops in north-west Africa to support the Allied cause, and discourage the Spanish from intervening on Hitler's behalf.

Churchill urged an immediate offensive, reminding Auchinleck that strong reinforcements were on their way to Rommel. Auchinleck argued that he needed at least until mid-September. Churchill was unhappy with this answer. On 5 August the debate came to a head during a miserable few hours inside Auchinleck's command caravan. Churchill arrived for an early breakfast, which was spoiled by swarms of flies. Amid the insects, sweat and cigar smoke, Churchill pressed again for his offensive. Auchinleck and Dorman-Smith refused to yield, explaining that the different parts of the army needed to be better trained before victory was possible. Chink became more and more irritated as Churchill thrust his 'stubby fingers against the talc of the wall maps', demanding attacks.

It was a little like being caged with a gorilla. Eventually the Auk said, 'No, sir, we cannot attack again yet.' Churchill swung around to me. 'Do you say that too? Why don't you use the Forty-Fourth Division?' 'Because, sir, that division isn't ready and anyhow a one-division attack would not get us anywhere.' Churchill rose, grunted, stumped down from the caravan and stood alone in the sand, back turned to us.

Breakfast was followed by lunch with the RAF. Food was brought up from the Shepheard's Hotel kitchens and a table was laid out on the beach. The cooling breeze, the claret and the absence of flies did much for the Prime Minister's temper. The tough, professional men of the desert air force were succinct and forthright. Air Marshal Tedder, who had concluded some time ago that the army was characterised by 'an excess of bravery and a shortage of brains', told Churchill that Auchinleck was not ruthless enough with his subordinates and was consequently surrounded by too many 'nice chaps'.

Churchill retired unusually early that night, saying that he needed to think. The following morning he burst into Brooke's bedroom while the Chief of the Imperial General Staff was still only half dressed. The Prime Minister had decided that Auchinleck's command should be split. The Auk should be given Syria, Mesopotamia and Persia and a new Commander-in-Chief found for the Eastern Mediterranean and the desert.

For Brooke, 6 August was 'one of the most difficult days of my life, with momentous decisions to take as far as my own future and that of the war was concerned'. At one point Churchill offered *him* the new job. Brooke was very tempted, but felt that he had taken some pains to establish a moderating influence over Churchill, and feared what might happen if a weaker-willed man replaced him. They decided on General Harold Alexander.

A new leader was needed for Eighth Army too, to work under Alexander. Churchill favoured Gott while Brooke recommended Bernard Montgomery. Churchill, who wanted to use Montgomery for Operation Torch, prevailed. He sent the suggested changes to London for approval by the War Cabinet, concluding that he trusted that this would 'impart a new and vigorous impulse to the Army and restore confidence in the Command, which I regret does not exist at the present time'. On 7 August Churchill visited the newly arrived 51 Highland Division and then attended a dinner at the British embassy.

He met Viscount Cranley there. Cranley had gone down with dysentery in late July and, running a temperature of 104 degrees, was sent to hospital in Cairo. While convalescing, he had been invited to the embassy dinner and found himself recounting to Churchill his own experience of the recent fighting. Churchill, attentive, heard him out and then announced, 'I have listened to this boy with great interest, as only those who have been in the frying pan have the right to speak of the heat of the fire.'

Later Churchill received word that Gott had been killed in a plane crash that afternoon. With his death, an urgent decision about Eighth Army was required. Brooke recommended Montgomery again, and this time Churchill agreed. He announced the appointment that night and wrote a letter to be handed to Auchinleck. The next day Auchinleck met Brooke 'in a highly stormy and unpleasant mood'.

> He wanted to know what the decision had been based on, and
> I had to explain mainly lack of confidence in him.

Auchinleck refused his new appointment. Brooke considered that he was behaving 'like an offended film star'. Churchill and Brooke decided that Dorman-Smith should go too. No new job was offered to him. He was obliged to hang around in Cairo, carefully avoiding all the clubs and bars where he might meet his peers. Then he was ordered back to London to await further instruction. He lost his temporary general's rank and was a brigadier once again.

> To see the Auk wrecked after he saved Egypt and to see how it's
> all been done. It's quite enough. There is nobody I want to serve
> now . . . not the High authorities at home, nor Churchill. The
> feet of clay are too apparent.

At Alamein, Peter Vaux was planning for the next German attack. He knew that Rommel was receiving a lot of new tanks. Good ones too, including a couple of dozen of the latest Panzer IV with the new long-barrelled 75mm gun. Reinforcements were on their way to Eighth Army as well, but whereas Axis supply ships only had to cross the Mediterranean, British ones still had to circumnavigate Africa. Not much would arrive until September. It was likely that Rommel would strike while he held a temporary advantage.

Vaux's Intelligence Summary No. 76 concluded that

> *All these factors, combined with his much improved situation in Russia, must soon persuade the enemy to resume the offensive which was so nearly successful.*

But where would the attack come? Rommel had tried to break through at el Alamein itself and he had tried the Ruweisat ridge. Vaux reasoned that this time he would break out between his two rocky strongpoints at Qarat el Abd and Jebel Kalakh. After this he might go straight down the barrel track to Cairo, but that was a risky waterless route, or else he might cut round to the coast. 'It would be typically German', Vaux decided, 'to attempt again the encircling tactics which proved so successful at Gazala.'

> *If any move of this nature is contemplated it will almost certainly be preceded by the move of 90th Light Division (always the key to German intentions in the southern sector); furthermore a break-through north of Mount Himeimat will first require a close recce (unlike the position at Hacheim) so that from the enemy's moves during the next week or two we should obtain some indications of his intentions.*

In May, Vaux had predicted an almost identical southern overlap, and he had not been believed. This time the army command was in complete agreement. Vaux was instructed to watch German patrol activity closely and, in particular, to alert them the moment he had any clue that 90 Light Division might be moving south.

Chapter 15

10–13 August

Sergeant Szima was handing out some advice.

OK, here's how it works. You go into the bar, or the pub or whatever. You look to see if there are any pretty girls by themselves. Then you send the barman over to her to ask what she'd like. She says, 'Why?' He says, 'Because the guy over there wants to buy you a drink.' She checks you out. You walk over and say, 'Look, I don't mean to be rude, ma'am' – and the 'ma'am' is very important – 'but where I come from we have this tradition. You have to offer the prettiest woman in the bar a drink.'

By now she's laughing and chances are she's real impressed. Treat her right, no profanities or anything, just let her know that you're interested but also be real respectful. Never fails.

Alex Szima and his men were based just outside Belfast. They practised marching and conducted night manoeuvres across the green fields and hedgerows. Life was good. There was plentiful food and ample time for visiting the local towns. Everyone seemed to love them: old men on their bicycles, kids hanging around the base waiting for chocolate and gum, and the girls in the dance halls and the pubs.

Yet Szima was dissatisfied. He looked forward to combat and he'd promised his mother that he would find a way to get to Hungary to find out how their relatives were faring. At first, some kind of mission in northern France seemed possible, but when only a trickle of new soldiers joined them, their hopes for action began to fade. Then, in the middle of June, a printed circular appeared on the company bulletin board. It offered 'hardy soldiers a rugged future in a job where a man could call his soul his own'. The ornate phrase was the creation of William Orlando Darby, an artillery officer who was also hungry for action. Darby was building an American version of Britain's commandos, an élite force called the US Rangers, after 'Rogers's Rangers', a backwoods militia from colonial times.

Selection began at Carrickfergus. Two thousand volunteers were made to run up and down hills to weed out the unfit; 550 were selected. Szima had been shot in the leg during a training accident and was spared the more strenuous parts of the selection process. But in his case they weren't necessary. Soon after he applied, Darby asked him to be one of his senior NCOs.

I had been injured in the upper thigh on the sub-Thompson range during my recruit training. Three of us were hit by one round, which in my case stopped just short of getting the family jewels. The range officer that day had been Darby's classmate at West Point, and I'm positive he was responsible for me being Darby's first choice for battalion sergeant-major.

Szima declined the offer, fearing that his gift for administration would keep him away from the battlefield. Instead he accepted the lesser job of 1st Sergeant of Headquarters Company, but on condition that he was sent on their first mission. The new Rangers were sent to Scotland to train alongside the commandos. A bagpipe band from the Cameron Highlanders greeted them at Spean Bridge railway station. Everyone formed up and then, to a screamed command from a British sergeant-major, they set off at a brisk pace. William Darby was feeling proud of his men.

> The brawny Scots strode off up a hill as if glad to show us their country. We stretched our stride, lifted our heads, and set out behind them for the hills in the distance.

The Americans were in good heart, striding smartly through groups of cheering civilians. But Achnacarry Castle, the commando headquarters, was seven miles away across undulating hills. The sun beat down, the Rangers' legs grew heavy, and their formation began to unravel. 'Mile after mile, we plodded ahead, and perspiration trickled down our backs . . . Where was this castle? How much farther?'

At last they reached the ivy-covered walls of the ancient castle, where the British colonel, barely out of breath, complimented his new guests on the vigour of their marching and promised them many more opportunities to practise in the near future. Had the Rangers not been so exhausted, they might have detected an impish grin beneath his ruddy features. And they got the message: they weren't commandos yet.

Achnacarry stood in a landscape of forests, hills and streams. Near by were beaches, lakes, sheer cliffs and deep peat bogs. Under the not so gentle instruction of the commando NCOs, the Americans marched, ran, climbed, swam, shot, abseiled and performed innumerable bayonet charges. Every second of every day was accounted for. In the castle grounds they slept fifteen to a large canvas tent, their feet all tangled up by the centre pole. It was cold, windy and damp, but they were so worn out they barely noticed.

Although there was a natural rivalry, Szima realised that, as individuals, Rangers and commandos had a lot in common.

> Units like these were made up largely of misfits, people who were dissatisfied in some way with their lives, who were looking to do – or be – something different.

He was impressed by the toughness and professionalism of his hosts, but determined not to be overawed by their cocky NCOs.

> As a sergeant-major I was instructed to eat at the British sergeant-majors' mess, opposite a row of our British instructors. One day a loudmouthed sergeant-major up from London asked my age and how long I'd been in the Army. I answered, twenty-two years old and two years in the army. He shouted to his captive audience of British instructors, 'By God, it took me seven years to make corporal.' My answer: 'Some people are just naturally slow.' It cost me a pound for a bottle of VAT 69 to calm him down!

Food caused the most complaints. After years of US army catering, the products of this Scottish cookhouse were meagre by comparison:

> Tea, fish and beans for breakfast, and tea, beans and bully beef for lunch; and tea, beans and beef for dinner. This was varied occasionally by porridge without sugar or milk and by some ungodly concoction peculiar to only the British and known mysteriously as 'duff'.

Sometimes the British mistook the generally more relaxed American attitude for sloppiness, and there was resentment once the commandos discovered what the Americans were getting paid. In June 1942 a private in the British army received under a pound a week, while GIs got four times as much.

Commandos were expected to make over 4 mph over varied terrain, with full equipment on their backs. Soon the Americans could manage this over a fifteen-mile hike. Then came 'battle preparedness', three-day exercises under live fire, made as true to life as possible. They crawled under barbed wire while machine-guns blasted over their heads, they ran through woods with grenades exploding in the trees, they swam in full equipment.

Punishment for lapses in discipline or performance involved fists rather than charge sheets.

> Our preparation was designed to untrain the mind from the fear of dying. There was a lot of violence, official and unofficial. We would literally beat the hell out of one another. One guy drowned in a freezing river crossing, another was blinded by a mine on a landing exercise.

The American contribution to the Pedestal convoy consisted of the *Santa Elisa* and the *Almeria Lykes*. The US tanker *Ohio* was crewed by British merchant sailors, as were the other eleven merchant ships, and the escort was entirely British. Most of the ships refuelled at Gibraltar and then passed through the straits in the early hours of 10 August in thick fog. But any delight they may have felt at thus evading fascist spies operating from Spain was short lived. At first light the fog cleared. The admiral signalled, 'All crews to action stations until further notice.' Minutes later a Vichy French airliner flew overhead. 'Oh, bollocks!' said the British gunner standing next to Lonnie Dales. They were both at their action station on the single-barrel 20mm Oerlikon on the 'flying bridge' over the wheelhouse as they watched the plane disappear into the distance. Sure enough, they had more company soon. German reconnaissance planes circled high and distant like vultures. The crew scanned the horizon for bombers, but all they could see were their own fighters, flying patrols in rotation from the carriers.

At noon on 11 August *Furious* turned into the wind and flew off her Spitfires for the 550-mile flight to Malta. Those remaining with the convoy watched the carrier and her escorting destroyers fade into the distance. Then, with no warning, a huge explosion shook everyone on the *Santa Elisa*.

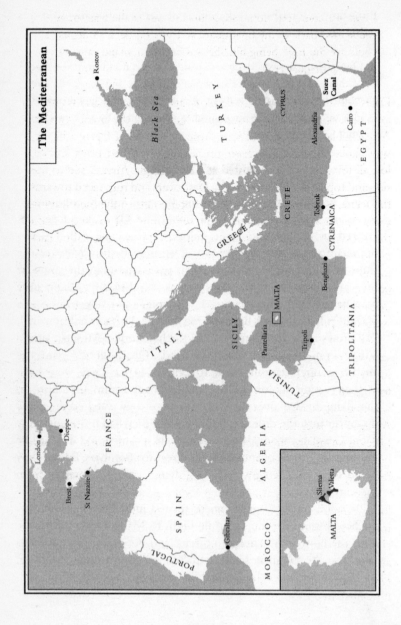

The Mediterranean

> I had just come out from eating lunch – out of the wardroom – and started back to my own quarters. I was on deck alone and I could see the *Eagle* being hit. She was only a thousand yards away on our port quarter.

Dales felt the explosive force ripple over his own ship and watched as the last of a full salvo of four torpedoes struck the aircraft carrier. At each blast a column of spray rose hundreds of feet in the air, way above its mast. The *Eagle* immediately belched black smoke, lost all forward speed and listed at a crazy angle. Aircraft slid to the side and toppled over into the sea. Destroyers and tugs raced towards the scene, hunting the U-boat or dropping rafts to the men leaping from the flight deck into the water, swimming fast to escape from the slicks of oil that poured from inside the sinking ship. Dales could hear them screaming for help. The huge vessel went down in just eight minutes but, owing to the quick action of the escorts, 900 of her crew of 1,160 were saved. Four of *Eagle*'s planes had been in the air and managed to land on other carriers but the rest were lost. Now they had only fifty-nine fighters left.

Soon afterwards more reconnaissance planes were heard, but not seen, far overhead. For some hours nothing happened. Then, early in the evening, Dales watched as the destroyers moved outward to form a defensive ring around the convoy. Over the Tannoy came warning of an imminent air attack. It had been a burning mid-August day and was still hot. The men were stripped for action, Dales wearing his steel helmet, white T-shirt and shorts. The sun began to sink bright gold in the sky behind them. Somewhere to their right lay Algiers and way ahead of them loomed Sardinia.

From out of the setting sun came the noise of aeroplanes. Six lumbering Heinkel 111s and thirty faster Junkers 88s, all carrying torpedoes, swooped down low. The guns on the outer destroyer ring opened up, and little black puffs of smoke followed the planes as they passed overhead towards the fire of the merchant ships. Dales added his own contribution to the criss-crossing coloured lines that filled the air.

It was the noise of battle which surprised him the most. The guns, the aircraft engines, the sirens, the urgent Tannoy instructions for ships to alter course to avoid torpedoes, the ships hooting as they turned to warn others of a possible collision, the British gunners screaming obscenities at the attacking planes and the entire German race. With its metal brace digging into his shoulders, Dales swung his shuddering gun round and poured cannon shells towards the bombers as they streaked past, aiming just ahead of them as he had been taught.

The planes disappeared as suddenly as they had come. Four had been shot down and none of the ships had been hit. The gun crews on the *Santa Elisa* cheered. As the British fighters abandoned the pursuit and returned to their carriers, half of the ships opened up again in their nervous enthusiasm.

Churchill flew to Moscow via Tehran, travelling high above the Volga river. About a hundred miles to the west, Russian armies were struggling to defend the line of the River Don. He landed in the evening of 12 August, and began his first visit to the capital of the communist world. He thought back twenty-three years to the time he had led French and British efforts to destroy the new Bolshevik regime. But this was not a moment to dwell on past antagonisms. At any moment the Germans threatened to pour through into the Caucasus.

The British party was entertained in a style that would not have disgraced Tsar Nicholas. Luxurious villas, servants in immaculate uniforms, tables piled with every delicacy: 'Totalitarian lavishness' was Churchill's description. Averell Harriman had flown in to offer America's endorsement to what Churchill had to say. Soviet chauffeurs drove the two of them into the Kremlin for their first meeting with Stalin.

The dictator was clipped and coldly formal. He began by telling Churchill that the news from the front was not good and that, although Moscow was safe for the moment, the Germans had enough forces to present a grave threat to it whenever they chose. After receiving this dismal account, it was Churchill's turn to report on the state of the war in the west. He began by explaining why an invasion of France was impossible in 1942. Instead, he offered a significant operation in mainland Europe in 1943. Stalin, looking grave, suggested a series of places on the French coast where a demonstration with six divisions might seriously damage the German armies in the west. Churchill maintained that any such operation risked handing the enemy a propaganda coup when it went wrong, as it surely would, and would only fritter away troops that could be better employed in 1943.

Stalin argued that the German forces in France were second rate and that Hitler's best troops only fought in the east. Churchill disagreed and said that his intelligence services had identified many first-class German units in France, Norway and the Low Countries. Stalin countered with his own, contradictory, intelligence reports and, as the atmosphere grew more sombre, the two men traded opinions about the quality of the German army in France. War, Stalin said, was war, and involved some risk.

Churchill, adopting a tone that had certainly been used to *him* by generals such as Auchinleck, said to Stalin that risk was one thing, folly quite another. The British officials taking minutes reported that Stalin was now looking both glum and restless, and at this point diplomacy gave way to insult. Stalin said that, as far as he was concerned, the British were unprepared to face the necessary challenges of war. He advised his opposite number that Britain 'should not be so afraid of the Germans'.

Churchill tried to turn the meeting. He spoke of the RAF bombing offensive and Stalin agreed that bombing was of 'tremendous importance' and necessary to break enemy morale. Churchill thought that the RAF could shatter almost every dwelling in every German city over the course of the following twelve months. This prospect cheered Stalin and the meeting grew warmer. They discussed the best way of dropping two- and four-ton bombs. Then Churchill took out a map of the Mediterranean and spread it out in front of the Soviet delegation. 'What is a Second Front?' he asked them. 'Is it only a landing in France?' With a jab of his finger he explained that, within three months, a large Anglo–American army would be on the north-west African shore. This action would, at a stroke, recruit a large slice of the French Empire to the Allied cause, neutralise the threat from Spain and threaten Rommel from the rear.

Stalin leaned over the map, smiled and showed great interest in every detail of the landings. Would this mean an attack on Tunisia and the removal of every German base in Africa? Hopefully, yes. And an attack on Sicily and Italy? Probably, yes. And what of the Vichy French? It might well split the government there and force the Germans to occupy the whole of France. As they speculated excitedly, Churchill drew a picture of a Nazi crocodile, meant to demonstrate that a victory in Africa would expose its 'soft underbelly' in southern Europe. Stalin looked pleased at last, and turned to Harriman to hear the American saying that Roosevelt stood four-square behind the strategic thinking that had been outlined by the British Prime Minister.

The meeting had lasted three hours. Churchill sent a cable to Clement Attlee, the Deputy Prime Minister: 'He knows the worst, and we parted in an atmosphere of goodwill.' Then he returned to the totalitarian comforts of his villa.

The night passed without incident and at dawn a pair of fighters took off from *Victorious* and *Indomitable*, climbing into the pale blue sky over a calm sea. As the light grew brighter the standing patrol of Fulmars and Sea Hurricanes was increased from four to twelve. At 0910, nineteen Junkers 88s attacked. Two were shot down by the fighters and four more fell to another great barrage of anti-aircraft fire. Once again, no merchant ships were damaged. On board the *Santa Elisa*, Lonnie Dales was recovering from the shock of seeing the *Eagle* sink and beginning to think that they might make it through unscathed after all.

It grew quiet again, except for the odd lone plane snooping around, whisking away when the guns fired. They were approaching the passage between Tunisia and Sardinia now. The enemy bases were close and the U-boats were near their favourite hunting grounds. ASDIC reports came in more frequently and ships could be seen turning sharply, avoiding phantom torpedoes. The destroyers had been forbidden to chase probing submarines; their job was to preserve the convoy.

The next attack came just after midday when Italian S84 bombers dropped large black canisters on parachutes just ahead of the convoy. These were obviously some kind of mine, and all the ships were ordered to make an emergency turn of 45 degrees to port to avoid them. Then everyone watched with fascination as the mines hit the water and began to move. A propeller drove the secret weapon, called the 'Motobomba FF', round and round in a circle of about a ten-mile radius until eventually they exploded harmlessly. Hardly had this mysterious if somewhat comical threat been avoided, and the fleet returned to course, when a second wave of attackers appeared. In fact a combination of misfortune and disruption by the British fighter screen had prevented them striking immediately after the first wave, to exploit the confusion caused by the novel 'Motobombas'. Thirty-three Italian Sparrowhawk fighter-bombers and ten more S84s came in with an escort of twenty-six Italian fighters. The British fighters broke up the formations but could not stop some planes getting over the ships. Dales was blazing away with his Oerlikon once more:

The noise was extraordinary – the 16-inch battleship guns were fired at planes! I think it was the first time that had ever happened and tons of shrapnel rained down on us all. I never will forget how one of the Italian pilots came down between us and another ship, really close, and he looked out and he waved at me. I waved back.

Even as the Italians pulled away, with no merchant ships damaged, a new wave of about forty German attackers moved in. The Fulmars and Sea Hurricanes fought off most of them, but about twelve broke through and penetrated the barrage put up by the destroyers, cruisers and battleships. They crossed the convoy from the starboard side and hit the freighter *Deucalion*. Some of her crew immediately abandoned ship, only to be sent straight back to her by the captain of the nearby destroyer HMS *Bramham*, who ordered his men to step on the fingers of anyone trying to clamber up the scrambling nets on the side of his ship. *Deucalion*, duly recrewed, could now only make 13 knots, so *Bramham* was ordered to escort her separately on a different route along the North African coast.

Around lunch-time most of the British fighters had to return to the carriers to refuel. Two Italian Reggiane 2001 fighters followed them in undetected and dropped bombs on the carrier *Victorious*, but they exploded on the armoured deck without doing serious damage. By now Dales was smeared with oil and sweat, half choked by cordite and near deafened by the massive barrage.

As the planes disappeared, the U-boats closed in again. But the perfect weather and calm seas that were so suitable for air attacks were much less welcome to the submariners. At 1640, just south of Cagliari, the destroyer *Ithuriel* sighted and rammed the Italian submarine *Cobalto*, crippling herself in the process. The afternoon was drawing on and the fleet was nearing the point just beyond Bizerta where the battleships and carriers would turn about and return to Gibraltar. The risk was judged too great for them to navigate the narrow sea lanes between Cap Bon and Marsala. But before they left there was one last alarm.

Again there was early warning, the result of the radar carried by the larger ships. Aboard the carriers, riggers, fitters and armourers worked to get tired pilots back into the air to face 120 bombers supplemented by fighter protection from Messerschmitt 109s that outgunned and outran the British fighters. Attacks came from all directions and all angles. Most of them broke through and reached the convoy. It was the first time Lonnie Dales had heard the unnerving wail of a diving Stuka. The German pilots ignored the merchant ships and fixed on the carrier *Indomitable*. *Nelson's* 16-inch guns opened up again in a vain attempt to thwart the attack. Dales was a distant onlooker as four Junkers 88s and eight Stukas dived and *Indomitable* disappeared among huge columns of water. From inside the spray came a great orange flash and then billowing columns of smoke. Three armour-piercing bombs had penetrated the deck armour, tearing a gaping hole six yards wide in the upper deck and stopping any more air operations. One of the bombs destroyed the wardroom. It had been packed with pilots and observers who were all killed.

They had reached the turning point, and *Indomitable* limped off into the sunset with *Victorious* and the battleships. With no more close air support, the convoy headed on. The cruiser *Nigeria* was flagship now, and with her were three other cruisers and twelve destroyers. Despite all the attacks, the convoy was almost intact and would be under cover of fighters from Malta the next morning. But this was the beginning of the most dangerous part of the journey.

Sandbanks left only two possible routes for the heavily laden merchant ships. The obvious one passed close to the Italian bases on the island of Pantellaria. It had been judged too dangerous. But the chosen course was almost equally unpleasant. Called the Skerki channel, it was a narrow and winding deep-water route through the sandbanks near the Tunisian coast. It was mined and, in the approaches to it, thirteen submarines were strung out across Pedestal's track. The minesweepers moved to the front of the convoy as it manoeuvred from four columns into two and approached the entrance to the channel in the gathering dusk.

The first ambush was executed to perfection. At 1945 the *Nigeria* suddenly heeled over to starboard; almost simultaneously the stern blew off the cruiser *Cairo* and she swung to port and stopped, and a second later, with another shattering explosion, a great sheet of flame soared above the masthead of the tanker *Ohio*. At first they thought they must have hit a minefield. In fact, in a quite brilliant attack, Lieutenant Renato Ferrini, in the Italian submarine *Axum*, had hit three ships with a single salvo of torpedoes. For a time the *Ohio* looked like a floating bonfire, but the hole that had been ripped in her side allowed seawater to flow in and this helped put out the flames. Within half an hour she was under way again, the bulk of her cargo untouched. *Nigeria* was too badly damaged to continue and the admiral decided to send her back to Gibraltar with a pair of destroyers for escort while he shifted his flag to the destroyer *Ashanti*. *Cairo*, a veteran of many Malta runs, was so badly damaged that she had to be sunk. Only *Cairo* and *Nigeria* had the sophisticated radio sets that were necessary for effective fighter control. Pedestal had lost its ability to vector in fighter cover from Malta.

The surviving ships fled south at speed to avoid the menace, but they were strung out and disorganised when, at 2035, the Luftwaffe discovered them with many of their principal anti-aircraft ships disabled. As the bombers swooped, the merchant ships were silhouetted against the last glowing light on the western horizon. The *Ohio*, marked out by her distinctive profile, was well to the rear. Thanks to her diesel generator she had restarted her engines, but with her steering damaged she was, for the moment, only capable of going round in circles. Forty bombers came out of the gloom. Combining high-level bombing with low-level torpedo runs, they picked out the merchant ships at leisure. *Empire Hope* was set ablaze and abandoned; *Brisbane Star*, badly damaged, struggled on. *Rochester Castle* was also damaged and lost way. *Ohio* rigged emergency steering gear aft. HMS *Ledbury* dropped back to help, guiding her through the night with a blue light on her stern. The bombing continued for another half an hour and an aerial torpedo hit the *Clan Ferguson*, which blew up spectacularly. A pair of torpedo-bombers picked out the limping *Deucalion* and sank her too. As the bombers pulled away, the convoy ran into a second Italian submarine pack. The cruiser *Kenya* was hit and damaged by a torpedo from the submarine *Alagi*.

By now the *Santa Elisa* had almost been hit several times. In the final raid of the day she was straddled by four bombs, forcing her to reduce speed. She fell behind. Dales and the rest of the gunners were still blazing away at anything that crossed their sights, but they all paused when the *Clan Ferguson* was hit. The explosion was colossal. Dales watched as a cloud of flame rose hundreds of feet out of the sea. Each merchant ship in Pedestal carried the exact same mix of cargo, so that a quantity of everything would get through even if only one of them made it. This meant that whatever mix of aviation fuel and ammunition that had just made the *Clan Ferguson* explode so violently was also sitting a few yards under Lonnie Dales' feet.

By the time the final air raid had finished, the *Santa Elisa* was out of touch with the rest of the convoy. They tried to navigate through the Skerki channel in the dark, helped by, but also illuminated by, the lighthouses off the Tunisian coast. They rounded Cap Bon at midnight and continued to hug the shore heading towards Kelibia, keeping as far as possible from Pantellaria. This section of the journey, forty nautical miles from the Italian naval base, was known as 'E-boat alley'.

Brooke had travelled to Russia on a separate aircraft and had been delayed by engine trouble in Tehran. He arrived in Moscow on 13 August, and later that day joined Churchill for a second meeting with Stalin. The good humour with which they had parted the previous evening had disappeared.

It crossed Brooke's mind that Stalin had taken the bad news about the Second Front to his Politburo and had been shaken by their reaction. Whatever had happened, Stalin had returned to the theme of an invasion of France in 1942, his insistence reinforced with more insulting attacks on the British, culminating in some withering criticism of the Royal Navy for their conduct during the PQ17 convoy.

This is the first time in history that the British Navy has ever turned tail and fled from the battle. You British are afraid of fighting. You should not think the Germans are supermen. You will have to fight sooner or later. You cannot win a war without fighting.

Churchill, beginning to lose his temper, defended British courage and described the months during which his country had fought on alone in 1940 and '41. He did not go so far as to point out that at that time Stalin had been allied to Hitler, but doubtless meant Stalin to reflect on the fact. Churchill became so transported by his own passionate eloquence that he barely left time for the translator and had to keep stopping to ask, 'Did you tell him *that*?' He concluded by saying that he would pardon Stalin's abuse of the Royal Navy, but only 'on account of the bravery of the Russian troops'. Stalin laughed. He replied that although he had not understood everything that Churchill had said, he could tell from his demeanour that Britain's fighting spirit burned brightly in her Prime Minister.

The eleven remaining merchant ships of the Pedestal convoy were 120 miles short of their destination. Somewhere ahead of the *Santa Elisa* minesweepers were trying to cut a safe channel through, but Lonnie Dales' ship was so far behind that it was difficult to tell in which direction to steer. On one occasion Dales saw a mine, caught in the glare of the searchlight, painted green, bobbing in the water some distance off the bow.

Off the Cap Bon peninsula, the Vichy French authorities ordered us away from their shores and began firing their shore batteries at us, so we had to alter course back out into the channel trying to avoid the minefields.

At two in the morning there was another orange flash in the sky and some time later they passed the burning wreckage of the *Glenorchy*, floating in a sea of oil. The ship had been abandoned. An hour later there were more explosions in the distance, where torpedo-firing E-boats sank the *Almeria Lykes* and the *Wairangi*. The men were almost worn out with the strain of watching and waiting, the sudden turns to starboard or port to avoid real or imagined mines and torpedo tracks. The master and lookouts on the bridge were peering into the darkness. It was the hour before dawn, almost five in the morning. It would be light soon and the horrors of the night would be over.

Suddenly Captain Thomson saw the dark shape of an E-boat appear almost alongside the ship and ran along the bridge. There was a stab of light in the darkness to port and machinegun bullets rattled on the gun shield in front of Lonnie Dales. Captain Thomson yelled, 'Get that son of a bitch!' Dales' loader fell away with blood gushing from his throat. Dales wrenched the gun round, trying to pick out the position of the attacker as he spat shells into the night. Another burst swept the flying bridge. Thomson threw himself to the deck to avoid being hit. Pieces broke off Dales' gun shield, but he had the shape of an E-boat in his sights and his last burst was answered by a great explosion out to sea, revealing the outline of his stricken enemy, but also illuminating a second E-boat approaching from the other side of the *Santa Elisa*, ready to launch its torpedoes. He swung around and tried to fire but had no more ammunition.

All my gun crew were dead. I didn't notice until I ran out of ammunition. No one would pass me the drum. When I ran out and hollered for ammunition there wasn't any, just bodies and blood everywhere.

Two men were lying dead in the turret and another was near by. Dales saw the E-boat fire and turn away in the darkness. The deck buckled and swayed under his feet as the torpedo struck the starboard side of number-one hold. Simultaneously, the petrol stacked inside went up with a roar and a great blaze of flame.

> When the torpedo hit the gasoline there was an explosion that blew the hatch covers and a solid wall of fire went over the smokestack. The British naval crew on the stern guns jumped for it as the flames lapped right around them; one of them got caught up in the anchor on the side of the ship.

As Dales ran with Captain Thomson and Fred Larsen to launch the lifeboats, fire engulfed the whole ship.

> Captain Thomson ordered 'Abandon ship' because our propeller had come out of the water, and we were unable to make any kind of steerage. We rounded up the survivors of the gun crews and others who hadn't already got into the water. We swam around, talking to each other and hoping for the best. The water wasn't too cold and I reckoned we had a good chance of being rescued. About daylight, or shortly thereafter, HMS *Penn* came over the horizon looking for survivors, and we were picked up.

At dawn a Junkers 88 swooped low to finish off the *Santa Elisa*.

Chapter 16

13–18 August

In Moscow the mood thawed again. Having vented all his anger, Stalin asked Churchill and his party to join him for a banquet. A hundred people gathered in one of the Kremlin's most ornate dining rooms: ministers, diplomats and Soviet generals festooned with medals. Just before he was driven there, Alan Brooke received the latest, depressing news from the Pedestal convoy. As if this were not enough to put him off his food, the sight of it made him feel distinctly queasy. The tables were piled high with every kind of roast meat, poultry and fish, with generous quantities of caviar and dozens of bottles of vodka. Brooke spent most of the evening trying to avoid the gaze of a small sucking pig, smothered in an unappetising white sauce, and equipped with a black truffle eyeball that threatened to drop out. Whenever he felt that no one was looking he carefully refilled his vodka glass with water.

Churchill, however, was in his element. Piling food on to his plate with aplomb, he joined in enthusiastically as Stalin toasted all of his generals and admirals in turn. Stalin toured the room, insisting on clinking glasses with the recipients of his toasts, some of whom, Brooke noted disapprovingly, were soon glassy-eyed and unsteady on their feet. Churchill drank to Stalin's own health while other guests proposed 'Death and damnation to the Nazis!'

and suchlike. Stalin teased Churchill by recalling pre-war visits to Moscow by sympathetic British politicians who had told him that 'Churchill, the old warhorse' was finished. Stalin claimed to have predicted even then that the warrior would make a comeback. Later, he told Harriman that he had meant what he had said about the British army and navy lacking the will to fight, but added that the RAF was good and that he had high hopes of the US forces.

The next day was spent recovering from the banquet. Stalin and Churchill had parted on extremely good terms the night before, with Stalin taking the unusual step of escorting his guest to the gates of the Kremlin. Then, during the evening of 15 August, Stalin asked to see Churchill again in private. He arrived at seven in the evening and stayed until three in the morning after Molotov joined them for another boozy dinner. Abuse had now softened into jokes, and even nostalgia. Stalin remembered London where, in 1907, he had been a young Bolshevik agitator alongside Lenin, while Churchill was already a minister in the British government. Stalin asked Churchill why he had 'bombed his Molotov', reminding him of the moment when the RAF had attacked Berlin during one of Molotov's meetings with his German opposite number in the days of the Nazi–Soviet alliance. The Germans were talking of Britain's imminent defeat, as they cowered in a shelter from British bombs, something that Stalin and Molotov thought very funny indeed.

The talk ranged over history and morality. At one point Churchill questioned Stalin about the peasant landowners who had stood in the way of his collective farm schemes during the 1930s. Millions had been killed. Stalin expressed a passing regret but then said that such things were sometimes necessary to help modernise a country. Churchill kept his own counsel.

> I did not repeat Burke's dictum, 'If I cannot have reform without injustice, I will not have reform.' With the World War going on all round us it seemed vain to moralise aloud.

Churchill did not have time to go to bed that night, as he was due to meet Brooke for an early flight to Tehran. The visit had been a singular personal triumph. He'd broken bad news, dealt with complaints and anger and established some kind of personal rapport with Stalin. He felt sure now that Russia would not make a separate peace and was confident that the future course of the war had been set, and set to his and Brooke's timetable. Catching his Prime Minister's mood, General Wavell wrote the 'Ballade of the Second Front' on the plane.

> I do not like the job I have to do.
> I cannot think my views will go down well.
> Can I convince them of our settled view;
> Will Stalin use Caucasian oaths and yell?
> Or can I bind him with my midnight spell;
> I'm really feeling rather in a stew.
> It's not so hot a thing to have to sell;
> No Second Front in 1942 . . .

The *Ohio*, doing 13 knots, caught up with the remnants of the convoy, although her captain, Dudley Mason, worried that she might break in two at any moment. Of the other merchant ships, the *Rochester Castle*, *Waimarama* and *Melbourne Star* were still together, with *Port Chalmers* lagging a little behind. *Dorset* and *Brisbane Star* had become detached and isolated. At 0800 on 13 August the convoy crossed the edge of a hidden screen of eight British submarines to guard them from surface ships. They had also been located by a patrol of Beaufighters flying in from Malta.

Twelve Junkers 88s arrived, aiming chiefly at *Ohio*, the most important vessel still afloat. But it was *Waimarama* that they hit, and her cargo went up in a similar sheet of flame to that which had crippled the *Santa Elisa*. The sea was soon on fire all around her, with burning fuel spread two or three hundred yards in every direction. Captain Roger Hill ordered his destroyer HMS *Ledbury* into the flames to pick up survivors. His had been one of the ships to leave the convoy PQ17 to their fate. Now he felt he was expiating his sense of guilt. He talked to the men in the water through his loudhailer even as more planes tried to machinegun the wreckage and his own anti-aircraft teams poured fire into the sky. Most of the crew were picked up, the last when the *Ledbury*'s own bows were in the flames and her crew were spraying the decks with water to stop them catching alight.

Melbourne Star was close behind *Waimarama* and had no choice but to plunge straight on into the flames. Her crew abandoned her, thinking she would blow up, but she sailed through unharmed and was then reboarded. *Ohio* turned hard to port just in time to avoid the burning area. *Dorset* saw the fire in the distance and changed course to rejoin the convoy.

More planes attacked at 0900, aiming for the tanker again. The gunners hit a Junkers 88. It crashed into the sea, bounced, and landed on the *Ohio*'s foredeck, throwing debris everywhere. A little later the chief officer telephoned Captain Mason to announce that a shot-down Stuka had just arrived on the stern. Mason answered nonchalantly, 'Oh, that's nothing. We've had a Ju 88 on the bow for nearly half an hour.' Shortly afterwards a near-miss right under the forefoot opened up both bow tanks and buckled the deck plating. The ship vibrated violently, but continued to make headway at 13 knots. What should have been the killer blow came at 1000, when *Ohio* was still a hundred miles from Malta. A stick of six bombs exploded close by and shook her violently. The two electric fuel pumps gave up. The crew managed to restart the main engines but could only make 4 knots. Then first one boiler blew, and a little later the other. The *Ohio* was dead in the water. The air attacks continued.

Some way ahead, *Dorset* took a direct hit. HMS *Bramham* stayed with her but she had to be abandoned. *Port Chalmers*, *Rochester Castle* and *Melbourne Star* steamed on. At 1120 the bombers attacked once more and a torpedo became entangled in the paravane floats streaming behind *Port Chalmers* which had been meant to catch mines. The crew carefully released the paravane, the weight of which pulled the torpedo underwater, where it exploded harmlessly. By now the surviving merchant ships were within range of Malta and squadrons of Beaufighters and Spitfires met the bombers, shooting down sixteen of them.

Malta was trying everything it could to help. Air Vice Marshal Keith Park discovered that an Italian battle fleet was at sea. With its big ships sunk or headed back to Gibraltar, the remnants of Pedestal would be no match for it. Park instructed his air controllers to announce in clear English that the Italians were about to be attacked by a huge number of non-existent British bombers. He hoped that the enemy would pick up the message, panic and order their warships back to harbour. They did. The RAF also bombed and strafed bases in Sicily to disrupt Axis attacks.

The American sailors from the *Santa Elisa* were slumped all over the decks of HMS *Penn*. Lonnie Dales thought that this was worse than manning a gun. Air raids were fine when you had something to fire back with, but when all you could do was sit or cower and think about what was going to happen if a bomb hit, then they were far less comfortable.

Penn's chief engineer came up on to the deck, sat on the hatch and smoked his pipe. He saw that Dales was shaken and gave him the benefit of an engineer's application of theoretical physics to the practical business of dodging bombs. 'You hear that, son?' 'Yeah, I hear it.' 'Don't worry. If you hear it, it won't hit you. It's a matter of physics. Sound waves travel in concentric circles. You won't hear the one that hits you.' Dales thought about this for a while. It was strangely reassuring. If you could hear it, you had nothing to fear. If you didn't hear it, there was nothing you could do about it.

He looked out ahead. It appeared that the theory would soon be tested again. *Penn* was steaming up at full speed towards the

Ohio, or what was left of her. Dales and Fred Larsen surveyed the tanker with astonishment. She was riding very low in the water, and as they got closer it became clear that the main reason for this was a gaping hole in her port side about 25 feet square from the main deck to below the waterline. Daylight could be seen streaming in from the starboard. The deck that side was peeled back and buckled. Paint was scorched and blackened from the fires and the superstructure and smokestack were pitted with bullet holes and shrapnel. The fuselage of the Junkers 88 lay on the forepeak and one of the wings straddled the side of the bridge. The deck was littered with shell cases, bomb splinters and pieces of aeroplane wreckage.

Discovering that *Ohio* was immobile, HMS *Penn* offered a tow. The weary crew cleared away enough debris for a line to be attached forward. As another bomber flew over, narrowly missing both ships, they tied a 10-inch manila rope between them. The little destroyer moved off, its engines straining as the much bigger tanker began to move. But the *Ohio* would not move straight. The hole in her side pulled her round and eventually the rope parted. Captain Mason signalled that the only hope was to tow from alongside or with one ship forward and another aft to steady her. They were still being attacked every few minutes, and Mason suggested that the destroyer, which, being mobile, was better able to dodge bombs, take off his crew until more arrived. At 1400 *Penn* drew up alongside and the exhausted sailors and gunners left the tanker and slumped down on the decks of the *Penn* alongside the men from the *Santa Elisa*. Nobody expected the tanker to survive, though *Penn* kept circling in case reinforcements arrived.

At 1600 Admiral Burrough turned back to retrace his steps to Gibraltar with the two remaining cruisers and five destroyers. An escort of four minesweepers and seven motor launches came out from Malta to escort the three merchant ships over the last few miles. *Rochester Castle*, *Port Chalmers* and *Melbourne Star* pulled into Grand Harbour, Valletta, at 1825 on 13 August.

Malta's Governor, Lord Gort, was on the Upper Barrakka gardens overlooking the harbour, listening to the cries of '*Wasal il-Konvoy! Diehel il-Konvoy!* (The convoy is here! The convoy is entering the harbour!)'. Amid the continuous roar of Spitfires overhead, a band struck up the Maltese national anthem and a selection of naval marches. The flags were out too – British, American and Maltese. The warships came in with their guns pointing up, and their crews standing on the edges of the decks stripped to the waist.

Meanwhile, seventy miles out to sea, two motor launches and the minesweeper HMS *Rye* had also gone to help the *Ohio*. Captain Mason asked for men to go back on to the tanker and prepare the towing ropes. His entire crew volunteered. *Rye* and *Penn* tried to drag her forward together. Half an hour later a bomber scored another direct hit on *Ohio* with a bomb that went into the engine room, destroying accommodation and choking many of the crew with asbestos dust from the lagging in the boiler room. One gunner was mortally injured. The attempts to tow were still proving unsuccessful, so Captain Mason ordered the crew to the boats and they abandoned ship once again.

At 1900 the crippled *Dorset* sank. Her guardian destroyer, HMS *Bramham*, picked up the survivors and steamed over to help *Penn* and *Rye* with *Ohio* because, in the captain's words, 'I could see even without using my binoculars that they had got it all arse about face and really were not achieving much.' *Penn* and *Rye* had tried towing with one ahead and one astern, but had been no more successful. They agreed that after dark they would try to move with a destroyer towing either side. But *Penn*, on the port side, found that she was getting far too close to the jagged metal of the hole in *Ohio*'s side and, fearing she might lose a propeller, cast off again. They gave up for the rest of the night.

When the sun rose on 14 August it brought a surprise. The *Brisbane Star* struggled into Valletta harbour, a gaping torpedo hole in her bow. She was the fourth of the fourteen merchant ships that had set out from Gibraltar to reach her destination. Of the rest, nine had been sunk and the *Ohio* was still wallowing without power. HMS *Ledbury* arrived to offer more assistance. It would not be long before the bombers came, too.

Lonnie Dales was now rested and restless. He had recovered his nerve and was bored rather than jittery at the prospect of doing nothing. It was clear that none of them was going to get to Malta until that tanker either got there or sank and, given the alternatives, he agreed that they might as well try and get it there. After a brief conversation he and Fred Larsen asked the captain of the *Penn* whether they could go aboard to repair and man the twin 40mm Bofors gun behind the stack.

> My biggest reason, I think, for volunteering with Fred Larsen was the great respect and admiration I had for his leadership. There was an ordinary seaman from the *Santa Elisa* who went with us and two Royal Marines, making a total of five.

The tanker's decks and superstructure were a ruin of twisted, smouldering metal. The three Americans and two Marines picked their way through the debris, avoiding the hot spots, looking for a gun that might still be useable. The 40mm Bofors turned out to be only superficially damaged and the Americans got on with repairing it while the Marines inspected the rest of the guns. When they were satisfied that the gun was working and had fired off a few bursts just to check, they settled down to wait. Larsen was singing quietly to himself: 'Sister Anne, Sister Anne, can you see anyone coming?' Then Dales heard the air-raid alarm from the bridge of one of the nearby destroyers.

> The only other people on board were crew members of the *Ledbury* or the *Penn* who were trying to adjust the cables holding the ships together and help fight fires when they broke out. But they immediately returned to their ships when the air attack came, and we were cut loose, so it left just the five of us on board.

The destroyer captains thought it better that they should be free to manoeuvre during air attacks. If they were near to the *Ohio* when all that fuel went up, then no one would be getting into Malta alive. Dales and Larsen fired the gun at anything that came close but saw a bomb fall near the stern, carrying away the rudder and opening up another hole in the side. The *Ohio* began to settle as the engine room flooded. The British warships came back alongside, much to the relief of the tanker's five defenders, and *Penn* managed to get a starboard tow attached by 1000.

They decided to try 'sandwiching' the tanker. *Penn* attached itself to the starboard side and *Bramham* to the port side, where, being shorter than *Penn*, she was able to stay clear of the dangerous flange of metal. It now appeared that the two destroyers were the only thing keeping the tanker afloat. Captain Mason was advising the captain of the *Bramham*.

> Through trial and error we discovered that if the *Ohio* took a swing to starboard the *Penn* should increase speed by a third of a knot which would very slowly check that swing and would bring her back again. And the swing would go past the right course and come towards my way so then I would increase speed slightly. So in fact the actual course was a zigzag, but it worked extraordinarily well.

Mason then went back aboard the *Ohio* to join Dales and the others.

> *Penn* was endeavouring to keep the engine room pumped dry but the water was gaining six inches per hour. The mean freeboard of the Ohio was now two foot six inches and the stern half of the vessel was expected to fall off at any time. She was drawing forty feet aft instead of twenty-nine feet.

At 1050 the bombers came again: five Italian Stukas and twenty fighter escorts. Dales' gun, and those on the destroyers, fired back, and British fighters joined the fray. A 1,000lb bomb landed close and holed her yet again. But the *Ohio* kept on its slow zigzag towards Malta, her decks little more than two feet above the water. Dales could reach down to get a bucketful to cool his gun barrels. Malta Spitfires circled overhead. The German pilots were evidently as desperate to sink her as Lonnie Dales, Fred Larsen and the Royal Navy were to keep her afloat.

> We took a bomb right down the stack. I thought that was it. It blew the bottom out of the engine room and threw up great clouds of asbestos, which fell on us like snow. But – somehow – the fuel tanks didn't blow. And the engineer had been right about the bombs. All I ever heard was a whirring noise from the ones that got us.
>
> Amazingly after all this she still managed to stay afloat. The *Penn* was circling and trying to protect us as best she could and we kept blasting away too with our guns, in between fighting the fires that kept breaking out.

During the night they tried to take *Ohio* through the British minefields. She made several final attempts to blow herself up as she swung off course. *Bramham*'s tow snapped once but it was made fast again despite the exhaustion of the men. They sighted the Dingli cliffs late in the afternoon, and the other escorts dropped depth charges in case U-boats were near. Lonnie Dales was still at his gun.

> There were still minefields to avoid, not easy when the heavy tanker was pulling the destroyers around, and with the threat of U-boats or E-boats, but all Malta's defences were on full alert to help get us in.

As night approached they could see Malta more clearly, and at 1800 tugs from Valletta came out to help, and HMS *Ledbury* was there for an extra push in the right direction.

At 0800 on 15 August the SS *Ohio* and the two closest escorts in naval history passed the ancient battlements of the Grand Harbour, her deck now freely washed by the sea. There were crowds waving and cheering the length of the Barrakka gardens. Lonnie Dales waved himself silly in reply.

> One of the most emotional sights I ever saw was arriving at Valletta with thousands of people standing on the walls cheering and singing. They had two military bands playing, and inasmuch as we, the survivors of the *Santa Elisa*, were the only Americans in the convoy left, they were playing 'The Star Spangled Banner' for us as we came in.

Immediately men swarmed aboard to pump out the oil. As it finally gave up its cargo, the *Ohio* sank lower and lower in the water. Mimi Cortis was off duty and she watched.

> What a joy to see every pair of hands working to unload the ship, with no time wasted. Any kind of transport was used to take the fuel to its destination.

Almost as soon as the last gallon had left, her keel settled gently on the bottom. Spitfires were constantly overhead and no enemy bombers attempted to disrupt the unloading. Lonnie Dales was taken off for some food and some rest.

> They took us to the underground shipyard, somewhere in a cave, and fed us a very wonderful meal considering the hardships they had been under. The first night I was ashore the building next door disappeared in a bombing raid and I didn't even wake up. I'll never forget the Maltese people stopping us in the street and thanking us. I'll never forget that.

Two weeks later Mimi's sister Mary was married. The reception-party fare consisted of some whisky and gin from a friend who was a quartermaster in the army and Mimi's one-tier wedding cake with its black-market eggs.

Peter Vaux kept dabbing iodine on to his desert sores but it didn't seem to do any good. The scratches he'd picked up when a pair of Messerschmitts had attacked headquarters a few weeks ago had turned nasty and wouldn't go away. But he couldn't afford to be ill now. Things were definitely hotting up again, and it was clear that a big rearrangement of enemy formations was under way. As yet 90 Light Division and the panzers still seemed to be in the north. But they would move late as usual. The full moon towards the end of the month had to be the most likely time.

7 Armoured Division was now based at the foot of Mount Himeimat, and some days Vaux climbed up the 700-foot conical hill to get a view of the next battlefield. Very early one morning his draughtsman, Corporal Barratt, came with him to draw the breathtaking view as the sun rose over the Qattara depression. Sunrise and sunset were the magic hours in the desert, the moments when the low light picked out everything in relief and threw pink and purple all over the drab brown. At times like that you could understand how people could come to love this barren wilderness. Vaux would scan the horizon with his binoculars, wondering what the enemy had hidden behind their ugly craggy stronghold of Jebel Kalakh. One day an RAF liaison officer appeared, complete with a radio truck. He and Vaux immediately struck up a firm friendship. The RAF man was fascinated by Vaux's intelligence maps and explained that he was empowered to call up a recce, so long as Corps did not object. After this they spent several days playing what amounted to a game of battleships, picking a square on the map where one or the other guessed the enemy might be hiding and sending a plane to see what was there. Gradually, they built up a picture of Rommel's latest dispositions.

Next Vaux tried to find out who was in these positions. He made some surprising discoveries. One day armoured cars patrolling the Qattara escarpment brought in thirteen Italians. They had been creeping round the foot of the cliffs and were already past Mount Himeimat when the armoured cars spotted them. First they tried to hide, then there was a shoot-out in a wadi. They had submachine-guns and it took a lot of infantry to overwhelm them. Even when they were finally hauled in, the Italians would not talk. Paxton soon had them identified: they were the colourfully named Cacciatori di Africa – the African hunters. But not one of them would reveal the purpose of their patrol, except to imply that it was secret and very important. And no one would say what division they were in.

Paxton and Vaux interrogated them one by one and got nowhere until Vaux discovered in one man's wallet a photograph of parachutists whizzing down a wire. 'Are you part of the Folgore parachute division?' he asked. The man wouldn't answer. But one of the soldiers who'd brought them in said, 'Actually, sir, I think one of them had something like "Folgore" written on his helmet.' 'Go and get it,' ordered Vaux. But the helmet had disappeared. Vaux separated the captain from the rest and, using just about the oldest trick in the book, told him a flat lie. 'Your men tell me you belong to Folgore Division, is that right?' The Italian immediately admitted that he did. So now Vaux knew who was positioned opposite.

A few days later they caught a German parachutist, who revealed that he belonged to an élite formation that Vaux had been worrying about for some time. The German's commanding officer was a Major Ramcke, a much-decorated war hero who was famous for the part he'd played in the capture of Crete in 1941. But now his men were being used as infantry of the line. Vaux wondered whether they were being introduced to desert conditions prior to some operation way behind 7 Armoured Division's lines. Rommel hadn't used parachutists before, but he was nothing if not adventurous.

From another prisoner Vaux discovered that a second celebrated parachutist, Major Burckhardt, was leading a unit near by, and was supposed to be trying out lots of new equipment, including a mysterious recoilless anti-tank gun. The picture was beginning to clear: Italians stiffened by German parachutists in the front line, and all the armour withdrawn and grouped together somewhere ready for the big offensive.

The last few days had seen a lot of coming and going on the British side, too. A remarkably youthful lieutenant-colonel called Mike Carver turned up at divisional headquarters as deputy to 'Wingy' Renton. Then Bernard Montgomery himself appeared, along with their new corps commander, Brian Horrocks. Horrocks was all toothy smiles; Montgomery barely bothered to smile at all. Small and birdlike, he looked faintly ridiculous in shorts, with reddening knees. He had acquired an incongruous hat from some New Zealander along the way. But his manner was fast and fearsome. 'He looks rather like a stoat', was Donald Reid's opinion. 'Very curious,' Vaux replied. 'We'll soon see how he turns out.'

Neville Gillman had a new gunner for his Crusader tank, an old and trusty trooper called Ernest Ickeringill, universally known as 'Gill', a quiet and very solid man from Lancashire. Gill was twenty-nine years old and married with two children. There was a new driver too, Corporal Kennedy, also in his late twenties, and someone who had seen plenty of fighting. The replacement radio operator, Lance Corporal Noel Willows, was younger. He came from Mill Hill and Gillman knew his aunt and uncle. He was confident that they would make a cracking crew.

Gillman's squadron commander, Viscount Cranley, had recovered from his dysentery and his dinner with Churchill. He travelled back from Cairo to the Sharpshooters' camp on a 15cwt truck loaded with beer, tea, sugar, tinned milk, tinned fruit and whisky. Thus fortified, the squadron began practising for its role in Rommel's expected offensive.

Although Churchill had insisted to his allies that an invasion of France was impractical, plans for a large-scale raid on the French coast, including tanks and six thousand men, were already complete. The intention was to kill and capture hundreds of enemy troops; force the Luftwaffe into a great battle over the sea, make the Germans deploy more men in western France to guard against future attacks, and learn valuable lessons about amphibious operations in the future. Lord Louis Mountbatten's Combined Operations headquarters was responsible for planning, along with General Montgomery in the weeks before he had left for the desert. They wanted to find out how easy it would be to get tanks ashore under fire, and whether it might be possible to seize a working port. There was a political motive, too: to demonstrate to the Russians and the occupied peoples of Europe that Britain could and would strike hard across the Channel.

The chosen target was Dieppe, a medium-sized commercial port in Normandy with a long-standing ferry link to Newhaven on the Sussex coast. The plan called for a frontal attack on the mile-long sea front, supported by two other landings, each about a mile either side of the town. In addition, two commando raids would take place near by. Canadians would make up 83 per cent of the assault force. Two hundred thousand Canadian troops were already stationed in Britain and many had been waiting for something to do since 1940.

When he learned of the plans, Roosevelt requested that some US Rangers join in. After six months of war, he wanted to see American soldiers in combat with the Germans and, after all the bad news from North Africa, it would be good for the American people to hear about this exciting new unit.

At Achnacarry, forty Rangers were assigned to 3 Commando and four to 4 Commando: William Brady, Franklin Koons, Kenneth Stempson and – as Darby himself had promised – Alex

Szima. The leader of 4 Commando, Lord Lovat, was already a legend, famous for taking his hunting horn into battle.

> Darby personally instructed me on how to address Lovat and gave me a handwritten note: 'I am Sgt Szima, 1st American Commandos, reporting to Lt Col. *The Lord* Lovat', with a PS reading 'and by God don't forget the *Lord*'. He made me rehearse it several times. But when I finally met Lord Lovat he cut me off right after my name.

At Weymouth, Szima boarded the *Prince Albert*, the commandos' main assault ship. There he met Major Derek Mills-Roberts, who would be second-in-command on the raid.

> As we boarded the *Prince Albert* I mistook him for a common deckhand. So he had good reason to scrutinise me more than the rest of the Americans attached.

4 Commando and its four US Rangers practised together. Their target was a coastal gun battery near the village of Varengeville, six 150mm guns mounted on revolving platforms in individual concrete pits. In preparation they rehearsed street fighting and close assault tactics, crossing barbed wire and bayonet charges.

> We performed miserably at this while the commandos excelled and could hardly wait for the real thing.
> Finally we got a chance to do something we were good at. I was ordered to fire five rounds into a row of targets. I got an eight-inch grouping. Major Mills-Roberts and everybody else that was firing rushed down to inspect. The target keeper said, 'That's probably a record.' When I returned I was greeted by Mills-Roberts, who said, 'Are you a member of the US Army Rifle Team?' I replied, 'No, sir, I'm a bartender from Dayton, Ohio.'

Szima's success on the range had something to do with his

brand-new Garand M1 rifle, which had just been issued to American forces and was superior to anything the British had.

The enlisted ranks took notice and I was labelled a 'Mystery Man' because of my performance with a rifle, and the scar on my left cheek. I told them it was from a fight I'd had with a Chicago gangster.

Everyone was given a job to rehearse – or, in Alex Szima's case, several jobs.

I was told that, because of my performance on the rifle range, the M1 rifle was being classified as an automatic weapon and so I was to team up with a commando called Heggarty who had a tommy gun. Our first job was to clear some houses on the way up to the battery. Then we would snipe at the enemy for forty minutes or so until the main force assaulted the guns. After that my role was to establish a rearguard along with another commando called McDonough who would have a 'Boys' anti-tank rifle.

In the days before the raid, Szima and his fellow Rangers were based on the *Prince Albert* and subject, once again, to British cooking.

Breakfast at Achnacarry had introduced us to the delights of salted porridge with kippered herrings and tea. The menu was the same aboard the *Albert* with a rotation of sausage with seventy-five per cent oatmeal filler. For supper it was mostly mutton and we were forewarned of this when some time during the day you saw a frozen sheep carcass tossed up out of the hold, and hosed down with seawater to expedite thawing. However, all this was compensated for each noon, when everyone on board got a tot of 140-proof rum, while declaring 'God Save the King' – even we Yankees.

Szima didn't feel afraid, or at least he told himself that he didn't feel afraid. It was more the feeling you got before getting up on stage, like the time he'd been in the high-school tumbling team: anticipation, agitation, the urge to get it done and get it over with. 'Americans are a bit like the crusaders of old.' He'd said that to lots of people. 'They accept any challenge and they look fear in the eye.' Yes, this is what he had wanted all along, the chance to be part of something important and exciting, the chance to show what Rangers could do, what Yanks could do and, damn it, what a barman from Dayton, Ohio, could do.

Chapter 17

18–19 August

Alex Szima was aboard *Prince Albert* when Lord Mountbatten visited 4 Commando on the evening of 18 August. 'Tomorrow we deal the Hun a bloody blow,' he announced. 'We expect heavy casualties – maybe as much as sixty per cent – and to those of you that will die, may God have mercy on your souls.' Szima did not find this particularly encouraging.

Szima joined Brady and the other two young Americans below decks in an old pre-match basketball routine. Four hands joined in a tight clasp as Brady yelled, 'Sixty per cent casualties! Piss on that! We're going to be in the forty per cent, right?' 'Right!'

> I said to myself, Well, Szima, this is your chance; it doesn't come to all men so don't fail yourself, and I knew that – like any competition – if you go in scared you lose your edge. So it was easy for me to do some pre-raid psyching of myself. I knew I'd be important and I didn't want to let anyone down.

During the evening of 18 August 250 ships left England. At about 0300 they ran into a small German coastal convoy and the E-boats that were protecting it. Shots were exchanged and star shells illuminated the scene. The chance of surprise had now passed.

But the ships were told to proceed as planned.

As the main force moved towards Dieppe, 4 Commando steered for Varengeville and its gun battery. By now they were all wearing black face paint and dark knitted woollen hats, preferred to steel helmets because of the need for speed. Lovat reminded his men that commandos did *not* lie down under fire. He expected to see everyone running up the beach no matter what. Only the wounded were allowed to take cover.

Lovat had split his 250 men into two sections. Szima and Franklin Koons were with 86 others under the command of Major Mills-Roberts. They were to land at a small beach called Orange One, directly below the battery, while Lovat led the larger group to Orange Two, about a mile farther west. Mills-Roberts' team would pin the defenders down while Lovat's group worked their way around the back for the final assault on the guns.

They lowered themselves into landing craft and moved off towards the distant shore.

I was dozing, in part due to the rum I had purchased from a sailor and shared between the four of us on the *Prince Albert*. I stuck my head up in the landing craft and saw the cliffs and a lighthouse. There was so much light that you could have read a newspaper. Then crash! The ramp dropped, and we were ashore.

It was 0500 and, right on cue, cannon-firing Hurricanes roared in above to attack the gun battery, and distract any Germans who might be watching the commandos land. Mills-Roberts led his men on to the beach and over the sand at a steady run. At the top was the opening of a small ravine, the commandos' route up to a small group of houses and farm buildings and the gun emplacements that lay beyond them.

Thick entanglements of barbed wire and piles of railroad sleepers barred their way. These had been anticipated and long, thin explosive charges, known as Bangalore torpedoes, were brought forward. Mills-Roberts ordered everyone to hug the side of the cliffs. Szima clamped his hands over his ears as loose sand and dirt flew all around. He turned to see a neat hole cut right through the tangled wire.

We moved through the opening and went up the ravine, pushing through bracken. I could hear Mills-Roberts barking orders.

Some distance beyond the top of the ravine were two houses which, Intelligence had told them, were occupied by German soldiers. Szima's job was to clear them along with a commando called Heggarty. Szima eased the safety catch off his M1 and followed Heggarty towards the first house. Its occupants had already fled. They crossed to the second house and moved cautiously through an open door. The ground floor was deserted. Szima, with Heggarty covering him, began to climb the staircase, laying his boots on the steps as quietly as a man can with a full pack on his back. He was still having the conversation with himself that had begun on the *Prince Albert*. 'This is your chance.' 'It doesn't come to all men.' 'Don't fail yourself!' He tried the first handle he came across. It refused to move. He aimed a kick at the door and fired as it burst open. Heggarty was firing his tommy gun into a second bedroom. But both were empty.

With the two houses checked, Szima and Heggarty rejoined the other commandos as they made their way through the bracken towards the gun emplacements.

I went up there with a couple of guys, but Mills-Roberts ordered us back to do our sniping. So we crawled along a hedgerow – no more than a belly-button high – in the direction of an old barn.

About forty yards away Szima spotted a large, multi-barrelled anti-aircraft gun with car tyres piled around it. German soldiers were gathered around the gun. 'They looked like puppets just sitting there, not moving.' Szima and Heggarty reached the barn unobserved by the anti-aircraft gunners, just as a German soldier began to run down from its upper floor. This, he said to himself, is getting kind of hairy.

> I couldn't see the German, but I heard him coming. I said something to Heggarty, who was behind a tree. He lowered his sub-machine-gun and, as the guy came out of the barn, he emptied the entire clip or drum, whatever he had, right into him. I had all the rounds going right past me, no more than four feet away. As I looked towards the German, he was almost cut in half. Part of his body was forwards and the other part was backwards.
>
> I wanted to get the hell out of there. I started to make my way around the side of the barn, and I saw the front of a wagon. Heggarty then hollered, 'Look out, Yank!' I just made it around the bend and approached the wagon when a stick grenade came out of the window of the barn and went off near where I had been standing. Another commando yelled out, 'Jocko, I'll get him.' The commandos always referred to each other as 'Jocko'. Heggarty finally got a bead on this grenade-throwing guy and got him. He was up there in the barn screaming.

Slightly dazed by all the close-up gunfire, Szima fumbled for one of the grenades from his bandoleer. He withdrew the pin and – remembering the instruction that accuracy comes from 'shot-putting' rather than throwing – carefully pulled the grenade back to near his cheek. Then he pushed his arm towards the upper window of the barn and let go. There was a loud explosion in the room where the man had been screaming and, after that, no more noise of any kind. It's likely that at this moment Alex Szima became the first American to kill a German soldier in the Second World War.

William Spearman was a commando in Lovat's main group. He had recently rejoined the unit after recovering from an injury sustained during a raid on Boulogne. Lovat's men were not as fortunate as Mills-Roberts' had been. Just before they landed, machinegun fire sliced across their landing craft. This was armoured, which gave some protection, but Captain Gordon Webb was wounded in the right shoulder. 'Quick, get out of the boat! Over the side, now,' Webb shouted. 'Don't all file up at the front!' He put his rifle over his left shoulder because of the wound, and, as he passed him, Lovat called out that he would be on a charge for that the next day.

True to his words at the briefing, Lovat strode up the beach, ignoring the gunfire and the cries of the men who fell to it. Following his commander, Spearman crossed the sand and reached the safety of the sand dunes and the bracken.

> Your one inclination was to dig yourself a hole, but Lovat had made it quite clear that no one was to lie down on the beach.

Their landing craft pulled away, drawing fire and giving the commandos time to organise themselves. Their first obstacle was barbed wire so thick that the Bangalore torpedoes couldn't clear it. Men threw themselves on to the wire to make it sag, while others climbed over them to get through. By now mortars were falling, killing eight commandos. Led by Lovat, who was carrying his favourite hunting rifle, they set off up the left bank of the little River Saane, moving in single file and encountering no more opposition while they made good speed for their rendezvous with the Mills-Roberts group. But everyone knew that German reinforcements would soon be on their way.

Alex Szima was standing near the old farm wagon in the court-yard of the barn. By now the guards knew they were under attack by more than fighter planes. Szima spotted one carrying a rifle about a hundred yards away at a small crossroads. At the same moment he was himself spotted.

I hit the deck and said to myself, Oh, God! and bingo, one round hit the concrete near me. I rolled over, little bits of concrete in my eyes. I started to move under the wagon to try to get a shot at this guy. Then a round caught me on the top of my cap, went right through it and tore it off. By reflex, I took the trouble to pick the thing up.

Other commandos were near by. One stood next to the wagon and fired a submachine-gun.

He kept firing and all the spent cartridges were falling on me and on the back of my neck and all over my arms. He became my biggest problem. So I got up and threw myself right into a steaming manure pile. I put my cap back on and then I saw the guard, who was now hiding in a ditch.

I shouted out in excitement, 'I see him.' And one of the commando officers shouted back, 'Well, get him, then, Yank! Get him.' I barrel-sighted my rifle, since I had horse shit all over the sight, and I fired off six rounds. I think I got him with every one. That was the end of him.

From the walls of the courtyard Szima had a clear view of the battery as it came under attack from commandos moving forward through the woods and orchards. Ranger Franklin Koons was there too. He had found a good sniping position in a nearby stable. Szima caught sight of a group of German soldiers about 150 yards away. In their white T-shirts and shiny black helmets they were as clear to him as any rifle-range target.

I fired a couple of clips at this group and at the anti-aircraft gun position. Somebody told me to change position then because some rifle fire was coming down at us.

When a high-velocity bullet goes near you, the air current will suck by with a quick 'whoosh, whoosh' sound. Then you hear the crack of the shot itself. It's strange, but you get a sense of the ones that are after you. At least, that's how I found it, and this was the first time anyone had ever taken a shot at me in my whole life.

Before he could relocate, Szima looked up and saw a German moving over the roof of a barn. He stood up and fired eight rounds. As the man tried to escape over the ridge, the heavy roof slates jumped and cracked all around him, sliding down and breaking on the ground. An officer shouted, 'Hold it, Yank!' and told him to stop firing in that direction because Lord Lovat's group was due to come that way at any moment. Before he had a chance to explain that there had been an enemy soldier heading their way, Szima saw four more Germans appear on the roof of another small house. He rapidly shot off two clips of M1 ammunition, knocking two of them down.

The German anti-aircraft gunners were beginning to panic. As fire burst around them, some sought shelter behind piles of sandbags. Lovat was ready to assault the main gun emplacements. It was 0630 now, and more fighters swept down, releasing smoke bombs to cover the attack. Then Szima heard something that had not figured in any of his training – the tuneless whine of a Scottish piper. Lord Lovat ordered his men to charge.

The commandos believed in the shock effect of noise and violence. As Lovat's men drove forward, bayonets fixed, they let out cries that temporarily drowned out the sound of the pipes. These were soon replaced by the cries of the men on the receiving end. Alex Szima realised that this was what all the training had been for.

People like commandos and Rangers, we're turned into that one per cent of humanity that can be animal in their activity. When the commandos charged you could not tell the screams of the doomed from the doomers.

William Spearman was one of the 'doomers', running and yelling through the smoke. They crossed 250 yards of open ground, losing both officers at the head of the charge to machinegun fire. Captain Patrick Porteous took control and led them into the battery, winning a Victoria Cross in the process. Spearman knew what bayonets could do: he'd had a bayonet wound himself. He remembered the German standing over him and lunging down. Only the double thickness of webbing on his belt had saved him. A hundred commandos went with Spearman into the gun emplacements. Inside they found three hundred German gunners. Within minutes, almost all were dead.

> You don't have time to feel sorry for them; I mean, you kill people and afterwards you think, was it necessary? But at the time, there was no stopping us.

The guns were destroyed by explosive charges. It was time for 4 Commando to evacuate before German reinforcements arrived. Several commandos had been killed or wounded around the barn, and Alex Szima had lost contact with Franklin Koons.

> We took the doors off houses and put the wounded men on the doors. Four German prisoners carried some of the wounded men. They all made the trek back to the beach. I fell back with them before stopping en route and forming the rearguard.

All the remaining commandos had to withdraw past Szima and McDonough, who had the Boys anti-tank rifle. Their orders were to wait for the last straggler to disappear around the bend of the track down to the beach before following to their next defensive position. As no enemy came near, this gave Szima the opportunity to think for the first time since he had kicked open that bedroom door. But he was feeling strangely numb.

We lay there listening to the quiet of the many dead. There were over a hundred bodies all around. I was waiting for one of them to get up and start firing, but no one did.

For several minutes there was silence, punctuated by occasional explosions from the ruined gun positions and more distant echoes of the fighting in Dieppe. Szima listened out for a whistle in the dark that would identify an approaching soldier as a commando. He'd faced this test and not broken down, or rolled away to hide in a ditch or an outhouse. Was he proud? Yes, but not exultantly so. Mostly he just felt tired, and surprised that so much carnage could be created so quickly. He took a few deep breaths of the damp morning air and reminded himself that his test was not over yet.

Suddenly I heard heavy footsteps on the other side of the hedgerow, to my right. Logically I knew it had to be Germans. I took a position at the gate and raised my rifle. Out came Corporal Koons. I sent him up the road to catch up with the slowly withdrawing commandos.

Szima picked up the front handle of the anti-tank rifle and, with McDonough holding the other end, half ran and half stumbled to the bend in the road, his movement restricted by the heavy smoke generator in his pack. He had considered setting it off at the first rearguard position, but decided against it. That probably saved many lives, including his own, for if he had produced a thick smokescreen higher up the road it would have obscured the German lorry that suddenly drove around a corner and straight towards his new position.

Szima told McDonough that if the lorry came past the farmhouse about 200 yards away they should both open fire. It came to a sudden halt by the farm gate and a soldier climbed out of the driver's cab and went to investigate. Seconds later he returned to the truck.

I yelled, 'Fire!' and he hit it right in the engine. The whole thing shook and men started jumping out, about twenty of them. I stood up and fired eight rounds myself, then we both hauled ass to the next bend.

Szima grabbed the front end of the anti-tank rifle again as he and McDonough dashed to their third position. One of them tripped and they both went down. Rifle fire was now zipping through the leaves. They picked up their packs and rifles and stumbled on towards the beach.

We reached the perimeter and McDonough gave the password 'monkey nuts', which I can honestly say I had forgotten. I saw a dead German on the ground and I was going to take his helmet off for a souvenir. But it was all gooey and messed up, and flies were all over it, so I said, 'The hell with it.'

The perimeter line was a few hundred yards from the ravine that led down to the beach. Szima found an officer and told him about the lorry. The commando said that other German forces were around too and estimated that they had about fifteen minutes to get out. He ordered Szima and McDonough to run across a field leading to the top of the ravine. Although more bullets flew their way, they made it there safely to discover that their landing craft were hidden behind a smoke bank about seventy-five yards from the beach, and a steady line of commandos were walking in waist-deep water out into the smoke.

A stream of commandos ran and fell down the ravine. Every other one appeared to have a Bren gun. The ten or twelve of us just stood and hoped somehow that the smoke would return to the beach, because it became obvious that we no longer had a perimeter defence.

All their canisters were burning now, but the smoke was drifting out to sea, leaving the remaining soldiers feeling ever more exposed. As they crouched by the side of the cliffs they could hear German voices a few hundred yards above. It was beginning to look like a choice between surrender or a bullet in the back as they waded out to sea.

> Then a miracle, in the form of a Boston bomber, came down, made a 180-degree turn, and began laying smoke directly on top of us. This really helped us clear the first hundred yards of beach without the Germans firing.
>
> The smoke was thick and choking but very welcome. Vision was only a few feet but we could hear commandos shouting directions. I was holding the front end of the anti-tank rifle on my shoulder, hearing rounds hit the water, knowing that if I drifted either right or left the two of us were doomed. That was definitely the worst part of the whole thing.

McDonough was first to reach the waiting landing craft, as Szima began to drink salt water. A friendly Scottish voice told him, 'Don't worry, Yank, there will be another boat in a minute.' But he couldn't see one.

> So I clung to the side trappings and was dragged about a hundred yards. When they stopped to set up the anti-tank rifle, I hollered. They started to fire and finally someone took my rifle and my arm, but not before my head got the full effect of a muzzle blast about three feet away.

4 Commando had achieved all its objectives, but this was the only bright spot in an otherwise calamitous day.

The Royal Regiment of Canada landed at Blue Beach, a mile to the north-east of Dieppe, and failed to make any impression on the defences. The beach was short, narrow and dominated by cliffs. It was about 250 yards long and only 50 yards wide at high tide. There was a twelve-foot-high sea wall, topped with barbed wire and studded by concrete pillboxes, from which machine-guns covered the beach. All the defending troops were on high alert by the time the first Canadian landing craft came into view. Thomas Hunter was one of the first to make the shoreline:

> The raid was supposed to be in the dark, but we were delayed because a ship got tangled up. It was broad daylight as we approached the beach. They dropped the front and we jumped in. We were up to our chests in water, and I had to pull a buggy with the three-inch mortar and the mortar bombs up the beach.

Machinegun fire swept through the men, cutting down one after another.

> We were slaughtered. We were up against cliffs either side, and no way out, pillboxes with machineguns at either end of the beach, machineguns just raking away killing everybody that came off the ships.
>
> The guy who was pulling the buggy with me got shot, and I couldn't pull it by myself because it weighed three hundred pounds, so I left it.

Hunter crawled into a little niche in the cliffs and started aiming rifle fire at the tiny slits in the concrete pillboxes.

> Jimmy Elliot was firing into one and I faced another one, and we were just firing into them. We had rounds and rounds of ammunition, we just kept loading. I don't know how they missed us. They were throwing grenades, one came near me but I threw it in the water. I was very calm. There's nothing you can do about it, I told Elliot. 'Can't do much about it now, we're stuck here, we'll just survive as long as we can.'

(*Right*) Mimi Cortis

(*Below*) A Valletta street in
the spring of 1942

'Hornblower's navy in action'. The escort for Operation Pedestal

Pedestal under air attack

'Lonnie' Dales

The *Ohio* enters Valletta harbour between *HMS Penn* and *HMS Bramham*, 15
August 1942

The aftermath of the Dieppe raid: part of the main beach

Canadian prisoners in the centre of Dieppe

Alex Szima accepts a light from a commando on his return from Dieppe

Therese Steiner

A cinema in Guernsey showing *Victory in the West*

" La Gazette Officielle "

REWARD OF £25

A REWARD OF £25 WILL BE GIVEN TO THE PERSON WHO FIRST GIVES TO THE INSPECTOR OF POLICE INFORMATION LEAD-ING TO THE CONVICTION OF ANYONE (NOT ALREADY DISCOVERED) FOR THE OFFENCE OF MARKING ON ANY GATE, WALL OR OTHER PLACE WHATSOEVER VISIBLE TO THE PUBLIC THE LETTER " V " OR ANY OTHER SIGN OR ANY WORD OR WORDS CALCULATED TO OFFEND THE GERMAN AUTHORITIES OR SOLDIERS.

THIS 8th DAY OF JULY, 1941

VICTOR G. CAREY,

Bailiff.

Guernsey's Bailiff, Victor Carey, attempts to smooth relations between islanders and occupiers

A British policeman closes the door of a German staff car outside the German commander's HQ in Guernsey.

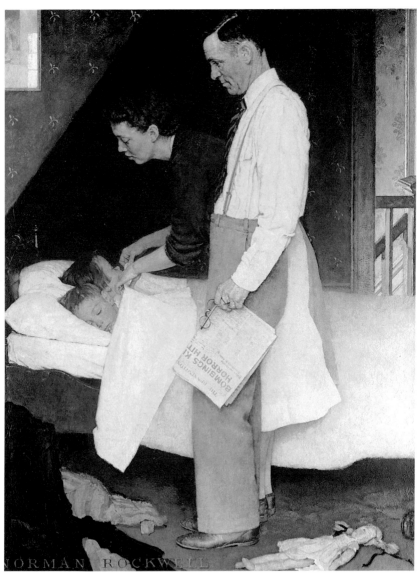

'Freedom from Fear' – Norman Rockwell's original painting for one
of Roosevelt's 'Four Freedoms' posters

All along the beach men were lying wounded with medical orderlies bandaging them as best they could.

> We honestly didn't expect to live. Just stay quiet and see what
> happens, I thought, and then, How did I get into this mess?

At the edge of the shore, red-tinged waves washed the bodies
backwards and forwards. Journalist Ross Munro called Blue Beach
'the grimmest beach of the Dieppe raid. It was khaki-coloured
with the bodies of boys from Central Ontario.' The scene was so
shocking that some of the landing craft were reluctant to approach
it. Seeing what awaited them, soldiers abandoned their equipment and leapt off their landing craft and tried to swim back out
to sea. As survivors hugged the sea wall and cliffs, an officer
screamed, 'It's hopeless, get back to the boats if you can.' At 0700
a call went out asking for vessels to evacuate survivors. Only one
responded. Troops soon surrounded it and the crew had to beat
them off with boat hooks. Then it capsized. The Royal Regiment
surrendered at 0830.

> Someone up ahead of us had put up a white flag. The Germans
> came down beside us. One of them spoke English quite well,
> he'd been to school in California. He said to me, 'What took you
> so long to give up?'

The main Canadian force landed on Dieppe's main beach, just
as an air and naval bombardment hit the German defences. Lt
Col. R.R. Labatt was proud to be leading the Royal Hamilton
Light Infantry into battle for the first time. On the landing craft
his men were calling out to each other. 'It's just like a normal
moonlight excursion, but without the girls.' 'Drinks on me in
Newhaven tonight!'

The smoke from the barrage cleared, revealing that few of the
strongpoints had been damaged. The Canadians could see German
soldiers setting up machinegun and mortar positions inside houses

and hotels facing the sea. As they struggled up the beaches, Labatt's men were caught in murderous crossfire. Some of them, with a handful of tanks, made the concrete esplanade and even captured a few buildings. But most remained pinned down on or near the beach. They had planned to follow the tanks deep into the town, but most of their tracked vehicles found it impossible to manoeuvre on the shingle and made easy targets.

Corporal Laurens Pals landed in the middle of the beach. All around him were bodies and broken-down tanks.

> The barges, soon as they hit the beach, they were lucky to get ashore at all. Some of them, instead of pumping water out of their bilges, you could see they were pumping blood. Then there was the continuous noise: dogfights overhead, planes hitting the water right alongside of you and bombs and shells.

Pals pulled his injured friends out of the water and carried them to a makeshift field hospital in one of the captured buildings. The Canadians had charged into a deathtrap and there was little they could do about it but try to bring small-arms fire on to the German positions and wait for evacuation. At 1100 Pals was ordered to surrender. He walked behind the one German prisoner his unit had managed to take, holding a white flag.

Of the 4,963 Canadians who had crossed the sea, 3,369 were killed, wounded or captured. Hunter and Pals were soon on their way to a prisoner-of-war camp in Germany, Stalag 8B, where Don Bruce had been held for the last month.

Chapter 18

19–26 August

Harry Hopkins had been an isolationist once, one of those who couldn't understand why Roosevelt wasted so much time on another European squabble. That was before his visit to London in early 1941, when he'd spent his first night in Claridge's listening to the bombs fall. An old friend at the US embassy, Hershell Johnson, told him that isolationism was like being caught in a burning building and not taking sides between the fire department and the flames.

He'd come to love England. After visiting Chequers he wrote, 'It is only when you see that country in spring that you begin to understand why the English have written the best goddamn poetry in the world.' And the English loved him too. He treasured a letter from a retired British naval officer from Farnham thanking America for her help and ending 'without you by our side, this inhuman tyranny would enslave the world'.

London's top people queued up to meet him. On one of his visits a message pad was waiting at the hotel reception desk:

1. Lord Halifax would like you to call him at the Dorchester Hotel. He is in room 708.
2. Lord Beaverbrook asked that you be kind enough to call him at Mayfair 1536.

3. The Lord Louis Mountbatten telephoned at 2025 hours. He will call you later in the evening. Should you care to reach Lord Louis contact could be made through his Flag Lieutenant at Whitehall 5422, extension 371.

4. Mrs Randolph Churchill telephoned to say that she has been advised of Major Churchill's safe arrival in New York. Her telephone number is Mayfair 5975.

Roosevelt – mindful of Hopkins' dreadful health – would send cables reminding him to take his medicine and get some early nights, but he escaped most evenings to play cards, visit a night-club or tour some bars. He walked the streets of the battered city. He found it inspired him. He wrote an article for an American magazine to answer the question 'What is the war for?'

> The war is to put free people's energy and creativity to work. To produce better homes, better clothing, more food, a surer rela-tionship with the land than they will find in any victory of this so-called superior Germanic race . . . Victory for the democra-cies will mean a new world order.

Hopkins drafted another paragraph to follow, which he then crossed out, probably because he did not want to give offence to America's allies.

> The democratic peoples do not propose to permit the minority of predatory interests among us to dominate policies which will control the world after Hitler's defeat. And just as that defeat must not result in the oppression of the German people themselves, by the same token it must result in the vast expansion of the good things of life to masses of people that for years have been disinherited.

'The minority of predatory interests among us.' Who did he mean? The old European empires whose feuding had created war and economic disaster? Or the rich in every country who shared too little of the 'good things of life' with their fellow citizens?

No matter how charming he found British lords and their ladies, the man who was responsible for all the Sherman tanks and Chevrolet trucks was motivated by factors that would not have been instantly understood in most London clubs. Hopkins' war was for social and economic change. It was the New Deal gone global. Although Churchill had got his way on the immediate war strategy, he was to discover that the future men like Harry Hopkins had in mind would be very different to the past.

At Newhaven the cameramen were waiting to capture the raiders' return. But only among the men of 4 Commando could they find the euphoria of a job well done. Alex Szima and the other Rangers were quickly pushed in front of the cameras.

> Commandos seem to be camera shy and with the four of us being interviewed and photographed extensively, it was very awkward. They were all impatient to get to the grog building for free beer and rum, and the cameraman wasn't allowed in the building.
>
> With my sensitivity to not being photographed from the left because of my scar, my only recourse was to take the initiative. I convinced the cameraman to find me a dry cigarette, which a commando then lit, making a great picture that went all round the world.

Szima couldn't settle. He felt exhausted but sleep would not easily come. The commandos were all issued with rail warrants for Troon back in Scotland. 'A fun place?' Szima asked. 'Avoid it if you can,' was the reply. So the Americans decided to stay in London instead.

Szima saw the morning newspapers, full of accounts of the raid on Dieppe and describing it as a huge success. He had seen many casualties during the journey back from France, and spoken to survivors from the shattered Canadian units. But he was proud of his own part, proud too that he had just helped write the first page in the history of the US Rangers. What he really needed was a drink.

There were girls along the fringe of Green Park, in the narrow streets running north from Piccadilly and all around the Regent's Palace Hotel, weaving between the glow of cigarettes, walking and bumping into the soldiers and the airmen. 'Oh, excuse me, handsome.' Some carried torches to illuminate their legs as they passed. Then a turned head and a smile. 'Like what you see, darling? *Heaven's* above!' Others huddled in doorways and the entrance to dark alleys, murmuring the age-old questions while their pimps offered bottles of whisky for four pounds ten shillings each. 'Fancy a good time, Yank?' Szima was soon talked into spending a pound on what turned out to be a not particularly good time after all. She kept talking about her husband in the Eighth Army.

The prostitute's husband was most likely sitting through one of the lectures that Montgomery made his soldiers attend, or undergoing fitness training, or familiarising himself with new equipment, all part of Monty's way of building his new model army.

Bernard Montgomery loved drills, sports, physical training routines, and would spend hours planning such things in intricate, even obsessive detail. Even as an officer cadet, he'd communicated a sense of keenness and efficiency. The Great War, during which he won the DSO and nearly died of his wounds, imbued him with a horror of bad generalship. 'Poor planning,' he would repeat, 'means the unnecessary deaths of brave men.'

Monkish in his private life, he told junior officers that they had to choose between being a good husband and a good soldier. He excelled at Camberley Staff College in the 1920s and won the admiration, if not the liking, of both Brooke and Alexander.

Then in 1927, to everyone's great surprise, he married. After bearing him one child, his wife died in 1937. This appeared to make Montgomery colder and more distant than ever, his air of superiority hardening into arrogance.

When he took over Eighth Army he was needlessly hard on Auchinleck, who had not yet formally handed over control, and took pleasure in giving orders to men still officially under his predecessor's command. 'It was with an insubordinate smile that I fell asleep: I was issuing orders to an Army which someone else reckoned he commanded.' At Sandhurst, he had once set fire to the shirt-tails of a pinioned victim and he was still capable of cruelty. He wrote twisted reports branding Auchinleck and Chink defeatists who had planned to retreat from Alamein as they had from Tobruk.

Montgomery was most decidedly not one of the 'nice chaps' about whom Air Marshal Tedder had complained to Churchill. Given the state of relations between the generals of Eighth Army when he took it over, this was probably no bad thing. Those who met him came away impressed with his quick confidence and the way he made it clear that orders were orders, rather than the basis for further discussion.

One of his favourite lectures at Camberley had been entitled 'The Registering of Personality' (Chink had cut the class). Now he put it into effect. He went among the men, dressed like them, and talked to them. If the past was all disaster and muddle and bad leadership – at least the way Montgomery told it – then the future would be different. He believed that his soldiers should know what they were being asked to risk their lives for, and he made a special effort to welcome the lecturers of the new Army Bureau of Current Affairs (ABCA). Doubtless some of the men smoked and sniggered at the back, but many others listened. In the 1945 general election, defeated Conservative candidates would blame ABCA's civilian lecturers for swinging the military vote against them.

Attitudes back home were shifting too. Ten million listened to the BBC's *Brains Trust* every week and heard academics, scientists and writers discussing the pressing issues of the war and the future. William Beveridge, George Orwell and J. B. Priestley were all regular panellists, and a generally left-of-centre tone dominated. There was a similar feel to Humphrey Jennings' cinema documentaries, which focused on the common man and featured scenes in which people gathered in pubs or amid bombed-out buildings and talked of the better, cleaner, fairer Britain that was to come. His *Listen to Britain*, released in 1942, opens with an evocative montage: a factory at dusk, men and women in a dance hall, farm workers walking down a country lane, a crowd at a railway station, smoke rising from northern mill chimneys; and then a Spitfire roaring overhead. The message was clear. This was a war not for God, King and Empire, but for the people at the bus stop.

The new spirit touched millions who would never consider themselves socialists. It was something collective, organised, professional; something *modern*. It was fed by the advice that flowed from Whitehall and by the everyday experiences of living in a newly centralised state. Economic planning, directed labour, factory committees, all prompted the question: if cooperation like this is possible in times of war, then why not later? And since public management seemed to be synonymous with efficiency, why not take control of railway companies, coal mines and hospitals too? By the summer of 1942 the number of pleats, the length of turn-ups, the width of lapels, the number of buttons, even the design of underwear were set by the state. Soon furniture designs, linoleum, sheets, blankets and mattresses were similarly controlled, and only available to those with the required chits and coupons. This was a mobilised, socialised, utility Britain whose people were busy fire-watching and digging vegetable patches from the brambles at the side of railway lines. 'I say to you,' said the minister on the newsreel, 'grow your own onions!'

'Why do the men not fight better?' The question had troubled Churchill earlier in the year. Perhaps they needed a future to fight for that *wasn't* the 1930s. Churchill had been a member of the Liberal government that had first introduced social security and state pensions. He'd called himself a 'Tory Democrat' then and had lambasted Conservatives for their lack of interest in the welfare of the poor. He'd been in the Conservative Party himself for decades now, but he hadn't forgotten his earlier interest in welfare. He enthusiastically supported the idea of asking William Beveridge to investigate health and social security with a view to extending state funding and management. Beveridge's report was a bestseller.

The new thinking extended to the empire. Pamphlets from left-wing organisations called for its 'democratisation'. Many were uneasy at this thought, but there was an unmistakable tension between Britain's role as colonial master and her current position as champion of human rights and national self-determination. George Orwell drew attention to 'the equivocal moral position of Britain, with its democratic phrases and coolie empire'. Orwell believed that Britain's war should be about building a fairer world rather than keeping its colonies. Most of the ABCA lecturers in the desert would have agreed.

In the egalitarian world of 260 Squadron, plain speaking was the rule. In this instance an Australian was addressing a Welshman:

> No offence, Shep, mate, but I reckon you'll be kipping on your own from now on. I can't see any other poor bastard sharing with you.

Sergeant Lionel 'Shep' Sheppard had begun by sharing a tent with five other pilots. One by one they were killed, wounded or captured. When anyone else joined his tent, they too soon disappeared. By early July he was sleeping alone, and new boys were warned to avoid him. In August one brave soul ignored the advice. For a while he seemed immune to the jinx, but then he was shot down. Now, as Cundy was telling Sheppard in his lazy drawl, the case was closed.

This was fine by Sergeant Sheppard. He liked having a tent to himself, and the curse evidently had no effect on him. He was confident and aggressive at the controls of a Kittyhawk. And they were good mates, him and Cundy. Indeed, all the squadron held Sergeant Sheppard in high regard. He stood a stocky five foot seven, with the pugnacious build of a rugby player, which is what he was. Proud of his Welsh ancestry, he took every opportunity to explain to rough colonial boys like Cundy that they should be grateful to make the acquaintance of one of God's chosen people. He'd always found it easy to get on with the Aussies, Canadians and Rhodesians who made up the bulk of 260.

Sheppard, from the industrial town of Newport in Monmouthshire, had been good with numbers and machines from the start. He joined the RAF as a nineteen-year-old in October 1940. He'd wanted to go in earlier as a 'boy entrant' but his family needed income so he got a job in the Post Office instead. At his interview to qualify for pilot training there were two graduates in front of him who both came out of the room looking crestfallen. But Sheppard breezed through, his mental arithmetic faster and more accurate than that of the officer who tried to catch him out.

He was sent to train in Rhodesia. There he had an idyllic time in the fresh air and the sunshine. The food was plentiful and good and he made some great new mates. He was selected to be a fighter pilot but, owing to a runway crash, was graded 'below average'. After being held back for a while as a result, he finally made the Operational Training Unit at Khartoum. Travelling via Luxor on Christmas Day, the trainee pilots wolf-whistled and waved at a most attractive woman they saw getting off the train there. They were arrested at Aswan. The attractive woman had been Egypt's Queen Farida, but she saved the pilots by informing the British authorities that she had not been embarrassed and they were not to punish the culprits.

The atmosphere in Khartoum was different. The instructor's opening words were, 'Don't think you are here to learn to fly. You are here to learn to kill.' Sheppard got his wings on 16 September 1941, by which time he had been regraded 'average' and joined 260 Squadron the following spring. It was not until May 1942 that his assessment finally rose to 'above average'.

One of his friends from training died on his first mission in April. Sheppard was badly affected by this, but he told himself he was a good pilot and sensed he would survive. He flew in combat for the first time on 31 May. The whole thing was a blur, and it was all he could do to stay in formation and follow his CO, 'Pedro' Hanbury. Sheppard never saw the enemy, even though the squadron leader was shooting at a Messerschmitt 109. But Hanbury was impressed that Sheppard had even managed to keep up with him. He brought the promising young Welshman on slowly, giving him flying experience ferrying damaged planes back to base, but keeping him out of the firing line until he felt he was ready. On 17 June, during the big raid on Gazala airfield, Sheppard made his first ground attack. He preferred it to dogfighting, despite all the flak. It was good to see the damage you were doing.

During the first week of July, flying over Alamein, he put in his first claim for a kill. He was behind Hanbury again, but the squadron leader's guns jammed so Sheppard followed in and they both saw bits fall off the German plane. He felt like a real fighter pilot now, but he quickly learned that in the air life or death might be determined by less than a second. On 10 July Cundy saved him with a sudden 'Look out, Shep!' over the R/T. Sheppard reacted without even looking.

> I turned so violently that I went into a spin. We were flying at around ten thousand feet. Down through the cloud I went, down and around, beginning to think I would never come out of it and preparing myself mentally to jump out. But I came out at fifteen hundred feet. Then I went back up through the cloud

determined to get the so-and-so who had forced me into the spin, but he and his friends had pushed off.

In August things quietened down. On 5 August the Prime Minister visited and Sheppard was one of the team of eight that escorted his plane back to Cairo. Squadron Leader Hanbury left to advise Group HQ on fighter-bombing, in preparation for the coming German offensive; 260 Squadron moved in with 112, Billy Drake's Shark squadron, and moved to Landing Ground 97 on the Desert Road. Here they practised new tactics, abandoning the old 'vics' of three planes. Instead, they adopted the preferred German pairs, with each pilot looking after the other, and with three flights of four to a squadron.

They also got a new kind of Kittyhawk to fly. The latest model, known as the Warhawk, had a powerful Rolls-Royce Merlin engine made in America. This meant they could now operate at 20,000 feet and get above the Messerschmitts for a change. It carried a 500lb bomb, twice the load of their old planes. Some American instructors with hundreds of hours on Warhawks moved in for a few weeks to teach them. The young pilots of 260 Squadron taught the Americans a few things about combat flying in exchange. The Warhawk was a plane to give real meaning to the squadron motto, *Celer et fortis*, swift and strong, and Sheppard, lying alone in his tent, looked forward to the next battle with eager anticipation.

Few German prisoners had been taken in mainland Europe, so the eight captives from Dieppe were given a thorough interrogation. Three were recently conscripted Poles, one of whom had actually fought against the Germans in 1939. They cooperated with enthusiasm. The Dieppe garrison, they said, consisted of unhappy foreigners like themselves and the very youngest and least warlike recruits from Germany and Austria. A doctor concluded that 'none of these men would qualify for a fighting unit of the British army'. The Poles complained that the German NCOs beat them if they misunderstood orders and, according to their interrogator, 'gave the impression of being like beaten, cringing animals, stupefied and bewildered by their inhuman experiences'.

The German prisoners complained about officers living it up in bars and trading on the black market while their men went hungry. The British concluded that the level of training and discipline in the German units was 'exceedingly poor', morale was low and they urgently wished for peace. Yet such military misfits – about a thousand of them in all – had wreaked havoc among the highly trained and aggressive Canadians.

The German army conducted its own investigation into the raid and concluded that:

> The Canadians on the whole fought badly and surrendered afterwards in swarms . . . on the other hand the combat efficiency of the commandos was very high. They were well trained and fought with real spirit. It is reported that they showed real skill in climbing the steep coastal cliffs.

The German analysts criticised the British for ignoring the strength of local defences, for sending tanks on to a shingle beach and for not landing artillery to tackle strongpoints. The fire of the naval guns, they concluded, had been poorly directed and ineffective.

Those who had planned and approved this raid, from Churchill down, put a huge amount of faith in Britain's vaunted 'sea wolves'. A series of successful commando raids had encouraged a feeling that all such amphibious assaults would be blessed with good chances of success, that every defending force – like the unfortunate guardians of the Varengeville battery – would be surprised and overwhelmed by the first shock of attack. But Dieppe was no isolated battery or lonely radar station, it was a heavily fortified port, and easily reinforced. In their overconfidence, Mountbatten's planners had grievously underestimated the difficulties.

After a night on the town, the US Rangers were feeling quite unprepared to meet one of the world's greatest film stars. But Douglas Fairbanks Junior very much wanted to meet them. As a naval officer with special publicity duties and a friend of Louis Mountbatten, Fairbanks had asked to take responsibility for promoting these first American heroes of the war with Germany. Alex Szima was soon swept up in his entourage.

> Fairbanks demanded and got the starring role in our activities for the next two days. This guaranteed VIP treatment, including a tour of Combined Operations HQ.

Outside Mountbatten's office Fairbanks did most of the talking, 'then a voice announced that his lordship was ready to receive us'. There were warm handshakes all round inside the large and beautifully furnished office. But Szima's attention was soon distracted by two large hand-drawn battle illustrations on the wall behind Mountbatten's desk.

> One was a battle involving large ships, aircraft, tanks and landing craft unloading commandos. It was titled 'COMBINED OPER-ATION'. Next to it was a huge 'OR' and then another drawing with planes falling out of the sky, ships sinking, tanks burning, and landing craft with bodies hanging out of the side. This was titled 'FLOPERATION'. This second one looked just like the disaster at Dieppe.

After some more small talk, 'we shook the royal hand and left for the dining room'. Fairbanks seated Szima next to a Lady Ashley, and told everybody at the table about the raid, while the soldiers concentrated on 'digging into the food'. When lunch was over the Rangers almost bumped into General Eisenhower, who had just arrived to see Mountbatten. They all saluted the general and told him about their part in the raid. After more handshakes and smiles Fairbanks led the group to the Savoy Hotel for the press briefing.

Another famous actor-soldier was there to meet them, Major Leslie Howard of the British army. Szima was a fan and had seen him recently in *Of Human Bondage* with Bette Davis. Press attachés milled around. Szima overheard two of them talking about their plans for the afternoon and was sure one of them whispered 'cosmetically unacceptable' while looking in his direction. It was the scar, he knew it.

The Rangers were shared out between the waiting journalists. It looked as if the photographers were being encouraged to focus on Franklin Koons, the well-built farm boy, whereas Szima was directed to the radio and newspapermen. He was the good talker, they said. Before he talked to NBC, Szima was reminded that the censor would only allow references to 'shooting at' the enemy rather than 'killing' them. Szima's tongue had been loosened by lunch-time alcohol, and part of him was enjoying the attention and all the famous faces. But another part was beginning to feel a little like a fraud.

> I knew this would create a lot of tongue-in-cheek comments and a credibility hurdle for us later with the other troops, when it came to explaining how we four overcame all obstacles, and obviously survived, while a lot of other people got caught up in a great disaster.

Fairbanks met the four of them in a nearby pub and more drinks were poured. Later they were taken to meet what seemed like a roomful of generals.

> Not knowing one general from another, I reported to the loudest.

In front of everyone this man asked me if I'd shat my pants, to which I said, 'No, sir.' Then, with a great laugh, he held the stage to declare that he had 'carried a turd' for two days after his first encounter in the Great War. Then he ordered us all another drink.

US newsreels portrayed Dieppe as a US commando raid. The headline of the *Daily News* of New York City for 20 August was 'Yanks in 9-hr Dieppe Raid: 200 Nazi planes blasted'. The *Chicago Sun* of 22 August – informed by the Fairbanks briefing – caught a similar mood.

> They were boys but they had grown up. Yet they were gay with victory, exactly like college football players – joking and laughing in the locker room after a big victory over a rival team which had been touted as the stronger.
>
> Ohio's Sgt Szima spoke for all. 'I didn't think we'd ever get back because of the way our officers talked to us before the raid. First we were talked to by the big boss, you know, that cousin of the King's' – he meant Lord Louis Mountbatten, Chief of Combined Operations – 'and he told us this job of ours was so important that it had to be carried out even if it meant every one of us lost his life, because if we didn't carry it out thousands of our men would lose their lives . . .'

By early September the Germans were dropping leaflets on the south coast of Britain featuring photos of the Dieppe aftermath.

After the Dieppe attack, Don Bruce and his new Canadian friends were punished for the behaviour of the raiders. The POWs were told that a dead German soldier had been found with his hands tied behind his back. Because of this they would receive no more Red Cross parcels and would have their hands tied in front of them with rope.

The Germans felt they had every justification for the shackling: they had written evidence that German prisoners were to be tied during the Dieppe raid. A brigadier had gone ashore with the battle plan, carefully wrapped to keep it dry. It stated that German prisoners should have their hands tied, to stop them destroying documents that could be of use to the Allies. It was written proof that the Allies were flouting the Geneva Convention.

We were all lined up one day and walked round to the hut where the tying was to take place. All the tables had been cleared out and at the door was a German guard with a machine pistol at the ready, in a semi-crouch with his tin helmet on. An interpreter said, 'There will be no talkings, whistlings or smokings.' We'd been warned that anyone who tried to resist would be beaten up.

It was a bit farcical. They'd tie us up at 8 a.m. and untie us at 8 p.m. They used a cross between rope and string, thickish stuff. It was a damned nuisance because it rubbed calluses on my wrists, and if you got a bloke who tied it on a bit tight it was very unpleasant. At the end of the day the tops of your arms begin to ache, for some reason.

Finally the German Medical Officer said that if we had our arms constricting our lungs like that then there would be a lot of cases of TB so they gave us handcuffs instead, with an eighteen-inch length of chain between the cuffs. It was actually possible to get these off, but if you were found with them off you got hit.

Bruce had a lot of time to think, lying on his rough bed and imagining life back at Marham. It would be getting too cold to swim in the lake now. Had anyone ever got the Canadians to take their hands out of their pockets? What was Len up to? At night he would imagine them preparing for another op, picking up their thermos flasks and their raisins, rumbling down the runway, every one of them counting down to the magic number thirty. A new batch of prisoners arrived. Bruce asked whether anyone was from 115 Squadron. Two men said they were. 'So I said, "Do you know Len Clough?" And one said, "Yes, he was our observer, but he's dead."'

He'd been on one of these stupid pointless daylight raids. If the weather was bad over Germany they used to put a few Wellingtons up on a pinprick raid. The idea was it got the German workers down into the shelters. But the planes were really exposed. Anyway, on this day they'd run out of cloud cover and been spotted. A front gunner from Len's crew had told everyone that, as they were going down over the sea, he had seen Len in the cabin directing the extinguisher on to a fire. Then they hit, and the only two who got out alive were the gunners.

Men played chess and cards and put on amateur dramatic shows. Some even tried to escape. But most settled down to boredom and privation, and some succumbed to despair.

Two friends had an argument. One beat up the other, then calmly walked to the wire and climbed over it. The guard shouted, 'Halt!' three times, but he didn't turn back and they just shot him dead. Another time someone went over to the forty-holer early in the morning and saw a shadow, looked up and there was a man hanging from one of the beams.

'Guys, will someone please tell this young lady that I am who I say I am?'

'Sure, Sergeant, we know you were at Dieppe. But I never saw you with Douglas Fairbanks. I think you made that part up yourself. Come over here, sweetheart, *I'm* Jimmy Cagney's brother.'

It had been too good to be true anyway. Taking a girl to a movie house in Dundee and finding *The Corsican Brothers* on the screen starring you-know-who. How was she going to believe that this American soldier had been eating lunch with him just two weeks ago?

Life in the Rangers' new base was good. They were back to American cooking and Dieppe veterans were treated to extra respect and extra rations. The routine was the Palais de Dance or the cinema followed by after-hours drinking at the Royal British Hotel, where all the Rangers with a pass congregated when the pubs closed. In Scotland, they had discovered, if you purchased a room you were entitled to drink for as long as you liked. So each night a different Ranger would get a room just to buy drinks for his buddies.

When you entered the lobby you would shout out, 'OK, who's got the room tonight?' And you gave him the money to buy all the drinks. Didn't make much sense, but what did in WW2?

It had been strange watching Fairbanks on the screen. Stranger still watching the newsreels that went on and on about Dieppe. By now Szima knew that what came out of the projector did not necessarily square with the memories that jostled for space inside his head. The cigarettes at Piccadilly that glowed like fire ants in the dark. The piper getting up and all the commandos charging. The Germans in the white T-shirts and black helmets. The man going backwards and forwards at the same time.

Boys from Dayton, Ohio, only saw men like Douglas Fairbanks on a screen, or read about war in a book. He'd wanted to see the world and experience its adventures for himself. He was glad that he'd done it; glad of the responsibility and the friendship. But he'd discovered that sometimes the storytelling was fake, that a 'Floperation' could be turned right back into an 'Operation' at the whirr of a camera and the stroke of a pen.

Chapter 19

26–30 August

At no other time since the beginning of the war has the British position in the Middle East been so desperate as it is now. Syria and Palestine are undefended; all Iraq and Iran are lightly held by two Indian divisions.

Colonel Bonner F. Fellers was writing another report. He was working for Military Intelligence in Washington now, and had been asked to assess what might happen in the Middle East over the next few weeks. To Fellers, what mattered most was not Britain's control of the Suez Canal, but the fate of the rail line that ran between the port of Banda Shapur in Iran and southern Russia. By August this was supplying Stalin's armies with some 1,000 tons of American equipment every day. In nearby Basra, American aircraft and trucks were being assembled from crated kits and flown or driven north. Keeping these supply routes open depended on the British holding on in the desert. But could they? Without further urgent American help, Fellers did not believe so.

During early July, Rommel's troops were exhausted, short of material and manpower. In spite of Rommel's weakness and with numerical superiority in every detail, the British Eighth Army failed against the Axis in its belated 22 July offensive.

From Washington's perspective it was ever more imperative to get supplies into the hands of struggling allies. Producing the equipment was not a problem. The American economy was surprising even Harry Hopkins. One illustration of the productive energy that had been unleashed concerned the Sherman tanks that Roosevelt had promised Churchill on that bleak June morning in the Oval Office. A convoy carrying the tanks was heading towards the Cape of Good Hope en route around Africa to Suez. Some spare engines were following in a separate ship that was sunk by a U-boat. Without even telling the British that there was a problem, Roosevelt personally ordered another supply of engines to be rushed to the coast and put on the fastest merchant ship that could be found. This overtook the original convoy and arrived at the Suez Canal ahead of the Shermans.

Fellers mentioned the tanks in his report, but added that US intelligence believed strong armoured and infantry reinforcements were also on their way to Rommel, and would be in position before the new American armour was ready for combat.

Three weeks is a liberal estimate of time before an Axis offensive may be launched. There is nothing in the past performance of 8th Army on which to base the hope that a reinforced Rommel can be stopped. Only an overwhelming British-American airforce can save this all-important theatre. Only air reinforcements can arrive in time for the impending Axis blow. The loss of the Middle East would be the greatest single blow to the Allied powers since the fall of France. It would eliminate the only remaining supply route to Russia and would relegate the British effort to a defensive role in the United Kingdom.

'One thing is certain,' he wrote, and he decided to underline what followed, 'unless both the United States and Great Britain extend every possible air aid to the Middle East at once, this all-important theater will be lost.'

Fellers turned to reports suggesting that powerful figures in the Muslim world would take the fall of Cairo as a sign that the time had come to drive the British out of the region. He knew something of this himself because he had cultivated senior Muslims in Cairo.

> For local leadership Moslems all look to Egypt. But in Egypt the British are not welcome. The attitude of the entire Moslem world toward the British runs from lukewarm to bitter hatred.

The answer, Fellers suggested, was an American diplomatic initiative to reassure local leaders that Allied victory would not mean enslavement to the West. 'Moslems are friendly, however, to the Americans, look to us for leadership and realise we are not imperialistic; they know we will go home when the war is over.'

When Churchill returned from Russia to Egypt he was greeted by news of anti-British rioting in Calcutta. It had been met by force and several protesters were dead. Gandhi had once again been placed under house arrest.

Churchill was able to talk to Montgomery about the most recent intelligence from Bletchley Park. The British decrypters had intercepted Rommel's latest message to Hitler, detailing his next offensive. He wanted to launch it on 26 August, but its success would depend on him receiving new stocks of petrol and ammunition. Montgomery planned accordingly. The line from the sea to the Munassib depression was held strongly by the Australian, South African, Indian and New Zealand infantry divisions. Below that the flank was open, defended only by a minefield and 7 Armoured Division. Auchinleck's plan had been to lure the Germans on to the British armour, dug in defensively on the Alam Halfa ridge and supported by anti-tank guns and strong field artillery. Montgomery decided to throw in a fresh infantry division as well. The British had 713 'runners' in the forward area, but only 164 of them were Grants. These, with supporting Crusaders and Stuarts, were deployed around Alam Halfa; 7 Armoured Division was given 122 Crusaders and Stuarts to stiffen up its force of armoured cars.

Churchill spent three days in the desert, visiting the troops. On 20 August he inspected the men on the Alam Halfa ridge. There he spoke warmly of the reviving morale of the army under Montgomery. In the evening, returning to the coast, he cavorted in the sea like a small boy.

Montgomery continued to 'register his personality'. After being handed an Australian slouch hat, he took to collecting hats wherever he went. He questioned the men about their positions and equipment. If the answers were unsatisfactory, officers were liable to be sacked. He would be heard to say, 'He must go. He must go at once!' and next day the officer would have disappeared. Montgomery wanted everyone to know his part. The troops rehearsed taking up their battle positions time and time again. A printed sheet was prepared explaining what the coming battle was about and handed to all the men.

Montgomery's chief of staff, Freddie de Guingand, had a bright idea. He arranged for the creation of a false 'going map' of the areas behind the British lines. Whenever troops went out on reconnaissance they were told to make maps of the 'going': where you could move fast, where you had to drive with caution, and where it was not possible to take vehicles at all. Terrain was divided into four kinds, differentiated on the maps by colours. Red meant that the ground was firm and clear. You could drive at more than 10 mph without worrying much. Yellow meant that you could drive at speeds between 5 and 12 mph, taking care to avoid rocks or soft sand. Green meant that a unit needed to check the area before driving over it. Low gear was essential. Blue was simply impassable. The area around and behind the present British positions had never been spied out by the Germans on the ground. For them, a new British map would be of huge value.

A map was prepared that marked as 'good' areas that were treacherously sandy and marked as 'difficult' areas that were, in fact, perfectly good. The idea was to persuade the enemy to move in the direction that the British wanted – towards their prepared position at Alam Halfa – and to persuade them that the route would be easier than it really was. That way the tanks would use up time and petrol travelling slowly over soft sand while, with luck, the lorries would get stuck in it and could be bombed while stationary.

Peter Vaux was ordered to make sure that the false map fell into enemy hands in such a way that they would believe it was real. He briefed a most trustworthy team. The map was tea-stained, folded, refolded and torn. They drove a scout car out towards a known German outpost. When they were shot at they all fled hurriedly, abandoning their kit with the map tucked inside a ragged haversack. From his favoured vantage point on Mount Himeimat, Vaux watched as a German patrol went over to the vehicle and came back with its contents. He smiled and crossed his fingers. After so many times playing the witless victim, it would be really *nice* to lure the Germans into a trap.

Intelligence was also helping choke off Rommel's supplies. British torpedo-bombers and submarines, some based on a revitalised Malta, hit the Italian merchant ships that were bringing Rommel's reinforcements and fuel across the Mediterranean. Using the increasing flow of decrypts from Bletchley Park, a committee in Cairo, set up by a young intelligence officer called Enoch Powell, predicted which ships offered the most juicy targets. In August 1,660 tons of ammunition, 2,120 tons of general supplies, 43 artillery guns, 367 vehicles and 2,700 tons of petrol and oil were destroyed, a third of what was sent. To protect the real source of the information, RAF reconnaissance planes were sent to precise locations and asked to give radio reports of sightings, so that the Italians would think their ships were being attacked after a chance discovery from the air.

Nazi propaganda played cleverly on every weak point. In the commentaries that came between songs on the radio, and in the cartoons dropped over their trenches, the message was always the same. Tommy risks his life in the African dust, while the people who are *really* behind this war live it up at home, most likely in the company of Tommy's wife or girlfriend. The seducers came in two stock caricatures: Jewish-looking businessman and big-spending American soldier, both laughing up their sleeves at the gullibility of anyone who believed in all Churchill's guff about democracy.

The same message, in a subtler form, was directed at British civilians. One Berlin-based radio station claimed to represent a group of independent-minded Englishmen broadcasting from somewhere in London, one step away from Churchill's secret police. It presented the British as the credulous pawns of the Jewish–American conspiracy, and their Prime Minister as the well-rewarded lackey of President 'Rosenberg'. The way this station told it, GIs were screwing Britain's women, Wall Street was screwing her economy, and the White House was screwing her empire.

Harry Hopkins was concerned enough to have transcripts cabled to Washington. One rambling analysis was typical. The Lend-Lease aid that was flowing across the Atlantic, the station explained, was not meant to help Britain, but to enslave her. The Americans were bartering Lend-Lease for trade and financial concessions that would leave Britain destitute. The 'help' from Britain's great ally was simply being used to advance a new 'Dollar imperialism'. The station described secret conversations between Roosevelt's men and the leaders of Congress:

> At each of these meetings it was pointed out that the Lend-Lease
> Act was no foolish magnanimity but the most effective way for

extending the influence of the USA and the regime of the dollar. Already by use of this weapon Britain had not only been persuaded to abandon a number of her colonies but that she had been largely deprived of her Latin American trade both now and after the war.

Why was Harry Hopkins so concerned at what the Germans were saying about Lend-Lease? Like all the best propaganda, it had hit on a *real* weak point, and some of it was true.

Churchill had only to look at the circumstances of his own birth to see that the future relationship between Britain and America was unlikely to be one of equals. His dissolute father, Lord Randolph, married his mother, the American heiress Jennie Jerome, only after lengthy negotiations had secured a huge dowry from her family: a classic alliance of cash-poor old-world aristocrats with wealthy new-world industrialists.

Churchill and Roosevelt's first wartime meeting had taken place in August 1941. Churchill sailed over in an appropriate symbol of British greatness, the battleship *Prince of Wales*. It was a good choice – Roosevelt was fascinated by warships. The two men established a warm rapport and their delegations set about drafting a statement of mutual beliefs. Although this was several months before America entered the war, the Atlantic Charter, as the statement was called, was the first expression of Allied war aims. It also established the political conditions under which America was prepared to send substantial aid to Britain.

Both sides were keen to assert the superiority of democracy over dictatorship, and to condemn those who used force to subjugate their neighbours. Roosevelt also wanted the Charter to declare the principles under which a fairer world could be constructed. Two American doctrines gave the British delegation palpitations: free trade and national self-determination. Ringing declarations about both were drawn up and debated back and forth. On the face of it both threatened the future of the empire, which existed behind the tariff walls of the Imperial Preference scheme.

Churchill was worried about signing anything that committed Britain to withdrawing from her colonies. He argued for the introduction of a clause that made a distinction between Britain's imperial possessions and the lands recently seized by Hitler and Mussolini. In the House of Commons he said that the Atlantic Charter was aimed at the peoples of Europe and not the 'separate problem' of 'the progressive evolution of self-governing institutions in the regions and peoples that owe their allegiance to the British crown'. In India, Gandhi was contemptuous.

The Charter's declaration on free trade was similarly softened. Roosevelt had wanted a commitment to removing all 'discriminatory tariffs'. Churchill held out for a vaguer form of words.

From Roosevelt, Churchill could always expect the most considerate answers, and the two men would always set disagreements aside in favour of the pressing business of war. Early in 1942 Roosevelt's suggestions about Indian self-government drove Churchill into a rage. Since then, the subject had not been raised. But the linked questions of empire and trade would not go away. Senior members of Roosevelt's administration pressed him continually about it. Secretary of State Cordell Hull, Treasury Secretary Henry Morgenthau and Vice-President Henry Wallace were all veteran 'New Dealers' from the 1930s. They believed that the war provided America's opportunity to set a sick world straight once and for all. First and foremost, this meant demolishing the armies that stood outside Cairo and Moscow, and removing the dictators who had sent them there. But it meant more than that – it meant establishing a new and fairer economic system after the war was won.

The British economist John Maynard Keynes spent most of 1941 and 1942 negotiating Britain's financial relationship with the United States. He soon discovered that, however polite Roosevelt was to Churchill, the idea of removing imperial tariffs was regarded as a 'neoreligious quest' in Washington, and pursued with relentless passion by the New Dealers. After much arm-twisting and agonising, Keynes's final deal included a specific promise to eliminate 'all forms of discriminatory treatment in international commerce'. Churchill wrote an angry note to Roosevelt to complain that Britain was not being treated like an ally but 'a client receiving help from a generous patron'. Then he thought better of the message and never sent it.

Berlin's fake British radio announcer could have had a lot of fun with that story.

The moon was approaching the full. Rommel would have to attack soon. The Italians had 240 M13 tanks and the Germans 203 of the most useful panzers, the Mark IIIs and Mark IVs, plus a few dozen of the near-obsolete Panzer IIs. Seventy-three of the Panzer IIIs had the accurate and powerful long-barrelled version of the 50mm gun. Twenty-seven of the Panzer IVs were truly fearsome beasts, the best weapons on the battlefield, with a brand-new long-barrelled 75mm gun that fired a 15-pound armour-piercing shell with accuracy and armour penetration far better than the Grant's.

On 23 August the RAF reported an increased number of vehicles in the southern area. The same day a radio intercept suggested that both panzer divisions' reconnaissance units were already in the south. For Vaux this triggered a frantic search for 90 Light Division. If they were there too, then an attack was imminent. And 25 August was the night of the full moon.

The game of battleships intensified as Vaux and the RAF liaison officer searched square after square. He sent out a section to probe towards the German lines, and then a whole platoon. Neither captured a prisoner. Finally an entire company advanced into an area where lorries had been seen. They captured a private who died en route and a captain who had to be dragged kicking and screaming all the way to Vaux's ACV.

They interviewed him before dawn but he refused to talk. His green shoulder tabs told Vaux that he was Lorried Infantry, but that was all they could get. Paxton put on his most sinister demeanour, trying to terrify the man, but he extracted only name, rank and serial number. Vaux offered a cigarette and changed the mood. 'The German army is well disciplined and we respect this. It's clear that you're not going to tell me anything that would dishonour you as an officer. The interrogation is over. My corporal will now take a few administrative details.'

As the man relaxed and lit up the cigarette, Paxton took up the baton. 'Your full name, please? Your age? Oh, and your wife's address would be useful; we may be able to get a message to her through the Red Cross. And your own field postal number, please, so we can get letters from her?' The German answered, clearly anxious to be in touch with his family. Vaux took out his list of identified mail numbers, cross-referenced with the units they served. Now he knew the man's headquarters, knew he was part of 90 Light Division, and knew they were based a few thousand yards away. 'How was Colonel Kreitzmann when you saw him last night?' he asked. The prisoner looked startled, but maintained his dignity. 'That was a filthy trick, even for an Englishman.'

Now Vaux had 90 Light pinpointed and his intelligence summary, though cautious, was phrased to remind anybody who might be complacent over the absence of tanks that tanks were capable of unexpected movement:

> There are more definite indications that the enemy is thickening up his forces in the South. 90th Light Division appears to be concentrated to the WEST and SOUTH WEST of DEIR EL QATTARA. It is doubtful, however, whether the German armour has moved. If the enemy thrusts in the SOUTH, as the evidence tends to indicate, then we may expect the armour to move at the last moment as it did at GAZALA.

That day Dougie Waller's holiday in Cairo ended. His territorial battalion of the Rifle Brigade had been disbanded and its men were divided between the two regular battalions, the first and second. In a sense this was a promotion. The regular battalions of the Rifle Brigade, the famous 'Greenjackets', had a great tradition in the army stretching back to famous service under Wellington in the Peninsular War. 'That means we're bound to get pushed in at the sharp end', was Waller's first reaction. The good news was that established gun crews were not to be split up. Waller, Alf Reeves, Bill Ash, Moggeridge and Sid the Bren gunner would be drafted to 1 Battalion as a unit.

They left on the morning of 25 August, and next day they were back at the front, one of four 6-pounders attached to 22 Armoured Brigade. They were ordered to dig concealed positions some distance out in front of the western end of the Alam Halfa ridge, covering an area of flat, unbroken ground between two foothills. Somebody handed Waller a piece of paper. It was a printed letter from General Montgomery. He studied it with astonishment and passed it to all his mates. It was the first time anyone had told them what they were actually supposed to be doing in the desert.

The guns were in a rough V shape, two forward, two set farther back. Lieutenant Paddy Biddell told them to hold their fire until the enemy was just 300 yards away. They would not get many shots before the Germans pinpointed their positions, so it was important that they made them count. Waller paced out the distance and put an empty petrol can on the exact spot. Then he set the dials on his gun sight to hit the can. On the ridge behind him the tanks of 22 Armoured Brigade were doing their best to construct defensive, 'hull-down' positions for their Grants. It was not possible to conceal a Grant completely because the main gun in the body of the tank had to be clear to fire, and if it *could* fire then the turret above it was bound to be exposed. The idea was that the Germans would be encouraged to close in on the Grants, and expose themselves to the hidden 6-pounders of the riflemen lying in ambush. It was all very well, Waller thought, until the Germans discovered *them*. Just what they were supposed to do in their shallow scrapes half a mile in front of the British line did not bear thinking about. He eyed the petrol can balefully. Perhaps the Germans wouldn't come.

Neville Gillman was not with the Sharpshooter unit behind Dougie Waller. Viscount Cranley's C squadron with its new Crusaders had been sent to stiffen up the armoured cars of 7 Armoured Division. Their job was to retire slowly in front of the advancing Germans to prepared positions on the escarpment to the east of Mount Himeimat. From there they could survey the whole battlefield looking north towards the next high ground at the Alam Halfa ridge. They were to let the heavy panzers pass through and then harry their supply vehicles.

On 28 August Montgomery held a conference of senior officers and told them, 'There will be no withdrawal; absolutely none; none whatever. None!' Mike Carver and Peter Vaux visited all the units in 7 Armoured Division, as well as those of 22 Armoured Brigade out on the Alam Halfa ridge. They talked to the men and took stock of the positions. They were still very cross about the behaviour of a signals colonel who, while visiting them, had remarked loudly on the lack of fighting spirit observed among troops in the Middle East compared with those training in England. They wondered what the arrogant newcomers would feel in a few days' time. From his armoured car, Vaux learned as much as he could about German preparations and their latest positions. The tank crews seemed cool and confident. Everything was prepared, and the only puzzle was what was keeping Rommel. The moon was beginning to wane. Next day Vaux's intelligence report emphasised the imminence of an attack:

the enemy is known to be strong in tanks and guns and has had considerable reinforcements of men during the last month. He realises that time is on our side and that he must strike as soon as possible to take advantage of his estimated present

superiority. Whatever has caused him to delay an attack may be
quickly remedied and we must expect an attack to be launched
at any time in the near future.

Rommel had indeed been delayed. Supplies of petrol and ammunition had arrived too late for him to attack on 26 August as he
had wished. Even with this shipment, he had barely enough fuel
and ammunition. His plan relied on speed and surprise. He
intended to shift his strike force southward suddenly, capture the
minefields at night, and drive on twenty miles beyond them before
dawn. Then the panzer divisions would wheel northward in a
wide sweep towards the coast and overrun the British supply
area. This, he hoped, would draw the British armour out to be
destroyed in the open; 90 Light and the Italian armoured divisions would protect his panzers' flank. He expected that, as so
often before, British reactions would be too slow to cope with
his speed and initiative.

On 30 August he was ready.

'Message coming in, sir.' Vaux put on his headphones and listened
with the radio operator. 'Forward patrols report Germans lifting
mines in front. Can hear tanks warming up.'

'Right, I'll have a word with the Brigade HQs. You'd better
go and wake Lt Col. Carver.' Carver arrived a few moments later,
shivering slightly. It was cold in the middle of the night even at
the end of August, but they were also tense and excited as they
listened to the latest reports from the patrols. There could be little
doubt about it: the Germans were crossing the minefield. Carver
woke General Renton.

'Well, if it's come, it's come,' he said. 'Issue Gamebirds.'

They listened as Carver spelled it out to the microphone:
'George. Able. M-m-Mike . . .'

He always stammered.

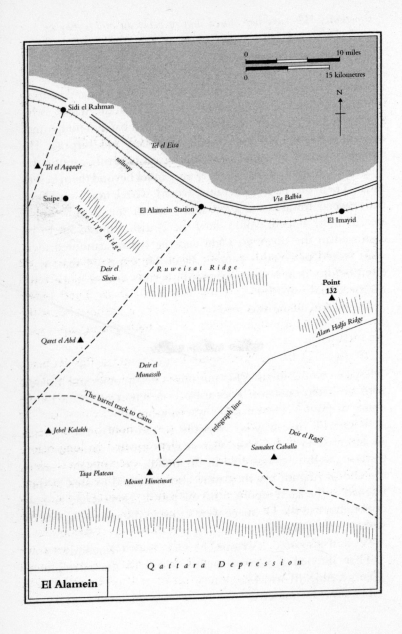

0   10 miles

0   15 kilometres

N

Sidi el Rahman

Tel el Eisa

▲ *Tel el Aqqaqir*

railway

Via Balbia

● Snipe

El Alamein Station

● El Imayid

Miteiriya Ridge

Deir el Shein

R u w e i s a t R i d g e

Point 132 ▲

Alam Halfa Ridge

Qaret el Abd ▲

Deir el Munassib

The barrel track to Cairo

telegraph line

▲ *Jebel Kalakh*

Deir el Ragil

Samaket Gaballa ▲

Taqa Plateau

▲ *Mount Himeimat*

Q a t t a r a D e p r e s s i o n

El Alamein

Chapter 20

31 August–15 September

'It's Gamebirds, Squeaker.' With a roar, engines started, crews put on headphones, and Neville Gillman and the rest of C squadron drove to their positions around Samaket Gaballa. Their orders were to hold the enemy on the minefields if possible, but if the Germans broke through, to retire at 1½ mph, putting up a spirited resistance.

At Alam Halfa, 22 Armoured Brigade, under Pip Roberts, moved to their battle positions. Dougie Waller's anti-tank platoon were a little farther down on the moonlit plain by their 6-pounders in the shallow pits they had dug for them. While Alf Reeves watched, the others tried to get an hour or two's sleep.

The RAF and the long-range artillery opened up long before dawn. Round the southern minefields everyone was alert, watching shellbursts turn the night sky bright white then orange. The British raked the minefield with fire, supported by mortars from the infantry. Lit up by flares dropped from Albacores, the German columns were bombed continually by Wellingtons as they concentrated on their side of the minefield. The defensive belt was deeper and stronger than Rommel had expected. General Georg von Bismarck, the commander of 21 Panzer, was killed by a mine while urging the troops forward on his motorbike. His immediate superior, General Walter Nehring, was wounded in one of the bombing raids. Instead of crossing the minefield in an hour or two, as Rommel had hoped, it took all night to force a bridgehead and push 7 Armoured Division far enough back to form up on the British side. Rommel contemplated calling the attack off, but decided to continue. By 0930 the panzers were finally ready to begin their drive north-east.

The men dozing on the lower slopes of the Alam Halfa ridge made themselves a brew and wondered where the Germans were. All through the long morning they waited, reading, talking nervously, drinking more tea, killing time. Dougie Waller took out a little wad of letters from Laurie. He read them through carefully once again. He had to make an effort because his mind kept wandering. He was always half straining for the noise of tank tracks that would bring them all suddenly to alert and have them crouching by the gun. He thought of Tottenham, of Laurie getting herself queened up for a night out in the West End, of the kids they planned to have, of watching Spurs beat the Arsenal and what he would say to his son when they won the FA Cup.

He folded the letters up and put his future back in his pocket. Then he checked the breech mechanism again, made sure the sights were still set on the old petrol can and rearranged the ammo. He looked at his watch; it was lunch-time. At home he would have been getting a sandwich and, perhaps, a pint. He opened his bottle. The brackish water had a head on it like beer. They broke open some bully and biscuits. The wind was getting up and sand blew into the tins of food.

Around midday the panzers paused to refuel a few miles west of Samaket Gaballa, where Neville Gillman's tanks were waiting. C squadron withdrew slowly, laying down harassing fire as they went. A sandstorm blew up properly then, stinging the eyes of the tank commanders on both sides and blowing grit into their mouths.

Peter Vaux and the RAF liaison officer were frustrated. The planes had not been able to do half the work they had wanted to because of the sandstorm. Otherwise things seemed to be going quite well. But the moment of truth was coming. On their false map they had marked the ground beyond Samaket Gaballa as soft sand in order to encourage the Germans to go farther north, towards the trap at Alam Halfa, where the going was marked good, though much of it was either very stony or very sandy. They waited for news of what the Germans decided to do.

At 1300, in continued poor visibility, the Germans resumed their advance, hampered now by soft sand. Rommel decided that a wide eastward sweep was no longer practical and instead elected to follow the line of telegraph poles that led towards Point 132, the highest feature of the Alam Halfa ridge. The map had worked, and the Germans now took precisely the route that Peter Vaux, and Bernard Montgomery, had hoped they would.

At 1530 the light tanks of 22 Armoured Brigade reported strong forces moving north-east. They were coming at last, but slowly. Dougie Waller thought he could hear shells exploding. It faded but then, unmistakably, he could pick out the sound he had been waiting for but dreading – the 'clank, clank, clank' of tank tracks over stony ground. The sound of machines coming to kill him. He glanced at his watch: 1825, long past time to knock off for the day. 'When's it get dark, Alf?' Two hours? Three? Time enough. Waller peered into the sandstorm. The wind was dropping and the dust was settling. He could just make out his silver petrol can, three hundred yards away, glinting as the sun broke through. He was lying full length at the front of his sangar. His throat was very dry. He had already drunk most of his water and he was saving the last tepid, salty gulps for later when it might be needed. The barrel of the gun was flush to the ground, a good position, very hard to spot, but not offering him much by way of a traverse, so he just had to hope the bastards didn't get around the flank.

There they were; squat dark tanks in several lines. Seventy, maybe eighty, of them, moving slowly. German, the new kind with the long guns, coming diagonally on. Might get a shot on the side. Peering through the sight, Waller watched the lead panzer slow and an officer peer out of its turret, searching ahead through binoculars. The sun was glinting off them. It must be right in his eyes.

'Bugger me! He's stopped right by the petrol tin.' 'All right, then, fire!'

'You fucking beauty!' They all stopped to look. A coil of black smoke was rising from the motionless tank, which now had a neat round hole in its side. It was the first time they had watched a tank die. Two men were scrambling out of the turret. 'Wake up, Sid!' Waller shouted. There was a spatter from the Bren gun in reply. 'Missed, you tosser.' Another tank wheeled around and started moving towards them.

'I've got him. Fire!'

'Just missed.'

'Get your head down. Now!'

The front gun shield shattered but the inner curved shield deflected the machinegun burst from the tank. 'He's smashed the sight.' Two tiny Germans made a dash from the back of their smoking wreck to the other tank. 'Let the poor sods go.' Sid just watched them run. The second panzer backed off slowly, its main gun still pointed straight at Dougie Waller. Perhaps he didn't know exactly where they were. Sand kicked up around the German tanks, fire from the Grants dug in above. Visibility improved again; Waller could see more of the Germans and a lot of them were smoking. He let out his breath and crawled back to the gun. It was still working even without a proper sight. 'Right, traverse ten. Shell in the breech. Fire!' 'Close. Try another. Ready? Fire!'

'Another hit! Who needs a sight, anyway?'

'Where's the one that knows where we are?'

Everywhere tracer, cordite and sweat as Waller reached for the warm, salty water. There goes the last drop. The Bren gun chatters again. The Germans were busy rescuing their own men and trying to drag away tanks that had lost their tracks.

The sun was helping them stay alive, very low in the sky but bright in the eyes of the Germans as they probed forward, searching for their enemies. Waller glanced behind him and saw some Grants burning on the hill. The Germans were moving in, coming closer again. They fired off another few rounds while their officer called up artillery support. Suddenly shells were exploding very close. 'Fuck me, it's our twenty-five-pounders.' 'Never mind us, will you?' They all lay flat. The artillery was firing a prearranged barrage to protect the 6-pounders, but to Waller and his crew it felt as if the shells were dropping right on top of them. A hundred yards away to the right a German infantryman threw a grenade into a 6-pounder gun pit. Waller didn't know all the other men in his platoon yet; here were some he would never know. He saw two slowly rise from the pit with their hands in the air; two Tommies with no more war to worry about. He peered forward. 'There's nobody coming this way.' The Germans were splitting up and trying to slide around the flanks. But the 25-pounders were pouring fire in again, and some of the panzers were losing their tracks. More British shells threw up columns of sand, and spat stone and shrapnel against the battered gun shield as Waller tried to make himself disappear into the ground once more. He was thinking, Make it be over, make it be over now.

Waller's gun crew had just played an important part in stopping the most dangerous attack of the Alam Halfa battle. The first shots of the new long 75mm guns had blasted holes in the Grant squadron immediately behind them. On the ridge, Pip Roberts had been forced to call in his reserve to fill the hole, but they were some distance away. In the meantime the Germans had advanced eagerly towards the gap and ran straight into the trap of the hidden anti-tank guns. Waller's platoon with their four guns claimed nineteen kills. The Germans had moved forward again, overrunning one of the four anti-tank guns, killing two men and taking prisoner the two that Waller saw with their hands up. Then the intense artillery fire that Waller had thought far too close for comfort had halted the Germans again. They split to move round the flanks. Then they saw what they had been hoping for all along – the British tanks moving forward. They retreated to lure the British on to their own anti-tank guns, but instead the British tanks halted and exchanged fire from a distance.

The last shafts of sunlight turned the whole dusty sky blood red. The panzers pulled back. Darkness enveloped the empty spaces, leaving just the dim light of smouldering vehicles, occasionally spluttering into flame. A firework display of Very lights began, to the right, to the left, and straight in front. The four Londoners crouching around the 6-pounder wondered what to do. They were clearly in no man's land now, and HQ didn't seem to care overmuch if the artillery fire caught them. But there was no question of abandoning the gun. They'd come to love it, come to enjoy having something that was efficient and deadly at last. But if they stayed the night they might get their throats cut by some German patrol. They could hear the loud drone of bombers flying overhead and moments later saw bright lights over in the Germans' direction and felt the crash of explosions shake the ground. The noise faded and still they waited, too frightened to sleep.

Someone was crawling towards them in the darkness. Waller's fingers tightened on his looted German Schmeisser. Ash had his tommy gun at his hip. 'Anyone still alive here?' It was Paddy Biddell, their platoon officer. He called for a vehicle to pick them up. They went back, threw themselves on the portee, and slept. Not even the waves of bombers passing overhead woke them up.

They returned to the gun at first light, ready to fight again, but there was nothing much happening on their bit of battle-field now. The panzers had not returned and all that was moving were the rival salvage teams of the two armies. The Royal Engineers were out lobbing grenades into the German wrecks, just in case. In the distance, German engineers were dragging disabled tanks on to transporters and carrying them away for repair, or crouching around the less badly damaged hulks, trying to replace tracks and sprockets. Waller and Reeves did some maintenance of their own, replacing the sight on their gun.

Then, to their great annoyance, they saw a British armoured car approaching fast in a great cloud of dust. 'Every bloody tank for miles now is going to know where we are,' muttered Waller angrily as he scampered towards the car to stop it coming right up to them. He ran crouching low until he got into the lee of the vehicle. 'I want you to fire on those men over there,' said the officer. 'They are recovering enemy tanks.' 'I can see that,' said Waller truculently, 'but my orders are to fire only at three hundred yards so as not to betray my position. In any case we only have armour-piercing ammunition. We don't have any high-explosive, so we wouldn't do any good.'

'If you do not fire on those men I shall go straight to your headquarters and report that you refused to obey my order.'

'You do what you want, sir, but I'm sticking to what I was told.'

'What's your name and number, soldier?'

'6919780 Rifleman Waller, sir.'

The armoured car pulled away, leaving Waller choking in its dust and furious. Eighteen Bostons and Baltimores with fighter cover passed overhead, and again there was the comforting sound of bombs hitting the Germans a few thousand yards away.

At 7 Armoured Division headquarters Peter Vaux learned, to his delight, that some German lorries were completely bogged down in the soft sand that had been marked red for firm going on the fake map in the area below Alam Halfa. Excitedly, he and the RAF liaison officer checked the grid references and called up the bombers. There had been little personal liaison with the RAF until this battle. Now a man with his own vehicle and radio was standing next to him. They had long conversations about what you could do from the air to discomfit the enemy and what you could do from the ground. As they surveyed the battlefield it was clear that in this battle a great deal was being done from the air. Now that visibility was better, a shuttle service of Bostons and Baltimores was flying up every hour from Alexandria, escorted by Kittyhawks. There was even a squadron of American Mitchells with white stars on their wings. Again and again the German columns were pounded. From the front line around Alam Halfa the news was that only one panzer division was active. The other was unable to move for lack of petrol, its supply lorries scattered over the desert by air attack and artillery.

At Alam Halfa, Dougie Waller was beginning to relax. He could hear the sound of fighting from farther north. The 25-pounders behind the ridge were whizzing shells over their heads rather than on top of them, and so far the Germans had not shown their faces. During the morning Bill Ash kept an eye out while the others improved their suntan and caught up on sleep. By the middle of the day the heat haze was distorting shapes on the horizon. Nothing ever happened at this time of day. If the Germans were going to do anything today they would do it in the evening. Leaving Alf and Sid to look after the gun, Bill and Dougie walked the three hundred yards across the desert to inspect their prize, the one that had stopped by the petrol can. It was a beautiful new Panzer IV. Only half of the driver was left. The loader and gunner were also very dead. 'Did we do that to them?' 'Jesus.' 'I reckon the engineers have been here. It might have been them with a grenade.'

'They must have been dead already, though.'

'Yeah, suppose they must.'

Holding a handkerchief to his nose, Waller clambered up on to the side of the tank and claimed the pennant in German national colours that fluttered on the aerial. It was only slightly singed. They began a search for loot: tubes of cheese, chocolate, any jerrycans. 'Here, look at this!' It was a postcard of Hitler meeting the Grand Mufti of Jerusalem. Waller put it into the back pocket of his lucky German shorts.

Neville Gillman was now up on the escarpment south of Alam Halfa.

Two hundred feet or so below us the whole German supply column was stretched out. We watched the bombers coming over again and again. It was a pretty impressive sight. The whole thing erupted in clouds of sand and smoke. You thought, There can't be anything left, but when the smoke cleared half a dozen lorries would be burning and the rest would be more or less intact.

C squadron added to the confusion below by shooting up armoured cars and supply lorries. Gillman's new crew was working well together in this, their first battle. Ickeringill was firing the main gun, his work faultless and his nerve steady. Willows was enthusiastic and positive, a distinct improvement on the previous radio operator. Kennedy, an experienced driver and ex-regular soldier, drove them around every obstacle and kept them well supplied with tea.

In the middle of the day, with the heat haze shimmering, Gillman had a moment of alarm.

I saw something moving, coming up the wadi, and thought it was enemy infantry. We all got ready to fire, but it turned out to be an Arab with a flock of sheep.

A Berber with a flock of sheep, unaware that the fate of the Middle East was being decided in his desiccated summer pasture.

The Panzerarmee was bombed and shelled throughout 1 September, unable to bring the British to the decisive armoured battle its leader sought. Next morning Rommel himself drove up. He soon saw the problem. He was forced to stop and hide from bombers six times in two hours, describing how 'swarms of low flying fighter-bombers' would follow up, leaving 'vast numbers of vehicles burning in the desert'. Again he wondered whether to call the offensive off. It was not just aircraft that were doing the damage. The light armoured units of 7 Armoured Division hit a supply convoy of 300 vehicles; 57 were destroyed and the rest scattered. Montgomery was also bringing in more artillery from the northern areas, and appeared to have shells to spare. Harold Harper's battery was set up behind the New Zealand positions where 90 Light Division was the principal adversary. Here, on 2 September, Harper was struck by one of the few German air attacks that got through the British fighters.

> We could see six or seven Stukas and when they turned we knew this one was for us. We all threw ourselves down on the ground around the gun. It was not my first attack but it was still terrifying. There was one new lad there and I had to hold him down on the ground. He wanted to run for it. You had thirty or forty rounds at the back of the gun pit and you prayed they didn't hit that. In the event they attacked just as the Matador was driving up to replenish the gun next to us. They hit it and it blew. Afterwards we all ran over to see if we could help. Two or three of the team were badly wounded. One lost both his legs and died.

That night Rommel decided enough was enough. On 3 September the morning air reconnaissance reported that all German vehicles were now facing west, and over a thousand of them were on the move near Ragil. To the staff of 7 Armoured Division, this seemed to be the moment to strike. They wanted to cut Rommel's tanks off before they regained their own lines. But Montgomery thought differently; he was still worried about his army's ability to attack. If Rommel were to turn and wipe out a big armoured charge with his fearsome anti-tank guns, then the course of the battle might suddenly change in a quite horrible and irreversible way. Monty wanted to fight things to his own pace and plan. It's possible that he missed an opportunity to wipe out Rommel's army cheaply, but with opponents as tough and resourceful as these it was difficult to be sure that you were winning. Montgomery's orders to Horrocks at 13 Corps were to close up behind the enemy, but to limit offensive moves to continued harrying of supply columns.

He preferred to use the RAF. On 3 September Lionel Sheppard and 260 Squadron used their new Rolls-Royce engines to the full for the first time, flying top cover high above a bomber squadron. The German and Italian fighters came looking for them at their normal 10,000 feet, but the British pilots were 10,000 feet higher this time. The heavy Warhawk built up an impressive speed in the dive and the Messerschmitts were taken by surprise. Sergeant Meredith shot one down and claimed another as probable, and Sheppard shot up an Italian Macchi 202 and was pretty certain he had destroyed it. Somewhat mysteriously, a few days later Sheppard's claimed kill was 'unofficially confirmed', most probably by an intercepted Italian damage report.

This was the first time the British army had been able to plan a battle with the benefit of really first-class intelligence: decrypts from Bletchley Park, Eighth Army's own 'Y' radio intercept service and the reports of intelligence officers like Peter Vaux. All combined to give clear and reliable advance warning of the enemy's strength and intentions. Unlike Ritchie in May, Montgomery believed what the intelligence staff told him and acted upon it. Better coordination had also helped. Air strikes had been called in successfully, and 22 Armoured Brigade had combined tanks, field artillery and Dougie Waller's anti-tank platoon to great effect. Indeed, the 6-pounder anti-tank gun had emerged as a real battle-winner, accurate, powerful and, most of all, reliable even in desert conditions. Until now much of the equipment being produced in Britain was known to have faults in design and performance. The government insisted on the highest possible pace of output, so factories sent machines to the Middle East that they knew to be poorly designed and faulty. But this was changing, and the public was assured that 'In the factories, the new 6-pounder is now being produced in great numbers and in a steady stream, and women workers are playing a large part in its production.'

The new gun had accounted for some of Rommel's best new tanks in the ground below the Alam Halfa ridge, but he still had over 450 left, including 200 panzers, and his own powerful anti-tank gun force was largely intact. German radio mocked the British claims of victory, calling the action 'a reconnaissance in force'. As they watched the enemy dig in for defence, the men of the Eighth Army knew that when the time came for them to move forward, it would not be pleasant.

When Ken Lee recovered from sandfly fever he was posted as a flight commander to 260 Squadron. He returned to Landing Ground 97 on the Desert Road. When he had left in July the airfield was still being bulldozed flat. Now it was finished, and so too were half a dozen more, spread out for miles either side of the road. As Lee arrived he saw an entire squadron take off in line abreast. He had never seen this happen before, and found it all rather inspiring. Then, seconds later, another twelve planes took off, then another, then a fourth batch, each rising in succession from a different direction to avoid the rolling cloud of dust that was thrown up by twelve aircraft racing in a line. Within five minutes the whole wing that operated from this landing ground was airborne. No, it was more than inspiring, it was awesome. There had obviously been a hell of a lot of new kit delivered while he was away. When he reached LG 97 he found that his new squadron was sharing it with Billy Drake and his old friends in 112 'Shark' Squadron.

Lee caught up with Drake. Life here was much more civilised than it had been 'up the blue'. Alexandria was only a short drive away, and on evenings when the flight was not at readiness it was possible to go out there. 'Alex' was very different from Cairo. Chic, like a fashionable French resort, with a smart sea front that would have graced the Riviera, it seemed to belong in a different world from the desert a few miles away. He and Drake drank in the bar of the Cecil Hotel and ate opposite in the square at the Petit Coin de France, and walked along the esplanade looking out over Aboukir Bay where Nelson had won the Battle of the Nile. Lee loved the new Warhawk, with which all four squadrons of this fighter-bomber wing had just been re-equipped. He also took an immediate liking to the Americans who were introducing the squadron to the new plane. Like himself, Major Salisbury and Captain Whittaker were experienced pre-war flyers, and they were delighted to meet a real Battle of Britain pilot. Then there was Captain Snead from Arkansas, who was fiercely proud of his home state and would fly into a mock rage if any fool of a Limey tried to pronounce 'Arkansas' as if it sounded like 'Kansas'. 'You can piss on the steps of the White House,' Snead would thunder, 'you can shit on the Stars and Stripes, but you can never, never defile the sacred name of *Arkensaw*.'

Someone mentioned a 260 pilot who always slept in a tent on his own. 'Who's that?' Lee asked. 'That's Shep,' came the reply. 'Nobody shares a tent with him.'

'What's wrong with him?'

'There's nothing wrong with him. It's just that nobody who shares a tent with him lives more than a week or two afterwards. So now nobody shares a tent with him. He's a pair leader in your flight.'

Lee's face displayed anxiety.

'Oh, it's all right to *fly* with him.'

The pilots who had flown together for months were sure of each other and very close. It was a little hard for an outsider like Lee, with his background as one of 'the few' from the Battle of Britain. He sensed that they were waiting to see how he would measure up to ground attack and the doubtful pleasures of German anti-aircraft fire.

But he did his best to fit in and soon they all knew him as 'Hawkeye'. There was no division between officers and sergeants here, just a single mess for all the pilots. They all ate the same food, mostly variations on fried bully beef with desiccated potatoes, or M & V stew. But Sheppard, who was the messing officer when he wasn't flying, had built up a special relationship with a Greek called Agnides who owned a grocery-and-beer franchise. Through him they supplemented their diet with tinned food and kept their bar, complete with ice chamber, satisfyingly well stocked.

Mid-September was quiet. Missions were infrequent and usually not too dangerous. In between they read and listened to the radio, or played Monopoly and other games. The Americans taught them to roll dice, playing craps on the floor of the big tent. It was too hot for baseball or anything energetic like that. Sometimes they would drink with the South Africans on the base, singing rugby songs like 'Get him down you Zulu warrior' and prancing around doing war dances: 'Ai ziga zumba zumba zumba!' The old hands had told the Americans all about the delights of Mary's House, which they had described as 'a paradise on earth'. The Americans didn't believe that such a place existed. Ken Lee was enticed along one September evening, when they all piled into a couple of American jeeps and drove into Alex.

Mary's House was several sophisticated steps up from the sailors' brothels in Sister Street. It had a restaurant and a bar, a dance floor with a little band and young ladies from Egypt, France and Turkey who wore evening dresses and would dance with you for the price of a drink. For a further pound you were given soap and a towel and directed discreetly to an upstairs bedroom with the girl of your choice. Lee danced and returned to his table, waving to a waiter for a drink. The table was almost deserted. To Lee's questioning look, one of the RAF men responded, 'Our American friends all appear to have disappeared!'

There was better news all round. As preparations continued in Britain for the Torch landings, Churchill sent Stalin and Roosevelt regular updates on the Alam Halfa battle, and the continued bombing of German cities. A new Arctic convoy, called PQ18, fought its way through to Murmansk. Thirteen out of its forty

'There will be no retreat, none whatsoever, none!' Bernard Montgomery
in front of a Grant tank

Dougie Waller's photograph of Laurie Richmond

Dougie Waller (*second left*) and friends in Cairo, August 1942

A 6-pounder gun comes off its 'portee'

The pennant Dougie Waller took from the first Panzer IV he
knocked out at the Battle of Alam Halfa

260 Squadron pilots. Left to right: Lionel Sheppard, Cundy, Edwards, Fallows, Gilboe

Ken Lee's snap of 260 Squadron pilots being briefed before a bombing raid near Alamein

260 squadron's Warhawks take to the air in line abreast

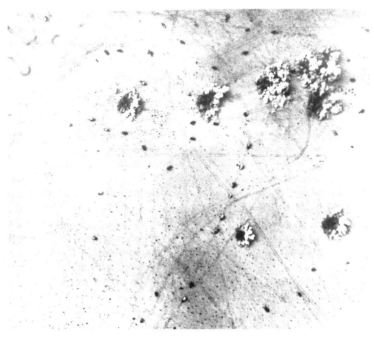

German vehicles under air attack

Neville Gillman's Crusader tank moves to Alamein on a transporter.
Left to right: Gillman, Kennedy, Ickeringill, Willows

Facing Gillman in the Alamein southern sector was 21 Panzer
Division and the Italian Folgore parachute division, as depicted
here in a postcard found by Dougie Waller

(*Right*) Sherman tanks in action during the Battle of el Alamein

(*Below*) Infantrymen near a burning German vehicle during the battle

(*Right*) The much-feared German 88mm gun, this one photographed on 10 November

German prisoners after the Battle of el Alamein

merchant ships were sunk, but forty-one German planes were shot down in return. The Royal Navy had expunged the shame of PQ17 and the northern supply route was open for business once again. From Iran, American equipment was still leaving for southern Russia. The threat to the Caucasus had abated because the German army, on Hitler's direct orders, was now diverting its main effort into capturing the city of Stalingrad.

Peter Vaux thought he had been sacked. Immediately after the Alam Halfa battle there had been an unpleasant row. Horrocks at 13 Corps had told Montgomery that 7 Armoured Division had not defended the minefield strongly enough and had withdrawn too rapidly. It was all very unfair: surely the delay imposed on the Germans in the minefield had been crucial. Nevertheless they were all under a cloud, and now he had received a piece of paper posting him away from the front line to join 1 Armoured Division at Cairo. He was very weary, still badly afflicted by desert sores, and feeling rather sorry for himself.

He had hardly been in Cairo long enough to report for duty and see a doctor when he got better news. He had been promoted to major and was to report to 13 Corps forthwith to become the senior intelligence officer to General Horrocks, a seriously important job. He asked whether he might choose his own assistants and, when told that he could, put in an immediate request for Corporal Paxton.

Life was very different at Corps HQ.

Horrocks had come from England and had very formal English 'white-kneed' ways at first. There were daily routines with fixed formal dinner. I had to put on a tie, something I hadn't done for months. Horrocks dined in the evening in 'A Mess' with half a dozen brigadiers. He liked to see things taken from prisoners and would hand them round for entertainment. He made me bring my tent closer to the mess so that he could get at these trophies more easily.

One of the first things that he was able to produce for the entertainment of General Horrocks' guests was Rommel's Order of the Day for the battle of Alam Halfa. It called for the final destruction of Eighth Army, the seizure of the delta and effectively exposed the lie of the 'reconnaissance in force'.

At first Vaux did not much like the static life, with telephones instead of radios and all the formal dining. On the other hand, the information coming his way was fascinating. All the latest details of enemy positions, to be circulated to the divisions, and reports on the private lives and personalities of the opposing generals from GHQ in Cairo. Vaux prepared briefings about them. He had two assistants as well as Corporal Paxton and access to the Corps wireless intercept station. This was in a lorry and manned by a group of multilingual Poles.

He watched the reinforcements arriving; 51 Highland Division marched proudly in with their pipers playing. The first self-propelled guns appeared, to match the ones the Italians and Germans had. Sherman tanks were parked in great long lines. They all had names painted on them in huge letters – cheerful names like 'Carefree', fierce ones like 'Widowmaker'. The old desert hands had given up naming their tanks years ago. The tank rarely lasted long enough for it to be worthwhile, and they did not like to dwell on what their gun did to the men that it hit. Vaux wondered how these gung-ho new arrivals would feel about widow-making when they had been fighting for as long as 7 Armoured Division.

Chapter 21

15 September–21 October

The delegates embroiled in John Maynard Keynes's economic negotiations in Washington often wondered which nation was doing the other one the favour.

The view from London was simple. Britain had bankrupted herself to fight this war, a war that was in America's interest. Why should she be further penalised by onerous financial and trade constraints?

But from Washington the issue looked very different. America was involved in a war to create world freedom, not reinforce the stupidities of the past. The New Dealers believed that two wars and one traumatic depression had been caused by European rivalries, and in particular by the closed trading regimes of the old empires. Since America was paying for everything, why should she be expected to subsidise a failed system?

Whenever Roosevelt grew soft, his Secretary of State, Cordell Hull, would remind him that they both wanted a more liberal post-war world, one that did *not* include the evils of imperialism and protectionism. Roosevelt's Vice-President, Henry Wallace, had an even more messianic vision of the US-led future and looked forward to the 'century of the common man'.

After months battering away at men like Hull and Wallace,

Keynes had been forced to the conclusion that the Americans were using Lend-Lease as a means of destroying the whole financial and trading system that Britain had built on the foundations of the 'sterling area' and Imperial Preference. It was Keynes's considered opinion that America intended to treat Britain 'worse than we have ever ourselves thought it proper to treat the humblest and least respectable Balkan country'.

Lend-Lease goods were delivered free of charge only when Britain's reserves fell below a certain level, so they acted as a very efficient means test. If there was money in the bank, then the bills had to be paid before the gifts could flow. This effectively allowed officials at the US Treasury to decide how much money the British government was allowed to possess at any one time.

Even some New Dealers thought that they were being too tough. Dean Acheson, a deputy Secretary of State, complained that the US Treasury envisaged 'a victory where both enemies and allies were prostrate – enemies by military action, allies by bankruptcy'. Acheson wanted Britain to finish the war solvent and accept a more liberal free trade system without coercion. But it was not to be.

Holding Britain's cash and gold reserves at a historically low level was official US government policy by 1942. This meant that Britain would start the post-war era with a giant balance of payments deficit, and financial reserves billions of pounds smaller than its debts. At one point Dean Acheson suggested that the Treasury permit London to expand its reserves, by loosening up the Lend-Lease terms. But the answer was 'no', a decision fully endorsed by Roosevelt.

Britain continued to rain its dearly bought bombs down on Germany. One of Peter Vaux's jobs was to gather information on the effect that it was having on enemy morale. He and Corporal Paxton studied whatever letters fell into their hands.

Hamburg, 31 July 1942

. . . this place looks terrible. Tommy visited us properly on two consecutive nights. They were nights of horror – the worst since the war started. Terrible fires everywhere, no part of the city has been spared.

Mainz, 16 August 1942

. . . But dear Ernst,
. . . the British airmen have completely ruined and wrecked our beautiful Mainz. When I say this to you, believe me, 70% of Mainz has been wiped out. In two nights the enemy have done this and brought misery and need on the population. If I only could, as I would like to, I would take my revenge on them . . . but we do hope that you will make it hot for them . . .

Paxton remembered Mainz-am-Rhein; he'd been there as a student. It had indeed been a beautiful city, set on a magnificent stretch of the Rhine, ancient capital of a principality with a castle, a fine cathedral and lots of elegant eighteenth-century squares. The fact that the Rhineland had consistently opposed Hitler in the 1920s and early '30s somehow made all this punishment seem worse. 'Poor old Jerry,' he said, mimicking Vaux's driver, who had taken to using the expression as the tanks with the bloodthirsty names rolled by.

Vaux's family lived in Devon, and his father had written to him about Exeter recently. The medieval heart had been burned out of the place; its wonderful old cathedral was a ruined shell. Exeter and Mainz, Cologne and Coventry: so much magnificence destroyed. Poor old all of them.

405 Squadron lost a Halifax bomber over Mainz. Edith Heap made another early-morning call from the ops room to the mess,

and the orderlies put the contents of seven more wardrobes into the storage shed.

If the voters of the Rhineland had managed to keep Hitler out of power, Edith would have been riding horses still, her great passion before the war. Her favourite mare, called Mouse, wasn't far away from RAF Pocklington, being looked after by Edith's elder sister, who lived in a village near York. Edith visited from time to time, but she didn't feel the need to ride any more. There were too many other things on her mind.

One of them was security. There had been a curious incident recently. An anxious woman called the station and asked to be put through to the ops room. Her husband had not rung her as he always did when he returned from a raid. Was anything wrong? Edith was able to reassure her that the man was safe, but had landed at another airfield. But she was determined to find out how his wife had known that there was an operation that night. There was supposed to be absolutely no contact with the outside world once an op was announced, families included. After a little detective work she discovered that the man was Catholic, part of a group who were allowed to travel to a nearby nunnery to give their confessions before every operation. On the way was a telephone box. It wasn't used again.

There was another problem – a notoriously promiscuous new WAAF who was causing a lot of bad feeling around the station, and whom the other girls had nicknamed 'Any Old Iron'. She would virtually drag men outside from the dances. The WAAFs got so cross about this that they physically restrained her one night and marched the unfortunate – or was it fortunate – man away. The girl was soon posted elsewhere.

Edith continued to visit London to see the Wisslers. By the autumn there were more Americans loitering around Piccadilly. 'Hey, babe, want a date?' they'd call out, oblivious to her rank. They received a terse Yorkshire reply: 'Get lost. I wouldn't be seen dead.' Some of these men expected the British girls to faint at their feet for a fancy line and a pair of nylons. Edith was responsible for transporting groups of WAAFs to dances at a new American base near Pocklington. When the bus was late one evening she cancelled the trip, much to the fury of the other girls. 'You wouldn't wait around for our boys like this,' Edith said, 'so why do it for the Yanks and their handouts?' To one of the sergeants, she added, 'You're newly married and shouldn't be thinking of going anyway!'

The great defensive advantage of the Alamein position – that there was no open flank – turned into a problem when the defender became the attacker. Montgomery was faced with a dilemma that was familiar to British generals of an earlier gener-ation: how to break an enemy with a frontal assault. For success, he needed to train infantry, artillery, tanks and aircraft to perform together with flawless coordination. Nevertheless, any attack on an enemy in well-dug defensive positions behind thick mine-fields was liable to be costly. In all essentials, the coming battle of Alamein would be a return to trench warfare.

Ground would have to be seized by infantry at first, moving forward at night in the face of mines, machinegun fire and mortars. A huge effort went into training mine-lifting teams. Electronic minesweepers were tested, as were 'Scorpion flails', Matilda tanks adapted to carry chains on rotating drums that would detonate the mines just in front of them. But the tanks often broke down in the clouds of dust generated by the chains, and the electronic sweepers were technically unreliable and exposed their upright operators to sniper fire. The favoured method remained the oldest: men crawling forward on their stomachs, testing the ground ahead with bayonets. In practice between 100 and 200 yards an hour could be cleared like this.

Half a million mines lay before them in what the Germans called their 'Devil's gardens'. Mined belts of ground were between 500 and 1,000 metres wide, followed by a strip of clear ground then another belt. In between were dug-in strongpoints containing machine- and anti-tank guns. The Germans laid all manner of booby-traps, some linked to explode together in long strings. There were the tiny 'S-mines', which jumped up and exploded at stomach height. Other anti-personnel mines were designed simply to blow off a foot. Large electronically controlled aircraft bombs were also planted here and there.

Montgomery announced his plan for 'Operation Lightfoot' to the corps and divisional commanders on 15 September: 30 Corps in the north would deliver the telling blows; 13 Corps in the south were to be the feint. A new armoured corps, called 10 Corps, would pass through the holes in the minefields cut by 30 Corps' infantrymen and proceed to destroy Rommel's armour in the open country beyond.

It was a simple plan but hugely ambitious in its logistical demands. The infantry were to cut through all the minefields in front of them in a single night, and the leading armour was to be out the other side by dawn to offer protection against a counter-attack. In the darkness, under fire and hemmed in by uncleared mines, all of the units involved would have to cooperate impeccably. To help them, Montgomery promised the biggest artillery barrage of the war. The attack would go in under the October full moon whose light would help the men creating and marking the gaps in the minefields.

When he heard the date of Montgomery's intended attack, Winston Churchill threw what Alan Brooke could only describe as a tantrum. Churchill wanted the offensive to begin a month earlier because he feared that Rommel's defences were growing more impenetrable by the hour. He challenged Alexander and Brooke on this point and a series of 'hammer and tongs' arguments resulted which left Brooke aghast.

[He adopted] the attitude that he was the only one trying to win the war, that he was the only one who produced any ideas, that he was quite alone in all his attempts, no one supported him. Indeed instead of supporting him all we did was provide and plan difficulties etc etc. Frequently in this oration he worked himself up into such a state from the woeful picture he had painted that tears streamed down his face! It was very difficult on those occasions not to be filled with sympathy for him when one realised the colossal burden he was bearing and the weight of responsibility he shouldered.

Montgomery finally settled the question with a blunt threat. If he could not attack in late October, he could not attack at all. If the Prime Minister wished to replace him, he was free to do so. Churchill backed down, although he may have reflected that even Auchinleck had promised to launch an offensive in September.

Montgomery's tank strength rose from 896 to 1,351, an increase made up almost entirely of Shermans and Grants. There were 1,021 tanks fit for action by late October, a two-to-one advantage over the Germans and Italians. The Shermans and Grants were given mainly to the newly arrived squadrons of 10 Corps that would make the breakout.

Anti-tank guns had also increased greatly in number. At Alam Halfa there had been 400 6-pounders in Eighth Army. Now there were 850, supplemented by 550 2-pounders. Each infantry battalion had eight 2-pounders, to help protect it against tanks, but a motorised battalion like Dougie Waller's now had sixteen 6-pounders instead of the four that had done so much damage at Alam Halfa.

Montgomery's intelligence team launched the largest deception programme to date. The idea was to make the enemy believe two things that were not true: that the attack would come in late November rather than late October, and that the weight of it would fall in the south. Dummy camps were built, with a fake freshwater pipeline with three make-believe pumping houses. The pipeline was aimed towards Samaket Gaballa, and the rate of progress indicated completion in mid-November. More dummy tanks and dummy guns appeared in the southern area where fake radio traffic indicated busy preparation for assault.

Real bombs were buried under the wooden depots and detonated electronically when German planes attacked, to imply that they had hit real ammunition stores. Up north, more dummy bases were established where the real ones would later go, so that the enemy would grow used to seeing forces there, and the arrival of the real ones would create no alarm. Actual deployments were made at night, with 'sweeper' teams following on to cover all tracks before dawn.

At 13 Corps HQ, Peter Vaux continued to build up a picture of the enemy's positions. He constructed a scale model of the terrain. Under an awning to protect it from the sun, a sturdy table with rimmed sides was filled with wet sand. Vaux and his assistants moulded it to imitate the contours of the land on the corps front. They built Mount Himeimat with its twin peaks, and Jebel Kalakh and Qaret el Abd, the German strongpoints, and scooped out sand for the Munassib and Mreir depressions. With white tape they laid out the minefields, then, using coloured wool, they marked in the positions of the Axis units. The sand table would be used for evening briefings during the battle.

13 Corps would attack at the same time as 30 Corps. Theirs was not to be as big an operation, but it was important nonetheless. They had to make enough of a dent in the Axis lines to keep Rommel guessing and hold 21 Panzer Division in the south for as long as possible. And if things went particularly well, Montgomery had the option of switching resources down to them.

Neville Gillman's squadron of Crusaders rejoined 22 Armoured

Brigade, which remained in 13 Corps. On 24 September the Sharpshooters were visited by Montgomery and their corps commander, General Horrocks. Peter Vaux accompanied the generals. When Vaux mentioned his sand table, the Sharpshooters asked to see it. Three days later the officers and NCOs came to Corps Headquarters to study the battlefield and the enemy positions laid out on the sand table. It gave them a much clearer overall picture of the battle to come. They practised crossing minefields at night. Viscount Cranley's dysentery returned and he went back to hospital in Cairo, leaving the squadron in the hands of Gray Skelton. Gillman's gunner, Ickeringill, had once been Skelton's batman and the two were great friends.

In the middle of this, Gillman was sent on an unusual reconnaissance mission. Skelton asked him to take his troop of three Crusaders down into the Qattara depression, to make sure that it was impossible for Rommel to move forces through it and around the British flank. There were steep tracks running down the escarpment that marked the edge of the depression, and they drove down very slowly. At the base was a wide salt flat, across which ran a narrow causeway of gravel and hardcore, about the width of a single tank. They drove on it for half a mile until the lead Crusader slipped off and had to be towed out of the marshy ground. By now Gillman was satisfied that there were no new roads, no evidence of any enemy patrolling and no realistic chance of anyone bringing a sizeable force across the wasteland, but he was enjoying his day of tourism. Leaving the other two tanks behind, he drove on, feeling rather like an explorer.

They came to an area of firmer ground, bordered by dunes of soft sand larger than a house. They all climbed out of the tank and scrambled to the top to find themselves looking out at a hundred miles of emptiness under the brightest of blue desert skies, surrounded by something they had rarely experienced before: absolute silence. Ickeringill, Willows, Kennedy and Gillman stood and enjoyed their moment of detachment from the war.

I'd never known anything like it, it was so clear and so quiet. The whole world felt like it was standing still, beautiful and peaceful.

After a while they broke away, returned to the tank and headed back to the world of noise to make their report and prepare again for battle.

Dougie Waller was also training hard. But he didn't object any more because he felt like a proper soldier now. The anti-tank guns of the Rifle Brigade were to be one of the first units through the southern minefield. It would be hard going. The Germans were defending the same British minefields, called 'January' and 'February', that had held up Rommel so successfully before Alam Halfa and had fallen into his hands afterwards when his retreat was uncontested. Mount Himeimat was in enemy hands too, and the Axis artillery would be directed from there.

In the weeks before the battle began, some familiar trouble broke out inside Eighth Army. The commander of 30 Corps, General Oliver Leese, was a newcomer to the desert. He was startled when three infantry generals, the Kiwi Freyberg, the Australian Morshead and the South African Pienaar, told him that they feared the armour would not do its job. Behind the old tension between tank men and footsloggers lay another divide. The infantry that would lead the attack came mostly from the dominions, whereas the armour was entirely British. Leese sent one of his staff officers to a 10 Corps conference and was amazed to discover that his generals had a point. Montgomery's plans were treated with some scepticism there. General Lumsden ruled at 10 Corps, and he did not conceal his doubts about Montgomery's tactics, predicting that the infantry would be unlikely to clear the required corridors through the minefield in a single night. Montgomery heard of the dispute and made it clear to Lumsden that, when the time came, he must send his tanks forward in accordance with the overall battle plan.

After this spat, Montgomery amended his tactics. Once through the minefields, the tanks would not surge forward in search of the enemy after all, but would form a defensive screen ahead of the infantry, inviting the panzers on to them.

After a quiet September, the RAF stepped up its operations again. Rommel's supplies remained the target for the heavy bombers, but the mediums attacked the Luftwaffe's airfields. On 6 October Intelligence learned that the Axis airfields were waterlogged after recent heavy rain and unlikely to be able to put up any fighters. Later that day Ken Lee, Lionel Sheppard and the rest of 260 Squadron flew top cover for a bombing raid on the field at Daba. They saw no enemy planes, but the aerodrome was heavily defended by flak and four of the bombers were shot down. Air Vice Marshal Coningham decided to attack the same target with the Warhawks three days later. Given their recent experience of the defences, and the fate of the bombers, this sounded like an alarming assignment.

As they came to thirty minutes' readiness, the pilots thought ahead while pretending to read the newspaper. As the clock ticked down, Sheppard felt

> a certain apprehension and nervousness come into the body system. It's not actual fear, but it is there. Your thoughts are in the aircraft – where are you going? Will there be a lot of flak? As soon as you get into the cockpit it all changes. The tension disappears. The ground crew checks your parachute and straps you in and you then become part of the aircraft.

The pilots went through the familiar cockpit checks, signalled for engine start and called 'chocks away'. With a thumbs-up, Sheppard and Lee taxied through the dispersal area, a fitter directing them to take their place in the take-off line. By the time the twelve planes raced off together, Sheppard's apprehension had been replaced by excitement.

Squadron Leader Devenish led the raid with Ken Lee as his number one. It was Lee's first big ground attack since he joined 260 and he wanted to give his best. They dived from 9,000 feet, dropped their bombs and came back around to shoot up everything worth shooting at. With so many of them attacking from all angles, the flak was not so concentrated as it had been before, and once again there was no sign of any fighters.

Lorries exploded as Lee roared overhead, the noise of his machineguns burning in his ears, his engine straining in the tight turns as he jinxed through the air in case the flak gunners had a bead on him. Sheppard watched men dive for trenches and anti-aircraft ammunition explode all over the place. It was thrilling, proof of a job well done. And they *were* good at their jobs, these 260 boys, aggressive, professional, and classy pilots too. They knew that the army was looking to them to prepare the way for the big push and they didn't want to let it down.

Some South Africans and a recently arrived American squadron joined the mêlée. It was the first time they had seen the Americans in action and Sheppard was impressed. 'The Yanks did bloody well. They were great pilots.' The attack destroyed ten aircraft in all and damaged twenty others, another sizeable blow to the Axis air force. They all returned to the Desert Road in high spirits, determined to do some serious damage to Mess Officer Sheppard's stock of imported beer, followed perhaps by another little familiarisation trip to Mary's House with their American friends. Ken Lee had a different kind of sensual treat in mind. He'd discovered the pleasure of having his hair cut and his chin shaved by a traditional Egyptian barber, finished off by a face massage and the exquisite pain of a facial tone-up with a large block of ice.

Peter Vaux was putting together the final details of the enemy positions; 13 Corps' immediate opposition consisted of the élite parachute brigades that had appeared in the summer. On the night of 19 October scouts captured a prisoner from Major Burckhardt's parachute commando group, and the next day one from the Italian Folgore parachute division. Vaux was pleased – it looked as if the deception plans were working, keeping some of the tougher Axis fighters in the south. This would help 30 Corps up north but, of course, it would make their own task more difficult.

The sand table's big day came when Montgomery visited 13 Corps headquarters to explain the final details to the divisional commanders and their chiefs of staff. Brigadier Erskine typed up a half-page outline of the plan and handed everyone a copy. Vaux attached his to his clipboard and sat next to General Nichols of 50 Division as Montgomery elaborated. At one point he ordered Peter over to the table. 'Come up here and point out what I'm describing on the ground as I speak.' Feeling nervous but proud, Vaux used his pointer to indicate the main lines of attack and the known enemy defences.

Questions were asked and answered in Montgomery's usual clipped, confident style and the briefing ended. The generals dispersed and Vaux went back to his seat for his clipboard. It was there, but the battle plan had disappeared. He searched under all of the chairs. It wasn't there either. He felt suddenly weak. The Battle of Alamein was to start the day after tomorrow and he had just lost the plan! Had it been stolen? Had he dropped it without noticing? There was a light breeze blowing towards the enemy lines. He felt panic rising. Surely it couldn't blow into enemy hands? He sent for the Military Police and had them line up and search downwind for his scrap of paper. Nothing. Could there have been a spy? If he owned up and Montgomery got to hear about it, it would certainly be the end of his military career. But if he didn't and if somehow the Germans had got their hands on the plan, then his carelessness could cost thousands of lives.

It could even jeopardise the course of the entire war. Embarrassed and fearful, he admitted his guilt to Brigadier Erskine, who told him to search again. Still they could find nothing. He had just reached the lowest pit of despair when he was ordered to report back to Erskine's office. Anticipating the biggest 'bollocking' of his life, he trudged over. Erskine saw his face and laughed. 'I've just had a call from General Nichols,' he said. 'He's terribly sorry and he can't imagine how it could have happened, but he appears to have two copies of the plan of battle.'

In an effort to protect Rommel's supplies, Field Marshal Kesselring had just launched another air offensive on Malta. It met with severe losses at the hands of the island's reinforced Spitfires – 131 Axis aircraft were shot down at the cost of 34 British fighters. The failure to invade Malta in the heady weeks after seizing Tobruk, Kesselring said later, had been 'a fatal blunder'.

Unknown to Kesselring, Operation Torch was drawing near. The Royal Navy was poised to escort the largest invasion fleet ever assembled into the Mediterranean. The question that preoccupied London and Washington was 'Will the Vichy troops in North Africa fight?' A big victory at Alamein would surely encourage them to lay down their weapons. It would also prove a very important point to the rest of the world: that a German army could be driven decisively out of territory it had conquered. In over three years of war this had not yet happened.

Ken Lee watched another procession of ammunition lorries moving up the Desert Road. For days now the convoys had been nose to tail. Nobody was telling them much, but it didn't take a genius to work out that something important was about to happen.

The RAF launched a new wave of attacks. On 20 October 260 Squadron flew top cover for a raid on Landing Ground 21. They approached over the sea at 14,000 feet, but were jumped. Back to his best Battle of Britain form, Lee saw them first. 'Break right, break right!' he called as he swerved out of the way of the black dots with the glittering, cannon-firing wings.

Suddenly there were 109s everywhere. 'Two on you, Eddy.' 'Look out, Shep.' 'Got you, got you!' 'Meredith's got one.' 'Thug's been hit.' Lee saw smoke trailing from one of the Warhawks. 'Blue Two down, anyone see a parachute?' 'I'm hit, glycol leak, heading home.'

Did he hate these men in the Messerschmitts? No, they were ciphers, potential scores.

> I mean, certainly the Poles hated the Germans but I don't think you'll ever find one British pilot that'll tell you that he hated them . . . It's rather like playing cricket, you wanted to score more runs than everybody else.

But scoring wasn't easy today. Lee remembered Group Captain Taffy Jones, MC, DFC, MM, and just about everything else. His motto was 'Don't shoot till you see the whites of their bloody eyes'. But he'd be lucky to see any bloody part of them. The 109s were scarily quick in the turn and could flick out of trouble like a darting swallow, leaving the Warhawk lumbering behind.

260 lost two of its planes, with both pilots missing, and three others limped home damaged. Although they'd got two of their attackers in return, everyone felt very crestfallen; they had been well and truly bounced. These latest Messerschmitts were very good, and the Warhawk, for all its fancy new engine, was no Spitfire. They arranged to do some practice dogfights to give themselves as good a chance as possible the next time. Lee didn't know the missing men very well, but was aware that the others did.

If it's a really close friend it would affect you particularly, but if it's just somebody in the other flight who you didn't know particularly well you'd just sort of think, hard bloody luck.

But getting bounced like this was an increasingly rare experience for Britain's desert pilots. Weeks of attrition had left the Axis air force with just 350 front-line aircraft to the RAF's 1,500, and little prospect of reinforcement. New planes were needed to defend the Reich from RAF Bomber Command, or else out in the east, and Kesselring could barely spare any after his recent mauling over Malta. The battle that was about to begin at el Alamein would be the first since the war began in which the British would dominate the skies.

Chapter 22

22–29 October

Neville Gillman spent two hours of 22 October in the dental van, having numerous fillings and crowns done. It was all very clean and professional, an impressive investment of government money in the health of a man who knew he was going into battle any day. As he left, Gillman told the dentist that he hoped he had not wasted his time.

Dougie Waller's anti-tank platoon would be accompanying Gillman's tanks. He spent 22 October on leave in Cairo, not knowing that the offensive was only twenty-four hours away. Waller had been saving up for one of the greatest treats the city had to offer. He booked himself into a posh hotel for the night where, for the first time since 1940, he wallowed in a gorgeous hot, deep bath in his own private bathroom.

That day in London Brooke chaired a long Chiefs of Staff meeting. Air Chief Marshal Sir Charles Portal was pressing for a further huge increase in his bombing force, which would mean less factory space for tanks and guns. Portal and 'Bomber' Harris were apparently 'convinced that Germany can be defeated by bombing alone', but the CIGS was not. Brooke delivered his counter-strokes, his mind wandering to the men on the starting line and wondering whether they would be unleashed that night.

He knew that Churchill's limited supplies of patience would be exhausted by now. 'I shall be lucky if I get through tonight without being called up by PM to ask how it is the Middle East attack has not started yet.'

But although the attack had not started, final preparations had. That night, the desert was filled with troops moving up to their battle positions. Military policemen directed units through the dust and the dark, down lanes marked by symbols illuminated by tiny guiding lamps: 'Bottle' and 'Boat', 'Hat', 'Diamond' and 'Boomerang'. Sappers laid out the start lines and the initial forward guidelines in telephone wire, to be replaced later with white tape. By dawn 220,000 men, 1,100 tanks and 2,000 guns were ready in their forward positions, equipped with enough supplies for two weeks' fighting. The ammunition stores were full to bursting, the hospitals were stocked and ready, the engineers had the recovery trucks prepared. Yet as the sun rose on 23 October hardly a trace of this activity remained. Every footprint and tank track had been brushed over. German and Italian forward patrols reported no unusual activity.

Montgomery had assembled the most powerful armoured force ever seen in the desert. Its real strength lay in the 210 Grants and 270 new Shermans. For the first time the Germans were not only outnumbered, they were bettered in quality too. The Sherman was essentially a sensible version of the Grant with the excellent 75mm gun mounted in the turret, allowing it to operate 'hull down' with a full traverse.

The men sat huddled in their trenches all day, smoking, writing letters, avoiding flies, waiting for the sun to set. Everyone knew that the enemy had spent weeks preparing the defence, and would put up the usual tough fight.

Rommel was not only an armoured specialist. As the author of the German army's manual of British infantry tactics, he had a shrewd idea of what Montgomery was going to do with his ground troops and artillery. In response, he had constructed a layered infantry and artillery defence, with the panzer divisions held slightly back, one in the north, the other in the south. In and behind the minefields bordering no man's land there were light outposts, designed to make clearing and crossing the fields as slow and costly as possible. The main defences, 2,000 or 3,000 yards deep, were up to a mile farther back, and in each of these the rear positions would be held more strongly than the forward ones. Rommel suspected that the attack would commence with a barrage aimed at his front lines, and hoped that it would leave the stronger rear positions unscathed to destroy any armoured thrust.

A shortage of infantry was his real difficulty. He only had 110,000 men, of whom slightly over half were Italian. He alternated units of the two nationalities in the hope that the Germans would stiffen the resolve of their allies. His tank force was also comparatively weak, as hardly any reinforcements had come through since Alam Halfa. There were just thirty of the latest Panzer IVs fit for action now, and eighty-eight of the long-barrelled Panzer IIIs. The remaining hundred or so panzers were nearly all Panzer IIIs with the less powerful 50mm gun, a good tank but inferior to the Sherman in almost every respect. The Italians had 318 medium and 21 light tanks left, but these had proved to be easy targets in the past.

But there was one arm in which Rommel remained formidably strong. With 500 artillery guns and 550 anti-tank guns, including 86 of the 88s, he could more than match the British in the one area that had been critical before. These guns would form the core of his defence. He would hold the panzers back for as long as possible, preserving petrol, waiting for a moment to catch Montgomery off balance.

The Panzerarmee faced a final problem: Rommel himself was not with them when the British attacked. He'd been ill for some time and had returned to Germany for a rest cure, and to lobby Berlin for more supplies.

The RAF was in action all day, maintaining continuous patrols over the enemy's battered airfields. In the morning Ken Lee led a sweep with twelve planes. He spotted a lone Macchi 202, dived on it and shot it down. It was his first desert victory, but as nobody else had even seen it, much less observed the result, he got no credit for it. A lively mid-air debate about what had happened followed. It was one of a sequence of phantom or real sightings, and during the investigations two of the planes became detached, lost the squadron and found their own way home.

As usual the ground crews were watching as the planes circled the aerodrome before landing. They ran over to 'their' plane, eager to check whether the guns had been fired. Lionel Sheppard was particularly friendly with his crew. They soon had the Warhawk back in tip-top order for the afternoon 'op'. Lee led the flight over Daba again, but the enemy was there in force for a change. Sheppard found a Macchi 202 smack in front of him. The Italian plane disintegrated as he hit it with all six machineguns at close range. 'Did you see that?' he shouted over the R/T. 'Yeah, saw that,' from someone. It was his first outright, indisputable kill. Elated with the success, he got in a second burst on a Messerschmitt 109. He sensed he must have hurt it, as it dived away fast. Sheppard followed, the heavier Warhawk diving faster than its rival. As the German turned away for Fuka, Sheppard cut inside and gave him another burst. It was all the ammunition he had left, but it seemed to have done the trick. The German suddenly shot upward. He's going to jump! he thought excitedly. He craned his head around to see the outcome, determined to confirm another kill, and, for a moment, forgot his normal routine of scanning the skies every few seconds. There was a small pinging noise and oil spurted over his screen. The stricken German disappeared from view, but his mate was obviously somewhere very close behind.

Peering through the few clear areas of windscreen, Sheppard dropped down and headed for the coast. A minute later he was skimming the bright blue waves five miles out to sea, beginning to feel safe. Then, with no warning, the waves were leaping up all round him. Behind, and slightly higher, was another Messerschmitt. Sheppard nursed the engine and simultaneously tried to weave but the German was faster and Sheppard couldn't really manoeuvre very well. Already the engine was spluttering as more oil escaped from it. Bullets splattered in the water again. For the first time in his war, he was really scared. He prayed, and spoke to himself out loud, 'I've got to do this.'

He'd slept with ghosts for months. It was funny, the business with the tent, but of course it wasn't funny at all. Good blokes, great mates, the adventures they'd had together, then gone, all gone, even the poor sod who'd tried to dodge the dreaded Welsh jinx. 'I've got to do this, I've got to do this.' Flying as low to the water as he dared, he turned towards Alexandria. It was simple now. If the German dared to go as low as Sheppard then the Welshman was dead. Every few seconds his pursuer put in a little burst but, as they approached the coast, the 109 suddenly came right alongside, only a dozen or so yards away. There he was, the German pilot, as clear as day, waving and smiling.

As his nemesis peeled away, Sheppard could only imagine that he had run out of ammunition. Any fighter pilot worth his salt would surely have made sure of his kill. He knew that he would. Or had the man felt sorry for him, seeing him struggle for life like that? Belching smoke from the engine shook him from his thoughts. It was dying completely now. The waving man had bumped up his score after all. There was the shore; he might just make the beach with the gentlest of glides.

The wheels touched the firm sand at the water's edge just as the smoke turned into flames. As Sheppard struggled with the cockpit release catch, an Australian officer ran over, hauled him out and helped him to a safe distance. Then he passed him a bottle of gin. He had contrived to land right next to a casualty clearing station just behind the Australian lines. Since he was apparently unhurt he was taken to a senior officers' mess, treated to a great deal of fuss and bother and offered a lift to the coast road. From there he stood waiting to hitch a lift home with his flying helmet in one hand and his parachute in the other. He felt very strange standing by the road in the early evening, wanting to go back west when everything else was moving east.

A jeep pulled up and the driver stuck his head out, asking where he was headed for. He was a brigadier and he said he could take Sheppard as far as the junction with the Desert Road. A few miles farther on they picked up a second pilot from 260 Squadron who had been shot down that morning. The brigadier told them both how much the army appreciated their efforts and, as he dropped them off, announced confidentially, 'The big push starts tonight!' The two pilots quickly picked up a second lift and returned to their airfield at about eight. Squadron Leader Devenish had just returned from a conference where he had been put in the picture too. He was less than pleased when he told Sheppard and the Welshman replied, 'It's OK, governor, I already know all about that!'

He felt weary and sick. Death had smiled and waved at him and it sounded as if the real battle hadn't even started yet.

As Lionel Sheppard was hitch-hiking home, the war correspondents were called to Montgomery's HQ. There, they listened once again to the slim man with the sharp little face and restless eyes.

> Well, gentlemen, the campaign starts tonight. In the moonlight there will be fought a terrific battle. My object is to remove the Germans from North Africa. It may take some time, but this is what we are going to do. I think this battle may well be the turning point of the war. It has always been my policy that we shall not have any more failures . . .

By now they had all registered Montgomery's arrogance and the cruelty with which he belittled his precursors. But he was confident and decisive too, a man with frightening quantities of willpower, a man who delivered platitudes as if he'd freshly minted them. He went on to say that most battles were lost by bad command and staff work. The soldiers rarely let you down. This was a bold thing for a general to say to a bunch of journalists at the outset of a battle, and again it seemed designed to besmirch his predecessors. He concluded with:

> Today every officer and man knows what is wanted. I have addressed all officers down to the level of lieutenant-colonel. They know all about the battle and they have passed it on to the men.

That night everyone received a 'Personal Message from the Army Commander' in the same forthright style:

> 1 – When I assumed command of the Eighth Army I said that the mandate was to destroy ROMMEL and his Army, and that it would be done as soon as we were ready.
> 2 – We are ready NOW.
> The battle which is now about to begin will be one of the decisive battles of history. It will be the turning point of the war. The eyes of the whole world will be upon us, watching anxiously which way the battle will swing. WE can give them their answer at once, 'It will swing our way.'

The Sharpshooters held a church service. Neville Gillman's friend Neville Burrell, also newly commissioned, said that he could not face it. He felt there was an irreconcilable gap between prayer and killing. Gillman went anyway and then returned to pack the tank. They made the time pass talking and dozing, reading letters or doing little jobs around the tanks. Ickeringill wrote to his wife Anne and to his two small children. About 1830 they started up the engines. It was already dark as they moved first through their own 'May' minefield and then through 'June', each well lit with yellow hurricane lamps for the southern and red lights for the northern passages. They were ahead of schedule, and at 2000 the column halted for half an hour. Unfortunately, by the time they restarted some of the hurricane lamps marking the lanes through 'Nuts' had gone out. To Gillman, well back in the column, everything looked wraith-like, enveloped in dust. In the six miles of no man's land between 'Nuts' and 'January' a single burning Bren gun carrier lit up the scene.

It was still late afternoon in London and, at another Chiefs of Staff meeting, Brooke's argument with Portal continued. The CIGS asserted that it would take more than just bombs to defeat the Germans. 'Mountbatten's half-baked thoughts thrown into the discussion certainly don't assist,' he noted irritably. Then the War Office finally called with the news he had been waiting for. It was tonight, it was about to start.

> There are great possibilities and great dangers! It may be the
> turning point of the war, leading to further success combined
> with the North African attack, or it may mean nothing. If it fails
> I don't quite know how I shall bear it.

Sergeant Harold Harper stood by his huge 5.5-inch gun and checked his watch. Moonlight filtered through the camouflage net overhead.

> 2140 hrs on Thursday night. We were very tense. They had told
> us it was now or never. At the cry of 'Take post', we all moved
> to the gun.

Harper's was the nearest British gun to the sea, the most northerly of the 882 guns in the artillery line. He called out the charge. The layer set the range reader and they loaded and rammed home the 100-pound shell. Harper called out the figures for direction and elevation and the gun moved to them. The layer reported, 'Ready.' The gun position officer ordered, 'Troop rest!' For a few minutes they stood around, joking. Harper kept glancing at his watch. He was thinking of that May morning and the armoured car with all the dead bodies in it. How they'd been outgunned and outfought. 'A minute to go, lads,' he said. Again, the officer ordered, 'Take post!' They returned to their places.

'Ten, nine, eight, seven, six, five, four, three, two, one, fire!'

No one who heard what followed would ever forget it. Waves of light rippled over the horizon 'as if some giant were playing crazy scales on a piano which produced flames instead of music'. Harper's battery all fired simultaneously, spitting flashes into the darkness and sending their high-explosive shells spinning out high above the British infantry, who were slowly moving through their own minefields or waiting nervously for the order to attack. Harper's men hauled another 100-pound shell into the breech. For thirty seconds he waited in severe pain; the gun stand had landed on his toe and it wouldn't move again until he was able to shout 'Fire!' Then he stood there with his torch and his firing plan, pounding the known German artillery batteries. While the 25-pounder field guns aimed at the nearer German positions, the forty-eight 4.5 and 5.5-inch guns in the northern sector fired ninety-six shells in two minutes on each German battery in turn. Wellingtons roared over to add their bombs. Then, just before ten, everyone paused. The layers put on a new range, much shorter, aiming now for the enemy front line. Again the countdown, again the crashing volleys of fire, but this time the infantry clambered out of their trenches and advanced as the ground exploded in front of them.

Inside Neville Gillman's stationary tank, the shells passing over-head sounded like an express train roaring through a station. The Crusader rocked slightly as they screamed by. Not long after-wards, radio silence was broken by the first reports from the men ahead forcing the gaps.

Ahead of the tanks were the motorised infantry of the Rifle Brigades. Ahead of Dougie Waller there was not very much except the Scorpion flail tanks that were sweeping the lanes. Waiting for them to break down or be knocked out were teams of engineers ready to continue the job by hand, and the men responsible for marking the lanes with tape. The entrances to the minefields were marked by red and yellow lights; within them the northern passage was marked amber and the southern green. 1 Rifle Brigade was the first fighting unit through.

The southern passage, through which Waller's B company moved, was exposed to artillery fire directed by German observers up on Mount Himeimat. The nearest Scorpion was knocked out about three-quarters of the way through. Then the fire hitting the Rifle Brigade grew more intense as they neared the German and Italian dugouts, with mortars and machineguns added to the mixture. They moved on very, very slowly, with dust dimming the moonlight and reducing visibility to almost nil. Drivers strained to track the movement of the vehicle in front, trying to spot the little coloured lights. They were placed only every fifty yards or so, so there was plenty of room to go wrong when the men were lucky to see ten yards ahead.

Waller's portee shook, stopped dead and began to smoke furi-ously. Something had got it right in the engine. They all leapt out as it caught fire. There was nothing for it now but to join the footsloggers, so they moved forward with their rifles, tommy guns and Waller's German machine pistol at the ready, through a scene lit by the flames of burning vehicles and the firework display of tracer cutting lines through the dust cloud. It was their job to destroy enemy strongpoints one by one, and they were up against tough Italian parachutists. They moved low to the ground, crouching behind vehicles and rocks, their mortars firing smoke to cover the advance. One by one, they drove their opponents out of their trenches by a combination of Bren guns, mortar fire and bayonet charges. The fighting was very confused. One dugout might be shooting back while another was trying to surrender.

Near Waller, a group of Italians came out with their hands up. Then the shooting started again from behind them and the surrendering troops threw themselves to the floor, exposing the riflemen to machinegun fire. Bill Ash was not amused – people either side of him had been hit. At the next position they saw some other Italians who looked as if they wanted to surrender getting sprayed by British submachine-guns. It just wasn't worth taking the risk. Waller looked for a moment at the motionless forms on the ground and ran forward.

The scene was similar in the north, but on a much larger scale. The infantry of 30 Corps – Aussies, Highlanders, Kiwis and South Africans – moved forward in waves through no man's land, towards the line of explosions ahead. In the Scottish sector pipes skirled above the clamour. Behind them came their vehicles, throwing dense clouds of dust into the night sky. The officers consulted compasses and the sappers rolled out the tapes.

The Australian attack went almost to plan. The Highlanders took heavy casualties in unexpected minefields swept by machineguns. They captured several strongpoints but most companies were still short of their final objectives when daylight overtook them. The difficulties in making progress hampered efforts to clear gaps for the armour of 10 Corps that was due behind them. The New Zealanders fought their way to their objectives, but had similar difficulties clearing routes for the tanks. The South Africans were mostly successful, except on the right where they failed to make contact with the New Zealanders.

In the places where the infantry were pinned down, chaos soon reigned. Darkness and dust combined with a featureless landscape to make accurate navigation almost impossible. On top of this, two distinct corps were trying to operate in the same restricted area, producing logistical confusion on a grand scale. Innumerable vehicles carrying equipment forward to the 30 Corps infantry were stuck in bottlenecks through which 10 Corps tanks were also supposed to pass, followed by their own support vehicles, ammunition and fuel bowsers. There were ambulances trying to go back the other way, there were breakdowns, there were uncleared mines, and there was enemy fire. By dawn few units knew for certain exactly where they were, and had less idea where their friends or their enemies were. According to Lt Col. Mike Carver:

> The congestion was appalling and the confusion considerable. The whole area looked like a badly organised car park at an immense race meeting held in a dust bowl.

On the German side, nobody knew what was going on either. The barrage had destroyed the land-line communication system and the Wellington bombers, equipped to jam radio communication, had finished the job. A couple of battalions of Italian infantry broke and fled from the impact of the barrage. There were reports of attacks in both north and south, and nobody knew which was the main one. General Stumme, commanding in Rommel's absence, went forward in search of information. His car was swept by machinegun fire and, as his driver tore away, he suffered a heart attack, fell off and died. Parties setting out to find him came under heavy fire. An SOS message was sent to Rommel in Austria.

By morning the Rifle Brigade had broken through the first minefield, taken 300 prisoners and was only 3,000 yards short of Mount Himeimat. But this progress had been achieved at a heavy cost.

A company was reduced from a hundred to forty men and amalgamated with the survivors of Dougie Waller's B company. There was no question of trying to get through the second minefield until the following night. There was nothing for it but to dig in as best they could in the flat open ground between the two minefields, exposed to the observers on the mountain ahead.

The Sharpshooters followed the riflemen through the minefield late in the night and formed a defensive bridgehead with their tanks and the riflemen's own 6-pounders around the exits. Dawn revealed weary infantrymen with fixed bayonets dug in all around Neville Gillman's tank. They were shelled throughout the day that followed, aware that when night came it would be their turn to lead the way forward, and that this time there would be no question of any surprise. Gillman, Ickeringill, Willows and Kennedy spent the whole time inside their cramped, stinking tank. From time to time shrapnel rattled harmlessly on the outside, and they all felt sorry for the men outside in their hastily dug trenches.

In the north the overlap between 30 and 10 Corps got worse. As his tanks struggled to force their way through the narrow lanes, Lumsden was soon clashing with Freyberg, one of 30 Corps' divisional commanders and a man who had never felt much confidence in Lumsden to begin with. At dawn on 24 October, Freyberg asked for more forward movement to protect his men, but Lumsden explained that his tanks were still stuck behind vehicles in the minefield gaps. Most of the day was spent disentangling units and getting the tanks forward under fire. By the evening Freyberg was complaining that the armour was still not properly set up for a second night of attacks and Lumsden's apparent lack of enthusiasm for the night's plan was reported back to Montgomery.

As they edged forward along the cleared paths through the minefields, the British tanks were taking a lot of punishment. Mostly it was long-range artillery knocking off their tracks rather than killing crewmen, but it all added to the confusion. Repair parties and supply lorries struggled past each other inside lanes that were barely wider than a single tank at some points. 10 Corps' forward officers requested that the night's attack should be abandoned. Lumsden agreed and told Montgomery so. In the middle of the night Montgomery summoned Lumsden and made it clear that the attack must proceed as planned, and warned that if he and his divisional commanders were not determined to break out, others could be found who were.

In the south, as darkness fell, the Sharpshooters formed up for the assault. Tonight they would be the leading regiment, and the Crusaders of C squadron would go through first. At midnight word came back that the gap was clear. When they advanced it turned out that there was still some way to go, so they settled down again to wait outside 'February', the second minefield. Eventually the news came back that the Rifle Brigade was through. The tanks advanced, passing the flashing light that marked the beginning of the cleared lane. Gillman strained to see the green lights and white tape that marked their path.

> We were fired on from the front and, as I remember, from one side. Something shot the periscope away about a foot in front of me, but as far as I can recall we all got through. Once through, our job was to form a bridgehead with the infantry. The big idea was to get the Germans to attack us. It was one or two in the morning and it was pitch dark. The first problem that we encountered was that there were mines scattered about outside the minefield. The second was that during the day the enemy had formed a ring of tanks and anti-tank guns around the minefield exits.

There were bursting shells and tracer everywhere. Ickeringill swung the gun, trying to shoot at the unseen foe, aiming at the flashes. All around crews were scrambling away from wrecked tanks. Many of the casualties had lost tracks on unexpected mines, so most of their crewmen were unharmed. Scout cars dashed around picking them up.

> Two tanks were knocked out near me. They were burning and you could see tracer and Very lights in the sky. I got between the two, each about fifty or sixty yards away. Gradually one tank after another went off the air. We switched off our engines and stopped firing. The Germans stopped firing as well.

The only dim light now came from the red glow from the wireless set, by which Willows crouched, silhouetted in profile. There was no forward movement from the British tanks.

> Then over the R/T we got an order. Any tank that was still a runner was to go back through the minefield. I ordered, 'Driver reverse left,' and we started the engine. As usual I was squatting on the commander's chair, searching for the gap in the dark. We were the only tank moving. Suddenly there was a hell of a thump on the back of the turret and the tank just stopped dead. Several things happened simultaneously. I felt as though my right leg had been hit by a stick, nothing worse, and there was a noise of tearing armour plate. I looked at the sloping sides of the Crusader turret and the top was sticking in the air. There was absolute silence for a second. I fell off the seat on to the bottom of the turret, which was revolving on the hydraulic spade grip.
>
> I could see that my leg was broken: it was sticking out at an impossible angle and I could smell burning. There was a hundred gallons of petrol in the tank so I only had a few moments. I hauled myself on to the gun casing and through the lid on to the top. The top is six feet or so up. I was remarkably clear headed. I remember thinking, If I try to jump with a busted leg it won't be good. If I roll sideways I'll land better. So I rolled off.

The enemy were firing again. Armour-piercing shot hit the ground close by, sending up showers of stones, sparks and yet more dust. Gillman hoped against hope that the others would emerge. What if Kennedy had been trapped? A Crusader's turret could stop in a certain position and block the exit from the driver's compartment. Gillman tried to crawl forward, his right leg dragging uselessly behind him in the sand, then he gave up. Moments later he raised his head to see Kennedy running towards him. He had been knocked out by the blast but the flames from inside the turret had burned the back of his neck and brought him to. His driver's hatch had opened freely. Kennedy hauled Gillman into a nearby slit trench and they both looked about for the others.

Flames were rising from the fighting compartment now, and there was no sign of Willows and Gill. There was nothing they could do. They had probably been killed by the impact of the shell. The force that had caught his leg and wrenched the turret up in the air had come from directly where they had both been sitting. It would have been very quick. Gillman prayed that that was so.

The firing died down. Kennedy said he'd see if he could get some help and set off back. Gillman sat there alone. Beyond his own tank were the skeletons of many more. Almost all of C squadron's tanks were there and none of them was moving. He wondered how many of the crews had got away. It seemed like another disaster. How many times this year had he been shot up by German anti-tank guns? Would it ever be possible to break through them? How many lives had been wasted trying to find out how?

He saw some movement not far away and waved and shouted. There were two or three 5cwt trucks and a Bren carrier. One of the men saw him and a truck came over. Gillman asked them to pick him up and take him back. They said they were under orders to reinforce the infantry holding the bridgehead.

I said my orders were to pull out. A shell landed on the truck in front and a couple of chaps were wounded. Eventually he said to

me, 'I think perhaps your orders are more up to date than mine.'
He drove me out and landed me at our rear HQ.

There, the doctor strapped Gillman's leg and gave him a shot of
morphine, though he wasn't in any pain apart from a dull ache
in his knee, and sent him to the casualty clearing station.

Despite more losses in the congested lanes, most of the tanks in
the northern sector finally broke through the main minefields
just before dawn. But they then became disoriented in the featureless plain beyond, where random mines were scattered and 88mm
guns from Rommel's rear positions preyed on them as soon as
it was light. Most soon withdrew behind the cover of the Miteiriya
ridge; others, with no ridge to gauge their position from, mis-
reported their true location. Montgomery issued orders on the
basis of what he had been told was happening, but they proved
impossible to execute in the real circumstances on the ground,
resulting in more confusion and relative inactivity. Limited enemy
counter-attacks were beaten off with comparative ease, but forward
progress was limited.

Ken Lee and Lionel Sheppard flew top cover to the medium
bombers, invariably twelve Bostons and six Baltimores in a rigid
formation. Axis fighters sometimes intervened but they were
always able to keep them off the bombers. They were bombing
tank concentrations now, 15 Panzer Division on 24 October. On
25 October six Macchis attacked. Sheppard found himself alone
with three of them. He shot down the leader, but was outpaced
by the others and returned to base alone, flying low over the
desert. On 26 October they escorted the usual eighteen bombers
on a run over the Fuka airfields. Meredith's flight took on five

Macchis. Meredith got one but was himself shot down. He radioed from the ground to say that he was OK, but they never heard from him again. On the way back they were jumped by a pair of Messerschmitt 109s, one of which picked off Sergeant Ody from behind. Two more of Sheppard's old comrades were dead.

Two days later he exacted some revenge. They met another pair of Messerschmitts hunting alone and Sheppard, with 'Thug' Thaggard, blew one of them out of the sky in a head-on clash at point-blank range. In the air, the Germans were reduced to skirmishing around the fringes now, trying to pick off any stragglers. Lee thought of how his own squadron in France had had to fight like that, small numbers throwing themselves in against huge odds, trying to cut a way through swarms of fighters just to get at the bombers that were the real target. The boot was on the other foot now; the RAF was throwing in masses of planes, the American bombers were there too, and the Germans just couldn't lay a glove on them.

On the ground things were different. By the morning of 26 October, the army in the north had just about reached its original objectives set for the morning of 24 October. But casualties were mounting. The New Zealanders and South Africans had each lost a third of their fighting strength, while the Highlanders, with 2,100 casualties, were in urgent need of relief. Intelligence was also giving very high casualties for the enemy, but although 10 Corps had undoubtedly destroyed some German tanks attempting counter-attacks, there was no sign that resistance was seriously weakening anywhere along the line.

It was clear that infantry would have to take and hold ground, and then defend it with armoured support. The Australians, who had so far moved forward successfully with relatively light casualties, were ordered to push on again in the north, and they did so, further extending their salient.

Rommel had returned. His tank commander, Von Thoma, reported that he had done all he could in the way of counter-attacks given the acute shortage of petrol, and that 15 Panzer was in consequence reduced to just thirty-one 'runners'. Unceasing air attacks and artillery fire had caused terrible losses and were badly affecting morale. Rommel's attention focused on two points – Hill 29 in the Australian sector and Kidney ridge a little farther south. The Germans tried to counter-attack again but coordinated air and artillery bombardments drove them back.

Eighth Army edged forward again. On the night of 26 October, 2 Rifle Brigade, under Colonel Vic Turner, was ordered to seize a position code-named 'Snipe', just south of Kidney ridge. They dug their eighteen 6-pounders in when the Germans counter-attacked, determined to eliminate the salient. Soon isolated, short of ammunition and without medical facilities, the battalion held out until late the following night when, having exhausted the ammunition available for the few surviving guns, they withdrew. When the position was studied later the wrecks of thirty-four tanks and self-propelled guns were found round it. How many more were towed away is not known. The 6-pounder had proved its worth again.

But after four days of fighting, the British had still not broken through Rommel's main defensive line. It was time to think again.

Chapter 23

29 October–10 November

Montgomery was still radiating confidence. Then again, so had Ritchie. By 29 October Churchill's anticipation had curdled into anxiety. He presented Brooke with a draft telegram to Cairo.

> Not a pleasant one and brought about purely by the fact that Anthony Eden [the Foreign Secretary] had come around late last night to have a drink with him and had shaken his confidence in Montgomery and Alexander, and had given him the impression that the Middle East offensive was petering out!!

Brooke's attempts to soften the cable were met by

> a flow of abuse of Monty . . . 'What was *my* Monty doing now, allowing the battle to peter out?' (it was always '*my* Monty' in a crisis) . . . 'Have we not got a single general who can win a battle?'

Brooke defended 'his' Monty and pointed out that he had just beaten off some determined counter-attacks and was gradually wearing Rommel down. But by now he was in agony too.

> On returning to my office I paced up and down, suffering from

a desperate feeling of loneliness. I had, during that morning's discussion, tried to maintain an exterior of complete confidence . . . but there was still just the possibility that I was wrong and that Monty was beat. The loneliness of those moments of anxiety, when there is no one one can turn to, have to be lived through to realise their intense bitterness.

Late that night Brooke was summoned to Downing Street again, where he discovered Churchill in a much friendlier mood. He asked whether Brooke wished he was out directing the battle himself, and he replied, 'Yes.' Churchill said that he knew why Brooke had turned down the chance to be Commander-in-Chief in Cairo, because Brooke felt that he would serve his country better by working with him. He thanked him for that.

This forged one more link between him and me! He is the most difficult man I have ever served with, but thank God for having given me the opportunity of trying to serve such a man in a crisis such as the one this country is going through at present.

Peter Vaux's main concern was trying to keep up with the changing German order of battle. He spent hours with his Polish linguists in their interception truck. As the fighting died down in 13 Corps' sector on the night of 30 October, 21 Panzer Division was pulled out and moved north. They had kept them down south for a week. Vaux discovered that the Germans were sending all their anti-tank guns up there too. Soon 13 Corps' sector had turned into a desultory sniping and mortaring contest.

On 1 November 260 Squadron escorted eighteen Bostons to bomb a concentration of vehicles on the Coast Road behind the German lines near Ghazal station. In the afternoon they were sent to bomb what was thought to be 90 Light Division's head-quarters. They dived from 8,000 to 1,500 feet and scored direct hits on the railway track and the road fork. Then the ground controller came on the R/T and vectored them to patrol over el Alamein, where troops were forming up for Operation Supercharge.

Supercharge was intended to be the final battle. Days of what Montgomery called 'crumbling' had created a large British salient in the direction of the Aqqaqir ridge, the dominant German position in the north. Under another huge night barrage, the infantry would advance once again, with General Freyberg's New Zealanders leading the way. 9 Armoured Brigade under John Currie was placed under Freyberg and became known as the 'Kiwi Cavalry'. Montgomery intended that Currie's 121 tanks would break through the German lines on the Aqqaqir ridge, cutting a path to the open ground beyond. Then 10 Corps would follow Currie out into the open ground beyond the ridge and there they would destroy Rommel's remaining panzers; 10 Corps readied 2 and 8 Armoured Brigades – 260 tanks in all – to do the job.

As the infantry were attacking on the night of 1 November, Vaux was with the Poles in the intercept truck. German radio security was breaking down in panic as every available 88mm and Russian 75mm anti-tank gun was ordered to line and dig in on the Aqqaqir ridge. He woke Brigadier Erskine, the Chief of Staff, and told him. He never knew whether Erskine woke Horrocks. It hardly mattered really; this was the crunch and the die was cast. Freyberg's New Zealanders had been reinforced by Geordies and Scots attached from other divisions. Currie's brigade moved forward behind the infantry but the familiar logistical and navigational problems delayed its attack until it was almost dawn. The anti-tank guns were ready. Currie's men charged the guns with all the courage of the Light Brigade. They overran some forward positions and destroyed thirty-five 50mm guns, driving over them and crushing their trails. One tank was knocked out by a gun twenty yards away.

But dawn broke with Currie's men still on the forward gun line. As usual the 88s were farther back in a second line of defence on the Aqqaqir ridge itself. The British tanks were silhouetted against the dawn light; 87 were hit, and 230 out of 400 men killed or wounded. There was no gap through the ridge for the other two armoured brigades to pass through.

Fisher's 2 Armoured Brigade was now close behind Currie. Should he attack immediately to exploit Currie's limited success, or should he dig in where he was? Fisher didn't want to charge the ridge, fearing a repeat performance of what had just happened. Currie and Freyberg furiously insisted that he attack immediately.

Fisher received various messages from his divisional commander – some to push on and some to destroy enemy armour where he could. He chose to obey the second order and stayed where he was, close to the 6-pounders and the field artillery. This decision turned the battle.

The Germans were massing their own armour. Rommel knew that the ridge could not last another night of infantry and artillery attack. His only chance was to clear the British tanks away now and drive the infantry back into their salient. But as he concentrated his panzers they were continually attacked by fighter-bombers.

What followed was the final, decisive tank battle of the desert war. Fisher's brigade, supported by 8 Armoured Brigade and the survivors of Currie's brigade, took Rommel's last throw. They were now in a situation that had so often been their enemy's, with all the high cards in their hands; 150 German and Italian tanks surged forward, supported by every gun that Rommel could lay his hands on. The Shermans and the Grants shot it out with them, supported by the 6-pounders and continual air support. After two hours only fifty Axis tanks survived, of which just thirty-five were panzers. The area between the salient and the Aqqaqir ridge was littered with burning tanks.

The tank battle was won, and the screen of anti-tank guns on the ridge had taken terrible punishment, but enough remained to force the British armour to remain immobile for the next twenty-four hours while Rommel tried to save what he could. He planned a general retreat, but was temporarily halted by a 'stand and fight order' from Hitler. It took him a day (during which he began to pull back anyway) to have this reversed.

The desperate messages between Rommel and Berlin were intercepted and reached London on 3 November. It was clear at last that Montgomery was winning.

With a feeling of savage joy, Lionel Sheppard put his plane into a steep dive and roared down, wishing he could make a sound like a Stuka to really frighten the arses off the tiny figures round the tents he was aiming at. Near to him, Ken Lee clenched his teeth. He still didn't really like this dive-bombing lark. If you got shot down doing this you were in for the quickest of top-speed deaths. But it was great to be part of a winning team. For today, for the first time, it was clear that they *were* winning. Below them, as they had flown up towards Ghazal, Germans and Italians were moving back everywhere, British tanks were forming up for the final breakthrough, and the RAF was rampant. In the morning they had bombed the runway at one of the Daba airfields, but the planes had all gone. This afternoon they were just behind the old German front line and there was hardly a German anywhere to be seen.

The little figures were diving for cover, their tents collapsing, bullets spurting in the sand. The Warhawks dropped their 500-pound bombs. A lorry burst into flame and a tent near to it caught fire. Lee glimpsed a man with his clothes burning roll over and over, and then they were past and turning for home. Very low now, moving fast east along the Coast Road with the setting sun behind them.

Sheppard's machineguns ripped into a wireless tender. A man disappeared inside a tank, slamming the hatch as machinegun bullets clattered into his armour. More lorries were spinning off the road in the soft sand, figures throwing themselves beneath them. Then another little convoy, trucks pulling guns behind them. They hit that too. There was one less 88. There was proper anti-aircraft fire now as they approached some gun pits. Lee blasted away with all six machineguns, but the tracer came straight up at him and bullets ripped through the windscreen and into the cockpit. In an instant he was past, unhurt, mumbling 'Thank God' and unclenching his teeth. Just ahead Sheppard was tearing after a half-track that was trying to escape him, looking as if he would follow it all the way to Tripoli if he had to.

By the morning of 4 November the British were on the Aqqaqir ridge at last, to find that most of the defenders had fled, taking their 88s with them. Peter Vaux got into his jeep and went out to the ridge to have a look. It was an astonishing sight. For hundreds of yards the ground was littered with burnt-out British and German tanks, their guns pointing in all directions. There were far too many to count. A lot of the Shermans were right up within a few yards of the gun pits, their muzzles pointing into them. He knew from experience what it must have been like for the crews; now he could see how it was for the gunners. Some of those pits were now empty, but by no means all. In many the guns lay shattered, their crews dead amongst the wreckage, the useless limbers burnt out behind them. In one group the blackened hulks of two Shermans almost teetered at the edge of a pit containing an 88mm. The pit was half-full of empty cases and every man of the crew had a bandage some-where on his body; the sergeant had two, one round his head, and his arm was in a sling. There was blood everywhere. The dead eyes glared up at Vaux. Idly, he noticed the Luftwaffe uniforms – of course, the 88mm anti-aircraft guns belonged to the air force. He looked at the undamaged tractor. Sure enough, the registration number began LH instead of the army WH. He turned away. So many brave men. War was a bastard.

22 Armoured Brigade assembled south of Tel el Eisa. It broke out across the captured minefields, led by Pip Roberts. The Sharpshooters came through with C squadron's Crusaders leading the way. The motorised infantry of 1 Rifle Brigade were right behind the tanks. Dougie Waller bumped along on the back of his latest portee with the wind blowing through his hair and the morning sun warming his back. Perhaps this time Eighth Army would not be coming back.

Soon after midday, ten miles south-west of the Aqqaqir ridge, 22 Armoured Brigade came up against the tanks and anti-tank screen of the Italian rearguard, Ariete Division. Waller had yet another portee shot from under him, but he, Bill Ash, Alf Reeves and Sid dug the 6-pounder in and brought it to bear on the M13s that stood in the way. For most of the rest of the day they slugged it out until finally, under the constant pounding, Ariete broke and ran, abandoning equipment everywhere. The southern flank of Rommel's defences had been utterly destroyed.

Waller's battalion camped on the ground that they had taken and in the evening they moved among the Italian dead, making a collection of useful guns and ammunition. The men they had fought were the Bersaglieri, mobile light infantry like themselves, supposedly an élite bunch. The cock-feather plumes in their helmets did not look so jaunty now as they lay twisted on the ground. The riflemen dug graves. They found piles of propaganda postcards, men in feathered hats marching towards Cairo. There was a songbook too. Waller went through it with Bill, trying to make out the meaning of the lyrics. '*L'Addio del Bersagliere*.' '*Addio* is goodbye, isn't it?'

> *Addio, mia bella, addio,*
> *io dissi, nel partire, al mio tesor.*
> *ti lascio il cuore mio,*
> *m'aspetta il Re sul campo dell'onor . . .*

'*Campo dell'onor* . . . Something about his field of honour, I think.'
The field of honour didn't much look like one. It was the same
for all of them fighting over this fly-infested, stony, stinking dump
of a desert. These poor sods in the silly hats had done their best.
Waller might still get home to his Laurie if he kept his head low
enough to the ground, but this one was staying in his field.

'Any decent boodle? I haven't tasted Chianti for months.'

The next day, with his gun attached to a big new truck, Waller
covered fifty-eight miles and in the evening was back on the
outskirts of Fuka. 'Sid,' he shouted, 'you're home.'

*The 125 Panzer Grenadier pocket was finally occupied on 3
November without opposition, the enemy having withdrawn to
approximately 869305. Before dawn on 4 November more of our
Armoured Cars passed west beyond the enemy's lines to join those
already disrupting his rear areas, and by 0800 hrs our armoured
forces were pushing forward beyond the Rahman track . . .*

Peter Vaux completed his report, with a sentence he had been
longing to write:

. . . The enemy is now in full retreat.

Then he went off to inspect the enemy lines. He wanted to find
out as much about the Ramcke parachute brigade as he could,
and especially about Lehrbataillon Burckhardt, the special unit he
had been curious about for months. He drove out in his jeep
with another officer to do a recce. They looked over the German
positions, pausing to study any abandoned equipment. Some of
the parachutists had abandoned their weapons and were sitting
there waiting to be taken prisoner. With no transport, not even
a stolen Italian lorry, they had been unable to escape. They spotted
a major sitting despondently on a petrol can. Could it be? He

had the right uniform. Vaux drove over and jumped out. 'You're Major Burckhardt, no doubt,' he announced with a triumphant smile. The German was astonished that they knew his name. They popped him into the jeep with the driver sitting behind him with a revolver and Vaux at the wheel.

Back at Corps HQ they introduced their new prisoner to General Horrocks, who took an instant dislike to him. He particularly objected to Burckhardt's yachting cap. Horrocks had spent the morning with a more agreeable prisoner, Generale Scattaglia, commander of the Pavia Division, who had been brought in in floods of tears. Scattaglia was charming, and Horrocks had found an ambulance for him to sleep in. Now he ordered Vaux that on no account was he to put Burckhardt in the ambulance 'with that nice Italian general'. In the end Vaux had to invite Burckhardt into the ACV. They opened a bottle of Bolinakis gin and sat up talking late into the night.

Burckhardt's English was excellent and they talked for hours about the fighting of recent months. Burckhardt spoke very freely – he saw no point in reticence. 'It's all over now,' he said. 'Africa's lost, you've destroyed us.' He talked a lot about personalities and about Germany too. Corporal Paxton's familiarity with the place opened him up further. Vaux believed that any time spent getting to know your opponents could not be considered wasted. Burckhardt talked about his time with the Kondor Division in Spain. He said that he had improved his English by going over to Gibraltar and drinking with the British officers there. Then he told them all about Crete, and how narrow the German victory had been. He had been dropped at Maleme airport and had fought against the Black Watch. He made them all laugh by telling them how the famous Olympic boxer Max Schmelling had refused to jump. Vaux asked him about his special equipment and he laughed, saying it was all buried where it wouldn't be found. Vaux forbore to mention that his men were digging out there now and had already unearthed that special lightweight airborne recoilless 75mm gun, neatly oiled and wrapped in blankets. It was a pity to spoil a long and memorable night. For a while Vaux felt as if he were an old soldier discussing a war that was already past. But, of course, for him it wasn't.

At the most basic level, Montgomery's tactics had worked. The relentless infantry assaults had caused Rommel to make counter-attacks in the face of Eighth Army's overwhelming artillery and air power. This had allowed the British to crumble their opponents to dust. Montgomery had been a good choice of leader for such a battle. The more nimble-minded Chink had once accused him of using sledgehammers to crack nuts. Well, Churchill had given him a very big sledgehammer in the shape of the re-equipped, lavishly supplied Eighth Army, and he had used it accordingly, drawing Rommel into a slogging match he could not hope to win. Such an approach may not have been exciting but it proved to be effective, and it employed two qualities that Montgomery possessed in abundance: implacability and mental strength.

But he had to recalibrate the battle several times, he'd lost more tanks than Ritchie had in the Gazala battles (500 in all, although only 150 beyond repair), he'd made mistakes that others had previously learned to avoid, and he'd caused logistical confusion by pushing units from different corps through the same narrow gaps to a timetable that was ambitious verging on fanciful. He'd also sent tanks charging at anti-tank guns again.

Some of his more experienced predecessors might possibly have made a better job of winning this battle. Certainly none of them had the numbers, the weapons or the intelligence that Montgomery enjoyed.

But he'd won through persistence, good morale and sheer weight of numbers. He'd kept on top of every detail of the battle and he'd created the impression of busy confidence that was so important in a general. His men attacked and kept attacking for him, which they had not always done before.

The army he had defeated was a tiny fraction of the one facing the Soviet Union, but what was important was that he had driven it back. For the first time one of Hitler's field marshals had been comprehensively vanquished. It showed a still-fearful world that such a thing was possible, it brought huge encouragement to those fighting elsewhere, and it provided the perfect background to Operation Torch. French and Spanish opportunists who might have acted on Hitler's behalf could now see that the Allies were the winning side, in Africa at least.

Churchill was already talking about church bells. Brooke advised a few days' delay to make sure that the victory was secure and Operation Torch a success. While he waited, Churchill sent messages everywhere, especially to America. He received one back from General Marshall:

> Having been privileged to witness your courage and resolution on the day of the fall of Tobruk, I am unable to express my full delight over the news of the Middle East and my admiration for the British army.

The Torch landings went more smoothly than anyone had dared to hope. Churchill got his national bell-ringing, creating a sound that was carried on radio stations to the desert, to Malta, and throughout occupied Europe. On 10 November he spoke at the Mansion House.

> I have never promised anything but blood, toil, tears and sweat . . . Now, however, we have a new experience. We have victory, a remarkable and definite victory. [The Germans have received] that measure of fire and steel which they have so often meted out to others . . . Now this is not the end. It is not even the beginning of the end. But it is, perhaps, the end of the beginning.

In late October British and American newspapers began printing the first details of Nazi extermination camps. Information about the use of gas had been smuggled through Switzerland. A public protest was held at the Albert Hall. Churchill wrote to the Archbishop of Canterbury.

> The systematic cruelties to which the Jewish people – men, women and children – have been exposed under the Nazi regime are amongst the most terrible events in history, and place an indelible stain upon all who perpetrate and instigate them. Free men and women denounce these vile crimes, and when this world struggle ends with the enthronement of human rights, racial persecution will be ended.

The regiments that fought at Alamein had rich, romantic histories – the Hussars, the Bays, the Black Watch, the Greenjackets and Lancers, the Gordons and Cameron Highlanders. Then there were the Australians, the Springboks and the Maoris, Kiwis and Indians, Sikh, Muslim and Hindu. Overhead flew pilots from Ottawa and Alberta, along with Rhodesians, Bermudans and men from every other corner of the 'far flung', that extraordinary empire of palm and pine.

What miracle brought volunteers from green, wet New Zealand, from Himalayan hill villages, from Canadian wheat farms, to fight and die on the other side of the world? Churchill's answer was the defence of a unique civilisation, a civilisation with a long history of constitutional government, rule not by dictators but by the law, and a decent record of colonial administration.

But, as her famous regiments advanced, the sons of empire were riding in Chevy trucks, under Warhawk fighters and Liberator bombers and behind Sherman tanks, the same tanks that Roosevelt had promised Churchill at his empire's lowest moment. A point of balance had been reached. The men who had sent the tanks and the lorries were destined to be the dominant force in the transatlantic alliance, and their ideas about the future would change Britain.

In London there had always been those who thought that the war was a great mistake. On the back benches of the Conservative Party, hard-core appeasers such as MP William Greene were heard grumbling that 'we should have backed the other side', and as recently as 1940 a sizeable proportion of Churchill's own cabinet had been unsure that fighting on against Hitler made sense. Cleareyed men like Foreign Secretary Lord Halifax could see that to continue risked economic ruin, even if Britain won. Churchill spoke of a great moral crusade, but what place should crusades have in the cold world of politics? Halifax had summed up his approach in 1938, the high-water year of appeasement:

The world is a strangely mixed grill of good and evil and for good or ill we have to do our best to live in it.

In 1940 Churchill had needed the close support of the Labour Party to sweep Halifax's 'mixed grill' off the cabinet table, and the British left was even more influential by 1942. By then, two years into the great moral struggle, the government had already made an explicit commitment to sweeping changes in social policy. Its propaganda emphasised human rights rather than imperial might. Britain's priorities were changing. That alone, notwithstanding all the economic pain being inflicted from Washington, suggested that the slender resources of post-war Britain would be spent on council houses and hospitals rather than battleships.

Some historians still think that Churchill got it wrong. In a phrase that evokes the old Berlin radio commentaries, one recently concluded that, in fighting World War II, 'the British had certainly gained a national myth, but they had also ensured that they would need one'.

But there was only one other path available, and it led to disgrace. Her ambiguous relationship with America cost Britain much of her economic independence, as became painfully clear in 1942, but it allowed her to preserve something rather more important: her real independence. Without those planes and tanks and lorries, without all those convoys of food and oil, she could so easily have become a second Vichy.

Neville Gillman's journey to Alexandria was dulled by morphine. He came to in a ward flooded by sunlight, lying on clean white sheets. He drifted in and out of consciousness, losing all track of time, then woke again to find a doctor examining him, and a strange smell.

> Mr Gillman, I'm afraid it's gas gangrene, there's really nothing we
> can do to save the leg. And if it doesn't come off, you're a goner,
> it's as simple as that.

Gillman had been unlucky. Sand had got into the wound, carrying bacteria that had multiplied beyond the control of any available medicine. Gillman's knee was blown up like a football and if the infection spread much farther he would most certainly be 'a goner'. There were others in the ward in a far worse state than him. One, in the corner, simply cried all day, sounding just like a little baby, until they moved him out because he was distressing everyone else. No, that wouldn't be Neville Gillman. He'd make the best of whatever else followed, leg or no leg.

A letter came from Gray Skelton.

> My dear Squeaker,
> I do most sincerely hope that you are making good
> progress. I could not sympathise with you more over the
> loss of your leg, but Thank God you are alive . . . Perhaps,

by now, you will have seen Cpl Kennedy – he was all right, although slightly burnt, but I sent him back to Sidi Bishr to get a thorough rest – he is a good chap and it is a pity to over work a willing horse – he must have had an unpleasant time, and nerves a bit shaken and no wonder. I am sorry that you have had the mental anxiety of wondering what had happened to him . . . It was a terrible blow to us when we heard that Neville Burrell had died of his wounds received in that minefield do on Oct 25 – he died on Oct 27th – a very sad loss to the squadron. I was terribly sad, too, about Gill, for as you know he was a particular friend of mine . . .

Ickeringill, Willows – oh God. He thought of Gill's calm voice and calm hands. How he had never been ruffled under fire, all his letters to the wife and two little children waiting for him in Lancashire. They would know by now. And Willows, young but already experienced, hard and trustworthy. He had been looking forward to meeting his family and telling them what a dependable and courageous comrade Noel was. He would *still* tell them.

'Right, you new boys, it's sung to "Waltzing Matilda", OK?'

> Now the first silly bastard climbed into his aeroplane
> Said he would fly over Germany
> But he sang, as he swang,
> And pranged it on the boundary,
> Who'll come on ops in a Wimpy with me?
>
> Ops in a Wimpy, ops in a Wimpy,
> Who'll come on ops in a Wimpy with me?
> And he sang, as he swang, and pranged it on the
>   boundary,
> Who'll come on ops in a Wimpy with me.

Reading those words on the faded sheet of paper, she's back there with the boys from 405, hearing the music, the tipsy male voices, Canadian, English, feeling the people pressed around. Some WAAF is sneaking off to the woods with her boyfriend, but there was a lot less of *that* than most people think. Just the people, that's what she remembers, all those young men singing away.

> And the next silly bastard, sorry, silly basket, ladies
> present . . .
> . . . he got over Magdeburg,
> Up came a fighter, one two three,
> And the rear gunner sang as he reached out for his
>   parachute,
> Who'll come on ops in a Wimpy with me?

Everyone standing around laughing and all knowing but never saying that some of them wouldn't be there the next time the song was sung, that there was a place they went in their Wimpies and Halifaxes that was cold and deadly.

> Now the third silly basket, he got over Nuremberg,
> Up came the flak like a Christmas tree
> And the crew all sang, as he put it in a power dive . . .

A man burst in on Edith Heap once. It was about midnight and she was asleep in the bed they kept in an office adjoining the ops room. He'd had some rough trips and was in a dreadful state and needed to talk to someone. No more ops, no more Wimpies, oh please God . . .

> I talked to him rather like I had to the horses frightened by rough
> handling when I was a girl. Holding his hand and trying to soothe
> him. 'Everyone's frightened, you know that, don't you? You'll be
> all right.' He said, 'I don't think I can go on and face another
> one. How can I?'

He spoke of fighters flashing by and fire raking the sides of the bomber, of the near-misses and the gunners screaming for the pilot to turn, or simply exploding as the cannon fire caught them. He was a navigator, sitting there, unable to fire back, body tensed for the impact. He was twenty years old. Eventually he went off to bed, joined in lustily at the next singalong and went back into action. There were lots of late-night talks like that.

They were sacrosanct. The boys knew they could trust us and there was no one else they could have spoken to like that on the base. Often, after a bad op, they would want to walk with a girl along the darkened country lanes, just getting it all off their chests, and then they would go back and sleep. Admin assumed we were making love in the hedgerows, but usually it was not that at all. We were keepers of confidences as much as girlfriends. 'England, Home and Beauty', as the poster of the time said. That was us.

Edith grew close to Hodge, a fighter pilot she'd known back at Debden. His first words had been jokey, as Denis Wissler's had been. Teasing her about an ill-fitting greatcoat. 'Good God, you look like an inverted teacup with two handles.' Hodge was a half-boyfriend, a sort-of boyfriend. They wrote, keeping it leg-pulling and light. There were dinner dates and a 'perhaps one day you might consider' sort of half marriage proposal. When he was posted to Malta they kept in touch and, yes, she might well have gone for him in the end. He was killed somewhere over southern Italy.

There was no time for sentiment. It was important to fight it out one day at a time and Just Carry On. When a WAAF whose boyfriend was killed broke down in the ops room, she got precious little female sympathy. She should never have shown her grief on duty. 'Our crying must be done in private,' Edith told her. The crews went through enough without harrowing scenes.

'There you go, you're on-line now. Welcome to the twenty-first century, Granddad.'

Neville Gillman moved the mouse. One of his friends had told him about the Commonwealth War Graves website at the last regimental dinner. He typed in the letters, I, C, K . . .

There it was on the screen.

In Memory of Trooper ERNEST ICKERINGILL 7912739, who died age 29 on Sunday 25 October 1942. Trooper ICKERINGILL, Son of Mr and Mrs Isaac Ickeringill; husband of Anne Ickeringill. Remembered with honour. ALAMEIN MEMORIAL

He thought for a moment of wide blue skies and stillness; and a sand dune the size of a house.

They're still within reach. Up country lanes, in city flats, at the end of Endcliffevale Road, Wells Walk, Greenways. Some vigorous, some not so now. Different sorts of people, just like in every generation, but never *quite* like every generation because it marked them as it had to do. Peter and Jean Vaux have been back several times. So has Dougie. Neville and Nancy Gillman have seen where he lost his leg; and searched for that peaceful corner of the Qattara depression.

This was the first victory, a dark victory that meant bursting the lungs of German children and Churchill biting his tongue when Stalin boasted of mass murder. But then, this war was getting nastier at every level. Nastier than any of them knew.

Edith misses it, for all the pain and tears. The intensity of feeling, the chance to make a difference, a cause that was clear and straightforward. Her frightened midnight visitor survived, and they still write every year. And she carried on; they both carried on, that was the main thing. A teenage showjumper turned cog in a killing machine, tough enough to last the course, meting out measures of fire and steel and learning how to win.

Epilogue

Claude Auchinleck
Was accepted back into the fold by Churchill and became
Commander-in Chief, India, where he supervised the war in
Burma with great success. After the war he oversaw the splitting
up of his beloved Indian army, then retired to Marrakesh. He
denied forcefully, in person and in print, that he had ever intended
to retreat to the Nile delta rather than fight on against Rommel,
as Montgomery implied in his memoirs. Nevertheless, he also
had many kind and complimentary words for both Montgomery
and Churchill. The Auk was revered throughout the British army
and was widely mourned when he died in 1981, aged 96.

Don Bruce
Survived increasingly tough conditions in his prison camp as the
war went on. When the Russian army approached the prisoners
were marched west, and some of the weaker men died. Bruce
survived beatings and a serious bout of dysentery and was finally
liberated by American soldiers. After the war he married Jean,
and they have two children. He decided not to continue in the
RAF and spent his career as a secondary school teacher. Retired,
he now lives in Yorkshire.

Mimi Cortis
Came to London and qualified to work as a nurse in the UK.
She married Len Turner, a former sailor, and settled in London

where she worked as a nurse for many years. She now lives in Northolt, in a spotless house behind a front door with a huge brass Maltese door knocker.

Lonnie Dales
Served in the US Merchant Marine throughout the war. After that he married Marjorie and eventually settled in Waynesboro, Georgia, where he still lives in a home they built amid the pines, close to their three children. Along with Fred Larsen, he received the US Merchant Marine Distinguished Service Medal for 'heroism above and beyond the call of duty' for the part he played in the Pedestal operation.

Eric 'Chink' Dorman-Smith
After a further unhappy period in the army, he returned to his family's estate in Ireland. He challenged both Montgomery's and Churchill's accounts of the desert war, and threatened Churchill with a libel case over the 'retreat to the delta' claim. To spare the Prime Minister a court appearance, Basil Liddell Hart was asked to adjudicate in 1954. Churchill's book was amended to include Rommel's praise for Chink and Auchinleck's defence at Alamein. A sign of his continued bitterness was that he became involved with the old 'Official' IRA in the 1950s, allowing them to train in his grounds. He fitted out his cellar as an operations room with maps of Northern Ireland pinned on the wall and drew up plans for an invasion and the capture of Belfast. He died in 1969. Auchinleck wrote: 'He was tragically mistreated and betrayed ... envy and malice pursued him but he never gave in.'

Claude Earnshaw
Spent the rest of the war in a prison camp, and afterwards for many years ran the 'Knightsbridge' garage at Jacksdale, Nottinghamshire. He also became a very useful bridge player.

Bonner Fellers

From September 1943 until his retirement in 1946 Fellers served on General MacArthur's staff. After the war he was active on the conservative wing of American politics. He died in 1973.

Neville Gillman

Was awarded the MC for his courage at Alamein. He spent eight months in hospital in South Africa, worked briefly in Egypt and was attached to the War Office Selection Board until 1946. He then completed his training as a chartered accountant. He married Nancy, a former Wren, in 1952. They have two sons and a daughter and live in retirement in a village near Amersham. He is President of the Sharpshooters Association.

Harold Harper

Fought in Normandy with the reconstituted South Notts Hussars and became 426 Battery Sergeant Major. He married Doreen in August 1945 and they had one daughter. He worked for Boots the Chemist for forty-seven years. He is now the curator of the South Notts Hussars Museum and lives in West Bridgford on the outskirts of Nottingham.

Edith Heap

Continued in Bomber Command until the end of the war. After that she worked as a social worker. She married and raised two daughters, one of whom served in the RAF. Now retired and living in Yorkshire she works part-time in her local library assisting readers with the large-print books.

Harry Hopkins

Worked closely with Roosevelt until the President's death in 1945. Hopkins' own health failed shortly afterwards and he died in 1946. His last letter was to Winston Churchill, complaining that he'd developed cirrhosis of the liver but not – he regretted – due to drink. Churchill later wrote that 'a strong, bright, fierce flame has burned out a frail body. His love for the weak and the poor was matched by his passion against tyranny, especially when tyranny was for the time triumphant.'

Ken Lee
Left 260 Squadron in November in order to lead 123 Squadron at Abadan in Persia. He was shot down over Crete in 1943 and spent the rest of the war in Stalag Luft III. He now lives with his wife Mary in Sheffield.

Lionel Sheppard
Won the DFC for his service in the desert, and then flew in Italy, where he was shot down by ground fire and seriously wounded. After months of painful treatment for a broken back he recovered and walked normally again, but was invalided out of the RAF in June 1945. After working in the family business for some years he opened the first supermarket in Wales. He retired in 1981 as director of a number of supermarket chains. He married Brenda in June 1944 and they have two daughters and a son. They live near Hull and he is still in touch with his many Australian and Canadian friends from 260 Squadron. A poster in his house states that 'It's hard to be humble when you're Welsh.'

Alex Szima
Fought in Tunisia and Italy. After the war he married Madeline, an old school-friend. Thirty-five years after the Dieppe raid, Szima finally got to deliver the full address to Lord Lovat that William Darby had made him practise in 1942. Mills-Roberts, Brady and Koons were also present at the reunion and 'we finished up two bottles of whisky and a very good dinner'. He retired to Florida, where he 'wore out two boats', and is now back living in Dayton, Ohio.

Peter Vaux
When Peter Vaux ceased writing the headquarters war diary and

turned his attention to intelligence summaries, he signed off with characteristic self-mockery: 'His wit, élan and industry in maintaining this historic document since 28 July 41 are unlikely to be missed by future historians.' How wrong he was! Peter and his wife Jean have revisited Libya three times in recent years, though nowadays he professes to be more interested in archaeological sites than old battlefields.

Dougie Waller
Married Laurie in 1944 before he went to fight in Normandy. After being demobbed in 1946 he went back to his old job in the city. He took his son to see his first Spurs match when the boy was about two. Then, with a thought about saving lives rather than taking them, he went into hospital management, eventually settling in Sunderland. Laurie died in 1988. Until Bill Ash's death in 2001, they remained the best of friends.

Western Desert
Parts of the desert – at the southern end of the Alamein line, and at points along the Gazala line especially – are still littered with WWII landmines. The British army had cleared the minefields around inhabited areas but its post-war clearance programme ceased when Colonel Gaddafi ejected it from Libya. In 2002, for the first time, the area around Bir Hacheim was declared safe.

Acknowledgements

Our first and most deeply felt debt is to those who allowed us to make their stories part of our book, underwent interrogation and subsequent re-interview and then, at the last minute, saved us from numerous gaffes by reading and checking the text. From those errors that remain we should like to absolve Don Bruce, Lonnie Dales, Neville Gillman, Harold Harper, Edith Kup (Edith Heap), Ken Lee, Lionel Sheppard, Alex Szima, Mimi Turner (Mimi Cortis), Peter Vaux and Douglas Waller. Peter and Jean Vaux have been pestered most and Peter has kindly acted as an unofficial consultant. His 1942 British army maps of the desert have been invaluable.

A number of others gave us supporting interviews or were approached in connection with avenues of research that we were unable to pursue. For their kindness or forbearance we should like to thank Molly Bihet, Nelson Dorey, Ray Ellis, Richard and Jean Evans, Jack Fisher, Dorothy Langlois, Bunty Lawson, Kaye le Cheminant, John McGregor, Olive Marquis, Jim Marshall, Gino Mercuriali, Barbara Newman, Ken Rogers and Moira Rolleston. Martyn Thompson, especially, put in a great deal of effort on our behalf in New Zealand; we very much regret that in the end we were unable to go there to take advantage of his generous endeavour. Special thanks to Iain Nethercott, who would have been in the book had he not spent so much of 1942 on a training course, but whose letters have kept us entertained and fascinated throughout the project.

We are especially grateful to Frances Craig, who researched and drafted the sections of this book that deal with Malta, Guernsey, the US Rangers and Bomber Command. She discovered and interviewed several of our contributors and made numerous telling contributions to the final manuscript.

Research in the National Archive in Washington was conducted for us by C. J. Jenner, who put his skill, experience and good judgement at our disposal in navigating the complexities of the filing system to unearth some fascinating new material about Colonel Bonner Fellers. We are most grateful for his efforts.

We wish to thank Sheila O'Connell for the loan of her father's diary and photograph album, Neil Clayton for numerous books and leaflets, and especially Avril Randell, who put not only her contacts but also her splendid library at our disposal. Thanks also to her daughter Louise for the line about the pink stone.

Frances received invaluable help in Malta from John Agius, Frank Rixon and Tony Spooner of the George Cross Island Association and the staff of the National Library of Malta and the Lascaris Bastion Museum. Additional medical information came from Clare MacArthur.

Tim Clayton would never have got to Libya without the help of Lady Avril Randell and her friends at Apollonia Tours. Special thanks to Ahmed and Younis, to the drivers who took us out into the desert and to Mr Mohammed and his wife for their garden in the desert at the Knightsbridge Acroma cemetery. Thanks also to everyone on the coach whose expertise was plundered, to the Kiwis for being the best of company, and to the staff of Monty's Bar at the Cecil Hotel, Alexandria, on the occasion when the Sharpshooters returned and once again emptied it of gin (both bottles!).

Phil and Tim incurred numerous debts on their trips to the

USA. For hospitality we should like to thank Alex and Madeline Szima, Lonnie and Marjorie Dales and their children Donna, Dottie and Cliff, Whitelaw and Brooksie Reid and Richard and Emily Lewis. Help and advice were also provided by Emory S. Dockery of the Darby Foundation, the US Merchant Marine Academy, Jimmy Ezzell of the *True Citizen* of Waynesboro, Georgia, Diana Hopkins and Page Wilson.

In the Channel Islands we are especially grateful to Richard Heaume of the German Occupation Museum, Guernsey, and Freddie Cohen of Jersey Jewish Congregation.

The staff of the Imperial War Museum gave us their usual good advice, especially the departments of books, documents and sound. We'd particularly like to thank Peter Hart and Richard McDonough. Thanks too to David Fletcher, curator of the Tank Museum, Bovington; Nancy Snedeker and her colleagues at the Roosevelt Library, Hyde Park; and the staff of the Twickenham Library for their unfailing helpfulness when faced with requests for obscure books.

As he did with *Finest Hour*, David Wilson read and gave helpful comments on the early drafts of this book.

Winston Churchill's words are reproduced with permission of Curtis Brown Ltd, London, on behalf of C&T Publications Limited, copyright © C&T Publications Ltd. Extracts from *Lord Alanbrooke's War Diaries*, edited by Alex Danchev and Daniel Todman and published by Weidenfeld & Nicolson, are quoted with permission. Quotes from Lavinia Greacen's biography of Eric 'Chink' Dorman-Smith are reproduced by permission of Macmillan. The quotation from Hornblower is reproduced with the permission of Penguin.

For the loan of and permission to reproduce photographs we are indebted to Don Bruce, Neville Gillman, Harold Harper, Edith Kup, Ken Lee, Lionel Sheppard, Mimi Turner, Peter Vaux and Douglas Waller, and the Imperial War Museum.

Once again we should like to thank our indefatigable and extremely supportive editor, Rupert Lancaster, and his assistant,

Hugo Wilkinson. We're also grateful to Kerry Hood, Briar Silich and Roland Philipps from Hodder, our agent Elaine Steel, our copy-editor Ian Paten, our proof-reader Jane Birkett and our map-maker Raymond Turvey.

Every reasonable effort has been made to acknowledge the ownership of the copyrighted material included in this volume. Any errors that may have occurred are inadvertent, and will be corrected in subsequent editions provided notification is sent to the authors c/o the publishers.

Notes on Sources

The action described in this book was based principally on interviews specially conducted for the purpose with Don Bruce, Lonnie Dales, Neville Gillman, Harold Harper, Edith Kup (Heap), Kaye le Cheminant, Ken Lee, Lionel Sheppard, Alex Szima, Mimi Turner (Cortis), Peter Vaux and Douglas Waller. These have been supported, where appropriate, by the war diaries of the units with which they fought and by other relevant accounts. Thus, we have attempted to reconcile Neville Gillman's recollections with the War Diaries of 4th County of London Yeomanry, Harry Ramsbottom's *Memory Diary*, and Viscount Cranley's book *Men and Sand*. Claude Earnshaw, who died some years ago, is based on Harold Harper's recollections and those of other South Notts Hussars.

Several of our interviewees had already been interviewed by the Sound Department of the Imperial War Museum and occasionally quotations or details taken from these very full and graphic interviews were also used. The reference numbers for the most important are: Harold Harper 10923, Edith Kup 13927, Peter Vaux 20950. We surveyed all of the South Notts Hussars interviews conducted by Peter Hart and used as the basis of his excellent oral history of that unit, *To the Last Round*. We found the interviews with Harry

Day 12412, Ray Ellis 12660, Bobby Feakins 15607, Charles Laborde 15103, William Pringle 14790, Albert Swinton 15104 and Edward Whittaker 12409 especially helpful. Our account of the Dieppe raid made special use of interviews with Thomas Hunter 18420, Laurens Pals 4642 and William Spearman 9796. A considerable number of other IWM interviews were consulted in the course of research.

All reconstructed dialogue, thoughts and feelings were based closely on the above sources. Contemporary atmosphere and dialogue were also adapted from books written at the time or soon after, such as Alex Clifford's *Three against Rommel*; Alan Moorehead's *African Trilogy*; *On Active Service*, Martyn Thompson's edition of his uncle Owen Gatman's moving correspondence; Jim Henderson's *Gunner Inglorious*; Cyril Joly's *Take These Men*; *Tanks across the Desert* George Forty's edition of Jake Wardrop's diary.

The historiography of the desert war has continued to reflect the clashes of ideas and personalities that characterised the British army in 1942. The pro-Montgomery orthodoxy of Sir Francis de Guingand's *Operation Victory* found a powerful riposte in Correlli Barnett's *Desert Generals*. Where Liddell Hart defended the tank men, Barrie Pitt championed the footsloggers. The South African official history is one of the more thorough accounts, and takes a charitable view of the South African contribution to the fall of Tobruk. Montgomery's autobiography and subsequent biographies of the general should be balanced against Lavinia Greacen's colourful biography *Chink*, which defends Eric Dorman-Smith and makes a powerful case that he was unfairly hounded out of the army after the campaign. Philip Warner's *Auchinleck, the Lonely Soldier* is a sympathetic portrait of a man who might conceivably have made a better job of el Alamein had he been given Montgomery's resources. Few histories of the desert war are not tinged with admiration for the professionalism and determination of General Rommel and his army. We have tried to give the Italian element in it a little more credit than it sometimes receives.

It need not damage Rommel's reputation as a general that some of his bolder decisions appear to have been founded on information inadvertently supplied by the American military attaché. We have unearthed new details of the story of Colonel Bonner Fellers in previously unpublished documents from the Public Record Office and from the National Archive in Washington, specially declassified for this book.

Quotations from sources other than our own interviews are listed below:

p. 5 'Report on Interrogation', Tank Museum, Bovington

Chapter One

p. 7   7 Armoured Division Intelligence Summary No. 33, Tank Museum, Bovington

p. 15   'about the Battle of Austerlitz', Alanbrooke, p. 260

p. 16   'When General Marshall, Brooke's opposite number', ibid., p. 247

p. 17   'He knows no details', ibid., p. xxi

p. 25   'Cannot work out why troops are not fighting better', ibid., p. 231

Chapter Two

p. 35   'Half our Corps and Divisional commanders', Alanbrooke, p. 243

Chapter Three

p. 43   'an original and delightful person', Ranfurly, p. 78

p. 44   'The trouble is your top brass', ibid., p. 117

p. 45   Acquisition of 'black code' by the Axis from Kahn, *Hitler's Spies*, pp. 192–3

p. 45   'Estimates (Cairo) on equipment', NA, RG 165, Box 760, 6900

p. 45   '2 Armoured Brigade of British 1 Armoured Division', NA, RG 165, Box 759 6910

p. 45   'Malta air forces report two [Axis] merchantmen . . .,' ibid.

p. 45   'To oppose Rommel in the desert the British have', ibid.

p. 46   'It will be the end of March before', ibid.

p. 46   'his outposts on the Tmimi–Mechili line', RG 165, Box
         759/6910 Egypt, I.G. No. 6910: HQME intelligence
         newsletter, week ending 16 April, forwarded by Fellers to
         Washington

p. 46   'Rommel used to wait for the dispatches', Irving, p. 142

p. 47   'It was only to be hoped that the American Minister', *Hitler's
         Tischgesprache*, evening 28 June 1942, quoted in Kahn, *Hitler's
         Spies*, p. 195

p. 47   'Please report on this', PRO HW 1/537

p. 47   Reference to 'a good source' sent to Churchill on 24 April,
         PRO HW 1/537

p. 48   'On 2 May the British discovered another reference', PRO
         HW 1/545

p. 50   'This is the most important battle', war diary of 3rd CLY, PRO
         WO 169/4495

p. 51   Details of German anti-tank guns from Agar-Hamilton and
         Turner, *Sidi Rezegh*, p. 45 and p. 46n.

p. 52   'The enemy armour was frustrated', 7 Armd Div. Intell. Summ.
         No. 34, 28 May, Tank Museum, Bovington

p. 56   'It is essential to avoid giving offence', PRO WO 201/2158

p. 56   'I am glad this list is being reconsidered', ibid.

p. 57   'ask Colonel Fellers to give us an assurance', ibid.

p. 57   'The Joint Planning Staff are authorised', ibid.

Chapter Four

p. 62   'In April Squadron Leader McCormack', 405 Sqn RCAF, ops
         record book; PRO AIR 27/1787

p. 66   'using a sledgehammer to crack a nut', Greacen, p. 100

p. 66   'Dorman-Smith allows cleverness to precede thoroughness',
         ibid.

p. 66   'a shared horror of military backwardness', ibid., p. 141

p. 67   'Brains? We just haven't damn well got any', ibid., p. 188

p. 68   'Four of the aircraft carrying 4,000-pounders', 405 Sqn RCAF,
         ops record book; PRO AIR 27/1787

p. 69   'All leave cancelled and men on leave recalled to unit', ibid.

p. 71   'the force of which you form a part tonight', Richards, p. 129

p. 72   'aimed at areas not already ablaze', 405 Sqn RCAF, ops record book; PRO AIR 27/1787

p. 72   Richards, p. 141. Figures for damage to buildings and factories vary.

p. 72   'You have no idea of the thrill', Sherwood, p. 553

p. 73   'at night the sirens wail', PRO Air 14/572

p. 73   'as men lost in a raging typhoon', *Bomber Command Continues*, p. 45

p. 74   'I am much distressed over the loss of 150th Brigade', Agar-Hamilton and Turner, *Crisis in the Desert*, p. 39

p. 75   'I am glad you think the situation is still favourable', Liddell Hart, p. 143.

p. 75   '[They] seem firmly to believe', PRO HW 1/615

p. 75   'British training [was] very inferior', PRO HW 1/636

p. 76   'The U.S. must absolutely have its own separate theaters', NA

Chapter Five

p. 84   'one of the most ridiculous attacks of the campaign', Pitt, 11, p. 216

p. 87   'a really bad day', war diary of 4CLY, PRO WO 169/4496

p. 88   'a nagging, aching doubt', Joly, pp. 302 and 307

p. 89   'In a moment so decisive', *Rommel Papers*, p. 217

Chapter Six

p. 91   'The Russians had already lost four million men', Overy, p. 19

p. 91   'Americans were saying Britain was yellow', Nicolson, p. 228

p. 91   '"intense" anti-British sentiment', Alanbrooke, p. 230

p. 91   '"oft-burned, defensive-minded" Britain', Gilbert, *Road to Victory*, p. 117

p. 92   'Our men cannot stand up to punishment', Nicolson, p. 225

p. 92   'The English promised the Russians two divisions', Blum, p. 81

p. 93   'The night-fighter force was expanded by 50 per cent', Murray, p. 191

p. 99   'There are so few men in our army', Greacen, p. 198

p. 100 'Atmosphere here good', Pitt, 11, p. 230

p. 100 'Retreat would be fatal', Gilbert, *Road to Victory*, p.122

p. 100   'embarras de Ritchies', Greacen, p. 196
p. 100   'another long report to German Army in AFRICA', PRO HW
          1/636
p. 101   'Prime Minister, I am satisfied', ibid.
p. 101   'Previous material on the security leak', PRO HW 1/641
p. 102   'Here I am with a head running wild', Greacen, p. 200
p. 103   'Fatigue in tanks', Liddell Hart, pp. 183–4
p. 103   'such was the fatigue of everyone', Cranley, p. 80

Chapter Seven

p. 115   'Nights of June 12th June 13th', Kahn, *Hitler's Spies*, p. 194
p. 117   'Sir, sir, you buy amber grease . . .', Ranfurly, p. 22
p. 124   'There are at least three American cyphers', PRO HW 1/652
p. 124   'PM directed me to wire Washington', ibid.
p. 124   'Please inform General Auchinleck', ibid.

Chapter Eight

p. 128   'We're here, because we're here', Alanbrooke, p. 266
p. 128   'strong adherent of breaking our heads', ibid., p. 268
p. 137   'We are Rommel's soldiers', Cooper, p. 161
p. 139   'Today the enemy has pushed down', 7 Armd Div. Intell. Sum
          No. 52, 20 June, PRO WO 169 4086

Chapter Nine

p. 144   'Tobruk has surrendered', Gilbert, *Road to Victory*, p. 128
p. 144   'neither Winston nor I', Alanbrooke, p. 269
p. 144   'Defeat is one thing', Gilbert, *Road to Victory*, pp. 128–9
p. 144   'like a thunderclap', Nicolson, p. 231
p. 145   'Anybody knowing what it entails', Alanbrooke p. 269
p. 148   '"Our commanders," reported *The Times*', Greacen, p. 201
p. 149   'fatuously numb', ibid., p. 202
p. 150   'Written appreciation by the German commander', PRO WO
          169 4086
p. 151   '"C", is this still going on?', PRO HW 1/676
p. 151   'we will not be able to count on these intercepts', Irving, p.
          180

p. 152 'I am informed that the brilliant', NA, RG 226 COI/OSS files, Box 103, 9457

p. 152 'contributed materially to the tactical', Kahn, *Codebreakers*, p. 255

p. 156 'the intriguer from Iowa', Sherwood

p. 157 'My Dear Harry, Be kind to the bearer', Hyde Park, Hopkins papers

p. 158 'This house, while paying tribute', Gilbert, *Road to Victory*, p. 33

p. 159 'Now for England, home, and a beautiful row', Alanbrooke, p. 274

p. 160 '11.30 pm. Just been told guardedly', Greacen, p. 203

Chapter Ten

p. 161 'I had the strangest feeling of certainty', Greacen, p. 206

p. 162 'At all costs and even if ground', Pitt, 11, p. 272

p. 162 'Your instructions regarding fighting manpower', PRO WO 201 400

p. 162 'and at night sometimes held hands', Greacen, p. 208

p. 163 'I think what sticks most clearly', ibid., pp. 208–9

p. 174 'It is again emphasised that THE ENEMY LISTENS', PRO WO 169 4087A, 7 Armd Div. Intell. Summ. No. 55, 1 July

p. 176 'The enemy is stretched to the limit', Jackson, p. 251

p. 176 'we are still sorting ourselves out', Greacen, p. 209

Chapter Eleven

p. 177 'We want "Might" in our propaganda', Beaton, *Near East*, p. 27

p. 177 'badly shaken, tired and discouraged', Beaton, *Years Between*, p. 186

p. 178 'Navy gone . . . Rumour in Cairo', Greacen, p. 212

p. 178 'a BBC announcer told Beaton', Beaton, *Near East*, p. 132

p. 181 'British shells came screaming in from three directions', Rommel, p. 246

p. 182 'On a brilliant starlit night', Cranley, p. 84

p. 183 'the saviour and protector of Islam', Cooper, p. 56

p. 183 'The Mohammedan leaders are in continued conference', PRO FO 208 21390

Chapter Twelve

Chapter Thirteen

p. 215 'Every day I lived in fear and terror', ibid., p. 39
p. 215 'bad-tongued Jew', ibid., p. 20
p. 215 'maniacal exhaustion', ibid., p. 40
p. 215 'I do remember – well – Therese coming', ibid., p. 45
p. 216 'had to report the next morning', ibid.
p. 216 'We got down there at half past seven', Newman interview
p. 217 'I still feel ashamed', Bunting, p. 106
p. 223 'herded together', Cohen, p. 48
p. 224 'the deportees were loaded', Patzold, p. 34
p. 224 'During the journey, crammed', Bunting, p. 110
p. 224 'A Jewish woman who was transported from Poitiers to Auschwitz', details from Patzold, p. 180.
p. 228 'They ordered us to stand', Cohen, p. 49
p. 228 'anyone who tried to put on his waterproof', Bunting, p. 110.

Chapter Fourteen

p. 236 'VD centres', see Cooper, p. 115
p. 242 'stubby fingers against the talc', Greacen, p. 236
p. 243 'an excess of bravery', Tedder, p. 217
p. 243 'one of the most difficult days', Alanbrooke, p. 293
p. 243 'impart a new and vigorous impulse', Gilbert, *Road to Victory*, p. 165
p. 244 'I have listened to this boy with great interest', Cranley, p. 89
p. 244 'in a highly stormy and unpleasant', Alanbrooke, pp. 296–7
p. 244 'To see the Auk wrecked', Greacen, pp. 244–5
p. 245 'It would be typically German', 7 Armd Div. Intell. Summ. No. 76, 7 August

Chapter Fifteen

p. 248 'hardy soldiers a rugged future', Darby, p. 25
p. 249 'The brawny Scots strode', ibid., p. 27
p. 249 'Mile after mile, we plodded ahead', ibid.
p. 251 'Tea, fish and beans for breakfast', ibid., p. 28
p. 252 'All crews to action stations', *Saturday Evening Post*, 9 January 1960, p. 75
p. 254 'Totalitarian lavishness', Gilbert, *Road to Victory*, p. 173
p. 256 'He knows the worst', ibid., p. 183

p. 262   'This is the first time in history', ibid., p. 185
p. 262   'on account of the bravery', ibid., p. 187

Chapter Sixteen

p. 265   Details of banquet, Alanbrooke, p. 301
p. 266   Details of 'another boozy dinner', Gilbert, *Road to Victory*, p. 200
p. 266   'I did not repeat Burke's dictum', ibid., p. 204
p. 267   'Ballade of the Second Front', Alanbrooke, p. 307
p. 268   'Oh, that's nothing . . .', Arthur, p. 148
p. 269   Malta minesweeping, details from *Malta Remembered*, p. 59
p. 272   'Sister Anne, Sister Anne . . .', Shankland, p. 225
p. 273   '*Penn* was endeavouring . . .', Arthur, p. 150

Chapter Seventeen

p. 287   'Your one inclination was to dig yourself a hole', IWM Sound 9796
p. 294   'The raid was supposed to be in the dark', IWM Sound 18420
p. 294   'Jimmy Elliot was firing', ibid.
p. 295   'the grimmest beach . . .', Atkin, p. 121
p. 295   'It's hopeless, get back to the boats . . .', ibid., p. 128
p. 295   'Someone up ahead of us had put up a white flag', IWM Sound 18420
p. 295   'It's just like a normal moonlight excursion', PRO DEFE 2/338
p. 296   'The barges, soon as they hit the beach', IWM Sound 4642
p. 296   Casualties, details from Atkin, p. 132

Chapter Eighteen

p. 297   'Hershell Johnson, told him . . .' Sherwood, p. 236
p. 297   'It is only when you see . . .', Hyde Park, Hopkins Papers
p. 297   'without you by our side . . .', ibid.
p. 297–8 Hopkins' hotel messages, ibid.
p. 298   'The democratic peoples do not propose . . .', ibid.
p. 301   'It was with an insubordinate smile', Montgomery, p. 103
p. 303   'the equivocal moral position', Orwell, p. 487

p. 307   'none of these men', PRO DEFE 2/338
p. 307   'gave the impression', ibid.
p. 307   'The Canadians on the whole fought badly', ibid.

Chapter Nineteen

p. 315   'At no other time since the beginning', Hyde Park, Hopkins
         Papers
p. 320   'At each of these meetings it was pointed out', ibid.
p. 322   'the progressive evolution of self-governing institutions'
p. 323   'neoreligious quest', Kimball, *Forged in War*, p. 101
p. 323   'all forms of discriminatory treatment', ibid.
p. 323   'a client receiving help', Kimball, *Forged in War*, p. 102
p. 324   'There are more definite indications', 7 Armd Div. Intell. Summ.
         No. 85, 25 August
p. 326   'the enemy is known to be strong in tanks,' 7 Armd Div. Intell.
         Summ., No. 86, 29 August

Chapter Twenty

p. 337   'swarms of low flying fighter-bombers', Rommel, p. 279
p. 339   'In the factories, the new 6-pounder', *The Sphere*, 19 September
         1942, p. 372

Chapter Twenty-One

p. 345   'century of the common man', Charmley, p. 51
p. 346   'worse than we have ever ourselves thought', Skidelsky, p. 103.
         For Keynes's opinion that America intended the destruction
         of the imperial trade system, see p. xx
p. 346   'a victory where both enemies and allies', Acheson, pp. 28–9.
p. 347   'But dear Ernst', XIII Corps Intell. Summ. No. 199, 22
         September
p. 351   '[He adopted] the attitude that he was the only one',
         Alanbrooke, p. 324.

Chapter Twenty-Two

p. 361   'convinced that Germany can be defeated', Alanbrooke, p. 332.
p. 362   'I shall be lucky if I get through', ibid.

Chapter Twenty-Three

Bibliography

Manuscript

Roosevelt Library, Hyde Park, New York State
Hopkins Papers

National Archives, Washington (NA)
RG 165 Egypt
RG 226 Co1/o55 files

Public Record Office, London (PRO)
AIR 14 572 British propaganda to Czechoslovakia, featuring the Cologne raid
AIR 27 873 112 Squadron ops record book
AIR 27 889 115 Squadron ops record book
AIR 27 1537 260 Squadron ops record book
AIR 27 1787: 405 SQN RCAF ops record book
WO 169 4007 XIII Corps (G branch) Sep.–Dec. 1942
WO 169 4033 XXX Corps (G branch) May–Jun. 1942
WO 169 4086 7 Armoured Division (G branch) Jan.–Jun. 1942
WO 169 4087A 7 Armoured Division (G branch) Jul.–Oct. 1942
WO 169 4494 2 Royal Gloucester Hussars

WO 169 4495 3 County of London Yeomanry
WO 169 4496 4 County of London Yeomanry
WO 169 4563 107 Royal Horse Artillery (South Notts Hussars)
WO 169 4649 7 Medium Regiment, Royal Artillery
WO 169 5054 1 Rifle Brigade
WO 169 5057 9 Rifle Brigade (Tower Hamlets Rifles)
WO 201 2139–2150, 2158 papers on Ultra and Fellers
HW 1 537, 545, 615, 636–677, 1038–1042 papers on Ultra and Fellers
FO 208 21390 Egyptian agitation against the British
DEFE 2 338 debriefing of prisoners and report of Lt Col. Labatt on
  Dieppe raid

Tank Museum, Bovington, Dorset
7 Armoured Division Intelligence Summaries for May 1942 (the diary
and summaries for May were destroyed when ACV1 was captured and
are consequently missing from the PRO series; the Tank Museum has
Peter Vaux's copies)

Privately supplied memoirs
Ellis, Ray, 'Once a Hussar'
Kup, Edith, 'Memoirs of a Wartime WAAF'
O'Connell, F., diary for 1942
Ramsbottom, Harry, 'Memory Diary'

Published

Acheson, Dean, *Present at the Creation*, London: Hamish Hamilton, 1970
Agar-Hamilton, J.A.I., and L.C.F. Turner, *Crisis in the Desert, May–July
  1942*, Cape Town: OUP, 1952
——, *The Sidi Rezeg Battles 1941*, Cape Town: OUP, 1957
Alanbrooke, Field Marshal Lord, *War Diaries 1939–1945*, ed. A. Danchev
  and D. Todman, London: Weidenfeld & Nicolson, 2001
Alexander, Joan, *Mabel Strickland*, Malta: Progress Press Co. Ltd, 1996
Arbib, Bob, *Here We Are Together*, London: Longmans, Green & Co.,
  1946

Arthur, Max, *There Shall Be Wings: The RAF 1918 to the Present*, London: Hodder & Stoughton, 1993

——, *The Navy 1939 to the Present Day*, London: Hodder & Stoughton, 1997

Atkin, Ronald, *Dieppe 1942*, London: Macmillan, 1980

Barnett, Correlli, *The Desert Generals*, London: George Allen & Unwin, 1960 (2nd edn 1983)

——, *Engage the Enemy More Closely: The Royal Navy in the Second World War*, London: Hodder & Stoughton, 1991

Beaton, Cecil, *Near East*, London: Batsford, 1943

——, *The Years Between*, New York: Holt, Rinehart & Winston, 1965

Bennett, Ralph, *Behind the Battle: Intelligence in the War with Germany, 1939–1945*, London: Sinclair-Stevenson, 1994

Bickers, Richard Townshend, *The Desert Air War*, London: Leo Cooper, 1991

Bihet, Molly, *A Child's War*, Guernsey, Channel Islands: The Guernsey Press Co. Ltd, 1985

Blum, John Morton, *Years of War 1941–45, From the Morgenthau Diaries*, Boston: Houghton Mifflin, 1967

Bomber Command Continues, London: HMSO, 1942

Bunting, Madeleine, *The Model Occupation*, London: HarperCollins, 1995

Calder, Angus, *The People's War*, London: Jonathan Cape, 1969

Carver, Michael, *Alamein*, London: Batsford, 1962

——, *The Dilemmas of the Desert War*, London: Batsford, 1986

Charmley, John, *Churchill's Grand Alliance: The Anglo-American Special Relationship 1940–57*, London: Hodder & Stoughton, 1995

Clifford, Alexander, *Three against Rommel*, London: Harrap, 1943

Cloud, Stanley, and Lynne Olson, *The Murrow Boys: Pioneers on the Front Lines of Broadcast Journalism*, New York: Houghton Mifflin, 1996

Cohen, Frederick E., *The Jews in the Channel Islands during the German Occupation 1940–1945*, The Institute of Contemporary History and Wiener Library Ltd in association with the Jersey Jewish Congregation, 1998

Combined Operations 1940–1942, London: HMSO, 1943

Cooper, Artemis, *Cairo in the War 1939–1945*, London: Hamish Hamilton, 1989

Cranley, Arthur, Earl of Onslow, *Men and Sand*, London: St Catherine Press, 1961

Darby, W.O., and W.H. Baumer, *We Led the Way*, California: Presidio Press, 1980

de Guingand, Sir Francis, *Operation Victory*, London: Hodder & Stoughton, 1947

——, *Generals at War*, London: Hodder & Stoughton, 1964

Delaney, John, *Fighting the Desert Fox: Rommel's Campaigns in North Africa April 1941 to August 1942*, London: Cassell, 1998

Dilks, David (ed.), *The Diaries of Sir Alexander Cadogan OM, 1938–1945*. London: Cassell, 1971

Dobson, Eric B., *The History of the South Notts Hussars 1924–48*, London, 1948

Douglas-Hamilton, James, *The Air Battle for Malta*, Edinburgh: Mainstream Publishing Co., 1981, Airlife edn 2000

Farren, Roy A., *Winged Dagger*, London: Collins, 1948

Forty, George, *Desert Rats at War: North Africa*, Shepperton: Ian Allan, 1975

——, *Africa Corps at War*, Shepperton: Ian Allan, 1978

——, *Tanks across the Desert: The War Diary of Jake Wardrop*, London: William Kimber, 1981

——, *The Armies of Rommel*, London: Arms & Armour, 1997

——, *British Army Handbook 1939–1945*, Stroud: Sutton Publishing, 1998

Gardiner, Juliet, *Over Here, the GIs in Wartime Britain*, London: Collins & Brown, 1992

George Cross Island Association, *Malta Remembered*, Valletta, Malta: 2000

Gilbert, Adrian (ed.), *The Imperial War Museum Book of the Desert War*, London: BCA, 1992

Gilbert, Martin, *Winston S. Churchill, VII: The Road to Victory, 1942–45*, London: Heineman, 1986

——, *Auschwitz and the Allies*, London: Michael Joseph Ltd and George Rainbird Ltd, 1981

——, *The Holocaust*, London: Collins, 1986

——, *The Second World War*, London: Weidenfeld & Nicolson, 1989

Graham, Andrew, *Sharpshooters at War*, London: The Sharpshooters Regimental Association, 1964

Greacen, Lavinia, *Chink: A Biography*, London: Macmillan, 1989

Grigg, John, *1943: The Victory that Never Was*, London: Eyre Methuen, 1980

Harris, Sir Arthur, *Bomber Offensive*, London: Collins, 1947

Hart, Peter, *To the Last Round: The South Notts Hussars 1939–1942*, Barnsley: Leo Cooper, 1996

Hastings, Max, *Bomber Command*, London: Michael Joseph, 1979

Hastings, R.H.W.S., *The Rifle Brigade in the Second World War 1939–1945*, Aldershot: Gale & Polden, 1950

Henderson, Jim, *Gunner Inglorious*, Wellington, NZ: Harry H. Tombs, 1945

Hinsley, F.H., and A. Stripp, *Codebreakers: The Inside Story of Bletchley Park*, Oxford: OUP, 1993

Hinsley, H.H., Thomas, E.E. et al., *British Intelligence in the Second World War: Its Influence on Strategy and Operations*, London: HMSO, 1979–88

Hopkins, June, *Harry Hopkins*, New York: St Martin's Press, 1999

Irving, David, *Trail of the Fox*, London: Weidenfeld & Nicolson, 1977

Jackson, W. G. F., *The North African Campaign, 1940–43*, London: Batsford, 1975

Joly, Cyril, *Take These Men*, London: Constable, 1955

Kahn, David, *The Codebreakers*, London: Weidenfeld & Nicolson, 1966

——, *Hitler's Spies: German Military Intelligence in World War II*, New York: Macmillan, 1978

Keegan, John, *The Face of Battle*, London: Jonathan Cape, 1976 (new edn Pimlico, 1981)

——, *The Second World War*, London: Century Hutchinson, 1989

——, *Churchill's Generals*, London: Weidenfeld & Nicolson, 1991

Kemp, Paul, *Convoy! Drama in Arctic Waters*, London: Arms & Armour, 1993

Kimball, Warren F., 'Stalingrad: A Chance for Choices', *Journal of Military History*, 60 (January 1996)

——, *Forged in War: Roosevelt, Churchill and the Second World War*, New York: William Morrow & Co., 1997

——, (ed.), *Churchill and Roosevelt, the Complete Correspondence: The*

Alliance Emerging, October 1939–November 1942, Princeton: Princeton UP, 1984

King, William, *The Stick and the Stars*, London: Hutchinson, 1958

Kurzman, Paul, *Harry Hopkins and the New Deal*, Fair Lawn, NJ: R.E. Burdick, 1974

Liddell Hart, B.A., *The North African Campaign 1940–43*, Dehra Don: Natraj Publishers, 1978

Longmate, Norman, *The Way We Lived Then*, London: Hutchinson, 1975

Lucas, Laddie, *Malta, the Thorn in Rommel's Side*, London: Stanley Paul & Co. Ltd, 1992

Lysaght, Charles Edward, *Brendan Bracken*, London: Allen Lane, 1979

McGregor, John, *The Spirit of Angus*, Chichester, Sussex: Phillimore & Co. Ltd, 1988

McJimsey, George, *Harry Hopkins: Ally of the Poor and Defender of Democracy*, Cambridge, Mass.: Harvard University Press, 1987

McKee, Alexander, *El Alamein, Ultra and the Three Battles*, London: Souvenir Press Ltd, 1991

Martin, Albert, *Hellfire Tonight*, Lewes, Sussex: The Book Guild, 1996

Maule, Henry, *Spearhead General: The Epic Story of General Sir Francis Messervy and His Men in Eritrea, North Africa and Burma*, London: Oldham's Press, 1961

Middlebrook, M., and C. Everitt, *The Bomber Command War Diaries*, London: Viking, 1985

Mitcham, Samuel W., *Rommel's Greatest Victory: The Desert Fox and the Fall of Tobruk, Spring 1942*, Novato, California: Presidio Press, 1998

Montgomery, Field Marshal the Viscount Montgomery of Alamein, *Memoirs*, London: Collins, 1958

Moorehead, Alan, *African Trilogy: The North African Campaign 1940–43*, London: Hamish Hamilton 1944 (new edn Cassell, 1998)

Morgan, Kevin, *Harry Pollitt*, Manchester: Manchester University Press, 1993

Murray, Williamson, *Luftwaffe, Strategy for Defeat*, London: Grafton, 1988

Neillands, Robin, *The Desert Rats: 7th Armoured Division 1940–45*, London: Weidenfeld & Nicolson, 1991

Nicolson, Harold, *Diaries and Letters 1939–1945*, ed. N. Nicolson, London: Collins, 1967

Orwell, George, *The Complete Longer Non-Fiction*, London: Penguin, 1983

Overy, Richard, *Why the Allies Won*, London: Jonathan Cape, 1995

Padfield, Peter, *War beneath the Sea: Submarine Conflict 1939–1945*, London: John Murray, 1995

Parkinson, Roger, *Dawn on Our Darkness*, St Albans, Herts: Granada, 1977

——, *The Auk: Auchinleck, Victor at Alamein*, London: Hart-Davis, MacGibbon, 1977

Patzold, Kurt, and Erica Schwarz, *Auschwitz war für mich nur ein Bahnhof – Franz Novak, der Transportoffizier Adolf Eichmanns*, Vienen: Metropol, Friedrich Veitl-Verlag, 1994

Pelling, Henry, *Winston Churchill*, London: Macmillan, 1974

Phillips, C.E. Lucas, *Alamein*, London: Heinemann, 1962

Pimlott, Ben (ed.), *The Second World War Diary of Hugh Dalton 1940–45*, London: Jonathan Cape, 1986

Pitman, Stuart, *Second Royal Gloucestershire Hussars Libya–Egypt 1941–2*, London: St Catherine Press, 1950

Pitt, Barrie, *The Crucible of War*, 3 vols, London: Cassell & Co., 2001 (1st edn 1980–2)

Playfair, I.S.O. et al., *The Mediterranean and the Middle East. Volume III, British Fortunes Reach Their Lowest Ebb (September 1941 to September 1942)*, London: HMSO, 1966

Ponting, Clive, *Churchill*, London: Sinclair-Stevenson, 1994

Poolman, Kenneth, *Night Strike from Malta: 830 Squadron RN and Rommel's Convoys*, London: Jane's, 1980

Ramsbottom, Harry, *Memory Diary*, Epsom: Chiavari Publishing, 1995

Ranfurly, Countess of, *To War with Whitaker*, London: William Heinemann, 1994

Richards, Denis, *The Hardest Victory: RAF Bomber Command in the Second World War*, London: Hodder & Stoughton, 1994

Roberts, Andrew, *Churchill: Embattled Hero*, London: Weidenfeld & Nicolson, 1994

Rommel, E., *The Rommel Papers*, ed. B.H. Liddell Hart, London: Collins, 1953

Roskill, Stephen, *The War at Sea, 1939–1945, volume II, the Period of Balance*, London: HMSO, 1956

Shankland, Peter, and Anthony Hunter, *Malta Convoy*, New York: Ives Washburn Inc., 1961

Shaw, W.B. Kennedy, *Long Range Desert Group*, London: Collins, 1945

Sheppard, Lionel, *Some of Our Victories*, Warrington: Compaid Graphics, 1994

Sherwood, Robert, *The White House Papers of Harry L. Hopkins*, II, London: Eyre & Spottiswoode, 1948

Shores, Christopher, *Malta, the Spitfire Year 1942*, London: Grub Street 1991

Skidelsky, Robert, *John Maynard Keynes, Fighting for Britain*, London: Macmillan, 2000

Smith, Peter, *Pedestal, the Convoy that Saved Malta*, London: William Kimber, 1970

Spooner, Tony, *Faith, Hope and Malta GC*, Swindon, England: Newton Publishers, 1992

Tedder, Marshal of the Royal Air Force Lord, *With Prejudice*, London, 1966

Terraine, John, *The Right of the Line: The Royal Air Force in the European War 1939–1945*, London: Hodder & Stoughton, 1985

Thompson, Julian, *The Imperial War Museum Book of the War at Sea: The Royal Navy in the Second World War*, London: Sidgwick & Jackson, 1996

Thompson, Martyn (ed.), *On Active Service*, Auckland, NZ: Addison Wesley Longman, 1999

Travers, Susan, *Tomorrow to Be Brave*, London: Bantam Press, 2000

Warner, Philip, *Auchinleck, the Lonely Soldier*, London: Buchan & Enright, 1981

Wingate, J., *The Fighting Tenth: The Tenth Submarine Flotilla and the Siege of Malta*, Leo Cooper, 1971

Winton, John, *Cunningham*, London: John Murray, 1998

Wynter, H.W., *Special Forces in the Desert War 1940–43*, London: PRO, 2001

Young, Desmond, *Rommel*, London: Collins, 1950

Index

429